THE WORLD FOR SALE

THE WORLD FOR SALE

Money, Power and the Traders Who Barter the
Earth's Resources

Javier Blas and Jack Farchy

5 7 9 10 8 6 4

Random House Business
20 Vauxhall Bridge Road
London SW1V 2SA

Random House Business is part of the Penguin Random House group
of companies whose addresses can be found at global.penguinrandomhouse.com.

Penguin
Random House
UK

First published by Random House Business in 2021

www.penguin.co.uk

A CIP catalogue record for this book is available from the British Library.

ISBN 9781847942654 (hardback)
ISBN 9781847942661 (trade paperback)

Typeset in 12/15.5 pt Bembo Book MT Std
by Integra Software Services Pvt. Ltd, Pondicherry

Printed and bound in Great Britain by Clays Ltd, Elcograf S.p.A.

Maps by Darren Bennett.

The authorised representative in the EEA is Penguin Random House Ireland,
Morrison Chambers, 32 Nassau Street, Dublin D02 YH68.

Penguin Random House is committed to a sustainable future for
our business, our readers and our planet. This book is made from
Forest Stewardship Council® certified paper.

MIX
Paper from
responsible sources
FSC® C018179

CONTENTS

INTRODUCTION

THE LAST SWASHBUCKLERS

The plane banked hard as it started its descent.

Far below, the placid waters of the Mediterranean had given way to a barren expanse of North African desert. Columns of smoke dotted the horizon. Inside the small private jet, the occupants were stony-faced, bracing against their seats as they descended in a series of stomach-churning corkscrew turns.

This wasn't a normal business trip, even for Ian Taylor. In four decades trading oil, Taylor had set down in plenty of hot spots, from Caracas to Tehran. Yet this journey – destination Benghazi, Libya, in the midst of a civil war – was a new experience.

Taylor only had to look out of the window to be reminded of the risks he was running. A thousand feet below, a lonely NATO drone was chaperoning his plane. Taylor, chief executive of Vitol, the world's largest oil-trading company, found himself wishing his contacts in the British government had sent a proper fighter jet to escort him.

It was early 2011, and the entire region was in the throes of a wave of popular uprisings that came to be known as the Arab Spring. In Libya, forces revolting against the forty-two-year dictatorship of Colonel Muammar Gaddafi had just taken control of Benghazi, the

most important city in the east of the country, and founded their own government.

The rag-tag army of rebels had a big problem, however. It was running out of fuel. The rebels urgently needed diesel and gasoline for their military vehicles and heavy fuel oil to run their power stations. Libya's own refineries had been shuttered by the war, leaving only a trickle of fuel entering the country via hundreds of trucks making the arduous trip from Egypt.

If anyone could take the risk of supplying a rebel army in the middle of a bloody war, it was Ian Taylor.[1] Bald, wiry and tireless, Taylor had transformed Vitol from a mid-sized fuel distributor into an oil trading giant. In the process, he had made it a potent force in the global economy, handling enough oil every day to supply Germany, France, Spain, the UK and Italy combined.[2] Now in his mid-fifties, he combined the easy charm of a member of the British establishment with the taste for adventure that was a prerequisite for an oil trader. He had never been afraid to lead Vitol to places where others feared to tread. And, in a world where oil and money go hand in hand with power, he was not one to shy away from deals that carried wider geopolitical significance.

When, a few weeks earlier, the possibility of a deal with the Libyan rebels had come up, Taylor hadn't hesitated. Vitol's team in the Middle East had received a call from the government of Qatar. The small gas-rich Gulf state had become a key political and financial backer of the Libyan rebels, acting as a go-between for them with Western governments and supplying them with weapons and cash. But buying tankers full of refined oil products and delivering them into a war zone was beyond Qatar's capability. It needed the help of a commodity trader. The Qataris wanted to know if Vitol could supply diesel, gasoline and fuel oil to Benghazi.

Vitol had four hours to think about it, and respond. The trading house only needed four minutes to say yes.

But there was a big catch. The rebels had no cash. Instead, Vitol would have to take payment in the form of crude oil from the few

oilfields that the rebels controlled. In theory, that shouldn't have posed a problem: Vitol could deliver fuel across the Mediterranean to the port of Benghazi, while receiving crude oil via a pipeline to the coastal city of Tobruk, near the Egyptian border and far away from the fighting (see map on page 331).

Taylor and the rest of Vitol's top brass quickly put together a proposal. It was nothing new for a big trading house like Vitol to barter one commodity for another, particularly when facing a cash-strapped customer. Indeed, other traders were also vying to take part in the deal with the Libyan rebels. But Vitol was more aggressive: it was willing not only to handle the shipments of fuel, but also to extend credit to the Libyan rebels, effectively lending them money.[3]

The company had another advantage: its political connections in London and Washington. Taylor, a gifted social operator with the charisma of a born politician, was a leading donor to the ruling Conservative Party. His contact book in London's business and political elites was second to none. Only a few months later, he would join other financiers at a dinner with the prime minister at 10 Downing Street. 'Obviously, I got permission from the Brits to go in,' Taylor later recalled.[4]

In the UK, a covert 'Oil Cell' at the Foreign Office worked to prevent Gaddafi's forces from obtaining fuel or selling crude internationally. Washington granted a sanctions waiver to allow US companies to buy Libyan oil from Vitol. And, of course, there was the NATO drone.

But while London and Washington were supportive of Vitol's mission, they weren't prepared to intervene too overtly on its behalf. As Taylor descended into what was still a war zone, he knew that, if something went wrong, he was on his own.

The possibility of anti-aircraft fire from Gaddafi's forces meant that a conventional landing was too dangerous, so the pilot descended as fast as the jet could dive. Taylor was alone in the small plane apart from a pair of hired bodyguards and Chris Bake, a thick-set New Zealander who ran Vitol's operations in the Middle East.

If the descent made his stomach turn, Taylor didn't get much comfort from what he found on the ground. In the spring of 2011, Benghazi was lawless and unstable. The city, a collection of dusty concrete buildings clustered around a fetid lagoon, was located just a few hundred kilometres from the frontline of a conflict that was still raging. The air was thick with the sounds and smells of war. Putrid-smelling hospitals were overflowing with amputees and other casualties. The dusty streets were filled with men and boys with Kalashnikov assault rifles strapped to their backs.

At night, random blackouts left the city without electricity for hours at a time. Patrols of heavily armed youths set up checkpoints at roads around the city. Out of this lawless environment would emerge the armed mob that, a year later, stormed the US consulate and killed Chris Stevens, the ambassador to Libya.

Benghazi's citizens, exhausted by decades of dictatorship and months of war, cowered in their homes. Saif al-Islam, Gaddafi's son, took to state television to make a bloodcurdling speech in which he promised further carnage: 'We will fight until the last man, the last woman, the last bullet.'[5]

Benghazi had long been the hub of Libya's oil industry. The country's richest oil reserves were located in uninhabited expanses of desert in the country's east – nearer to Benghazi than Tripoli, the capital, which was still firmly under Gaddafi's control. Most of the oilfields had been abandoned as fighting swept the country, and Libya's top geologists and oil engineers would meet in the evenings in Benghazi's main square to discuss their country's plight. A couple of kilometres away, the regional headquarters of the national oil company of Libya stood next to the blackened shell of a former police station that had been torched by the rebels in the first days of their uprising.

This was where Taylor and Bake headed once their plane had touched down. The man waiting to meet them was Nuri Berruien. A veteran engineer, Berruien had been preparing for retirement before the civil war broke out. By spring 2011 he was running the rebel

branch of Libya's national oil company, cutting the deal that could save the revolution.

If Taylor was going to deal with the rebels, he wanted to know who was on the other side of the transaction. He knew from decades of experience in the Middle East that a personal assurance could matter more than a carefully drafted contract. And, in any case, a contract would be of little use when dealing with a rebel government operating in makeshift ministries a thousand kilometres from the country's capital.

Taylor was satisfied. The man on the other side of one of Vitol's riskiest deals ever was not some war-crazed loon, but an oil industry pro. He shook hands and returned to London. 'It was a gamble, but it was a reasonable gamble,' he later said. On the other side, Berruien was also content: Vitol had offered him 'the best terms' and had not even bothered to ask for war insurance.[6]

Almost immediately, Vitol's intervention shifted the balance of the war. Securing sufficient fuel had always been a crucial determinant of victory in North Africa's empty stretches of desert. It was here in the Second World War that the army of Erwin Rommel, the German general popularly known as the 'Desert Fox', foundered after running out of fuel.

Now Libya's rebel army had enough fuel to avoid Rommel's fate. Thanks to Vitol, it could power its tanks and 'tacticals' – the improvised combination of a pick-up truck with a machine gun welded to its flatbed, which was the rebel military's vehicle of choice.[7]

Despite air support from NATO and financial aid from Qatar, the rebels had failed to advance beyond their stronghold in the area around Benghazi. By the time of Taylor's visit in spring 2011, their territory encompassed only the eastern region of Benghazi and a strip of coastline for a further 150 km southwest.

The key strategic goal was to take the oil towns further west – Marsa al-Brega, Ras Lanuf and Es Sider – through which Gaddafi loyalists still controlled access to Libya's oil riches. Following the first deliveries of fuel from Vitol, Marsa al-Brega fell to the rebels

on 17 July. Within weeks, they had taken Ras Lanuf and Es Sider, and from there seized control of the inland oilfields of the Sirte basin, the spot where oil had first been discovered in Libya in 1959.

By October, they had cornered Gaddafi loyalists in a small area to the west of Sirte. One day, a group of rebel fighters surprised Gaddafi's convoy and the man who had ruled Libya with an iron fist for four decades fled, seeking shelter in a drainpipe. The rebels dragged him out and beat him to death – a gruesome moment of triumph that was filmed on a mobile phone and broadcast around the world.

For Vitol, though, triumph was still far away. The company's plans had started going awry only a few days after Taylor and Berruien had shaken hands in Benghazi in the spring. Despite a promise that the existence of the deal would remain a secret, it soon became public that the rebels had agreed to sell their oil and receive fuel in exchange. In response, Gaddafi's forces sent men across the desert to blow up the key Sarir–Tobruk pipeline, which linked the oilfields controlled by the rebels with an export terminal on the Mediterranean coast – the site where Vitol had anticipated taking delivery of the crude oil it was accepting as payment. 'That was the end of their crude exports for a while,' Bake recalls, grimly.[8]

Taylor had a dilemma. There was no longer any way for Vitol to get paid with crude shipments. Every cargo of fuel the trading house delivered now represented an ever-growing financial exposure to the rebels, who had no government, no central bank and little standing internationally. If Taylor continued supplying them, he was effectively betting his company that the rebels would win the war.

He decided to risk it. By then he'd spent thirty years building a network in the Middle East. If he walked away from the deal with Libya's rebels, he'd not only be letting them down, but also his long-standing contacts in Qatar – a country that had long been a lucrative source of business for Vitol.

Rival traders believe there may have been another reason why Taylor felt comfortable sticking with his deal with the Libyan rebels: Gaddafi had billions of dollars frozen in Western bank accounts. Had

the war ended badly for Vitol's deal, Taylor's friends in Western governments could have ensured that the trading house would be repaid from those frozen assets. (In September 2011, $300 million in Libyan assets in the West was unfrozen in order to help pay Vitol.)[9] 'We had no guarantees from anybody,' insists David Fransen, chairman of Vitol in Switzerland and one of Taylor's longest-standing partners. 'We just got a few "You'll be alright, do its".'[10]

Over the coming months, Vitol's tankers shipped cargo after cargo. The boats slipped into Libya's ports at night, with orders to complete unloading and steal away again before dawn. At times, fighting was raging within earshot of the ship's crew, who were standing on top of hundreds of thousands of barrels of highly flammable fuel.

With every shipment, the stakes grew higher for Vitol. Over five months, the trading house shipped thirty cargoes of gasoline, diesel, fuel oil and liquefied petroleum gas to Libya. At one point, as everyone waited for the war to end and oil production to restart, the amount owed by the rebel government to Vitol ballooned to more than $1 billion – a sum large enough to threaten the trader's survival, and that it would have struggled to recover if the war had ended differently. 'It was a deal which, to be honest, got much larger than it should have,' Taylor said. 'It could have gone very, very badly wrong.'[11]

It's impossible to say how the Libyan civil war would have turned out if Vitol hadn't taken on the deal to deliver fuel to the rebels, and then continued delivering even after it couldn't be repaid. Perhaps another commodity trader would have taken Vitol's place? Perhaps the Qatari government would have found another way to get fuel to the rebels?

But one thing is hard to dispute: without $1 billion of fuel in their moment of need, the rebels would have certainly been defeated. 'The fuel from Vitol was very important for the military,' Abdeljalil Mayuf, an official at rebel-controlled Arabian Gulf Oil in Benghazi, said in 2011.[12] It was not the first time an oil trader had shaped the history of the Middle East, and wouldn't be the last.

For Libya, however, the story didn't have a happy ending. In the years after Taylor flew into Benghazi, the country lurched from one conflict to another. Gaddafi's death didn't end the fighting: local warlords in the country's west and east continued to battle over its oil resources. In 2014, Libya descended into a second civil war – which, at the time of writing, is still smouldering. And the fall of Gaddafi had wider destabilising effects across the whole region, as the Libyan army's arsenal was smuggled out to conflict zones including Syria, where the terrorist group Islamic State was beginning to gain a foothold.[13]

As the dead bodies piled up in Libya and the effects of its civil war rippled across the Middle East, Taylor came to question the wisdom of his intervention. 'It's hard to know whether we got it all right,' he told an interviewer in 2019. 'I was thinking about Libya the other day and was really upset about it – maybe we shouldn't have done that one.'[14]

Vitol's deals in Libya are a demonstration of the enormous power that commodity traders wield in the modern world. Few of us experience their might as directly as the Libyans, but whether or not we know it, we are all their customers. Most of us take for granted the ease with which we can fill up our cars, buy a new smartphone or order a cup of Colombian coffee. But underpinning almost all of our consumption is a frenetic international trade in natural resources. And underpinning that trade, from their offices in sleepy towns in Switzerland or New England, are the commodity traders.

Little noticed and little scrutinised, the commodity traders have become essential cogs in the modern economy. Without them, petrol stations would run out of fuel, factories would grind to a halt and bakeries would run out of flour. They are, in the words of Ludwig Jesselson, one of the industry's pioneers, an 'international clearing-house for essential goods'.[15]

Their influence is not limited to the economy: the commodity traders' control over the flow of the world's strategic resources has

also made them powerful political actors. To grasp the interplay of money and power in the modern world, to see how oil and metals flow out of resource-rich countries and cash flows into the pockets of tycoons and kleptocrats, you need to understand the commodity traders. They usually say they are apolitical, motivated by profit rather than the pursuit of power. But there is little doubt that, as Vitol's deals with Libya's rebels show, they have shaped history.

In Iraq, the commodity traders helped Saddam Hussein to sell his oil, bypassing UN sanctions; in Cuba, they swapped sugar for oil with Fidel Castro, helping to keep the Communist revolution alive; and they secretly sold millions of tonnes of US wheat and corn to the Soviet Union, propping up Moscow at the height of the Cold War. When Igor Sechin, the boss of Russian oil giant Rosneft and an ally of President Vladimir Putin, needed to raise $10 billion in short order, whom did he call? The commodity traders.

They are the last swashbucklers of global capitalism: willing to do business where other companies don't dare set foot, thriving through a mixture of ruthlessness and personal charm. But while the importance of the commodity traders has grown in recent decades, their numbers have remained relatively small: a large share of the world's traded resources is handled by just a few companies, many of them owned by just a few people. The five largest oil trading houses handle 24 million barrels a day of crude and refined products, such as gasoline and jet fuel, equivalent to almost a quarter of the world's petroleum demand.[16] The seven leading agricultural traders handle just under half of the world's grains and oilseeds.[17] Glencore, the largest metals trader, accounts for a third of the world's supply of cobalt, a crucial raw material for electric vehicles.[18] But even those numbers understate the traders' role: as the fastest and most aggressive participants in the market, it is often their trades that set the price.

As journalists covering natural resources over the past two decades, we have been struck by the power and influence that is concentrated in just a few commodity traders' hands, and equally surprised by how little is known about them – particularly by regulators and

governments. To some extent that's by design. For the most part, the commodity traders are privately owned companies, with less obligation to disclose information about their activities than their publicly listed counterparts. Many have traditionally viewed their superior access to information as a competitive edge – and so have gone to great lengths to avoid giving out any information about themselves. As Ian Taylor, who died in 2020, said as he sat down with us for an interview for this book: 'We would prefer you not to write it.'[19]

So the industry has remained in the shadows, barring the odd flurry of interest – usually when prices surge or when scandals break. In three-quarters of a century, only a handful of books has been written about it. And journalists have, with a few exceptions, given up on trying to write about companies who greet their questions with a wall of silence (and, occasionally, threatening legal letters).

That's something we experienced at first hand working for the *Financial Times* and Bloomberg News. When we started writing about commodities in the early 2000s, we were intrigued by the traders. Many people in the natural resources industry seemed to believe they were the hidden hand behind moves in prices or political events. Yet they almost never appeared in public, or in the pages of the newspapers. Few of our colleagues had ever heard of them, let alone spoken to them.

Our curiosity only grew when we first tried to make contact. Glencore had deputised one of its in-house financiers to tell journalists, politely but firmly, that they could take their questions elsewhere. His first tack was to try to persuade us that our interest was misplaced. (Glencore was, at that time, already the world's largest commodity trader.) 'We are a little company of no interest to anyone,' the person said. We would do better to spend our time writing about more interesting companies, he recommended.

Louis Dreyfus, one of the largest agricultural commodity traders, employed an even simpler technique. It gave journalists the email address and phone number of an executive to contact with questions. But the phone was never answered, and the emails were never

returned. When, after weeks of fruitless attempts, the elusive executive finally answered the phone, he said that, yes, of course he had seen our emails. Why, then, had he not responded, even with 'no comment', long the favourite response of a stonewalling PR man? His lack of response, he replied enigmatically, should have been seen as a form of response in itself. And then he hung up.

This book grew out of a desire to understand and explain these enigmatic companies and individuals. We were lucky with our timing: our interest came at a moment when the commodity traders were coming out of the shadows. Most strikingly, Glencore went public in 2011, in the largest ever flotation on the London market – a move that forced it to start opening up about its finances, and submitting itself to questions from investors and the media. Its competitors, too, started hiring PR consultants, publishing information about their finances and giving interviews to journalists.

In over a year of research for this book, we've interviewed more than one hundred active and retired commodity traders. Some have turned us down, but many more have been willing to talk, perhaps encouraged by the passage of time to open up their world to outsiders. We've spoken to more than two dozen current and former Glencore partners, to every living founder of Trafigura, and to a dozen current and former executives of Vitol. The process of carrying out the interviews has offered its own insights into the riches that the commodity trade has generated. We interviewed Andy Hall, who has a good claim to being the world's most famous living oil trader, at his 1,000-year-old castle, bedecked with modern art, near Hanover. Another retired oil trader invited us to his stud farm in the English home counties. A third hosted us at his chalet in an exclusive Swiss ski resort.

Many of the current crop of commodity traders were more guarded in their interactions with us, although every major trading house offered us a meeting, with the exception of Archer Daniels Midland. The chief executives of each of the largest oil, metals and agriculture traders gave us an interview. Some were more forthcoming than others. Ivan Glasenberg, the boss of Glencore, whose company was

at the time of research being investigated by the US Justice Department in a corruption and money-laundering probe, invited us to an interview on the top floor of his company's boxy Swiss headquarters. Then, with his lawyer on one side and his PR man on the other, he parried our questions for five combative hours, insisting that large swathes of our conversation could not be quoted.

The history recounted in this book is based primarily on all those interviews. Where we've recounted historical events or encounters, we have based them on the accounts of at least one person who was involved. Where different people differ in their recollections of the details, we've noted that in the text.

Have the traders always been entirely honest with us? We'll leave the reader to judge. When it comes to the more dubious corners of the business of commodity trading, we've received a variety of responses. One former Glencore trader began his conversation with us with the words: 'What I'm going to tell you is *not* going to be the whole truth and nothing but the truth. There are things I'm just not going to tell you.' Another trader shut down the conversation whenever it turned to the more scurrilous moments of his career. But he would not have made a good poker player. When we asked how he had managed to secure such a lucrative oil deal in Nigeria or Iran, a smile flickered across his face and his eyes twinkled with everything left unsaid.

We haven't relied solely on the traders' own accounts of themselves. This book is the product of twenty years of learning about the commodity traders. In that time we've not only met and interviewed hundreds of traders, but also travelled to dozens of countries, from war-torn Libya to the US farm belt, to talk to the people who do business with the traders, the government officials who interact with them, and the ordinary citizens who are affected by their activities. We've also gathered thousands of pages of documents, many of which have never been published, detailing the traders' finances, the networks of companies they own, and the structure of their deals.

★

The term 'commodity trader' conjures a variety of different images, from the roaring trading pits of Chicago to the banks of computer screens on a Wall Street trading floor. But the focus of this book is the companies and individuals whose business is buying and selling physical commodities. It is they who control the flow of natural resources around the world; it is in their hands that an almost unique type of political and economic power is concentrated.

That definition excludes the Wall Street banks and hedge funds that bet vast sums on moves in prices without ever coming close to an actual barrel of oil, a bushel of wheat or a tonne of copper. It also excludes the big miners and oil companies that have sophisticated networks around the world to sell their iron ore, copper or oil, but wouldn't consider it their business to buy and sell commodities they hadn't produced.

Of course, the category of commodity trader is somewhat blurry around the edges: some large oil companies, such as BP and Shell, are also major traders above and beyond the oil that is produced at the fields they own. Banks like Goldman Sachs and Morgan Stanley have, at various points in history, also been significant traders of physical commodities. Japan too has a long history of general trading companies, the *sogo shosha*, whose principal role has been to secure the natural resource imports needed by Japanese manufacturers, but which have also dabbled in international commodity trading – occasionally with disastrous consequences.

While some of these feature occasionally in our story, our focus is on the companies and individuals whose main activity is neither producing nor consuming commodities, but trading them. These are the companies sometimes known as the 'independent traders' or the 'trading houses'. Even then, we can't hope to provide an exhaustive account of every trader of every commodity in history. Instead, we have focused on the companies that have dominated the traded markets in oil, metals and agriculture over the past seventy-five years, and which have had a critical role in the development of the global economy.

Many of those companies belong to a single corporate dynasty. While Glencore dominates commodity trading today, in the 1980s it was Marc Rich + Co that played the dominant role, and, in the 1960s and 1970s, Philipp Brothers. The companies have an almost familial connection: Marc Rich was a senior trader at Philipp Brothers before he left to found the company that bore his name; and Marc Rich + Co was renamed Glencore when the top traders ejected Rich from the company he had founded.

Today, Glencore is the largest metals trader, a top-three oil trader, and the world's largest wheat trader. The company has emerged from Marc Rich's shadow to become a blue-chip stock. From an unassuming building in a quiet Swiss town, it has interests stretching from Canadian wheat to Peruvian copper and Russian oil. Here, the traders are mirror images of their boss, Glasenberg – they talk in the same clipped tones, they join him on morning runs, and quite a few of them are, like him, South Africans with a training in accounting. And they match the tireless work ethic of a man who thinks nothing of calling a journalist at 6 a.m. on a Sunday morning to discuss a story.

Trafigura belongs to the same dynasty. It was started by a group of disaffected former Marc Rich employees who struck out on their own in 1993. The company, now the world's second-largest oil and metals trader, has held on to its underdog mentality, as well as a French sense of style inherited from its founder, Claude Dauphin.

In oil, the leading trader is Vitol, whose executives exude the confidence of the British establishment – as befits a firm whose office is just a few metres away from Buckingham Palace, and whose long-time CEO Ian Taylor was a regular visitor to 10 Downing Street.

In agriculture, Cargill is king. The US company, the world's largest trader of grains, carries itself with the quiet self-assurance of the generations of Midwest wealth on which it was built. As the major trading house that has been at the pinnacle of its industry the longest, it is also the most corporate – with its own archivist and its own authorised company history, which runs to three volumes, at a total length of 1,774 pages.

Within these companies there is an extraordinary cast of characters: manically hard-working, fiercely smart, disarmingly personable, and singularly focused on making money. One thing there is not much of in the commodity trading industry is women. The commodity trading companies make Wall Street banks look progressive on gender diversity. Glencore was the last member of the UK's FTSE 100 index of leading companies to have an all-male board, before it appointed its first female director in 2014.[20] Fewer than one in twenty senior executives in the commodity trading industry are women.[21] Some of the largest commodity traders, such as Vitol and Trafigura, don't have a single woman among their top executives. Glencore, in its annual report published in March 2020, said it wouldn't hit a target set by investors to have a third of its senior management made up of women by the end of the year: 'Still today we find it challenging to fill senior positions … by women.'[22] It's not just on gender diversity that the commodity traders fall down: their upper echelons are not only overwhelmingly male, but also overwhelmingly white.

The basic business of the commodity traders is disarmingly simple: buy natural resources in one place and time, and sell them at another – hopefully making a profit in the process. Their role exists because supply and demand of commodities often don't match. Most mines, farms and oilfields aren't located in the same place as the buyers of their goods. And not every copper miner or soybean farmer can afford to have a network of offices around the world to sell their products. What's more, much of the time, commodity markets are either over- or under-supplied. The traders, ever nimble and flexible, are always ready to take a commodity off a producer's hands as long as the price is right, or to supply it if a consumer is willing to pay.

For an example of how that works in practice, look no further than the oil price crash of 2020. As the coronavirus pandemic spread across the world, grounding flights and forcing people to stay at home, the price of oil spiralled lower and lower, briefly trading below zero for the first time ever. And so the traders stepped in, buying oil at dirt-cheap prices, and then storing it until demand recovered. Some

even bought a few barrels at negative prices, meaning that producers had to pay them to take it off their hands.

The commodity traders are arbitragers par excellence, trying to exploit a series of differences in prices. Because they're doing deals to buy and to sell all the time, they are often indifferent to whether commodity prices overall go up or down. What matters to them is the price disparity – between different locations, different qualities or forms of a product, and different delivery dates. By exploiting these price differences, they help to make markets more efficient, directing resources to their highest value uses in response to price signals. They are, in the words of one academic, the visible manifestation of Adam Smith's invisible hand.[23]

As they have grown, they've also become important conduits of finance for global trade – a kind of shadow banking sector that is willing to pay oil producers up front for their crude, or supply copper to manufacturers on credit. As Jim Daley, a former head of oil trading at Marc Rich + Co, puts it: 'Oil is just a form of money.'[24]

But while this book is about the rise of the commodity traders in the second half of the twentieth century, it also tells a wider story. Their tale offers an insight into how the modern world works – a world where the market is king, where international enterprises seem able to shrug off almost all attempts at regulation, and where titans of global finance hold more power than some elected politicians.

Commodity trading is as old as commerce itself, but the trading industry only began to take its modern form in the years after the Second World War. This was the era when trading companies became truly global for the first time – and, crucially, when oil started to become a tradable commodity. Where their predecessors had been operating in narrow niches, from the 1950s onwards the commodity traders suddenly found themselves on the crest of an enormous wave of global economic growth. As the US achieved superpower status,

it encouraged trade around the world – and the early traders were its emissaries. In dollar terms, the world's trade in manufactured goods and natural resources rose from less than $60 billion just after the Second World War to more than $17 trillion in 2017, a quarter of which was made up by commodities.[25]

And as economic prosperity spread beyond the US and Europe, the commodity traders were leading the charge. They were among the first Western companies to open offices in countries such as India, Russia, China and Indonesia, many years before other investors discovered the concept of 'emerging markets'. 'It's not for the faint of heart,' says David MacLennan, chief executive of Cargill. 'The history of Cargill has been to go into places where other people won't. That's where opportunity is. Whether there's crisis, or threat, or things that are high risk, that means there's opportunity.'[26]

At the centre of this book's story are four developments which moulded the global economy in the commodity traders' favour. The first was the opening up of markets that had previously been tightly controlled – above all, oil. The dominance of the large oil companies, known as the 'Seven Sisters', was loosened by the wave of nationalisations that swept the countries of the Middle East in the 1970s. Suddenly, oil that had been locked into a single company's supply chain from well to refinery to petrol station was freely tradable, and prices that had been fixed began to move. Middle Eastern and Latin American leaders alike now had oil to sell, and the commodity traders dealt with them indiscriminately. In the process they helped to create a new form of global power, the petrostate.

The second was the collapse of the Soviet Union in 1991, which, at a stroke, redrew a global network of economic relationships and political allegiances. Again, the commodity traders dived in, bringing the law of the market to what had previously been planned economies. Amidst the chaos, they became key lifelines for struggling mines and factories, even propping up entire governments. In exchange, they were able to secure access to natural resources at extremely favourable terms.

The third was the spectacular economic growth of China in the first decade of this century. As the Chinese economy industrialised, it created enormous new demand for commodities. In 1990, for example, China consumed the same amount of copper as Italy did; today, every other tonne of copper on earth goes to a Chinese factory.[27] And the shift of China's rural populations to the cities created new demand for imports of food and fuel. The result was another step up in the international trade in commodities, followed by a huge spike in prices. As the commodity traders scoured the world for commodities to feed the insatiable demand, they helped to forge new economic relationships between China and resource-rich countries in Latin America, Asia and Africa.

The fourth was the financialisation of the global economy and the growth of the banking sector, beginning in the 1980s. Where their predecessors would need to have enough capital to pay for each shipment of metal or grain they bought, suddenly the modern traders could use borrowed money and bank guarantees, enabling them to trade in much larger quantities and to marshal much larger sums of money.

The result of these four developments was an extraordinary expansion in the wealth and power of the handful of companies and individuals who dominate the global trade in commodities. The traders' aim is to take a small profit margin on a large volume of trade. And that volume is truly enormous: in 2019, the four largest commodity traders had a turnover of $725 billion – more than the total exports of Japan.[28] The industry's profits have been similarly impressive. Marc Rich + Co made so much money in the oil crisis of 1979 that it would have ranked as one of America's ten most profitable companies. In the decade of the China-led commodities boom leading up to 2011, the combined profits of the three largest commodity traders were bigger than those of better-known giants of global commerce, such as Apple and Coca-Cola (see table on page 332).

What's even more remarkable is that those profits have been shared among a very small group of people. The commodity

traders, with a few exceptions, have remained private, dividing up their profits between a handful of partners or founders and creating fantastic wealth for those individuals. Vitol, still owned exclusively by its employees, has distributed more than $10 billion to its trader-shareholders in the past decade alone. The family that owns Cargill contains no fewer than fourteen billionaires – more than any other family in the world.[29] Louis Dreyfus, the historic grain trader, is almost entirely owned by just one person. Glencore minted no fewer than seven billionaires when it floated in 2011.

This cocktail of big money, strategically important resources and a willingness to operate where others fear to set foot has provided no shortage of opportunities for skulduggery among the less scrupulous members of the commodity trading industry. That's largely been possible thanks to a remarkable lack of regulation or government scrutiny of their activities.

One of the reasons the activities of the commodity traders have escaped oversight for so long is that they operate in the most opaque corners of the international financial system. The commodities they transport are often to be found on the high seas, beyond the scope of any national regulator; they typically trade through shell companies in offshore jurisdictions; and the traders have based themselves in places like Switzerland or Singapore, which are famed for their light-touch regulation. As one prominent Zurich law firm puts it: 'Commodity trading activities are hardly regulated in Switzerland'. The company in question, Pestalozzi, is in a better position to know than most: its namesake, Peter Pestalozzi, worked for three decades as the lawyer for Marc Rich + Co and later Glencore, sitting on the company's board of directors until 2011.[30]

And so, when commodity traders have hit the headlines, it has more often than not been because of wrongdoing. Most famous of all, and most instrumental in shaping the popular perception of

commodity traders, is the case of Marc Rich. In many ways the founder of the modern commodity trading industry, Rich spent almost two decades as a fugitive from US justice, holed up in Switzerland after he was indicted for tax evasion and trading with Iran at the same time as dozens of Americans were being held hostage in Tehran.

Some of the traders we've interviewed have been remarkably blunt about the trading industry's reputation for bribery and corruption. 'Unfortunately this is something that has plagued the commodity industry,' Torbjörn Törnqvist, the co-founder and chief executive of oil trader Gunvor, told us. 'There's a lot of skeletons and many of them, most of them, will never be surfaced.'[31]

Another trader, who was one of Glencore's most senior partners until 2002, calmly told us how he used to travel regularly to London with a suitcase full of cash. Of course, he pointed out, in those days paying 'commissions' was both legal and tax-deductible for a Swiss company.[32]

Others have retreated to PR platitudes: the industry's reputation for wrongdoing is outdated, they say, insisting they have 'zero tolerance' policies on corruption. It's certainly true that things have changed. Overseas 'commissions' are no longer tax deductible as they once were; banks now ask tougher questions of the companies they lend to; and many commodity traders have compliance departments that act as internal policemen.

And yet the constant flow of stories – some of them extremely recent – that paint the industry in an unflattering light suggests that in too many cases, traders are still willing to put morality and the law to one side in order to turn a profit. From the Democratic Republic of Congo and Ivory Coast to Brazil and Venezuela, many of the world's largest traders are in the crosshairs of anti-corruption prosecutors.

The worst examples of commodity traders' behaviour do not define the whole industry, however. 'Just like not every Hollywood producer was a Harvey Weinstein, not every commodity trader is a briber,' argues Mark Hansen, who runs a mid-sized metals trader.[33]

Yet corruption is not the only sphere in which the commodity traders' reputation is far from glowing. Thanks to their bases in low-tax jurisdictions, many of the traders have paid remarkably little tax on their extraordinary profits. Over the past two decades, Vitol has paid just 13% in tax on its profits of more than $25 billion.[34]

And in a world waking up to the reality of climate change, the traders have been slow to reform a business that still relies heavily on commodities that pollute the environment. Coal is among the most important drivers of profits for Glencore, which is the world's number one exporter of the commodity. Glasenberg, who started his career in the coal business and once bragged that the world was 'horny as hell for coal',[35] is still a fan.[36] Oil and gas remain hugely important to many of the top traders. No one that we have interviewed appears to be ethically troubled by that: the traders simply argue that they will continue to trade fossil fuels as long as the world keeps consuming them. Yet even if they aren't concerned about their own impact on climate change, the shifting public debate on fossil fuels still represents a threat to their business.

Whatever their future holds, one thing is clear: the commodity traders have, over the past three-quarters of a century, become enormously important and influential actors in the world. For too long, their activities have been little understood and their significance has been underappreciated.

We hope this book will go some way to changing that.

ONE

THE PIONEERS

As Theodor Weisser approached the Soviet border, he felt a shudder of fear.

Travelling from Western Europe to the Soviet Union in 1954 would have been a daunting journey for anyone, but for Weisser it required particular courage. As a soldier in the German army, he had been captured by Soviet forces in the Second World War and made a prisoner on the Eastern Front.

Now in his forties, but with the memories of his time in a Soviet prison camp still fresh, this trip would be his first to Russia as a free man. At the last minute, fearing that someone he'd encountered during the war might recognise him, he bought a red cap and pulled it down over his eyes.[1]

Weisser was in ground-breaking territory. He was travelling to the capital of Communism at a time when the Cold War dominated public discourse in the West. Since a Soviet-backed coup in Czechoslovakia in 1948, Western Europe had become increasingly alarmed about the threat of an assertive Soviet Union on its doorstep. And America was gripped by the Red Scare whipped up by Senator Joseph McCarthy's public denunciations of suspected Communists.

But Weisser was not the kind of man to be easily deterred. He had set off from Hamburg determined to buy some oil, and he wasn't going to leave without a deal. He made his way through Moscow's wide, empty highways to one of the few hotels where foreigners were permitted to stay, and waited for the Soviet bureaucracy to take notice of him.

He didn't have to wait for long. Soon, he had succeeded in securing a dinner appointment with Evgeny Gurov: the head of Soyuznefteexport, the government agency that controlled the Soviet Union's oil trade. Gurov was an ideologue who recognised earlier than many others the potential for oil to be used as a strategic weapon.[2] Weisser, on the other hand, was not motivated by ideology, but by profit. His company, Mabanaft, was a distributor of fuel across West Germany. And it was losing money. Weisser needed to find new sources of oil to sell to his clients, and that meant going where few others would dare.

No record remains of where the two men dined or what they ate, but it must have been a peculiar affair: one of the Soviet Union's top trade officials sitting at a table with a former prisoner of war, toasting their new acquaintance under the watchful eyes of the KGB.

There was a period of negotiation, but Weisser's perseverance would ultimately be rewarded: Soyuznefteexport sold him one cargo of diesel for resale in West Germany. The trader's pioneering spirit would prove costly, however, at least initially. On his return to Germany, his willingness to deal with the Cold War adversary meant he was shunned by much of the oil industry. The shipping companies he had been using to transport his fuel around the country refused to do business with him, on the grounds that their other customers didn't want to charter ships that had previously held oil from the Soviet Union.[3]

But Weisser, a consummate networker with a broad, open face and a winning smile, knew he had secured the only thing that mattered from his trip to Moscow: a contact behind the Iron Curtain. His first deal marked the beginning of a relationship that would

continue for years, underpinning the profits of his trading business. In 1956, Gurov visited Weisser in return, and, in Munich, he signed a one-year contract to sell diesel to Mabanaft. Soon, the German trader was also buying crude oil from the Soviets.

The early deals with the Soviet Union were a personal triumph for Weisser, a testament to his courage, tenacity and charm. But they were also a sign of how the world was changing, and the increasingly critical role that commodity traders like Weisser would play in it.

After decades of economic depression, stagnation and war, the world was entering an era of stability and economic prosperity. The horrors of war had given way to a peace policed by the US's growing military might – the Pax Americana. Where living conditions in the mid-1940s had been marked by price controls and rationing, by the 1960s a growing number of households in the US, Europe and Japan could afford televisions, refrigerators and cars. Between 1950 and 1955, more than half of the households in America bought a television.[4]

Everywhere new trade routes were opening, as nationalism and protectionism gave way to free trade and global markets. The world economy was growing at the fastest rate on record, driving ever greater consumption of natural resources. The period became known as the Golden Age of Capitalism.[5] Weisser had understood that this new world held unprecedented opportunities for a company whose entire business was international trading – never before had a commodity trader been able to paint on such a global canvas.

He was not alone. Around the world, a new generation of commodity traders was exploiting the opportunities created by the booming global economy. In New York, Ludwig Jesselson, a brilliant and intense young metal trader who had fled to the US to escape the anti-Semitism of Nazi Germany, had a similar vision. He would lead his company, Philipp Brothers, to become so dominant that it took on the biggest banks on Wall Street, giving birth to a family of trading companies that still dominates the global commodity markets today.

In Minnesota, John H. MacMillan Jr, a grain trader who had taken over the running of his family company, was determined to turn its fortunes around. That family company, Cargill, would go on to become America's largest private corporation, making MacMillan's descendants some of the richest people on the planet.

These three men were the founding fathers of the modern commodity trading industry. Where their predecessors had focused on local niches, they saw that the whole world was becoming one market. Everything was for sale; potential buyers were everywhere. Decades before 'globalisation' became an economic buzzword, they created businesses that were based on it in all but name. As international trade expanded and became a central part of the modern economy, their companies would be its ushers, shaping it at the same time as profiting from it – and forging a business model that would define the commodity trading industry for decades to come.

Over the next twenty years, commodity trading would be transformed from a small-time business into one of the most important industries in the world economy. Traders such as Weisser, Jesselson and MacMillan would become paragons of the new economic order, amassing extraordinary wealth and being welcomed into presidential palaces around the world as masters of the earth's natural resources.

It was a revolution that largely went unnoticed by politicians and the wider public. Only after decades of quiet growth would the world understand how central the commodity traders had become to the global economy. When the realisation came, in the 1970s, it would bring the richest nations on the planet to their knees. All of a sudden, policymakers would wake up to the fact that the commodity traders – a group they had barely realised existed – had accumulated unprecedented power over the world's energy, metals and food.

The history of commodity trading goes back to the dawn of mankind, when the first settled humans started to buy and sell stones and

metals, perhaps in exchange for grains. Indeed, the tendency to 'truck and barter' – to trade – is seen by anthropologists as one of the activities that marked the beginnings of modern human behaviour.[6]

But the first commodity trading companies that bear any resemblance to today's traders did not appear until the nineteenth century. For centuries, bands of merchant-adventurers had been travelling around the world seeking valuable resources to sell back at home – the most successful of them, the East India Company, governed the Indian subcontinent for several decades.

With the industrial revolution, however, the trade in resources was transformed. The invention of the steamship meant that, for the first time, long-distance commodity trading wasn't at the mercy of the winds. The cost of transporting goods fell precipitously, and as a result it became viable to ship not just tea, spices and precious metals over long distances, but also lower-value goods like grains and ores. And the telegraph ushered in an era of near instant global communications. In August 1858, the first telegraph line across the Atlantic opened, immediately cutting the time it took to deliver a message from London to New York from nearly two weeks to just a few minutes.

With these technological developments came the first dedicated commodity trading companies. Merchants sprang up to buy and sell the scrap metal and residues that were the waste products of the burgeoning industrial age. And grain traders delivered food to the growing metropolises full of hungry workers.

The nineteenth-century metals trade grew up in Europe's industrial heartlands, dominated by three German companies: Aron Hirsch & Sohn, Metallgesellschaft, and Beer, Sondheimer & Co. Philipp Brothers, the company that Ludwig Jesselson would later lead, grew out of this German tradition. Its founder, Julius Philipp, had begun trading from his apartment in Hamburg in 1901, and in 1909 his brother Oscar moved to London to establish Philipp Brothers.

The first traders of agricultural commodities were more scattered, with different companies rising up to dominate particular regions or

market niches. In the world's breadbaskets, grain trading companies were set up to transport wheat and corn from the farms to the cities. In the United States, their number included Cargill, founded when the son of a Scottish immigrant opened his first grain silo in 1865.

The industry fell on hard times during the First and Second World Wars. Entire trading dynasties in Europe were lost, and the families behind some of them – many of which were Jewish – had to flee the advancing Nazi army. Not all of them got out in time: Julius Philipp was captured in Holland and died in 1944 in a concentration camp in northern Germany.

When the war ended, it opened up a new horizon of opportunity for the commodity traders. The ruined cities of Europe and Asia needed rebuilding, and that would require steel, cement and copper. The trade in natural resources, which had been tightly controlled by wartime governments, would be slowly freed in the new age of peace. And the dominance of the US on the world stage would herald a new era of growth and open markets.[7]

The pioneers of commodity trading had very different backgrounds and upbringings – MacMillan had been born into a wealthy family in the US Midwest; Jesselson was the son of a shopkeeper from southern Germany; and Weisser had grown up in a middle-class family in Hamburg. But what they shared was an instinct for internationalism and a willingness to travel the world in search of new opportunities. In the wake of the war, they set about building their companies into truly international enterprises, profiting from the globalisation of the world economy and shaping it in the process.

That meant adopting an outlook that many of their successors in the commodity trading industry still subscribe to: go everywhere, leaving politics and, in many cases, morality to one side. They traded with Communist and capitalist countries alike; with rapacious local businesspeople or government bureaucrats – the goal was to make a

profit. As one of Philipp Brothers' early traders put it: 'One of the basic rules of Philipp Brothers is that business is supreme; political matters are not business.'[8]

Of the three men, it was Ludwig Jesselson who most personified the globetrotting approach of the early traders. With a piercing gaze that magnified his ferocious intellect, Jesselson had arrived in the US in 1937 to escape the anti-Semitism sweeping Europe. He soon had a job trading scrap metal at Philipp Brothers in New York, and, while his fledgling career was put on hold by the Second World War, his ambition remained undimmed.

In 1946, already a senior trader at Philipp Brothers and determined to build the firm into a global business, he set out on a round-the-world trip. In the devastation left by the war, Jesselson, then thirty-six and fizzing with energy, saw only opportunity. From New York, he travelled to Japan and India, Egypt, Germany and Yugoslavia. It was years before commercial air travel across continents would become commonplace, and flights were irregular, long and bumpy.

But Jesselson was unfazed by a little discomfort. Described by a colleague as the 'spark plug of Philipp Brothers', he had supreme confidence in his conviction of the coming economic boom.[9] He set out to hire dozens of new traders and open offices around the world.

With his bald head, boundless energy and intense glare from behind his thick-rimmed spectacles, Jesselson inspired respect and devotion from his band of young traders. 'We all saw Jesselson as a father figure, somebody who gave young people a chance,' says David Tendler, who rose up under his tutelage and went on to run Philipp Brothers in the 1970s and 1980s.[10]

Under Jesselson, who took over running the company in 1957, Philipp Brothers would be transformed from a mid-sized scrap and ore dealer with a staff of about fifty into the world's dominant metals trader. And the DNA of the company would be passed down from one generation of commodity traders to the next, creating a family of trading companies that still defines the global commodities industry.

Just as Weisser had done in oil, Jesselson pioneered the metals trade with the Communist world. One of the first prizes was Yugoslavia, where he had travelled on his world tour in 1946. Philipp Brothers secured a contract with the state metals monopoly, Jugometal, to sell its entire metals output, linking the socialist government of Tito with capitalist America.[11] By 1950, that was worth $15–$20 million of metals a year – more than the company's entire sales just a few years earlier.[12]

By the late 1950s, Philipp Brothers was also buying ferroalloys from the Soviet Union and pig iron from East Germany. In 1973, it was able to boast in its annual report that it had 'for many years done a substantial business with the Soviet Union, as well as with other Eastern European countries'. As a result, it was one of the first ten American companies allowed to establish offices in Moscow.[13] The traders even supplied the US military stockpiles with metal from its Cold War adversaries. For Jesselson, the political implications were irrelevant: all that mattered was that it was profitable business.

John H. MacMillan Jr was from a different world to Jesselson – he was more than a decade older, and he had grown up in a prosperous Midwestern family of Scottish origin. But the two men shared a passion for the business of trading, and a tireless energy that exhausted all who tried to keep pace with them.

MacMillan – known to everyone as John Junior – was born into the commodity trade. His father had run Cargill before him, and his education took place on the floor of the Minneapolis Chamber of Commerce, where traders screamed orders at one another. It was a tough schooling, but an essential one: at Cargill, there was no greater insult than to be considered a 'businessman' rather than a 'trader'.

Always smartly turned out, with a square jaw and neat moustache, he looked the part of the head of a family enterprise. But behind his Midwestern poise was a driven businessman with a creative streak. He was an 'enormously restless person, who was constantly inventing and creating', according to his son's account of him. 'For my father, the corporation came first, even before family.'[14]

And in the early 1950s, he realised the corporation needed a new direction. Cargill was an insular company, focused on the US market, and it was missing out on a boom in international trade. 'We are all terribly upset over missing out on the big volume export business,' MacMillan told his senior staff.[15]

In part that oversight was a function of Cargill's good fortune to have been founded in one of the world's most rapidly growing bread-baskets. The company had developed a solid business moving wheat, corn and soybeans from the Midwest to the growing metropolises on the east and west coasts. While its European and South American rivals had been forced to look overseas for new business, Cargill hadn't needed to.

MacMillan would change that. Like Jesselson at Philipp Brothers and Weisser at Mabanaft, he set out to expand across the world. In 1953, he incorporated Tradax International, the unit that was to serve as his spearhead in the global market. In 1956, he opened the Geneva office of Tradax as Cargill's hub for international trading. The city was chosen for its 'excellent travel and communication facilities', its multilingual tradition, and its 'limited corporate taxes'.[16] The opening of the Tradax office would mark the beginning of a long and prof-itable partnership between Switzerland and the international com-modity traders.

MacMillan's strategy led Cargill – like Philipp Brothers and Maba-naft – to forge new economic links with the Communist world. But while the other pioneers were importing commodities from the Com-munist Bloc to the West, Cargill was building connections in the opposite direction, exporting American agricultural surpluses to the world – including to countries behind the Iron Curtain. The trade was encouraged by generous subsidies from the US government, seeking to support farmers whose ever-larger harvests couldn't all be absorbed at home. Washington financed billions of dollars of exports, helping to spread the American diet around the world. And the grain traders helped deliver this wave of American grain: Cargill quadrupled the volume of its American grain exports between 1955 and 1965.[17]

Initially, the grain exports went to US allies. But soon Cargill and other grain traders were also selling to the Communist Bloc. First came Hungary, which bought $10 million of American grain in late 1963. Next, Cargill dispatched its traders to Moscow to negotiate a bigger deal – for $40 million of wheat. The new business with the Communist nations was a boon for Cargill: in 1964, the company reported its second-highest ever annual profit. The Russian business, it told shareholders, was 'the underlying spark'.[18]

The sale of millions of dollars' worth of American wheat caused a stir in Washington. Port workers went on strike and refused to load ships taking grain to the Soviet Union, and unions urged their members to boycott Cargill and the other commodity traders. Some lawmakers even tried to block the sales, without success.

The furore was one of the first demonstrations of the political nature of the commodity trade, and the power that the traders were accumulating as pioneers of international commerce. In the course of establishing new trade routes between east and west, Cargill and the other pioneers were driving a commercial rapprochement between the US and the Soviet Union that politicians weren't prepared for. Within a few years, however, the deals with Moscow in 1963–64 would seem like a practice run for a much larger – and much more politically explosive – series of deals.

Cargill's strategy of internationalism was a runaway success. MacMillan, who died in 1960, wouldn't be around to see the company rise to the pinnacle of global trade, but there is little doubt that it was he who set Cargill on that path. 'John MacMillan Jr was a genius who set up the international expansion of Cargill,' says David MacLennan, the present-day CEO of Cargill. 'He created the modern company.'[19]

And then there was Theodor Weisser. If Jesselson and MacMillan were scions of the metals and grain trading industries that had been well established since the nineteenth century, Weisser was a maverick who invented a new business single-handedly. He had returned from captivity in the Soviet Union after the defeat of Nazi Germany only

to discover that his old job at an oil company no longer existed. That was all the encouragement he needed to follow his dream of creating his own business.

To kick-start his new project, he bought a dormant company called Marquard & Bahls for 70,000 Reichsmark (the equivalent of about $100,000 in today's money), largely for its import–export licence, a thing of value in a country that was still formally under foreign occupation. By the 1950s, when Weisser travelled to Moscow, the company was already well known throughout the primitive market for refined products by its telegraphic address: Mabanaft, a contraction of its trading name, Marquard & Bahls Naftaproducts.

But Weisser did more than just pioneer a new trade route – he helped to create a new industry where previously there had been none. When Weisser set off for Moscow in 1954, there was no real international oil trade – just a handful of huge companies with near-unlimited market power. Oil trading had briefly flourished in the nineteenth century after the first discovery of oil in America at Titusville, Pennsylvania, in 1859. But the trade abruptly dried up when John Rockefeller bought up control of nearly all the refining capacity in America for his Standard Oil Trust. With only one buyer in town, there was no competition, and so no market.[20] The price of oil was decided by Rockefeller.

The US government broke up Standard Oil in 1911, but the oil market continued to be dominated by an oligopoly of large companies that were vertically integrated to include oil wells, refineries and retail outlets. By the 1950s, the oil market was controlled by seven large companies. They came to be known as the 'Seven Sisters' – the forerunners of the companies that are today ExxonMobil, Royal Dutch Shell, Chevron and BP. Many of them were the descendants of Standard Oil, created in the wake of its break-up. Crude oil was purchased at 'posted prices' set by refiners in each region, a practice that had been started by Rockefeller. International trading outside the oligopoly of these major companies was virtually non-existent.

In the early days of the international oil market, the Seven Sisters avoided dealing with independent traders like Weisser, wary of any threat to their market power. Trying to break their clubby control of the oil market required creativity and a spirit of adventure – and Weisser was perfectly suited to the task. Known to his friends as Theo, he was a born adventurer with a taste for exotic travel, who thought nothing of the discomforts of setting out on a business trip for weeks or months at a time to unknown parts of the world.

He would fly first class, booking a full row of seats so he could keep with him several large suitcases full of paperwork that he carried with him everywhere.[21] In 1951, he set off on a three-month voyage through Africa, travelling across a continent that was on the brink of radical upheaval, as former French, Belgian and British colonies were soon to gain independence. From Tangier and Casablanca, he travelled to Dakar, then Elizabethville and Leopoldville (now Lubumbashi and Kinshasa) in the Belgian Congo. Everywhere he went, he negotiated contracts for Mabanaft to supply the African continent with fuel.

When he struck his deals with Moscow, Weisser became the first independent trader to circumvent the oil majors' club and trade crude oil outside their network of control. They punished him for his insolence, refusing to do business with him immediately after his return from the Soviet Union. And they had good reason to be concerned: Weisser's trades not only marked the start of the rise of the international oil traders, but also the beginning of a major increase in Soviet oil exports.

In 1954, when the Mabanaft boss first travelled to Moscow, Soviet oil production was relatively small, and almost entirely consumed within the Communist Bloc.[22] It was outside the control of the Seven Sisters, but it did not impinge on their empires.

Yet the export route that Weisser helped open would soon take on enormous significance for the global oil market. Until the 1950s, the Soviet Union's oil had come largely from Baku on the Caspian Sea, whose riches had been exploited since the nineteenth century.

But now geologists began to develop new deposits in the Volga-Urals basin, and Soviet oil output doubled between 1955 and 1960.[23] The Soviet Union displaced Venezuela as the second-largest oil producer in the world, behind only the US.

This geological boon coincided with a shift in political winds in Moscow as Nikita Khrushchev, the Soviet leader, pushed for an increase in foreign trade. Soviet trading agencies, such as Soyuznefte-export, became more active. Soviet exports of crude oil and refined petroleum products to the so-called Free World rose from a mere 116,000 barrels a day in 1955 to about one million barrels a day in 1965.[24] The oil export campaign became the most visible manifest-ation of what Western diplomats started to call the 'Soviet Economic Offensive'.

With little fanfare, the commodity traders were helping to change the world economic order. They were forging trade links between Western markets and suppliers that had previously been sealed off behind the Iron Curtain, and in doing so they were helping to unpick the oligopolies that controlled many markets. Within a few years, the ripple effects would be felt across the world.

Weisser, Jesselson and MacMillan were not just important because of their economic impact, however. They also created a model for the business of trading commodities that still holds today.

Where previously traders had focused on particular locations or markets, Mabanaft, Philipp Brothers and Cargill aimed for global mastery of the commodities they traded. Before the Second World War, metal traders such as Philipp Brothers had focused on deals where they could buy a package of metal having already agreed a deal to sell it onwards. A junkyard might call up the firm and offer to sell it a few hundred tonnes of scrap metal. It would then send a cable around to other dealers, and if one could be found who was willing to buy at a price that would give Philipp Brothers a profit,

the company would almost simultaneously agree deals to both buy and sell the metal.[25] Another line of business involved selling on behalf of a producer for a fixed fee per tonne. This was safe and predictable business, but had little potential for outsized profits.

Under Jesselson, Philipp Brothers became more ambitious. The company started doing larger-scale and longer-term trades. It began to negotiate long-term deals to buy from producers, often in exchange for loans. Now the company had a global network of supply deals – a 'trading book' – that could be extremely profitable when market dislocations caused prices to move sharply up or down. 'Always have something to sell,' explained Ernst Frank, the company's specialist in copper, lead and zinc. 'Always be in the business, then sometimes a real shortage develops and if one has material to sell one can make real money.'[26]

Trading on a larger scale required larger and longer-term contracts – and that required a large address book of suppliers and consumers of commodities. The pioneers incessantly cultivated relationships, spending enormous amounts of time and money to woo crucial business contacts. This focus on the personal connection became an obsession in the industry, giving some trading houses an air of old-world charm that they maintained even after email and video conferencing overtook the face-to-face meeting as the main form of business communication. At metals trader Transamine, for example, it is still said that a trader is more likely to be fired for taking a contact out for a bad lunch than for losing money on a trade.[27]

Networking was especially important in the emerging field of oil trading, where it was often in the hands of a few government officials to decide how to sell vast quantities of their country's petroleum resources. And Weisser was a born relationships man, who could strike up a friendship with anybody. Every year, he'd throw a lavish party for all his oil contacts at the St Moritz Hotel on New York's Central Park, replete with freely flowing Champagne and a banquet of delicacies from all corners of the globe. He had already built a relationship with Gurov at Soyuznefteexport, but he hardly restricted

himself to the Communist world. In Pittsburgh, he schmoozed the hard-dealing executives of Gulf Oil. In Texas, he scored a contract with Hunt Oil, owned by the wealthy Hunt family. In the Middle East, he was on first name terms with all the most powerful sheikhs and oil officials, including Sheikh Ahmed Zaki Yamani, the Saudi oil minister, whom he counted as a personal friend.

The savviest traders used such global networks of contacts to gain unparalleled insights into the state of the world economy. They invested not only in traders to staff their worldwide offices but also in communications systems to ensure that information could be rapidly shared across their companies. Dozens of staff spent their days sifting through telex messages to extract the gems of information. 'Our communication system is probably the most sophisticated in the world, with the possible exception of the Defense Department or the Central Intelligence Agency,' one Philipp Brothers executive boasted in 1981.[28] With this sophisticated network of market intelligence came a culture of secrecy, as the traders sought to protect their insights.

And the traders' intelligence networks were enormously valuable, allowing them to make better-informed bets on the market than their competitors. During the Suez Crisis in 1956, when Israeli, French and British troops moved into Egypt, Cargill's traders in Geneva bet that shipping costs would rise. Then the crisis closed the Suez Canal, forcing ships to take the long route around Africa, and freight rates soared. Cargill's ability to combine political and market insight had paid off.[29] It was a neat distillation of the strategy that the early traders had pioneered: build as large a portfolio of contracts as possible, squeeze your network of contacts for information – and then exploit that information to trade profitably.

But perhaps even more important than their business model was the pioneers' approach to their employees. The pioneers passed on to their successors a corporate culture that continues to influence traders to this day. While the early trading houses had different origins and different styles, they shared an emphasis on hard work, loyalty and partnership.

Junior employees were put through gruelling apprenticeships. At Philipp Brothers, every youngster would begin his career doing the company's most menial jobs, rotating through different departments until his bosses were convinced he understood the basics of the business and had proved his loyalty to the firm. Mendel Bernberg, who was hired by Julius Philipp as a *lehrling* – or apprentice – in 1919 at the age of fifteen, recalled that the average day began at 8 a.m., opening and sorting the mail, and ended at 10 p.m., after preparing the mail and cables and delivering them to the post office.

Several decades later, not much had changed. Felix Posen, who joined Philipp Brothers in the mid-1950s and much later became a top executive at Marc Rich + Co, also started in the mail room, coding and decoding messages to be sent by telegram. 'If you didn't want to work hard, you shouldn't join Philipp Brothers,' he recalls.[30]

Generations of young traders went through this initiation. The experience taught the apprentices grit, meticulousness and humility, as well as the fundamentals of the commodity business. Many went on to become some of the world's top commodity traders – among them Marc Rich, who started as a trainee in New York in 1954.

The long years of apprenticeship created a sense of loyalty at the trading houses. Weisser saw his staff as family, forgiving their shortcomings almost to a fault. But it was not just shared experience that made the Philipp Brothers traders so close-knit. It was also shared financial interest. In 1956, the company had distributed shares to about forty of its employees, creating several millionaires in the process. This partnership structure, with dozens of shareholders and not one dominant voice, became a model for the trading houses that came later. It bound the company's top traders together and created a greater incentive for them to devote their energies to the company. 'We handle our people like a family,' Jesselson said in 1981. 'We always work as a team. Nobody forces his will through. That has always been the strength of the organization.'[31]

It was a business model that worked. By the 1970s, the commodity traders had become significant participants in the new economic

order. Cargill's profits had risen from about $1 million in 1940 to $24 million in 1970.[32] Philipp Brothers, which had made a profit of just $550,000 in 1947,[33] was by 1970 making $38.7 million.[34] The traders did more than simply take advantage of the increase in global trade flows: they also facilitated it, organising shipping and financing and linking buyers with sellers across the globe.

But even as the commodity traders grew in scale and profitability, the world paid little heed to their increasing power. After all, supply of commodities had been plentiful for years, and prices had been low. Few noticed that a handful of traders had assumed a role of enormous importance in the flow of natural resources around the world, a flow that was becoming ever more central to global prosperity. They would soon be jolted out of their complacency as, one by one, the prices of the world's most important commodities shot higher in the 1970s. And the first shock came in the market for that most basic of commodities: grain.

In the summer of 1972, Cargill was riding high. Under the leadership of Erwin Kelm, the protégé of John H. MacMillan Jr, it had grown into a business with $5 billion in sales, claiming the title of the largest agricultural trader in the world. And it had weathered the criticism of its links behind the Iron Curtain impeccably. It hadn't been an easy few years – the company had been wrongfooted by the market and barely covered its costs in the late 1960s. But Kelm, a steadfast proponent of Cargill's global expansion, steered the company through the downturn with its appetite for international business undimmed.

So when Nikolai Belousov – the head of Exportkhleb, the Soviet government agency in charge of trading grain – arrived in New York in the summer of 1972, Cargill didn't think twice about working with him. In a meeting at the Hilton with Walter 'Barney' Saunders, Cargill's head of grain trading, Belousov negotiated a deal to buy

two million tonnes of US grain over the course of the next year. It seemed, at the time, like a good deal all round.[35]

But Cargill was in for a shock. Belousov – a grey, tall and slender man, who spoke perfect, almost unaccented English – may have been born and educated in the Communist system, but when it came to trading, he was as sharp as his American rivals. When he arrived in New York, he had called not just Cargill, but every single one of its rivals.

Each of the trading houses sprang into action. Executives from Cargill's competitors immediately flew in to New York from as far afield as Paris and Buenos Aires. Many remembered the sales of 1963–4, when the Soviet Union had bought $40 million of grain from Cargill. But this time Moscow was aiming for much more: a drab Soviet bureaucrat was about to conclude the largest deal in the history of agricultural trading.

One by one, Belousov negotiated with each of the largest grain traders. Before meeting Cargill, he had met with Michel Fribourg, the president and owner of Continental Grain Company, and struck a deal to buy $460 million of American wheat and other staples – one of the largest commodity trades that had ever been done. Later he met with Louis Dreyfus, Bunge, Cook Industries and André & Cie.[36] Belousov bought from everyone. Each trading house thought it was alone in cutting a big deal with the Russians, largely unaware of how much others had sold.

When it became clear how much Belousov had bought, traders realised there wouldn't be enough American grain to go around. In total, Belousov – spurred on by the risk of mass starvation at home after the Soviet crops had failed – bought almost 20 million tonnes of grains and oilseeds from the grain traders. The size of the wheat purchases was extraordinary: 11.8 million tonnes – equal to almost 30% of the US wheat harvest. When the market woke up to the sale, it was clear the US wouldn't have enough grain to meet the combination of its own domestic consumption, the demand from traditional importers, and the extra purchases from the Soviet Union.

Wheat, corn and soybean prices raced higher, triggering a bout of food inflation the like of which Americans hadn't experienced in a generation. On 3 July, just before the Russians started talking to Continental, milling wheat prices in Kansas were $1.44 a bushel; within ten weeks, the price had risen 60%. Worse was to come: in the year after the Soviet deal, wheat prices tripled. Corn and soybean prices also climbed. With grain prices rising, the price of meat shot higher too.[37] The public was outraged. The episode became known as the 'Great Grain Robbery'.

Cargill reacted to the outrage by trying to demonstrate that it hadn't profited from the hunger of American citizens. For the first time in its 107-year history, it made information on its trades public. It even commissioned its auditors to compile a report demonstrating it had lost money on the Soviet sales. It was true: Belousov had outsmarted the Western grain traders. The very secrecy so loved by the industry had backfired. The companies had all kept their contracts secret, and so they all suffered when they realised that they weren't the only ones with a deal. The traders had all sold grain they didn't yet own, hoping to buy it later on the open market. So when they all tried to buy at the same time, prices jumped. Cargill told Congress it had lost $661,000 on the Soviet contract.[38]

But those losses masked what was, in reality, a golden period. What Cargill hadn't told Congress was that it had made millions through speculative bets on the market. Cargill reported net income of $107.8 million in its 1972–73 fiscal year,[39] up nearly 170% from the previous year. 'It was a year of record profits, record dollar sales, record tonnage, record margins, record problems, record expense, record traffic jams, record prices and controls, record aspirin pills, and many record performances by a record number of people,' a Cargill executive said.[40]

A lot of the profit hadn't come from the traditional business of buying physical grain from farmers and selling to consumers, but from pure speculation. Cargill's bets on the market were largely placed by Tradax in Switzerland. The traders at Cargill's headquarters near

Minneapolis rarely took bets on the direction of grain prices, known in trader-speak as the 'flat price'. But at Tradax it was a different story. Realising that the Soviet purchases would cause shortages of wheat, the traders placed enormous bets that prices were going to rise. 'We took much larger flat price and premium position than ever before,' Tradax said. Of course, their bets came good: Tradax recorded profits of $60.17 million in 1972,[41] more than the earnings of American titans such as Boeing or Colgate-Palmolive in the same year.[42]

The sale of roughly $1 billion of grain to America's biggest geo-political rival right under the nose of the US government was a demonstration of the power that had accumulated in the hands of the commodity traders. As the US had become the world's dominant grain supplier in the decade after the Second World War, the trading companies were at the vanguard of a wave of US exports, acting as ambassadors for American grain around the world. Unlike actual ambassadors, though, the traders were not employees of the US government – not only did the government have little ability to regulate them, but it was almost entirely in the dark about the sales until after the fact. And thanks to generous export credits, the Soviet purchases made at rock-bottom prices had been funded to the tune of about $300 million by US taxpayers.[43] The public's reaction was instantaneous and damning: 'SOVIET GRAIN DEAL IS CALLED A COUP', blared a headline on the front page of the *New York Times* in September 1972.[44]

Belousov's deals in New York's hotels had helped the world wake up to the power that had accumulated in the hands of the commodity traders. After two decades of global growth, the world consumed more natural resources than ever. It was more dependent than ever on international trade of these resources. And that meant that the world was more reliant than ever on just a few men, the pioneers of trading, who had built their industry around this flow of commodities: Weisser, Jesselson, MacMillan and their heirs.

But the Soviet Union's surprise swoop on America's grain stores was just a prelude to what was to come. Soon, the same sort of chaos

that the grain market had just experienced would strike the most critical commodity of all to the twentieth-century economy, the resource that Theodor Weisser had coaxed out of the Soviet Union two decades earlier: oil.

TWO

THE GODFATHER OF OIL

On 25 April 1968, the 'President's Daily Brief' arrived on the desk of Lyndon B. Johnson, direct from the Central Intelligence Agency. The top-secret document is a succinct summary of world news, the CIA's version of *Reader's Digest*.

On this occasion, after updates on the war in Vietnam, the Soviet Union and the development of ballistic missiles in China, the president's eye was led to an item about the geopolitics of oil that America's spymasters thought needed his attention.

'Israel is about set to start work on a 42-inch oil pipeline by-passing the Suez Canal', began the brief. It included a map, showing the pipeline's route from Eilat, an Israeli port on the Red Sea, north through the country to the Mediterranean coast at Ashkelon (see map on page 333). The construction of the pipeline pointed to an alliance forged in oil and steel between Israel and a country that would go on to become its bitterest enemy, the CIA concluded: 'Iran is the only likely source of substantial quantities of petroleum for the pipeline.'[1]

The construction of the pipeline and the CIA's interest in it were a demonstration of oil's increasingly important role in the world economy – and its dependence on the febrile politics of the Middle East. For the American government, that was a growing concern. By

the late 1960s and early 1970s, a wealthier world was demanding vastly greater quantities of oil. Between 1948 and 1972, consumption tripled in the US – an unprecedented increase, except when measured against what was happening elsewhere. Oil demand in Western Europe over the same period increased fifteen-fold; in Japan it grew by more than 100 times.[2]

At the same time, the Seven Sisters' grip on the market was looking increasingly shaky. The chain of events that had begun with Weisser's trip to the Soviet Union in 1954 had made it easier for oil-rich countries to sell their crude outside of the network of the large Western companies. The market had begun to open up, with Moscow selling its oil far below the 'posted prices' set by the Seven Sisters.

The erosion of the power of the Western corporate oligopoly had reached a key juncture in August 1960. With Soviet oil undermining their market dominance, executives at Standard Oil of New Jersey (a forerunner of ExxonMobil) had taken it upon themselves to cut their Middle East posted price by 7% – without consulting the governments of the countries that were producing it. The sheikhs were livid. Resentful about the loss of income and furious that they hadn't been consulted on the price cut, oil-producing nations started agitating for action. A month later, the oil ministers of Saudi Arabia, Venezuela, Iran, Iraq and Kuwait gathered in Baghdad. After four days of deliberations, they announced, on 14 September 1960, the birth of the Organization of the Petroleum Exporting Countries – or OPEC.

It was the first step in a transformation of the energy industry that took place in the 1960s and 1970s. Increasingly assertive under the auspices of OPEC, countries began nationalising their oil resources, and where foreign companies were allowed to stay, they were forced to hand over more profits and taxes to their hosts.

The change marked the beginning of an era in which OPEC would turn the oil market and the world economy on its head, ending the dominance of the Seven Sisters for good and handing huge power

to the commodity traders. As oil-producing countries nationalised their petroleum industries, the traders became essential conduits to move their crude to the international market. It would increasingly be the traders, and not the large oil companies, who would determine who could buy or sell oil, empowering the new petrostates of the Middle East, Africa and Latin America.

As a result, the traders became the pioneers of a shift that was happening across the world, from a carefully controlled economy under the stewardship of a largely American oligopoly to a free-for-all in which the market was God. Over the course of the next decade, the oil price would fluctuate wildly, redrawing the contours of the global economy amid political upheaval everywhere from the US to Iran. And there was one trader who more than anyone saw the possibilities of this new era and grasped them with all his might. His name was Marc Rich.

Then a young trader at Philipp Brothers, Rich had just discovered what Weisser had shown more than a decade earlier – that crude oil could be traded. He would go on to become the master of the global oil market. But his training ground was the pipeline between Eilat and Ashkelon that was being built by Israel with secret Iranian support.

The two countries were strange bedfellows, even before the Islamic Revolution of 1979, but they were united by their economic interests. Iran had oil to sell and Israel was a buyer, but both countries wanted a way to get oil from the Persian Gulf to the Mediterranean without having to go through the Suez Canal.

They had been working on the pipeline in secret for several years, but had made limited progress. Everything changed in 1967, when, amid escalating tensions, Israel launched a surprise attack on Egypt and Syria. Egyptian President Gamal Abdel Nasser responded by closing the Suez Canal. The war was over within six days, but the canal wouldn't reopen until 1975. The shutdown was so sudden that fifteen vessels were trapped inside the canal, unable to leave for eight years.

The closure of the Suez Canal had a major impact on global trade. The waterway was then, and remains today, a crucial shipping route for the oil market – the most direct route to deliver oil to Europe and the US from the massive fields of Iran, Saudi Arabia and the United Arab Emirates. When Nasser closed it, Middle Eastern oil was forced to travel all the way around the horn of Africa, delaying deliveries and adding significant costs.

Iran and Israel responded by fast-tracking their plans for a pipeline that would span the 254 kilometres between Israel's Red Sea and Mediterranean coasts, bypassing the canal. Envoys from the two countries met in secret to thrash out the details. After the personal intervention of the Shah, the two countries agreed to create a jointly owned entity, the Trans-Asiatic Company, based in Switzerland, to build and manage the new oil pipeline. The Iranians used a shell company in Liechtenstein to hide their ownership of half of the company, while the Israelis used a Panamanian entity.[3] Even today, the Israeli newspaper *Haaretz* describes the company as 'the most secretive firm in Israel'.[4]

Into this shadowy world stepped the commodity traders. Oil importers in Europe were worried about handling oil from the pipeline, fearful of antagonising Arab countries that were boycotting Israel. The Iranians and the Israelis needed help to keep their new trade route flowing – and who better to turn to than the new breed of traders who, equipped with little more than a telephone and sharp wits, could buy and sell oil anywhere in the world? It was the perfect opportunity for an ambitious and aggressive trader like Marc Rich.

The man who would become the godfather of the oil market was born Marcell David Reich to a Jewish family in Antwerp, Belgium, in 1934. His father, who made a living trading textiles and shoes, had grown up in Germany, so young Marcell grew up speaking German and French.

His early years, like so many of the Philipp Brothers traders of the era, were shaped by the rise of Nazism in Europe. In May 1940, his father packed the family into a black Citroën bought specially for the purpose and drove the family into France – just a week before the German army marched into Antwerp. From France they managed to board a ship to Morocco, where they spent several months in a refugee camp. Eventually, they managed to get visas for the US, and, in 1941, at the age of six and speaking not a word of English, Marcell Reich arrived in America.

The family first lived with an aunt in New York, then moved to Philadelphia, then Kansas City. As a result, Marc Rich – the Americanised name he had taken for himself – attended a different school virtually every year.[5] From this point onwards Rich had a feeling, which he never lost, of being an outsider. And it was also during this period that he discovered a passion for business. By the late 1940s, the family had moved back to New York, and Rich was spending his spare time helping out with his father's business importing jute for burlap bags. Writing in his high-school yearbook, the teenage Rich already knew what his dream job was: 'business'.[6]

Rich enrolled at New York University, but never graduated. Instead, thanks to an acquaintance of his father's, he got a position as a trainee at Philipp Brothers. In 1954, aged nineteen, he started working at the company's office at 70 Pine Street, a skyscraper just around the corner from Wall Street in the financial district. Like all the trainees, he began in the mailroom.

He wasn't to be there long, however. Rich had a talent and a drive that was hard to miss. 'He was a great colleague, a very bright guy, multilingual and enormously hardworking,' recalls Felix Posen, who worked with Rich at Philipp Brothers and later at Marc Rich + Co.[7] Another of his contemporaries remembered Rich always arriving first in the morning, greeting the other juniors with a sarcastic 'good afternoon' as they tramped in at 8.30 a.m.[8] It wasn't long before he had moved up from the mailroom, and was working with one of the company's senior traders.

Already at this early stage, he showed the combination of business acumen and appetite for taking risks that would make him fantastically successful. Rich took responsibility for trading mercury, a niche commodity unimportant enough to be given to a junior trader. Mercury had historically been used to extract silver, in thermometers, and to treat syphilis. By the 1950s, it was also being used in batteries, particularly in military equipment. Rich became convinced that demand would rise rapidly, and he set about negotiating with producers to secure supplies. With Washington full of dire warnings about resource scarcity, he was soon proved right. A massive government stockpiling programme launched in mid-1954 mandated purchases of an amount of mercury equivalent to almost a third of global production. Marc Rich's mercury was suddenly in high demand.

From then on Rich was a rising star of Philipp Brothers, posted around the world to secure business or resolve problems. He spent six months in Bolivia; he flew in to Cuba in the wake of the revolution to negotiate with the new government of Fidel Castro; he had spells in South Africa, India and the Netherlands. In 1964, at the age of thirty, he was appointed office manager in Madrid, firmly establishing him as one of the company's next generation of leaders.

Rich could turn on the charm when he needed to, but he had few close friends. One mining executive who dined with him remembers him being pleasant, but cold.[9] And while he inspired huge loyalty from many of his employees, none doubted where Rich's priorities lay. 'His business and his hobbies were one and the same,' says Danny Posen, who recalls, as a junior employee, waiting late into the evening outside Rich's limousine, only to find him still inside surrounded by the day's telexes and deep in debate about the business.[10]

That single-mindedness extended into his personal relationships. Even when he was being warm and generous, it was hard to escape the feeling that he was trying to gain some information or advantage from the other person. Roque Benavides, whose family owns a mining business in Peru, recalls dining at Rich's house: 'He was a great

host.' The wine flowed freely, and Benavides returned to his hotel 'absolutely drunk'. But Rich also got what he wanted from the encounter: a ten-year contract to buy from Benavides's mines.[11]

Rich had not been the first trader at Philipp Brothers to deal in oil. That honour fell to Alan Flacks, the head of the company's Milan office, who had got wind of a 25,000 tonne cargo of oil that might be for sale when visiting clients in Tunisia in 1969.

Flacks, a metals trader from Manchester, knew little about oil – neither did anyone else at Philipp Brothers. But he figured it couldn't be so different to trading metals. He made some calls, and found a refiner willing to buy the cargo. After a few days of talks, he agreed a price with the Tunisians, then immediately sold it on for a little bit more. The deal was effectively riskless, and Philipp Brothers ended up making about $65,000 from the operation – a tidy sum at the time. 'It was a back-to-back deal, very safe because there was no storage involved and the money was right up front,' Flacks said.[12]

But Rich's natural aggression and raw enthusiasm for the new commodity meant that he soon supplanted Flacks as the company's principal oil trader. 'I was working in a commodity trading house and the oligopoly of the Seven Sisters was coming to a halt. Suddenly, the world needed a new system of bringing the oil from the producing countries to the consuming countries, so that's exactly what I did,' he told his biographer a few years before his death in 2013.[13] 'I just thought it should be possible to trade oil despite the Seven Sisters.' The key to his early success was the Eilat–Ashkelon pipeline.

Trade through the pipeline was shrouded in secrecy. At the Iranian end of the trade, tankers would load oil from Iran in the Persian Gulf and the crew would tell port authorities that they were heading to 'Gibraltar, for orders'. But the tankers would never appear in Gibraltar. Instead, they would sail in secret to Eilat, unload their oil, and

reappear empty in Iran. Anyone watching could only guess where they might have offloaded their cargo. *The Sunday Times*, which published an account of the trade in 1970, called it the 'mystery of the disappearing tankers'.[14] The Israeli end of the business was equally secretive. The Israeli government imposed a complete blackout on reporting information about any vessel picking up crude at its ports to supply European customers, effectively keeping the whole flow in the shadows.

Rich couldn't have pulled off the trade without a colleague who would become his life-long collaborator: Pincus Green. Green, known as 'Pinky', had cut his teeth trading chrome, a metal used in stainless-steel alloys. Back in 1968, Iran was the world's eighth-largest producer of chrome,[15] so Green travelled back and forth to Tehran to negotiate deals.

While Green brought the Iranian contacts – and a mastery of shipping that earned him the nickname 'The Admiral' – Rich had the swashbuckling edge needed to find a way to get the barrels on to the market. 'The pipeline was there. I decided that it was attractive,' he said. 'People were reluctant to use the pipeline because the oil had passed through Israel.'

But Rich didn't hesitate. He and Green exploited the pipeline with gusto, using it to sell Iranian oil all over Europe. With Philipp Brothers standing between them and the politically sensitive pipeline, the buyers of oil couldn't turn down the chance for a bargain. 'There was a big price advantage,' Rich said. 'The transport of Iranian crude through the pipeline was much cheaper than going all the way around Africa.'

The 'landlord', as the Shah was referred to by the Israelis, was delighted: the 254 kilometres of pipeline saved roughly 22,000 kilometres circumnavigating Africa, making Iranian oil far more cost competitive than any of its rivals in the Mediterranean (see map on page 333). The oil started to flow in December 1969, and the following year 162 tankers unloaded nearly 75 million barrels into the pipeline (about 200,000 barrels a day).

Inside Philipp Brothers, however, the Israeli pipeline was seen as a risk. Rich received such a dressing-down from the company's bosses for not insuring the oil shipped through the pipeline that he worried he might be fired.[16] But the reprimand didn't slow him down. Over the years, first for Philipp Brothers and later for his own company, he shipped between 60 and 75 million barrels per year of Iranian oil via the Eilat–Ashkelon pipeline. It was, in his words, a 'very, very important business'.[17]

Rich couldn't have got his start in oil trading at a better time.

From 1960 to 1970, in spite of the growing challenge posed by the independent oil traders, the Seven Sisters had largely kept control of the market: oil prices had barely moved. Arab Light, the benchmark for Middle Eastern crude, started the 1960s at $1.90 per barrel and ended the decade at $1.76 – a decline prompted by the rising Soviet exports shepherded on to the market by Weisser and others. But by the beginning of the 1970s, the trend had reversed and oil prices were on the rise. A crisis was brewing in the oil market. Its ingredients were there for anyone to see, though few paid much attention.

In 1971, US President Richard Nixon dropped the gold standard, which until then had underpinned the value of the US dollar. His motives had little to do with oil, and more to do with trying to support the US economy. But the impact on the oil market was dramatic. As the American currency lost value, the earnings of Middle Eastern countries, which sold their oil in dollars, were also devalued. Within OPEC nations, it sparked new calls for governments to seize control of their natural resources from Western companies. From Algeria to Iraq, producers demanded a greater share of the earnings from their oil industries – which had, until then, been largely controlled by the Seven Sisters. Soon, their demands were so strident that they amounted to full-blown nationalisation.[18] Saudi Arabia, which had long resisted the trend, began agitating for a stake in the

vast reservoirs of oil controlled by American companies through Aramco. Country by country, the vice-like grip of the Seven Sisters on the global oil market was being broken.

The companies had little choice but to raise prices. By 1971, Arab Light cost $2.24 a barrel; in 1972, it was $2.48; and in 1973 it was $3.29. Worse was to come. In April 1973, James Akins, a US diplomat, published an essay in *Foreign Affairs* titled 'The Oil Crisis: This Time the Wolf Is Here'.[19] Whether Marc Rich read the article or not, he too was convinced oil prices were about to shoot higher.

In the spring of 1973, the National Iranian Oil Company offered to sell Rich and Green one million tonnes of crude (about 7.5 million barrels). It was a huge contract, but there was a catch: rather than the prevailing $3.29 a barrel official price, Tehran wanted to sell the oil at $5 a barrel. Convinced that oil prices were about to rise further, Green, who was in Tehran leading the talks, took the deal. It was a gamble, but a calculated one. Thanks to their contacts, Rich and Green had heard that something big was about to happen in the petroleum market. They weren't sure what, but they took the deal all the same.

When Jesselson heard about it, he was beside himself. 'Irresponsible, that is what they were,' he seethed.[20] For months, Jesselson had been urging Rich and Green to slow down, telling them to avoid undue risk and 'not expose the company to adventures'. He and his colleagues in New York had been 'shocked', he said, at some of the trades they had agreed 'without the corresponding sales being concluded at the same time'.[21] While metals traders like Jesselson were able to offset their exposure to market gyrations using the London Metal Exchange, Rich and Green could not eliminate the risk to their oil contracts of a sudden move in prices, because there was no exchange for oil. When Rich and Green bought a cargo of oil, they fixed the price then and there. If prices went up, they made a killing; if prices fell, the losses would be just as large.

The deal with Iran was the last straw for Jesselson. The contract was worth $37.5 million. If prices didn't rise as they hoped and they

were forced to sell the oil at the official price, Rich and Green would suffer a loss of nearly $13 million – a fortune for Philipp Brothers at the time.

After frantic conversations across the Atlantic, Jesselson had had enough. He ordered Rich and Green to find a buyer and get rid of the Iranian oil immediately. 'Nobody could control them, or the business, as it, and they, were too fast moving,' recalled Tom O'Malley, who would go on to become head of oil trading at Philipp Brothers.[22]

Still, Rich and Green had no trouble finding a buyer for their oil – and they sold it at a price of just over $5 a barrel, enough to make a small profit, to an American refiner, Ashland Oil (today part of Marathon Petroleum). That should have been a signal to their bosses that Rich and Green were right about the market. By the middle of 1973, it was clear that $3.29 a barrel, the official price, was no longer the real price. Oil was already being bought and sold for more than $5 a barrel. Jesselson didn't care. It would only take a few weeks for him to see how wrong he had been.

In September 1973, the international oil companies and OPEC sat down in Vienna for talks. For many, it seemed obvious that it was a question of when, not if, the world would see drastically higher oil prices. In a television interview, the Japanese prime minister gave what must have felt like a dire warning: 'An oil crisis ten years from now is clearly seen.' It turned out to be more like ten days.[23]

On 6 October 1973, Israel went silent to mark Yom Kippur, the holiest day of Judaism. At the same time, Egypt and Syria were preparing for war, in an attempt to recover the territories they'd lost in 1967. That afternoon, Egyptian forces crossed the Suez Canal while Syrian troops moved on the Golan Heights in a coordinated offensive against Israel.

With war raging, the talks between OPEC and the Western oil companies in Vienna, now in their second month, ground to a deadlock. The producers wanted prices to be doubled; the oil companies, under pressure from their governments, were prepared to offer at

most a 15% hike. The meetings ran late into the evenings as the negotiating rooms grew fuggy with cigarette smoke. Arab oil officials passed around newspaper clippings about the war, furious at Western governments' perceived support for Israel. The oil executives could sense the mood was turning against them. They were terrified that the OPEC nations might use oil as a weapon.

George Piercy of Exxon and André Bénard of Shell, who led the talks on behalf of the oil companies, asked their headquarters for guidance. The companies passed the question on to their governments. The response was nearly unanimous: Washington, Tokyo, London and several other European capitals told the companies to hold firm. The world economy, they argued, would not be able to withstand the huge price increase that OPEC was demanding.

On 12 October, six days after the war had started, the oil executives went to see Sheikh Yamani, the Saudi minister, in his suite at the top of the Intercontinental Hotel. They had bad news. Actually, they had no news. The companies simply weren't willing to meet OPEC's demands. Yamani, a Saudi diplomat with years of experience, prepared for a long night of negotiations. Fearing that a failure to reach a deal would bring even more chaos to the Middle East, he warned the oilmen that their position was a mistake. The Saudi minister ordered a Coke for one of them and slowly squeezed a lime into it, awaiting the executives' next move.

But none came. Piercy, a rugged engineer, had no time for diplomatic niceties. As far as he was concerned, there was no point in any more talk. Yamani sighed and, in front of the executives, started to ring his counterparts to break the news. He phoned Baghdad, talking agitatedly in Arabic before telling the oilmen: 'They are mad at you.' The Kuwaiti oil minister, who was staying in the same Vienna hotel, joined them in the early hours of the morning in his pyjamas. But there wasn't much to discuss.[24]

Eventually, the group broke up. As they were leaving Yamani's suite, one of the executives asked what would happen next. 'Listen to the radio,' the Saudi oil minister replied.[25]

The radio reports from Kuwait, where the oil ministers convened a few days later, soon made Rich and Green's bet on higher oil prices look prescient. On 16 October, they announced a unilateral 70% hike. Yamani was euphoric. 'This is a moment for which I have been waiting a long time,' he said. 'The moment has come. We are masters of our own commodity'.[26]

The following day, 17 October, there was another OPEC meeting, this time just for the Arab member countries. With war raging, some ministers were pushing for an all-out economic blockade of Israel and its allies, including America. When the meeting concluded, the Arab countries announced they would cut their production by 5% per month 'until Arab political demands on Israel are met'[27] and launched an embargo on the US and other countries they perceived to be friendly towards Israel. The old era of stable, boring oil prices was over. From now on, the price of the world's most important commodity would be at the mercy of Middle Eastern politics.

Oil prices shot up to $11.58 a barrel, more than double the price at which Rich had agreed to buy crude from Iran a few months earlier. Ashland Oil, which had taken over the contract from Philipp Brothers, made a fortune. If Rich and Green had been allowed to hold on to their contract, they could have made extraordinary profits: nearly $50 million from a single deal, far more than Philipp Brothers had ever earned in a year.

Rich and Green had understood that the oil market was entering a period of upheaval. And it was one in which the traders, rather than the major companies, were in the ascendant. 'What we have witnessed is a shifting of the centre of gravity of the oil industry,' wrote Jan Nasmyth, an early chronicler of the market. The oil industry's power centres were no longer the major oil companies' headquarters in London, New York and San Francisco, but the towns in Switzerland from which the traders operated. 'There are offices in Zurich, in Geneva and in Basel offering crude on a scale that would formerly have given satisfaction to a major oil company and which now include majors among their customers,' Nasmyth wrote.[28]

For the global economy and for world politics it was a seismic shift. Over the course of a few decades, oil had quietly become the critical commodity for the world's economic health. The market had been stable and predictable for many years. But now the oil price was unleashed, tripling or quadrupling overnight, and ushering in an era of unprecedented volatility (see graph on page 334). The global economic boom that had lasted since the Second World War came to an abrupt halt. Economists started to talk gloomily about 'stagflation' – a combination of economic recession and high inflation that scarred an entire generation. The shock was particularly profound in America, which more than anywhere else had embraced the cult of the automobile. Suddenly, American drivers had to wait in line to fill up their cars.

The nationalisation of Middle Eastern oilfields had cracked open the oligopolistic system that had been carefully built and nurtured by the Seven Sisters for decades. As OPEC nations seized control of their oil resources, they diverted the flow of petrodollars from the companies' coffers to their own. Western countries began to worry about their dependence on Middle Eastern oil, a concern that would be a major driver of foreign policy for the next half century.[29]

As more and more oil began to be sold outside the control of the Seven Sisters, so the opportunity for independent traders such as Mabanaft and Philipp Brothers grew. And with less of the market under their control, the Seven Sisters also lost the ability to dictate prices. Instead, the price was set in a competitive marketplace amid a cacophony of buyers and sellers. And the kings of the marketplace were the traders.

The oil market began to look more like those of other commodities, such as wheat, coffee and copper, where the traders had long acted as middlemen, helping to smooth the flow of global trade. And the surge in prices meant the profits could be extraordinary. Old commodity traders like Philipp Brothers soon realised they could make more money buying and selling crude than they had done in

decades of trading metals. Soon it had expanded into grains, coffee and sugar trading. The agricultural commodity traders, flush with cash from the Great Grain Robbery, also began to look to other markets. Cargill broke into metals in 1972 by buying C. Tennant, Sons & Co, a metals trader, for $5.95 million.[30] Over the next few years, it went into steel and oil too. The first global commodity trading houses, capable of dealing in energy, metals and agriculture simultaneously, had emerged.

Oil also brought the traders closer to power. Governments had often looked on metals, minerals and agricultural commodities as strategically sensitive resources. But oil was different: the money was bigger, and the governments of oil-producing countries were almost entirely dependent on petrodollars. The traders became friends with oil-rich leaders in the Middle East, Africa and Latin America, while Western governments, desperate for cheap oil, turned to them to secure supplies. Oil from where? Only the traders, now at the centre of global finance and politics, appeared to have the answer – and they weren't telling anyone. 'Why should we lead the bees to the honey?' asked a Philipp Brothers executive during the oil price spikes of the 1970s. 'Let's just say that we have gotten oil from all over the world and have distributed it throughout the world.'[31]

Even Marc Rich couldn't have foreseen all of this in 1973. Back at Philipp Brothers, he and Green were seething about something more immediate: the fortune they could have made if it hadn't been for their superiors' lack of courage. Nonetheless, their oil trading business still delivered abundant profits: Philipp Brothers' earnings before tax were a record $54.9 million in 1973, up 75% from the previous year.

But Rich wasn't happy. Not only were the Philipp Brothers bosses clipping his wings and preventing him and Green from trading at

their full potential, they also weren't paying them sufficiently. He started to lobby Jesselson for more money. Rich, who at the time was making about $100,000 a year, including his bonus, wanted $500,000 each for himself and Green (equivalent to about $3 million in today's money). It seems like an unspectacular sum by comparison to the bonuses of some modern-day executives, but for Jesselson, it was an unconscionable amount of money.

For weeks, a pitched battle took place. Rich said that his and Green's oil trades had delivered tens of millions of dollars in profit, with tens of millions more that would be realised the following year. Jesselson was more conservative, arguing that the company should be cautious booking profits from the wild new world of oil trading. 'These oil contracts that Rich had in the books, from all kinds of sellers, many rather unusual governments, would they all be honoured in a rising market?' Jesselson recalled later. 'Wasn't the price fever, the unsettled international situation, inducive to cancelling contracts? And much of what Rich figured would become a profit could well have turned into a huge loss.'[32]

Rich flew from Madrid to Philipp Brothers' European headquarters in the Swiss town of Zug in February 1974 to try to reach a deal. Jesselson was visiting as part of a skiing holiday in the Alps. Once again, the old master of commodity trading clashed with his younger protégé on the subject of remuneration. Rich again demanded $1 million, to be shared between Green and himself. Jesselson countered with an offer that Rich should move back to New York and be anointed as his successor at the helm of Philipp Brothers. Rich didn't lose focus, however. He told Jesselson he was interested, 'provided we come to an agreement on the remuneration'. But Jesselson was unmoved: he had grown up in a company that had seen its traders as a family, a company in which there was no place for too much personal ambition. As a matter of principle, he would offer Rich and Green only a fraction of what they were asking for.[33]

Rich, who had already discussed it with Green, told his boss he was leaving to set up his own company. Jesselson, perhaps in a flash

of arrogance, perhaps not understanding the significance of the moment, wished him well and then donned his ski boots and set off for the pistes with the head of Philipp Brothers' European operations. 'So I had to leave,' Rich told his biographer. 'I didn't want to leave. I had been there for twenty years, I liked the company. I liked Jesselson, and I think he liked me.'[34]

A few days later, Jesselson's vacation was interrupted by urgent calls from Zug and Madrid. It was not just Rich and Green who had left the company – other senior traders were also defecting. The top brass of Philipp Brothers was in shock. A job at Philipp Brothers was a job for life. It was rare for people to be fired or to leave. And rarer still for them to leave to go to a rival trading company.

Jesselson was immensely hurt. In a candid interview in 1979, he recalled the departure of Rich as a 'very sad chapter' in his life. 'They were like my own sons. I brought them up from nothing, and then they turned their backs on me.'[35] (That may be the case, Rich would respond sardonically, but 'he forgot me in his will'.)[36] The top Philipp Brothers managers in Europe learnt the news when they gathered to be photographed for the annual report, a few days after Jesselson and Rich had parted ways. To their surprise, Rich wasn't there. Jesselson broke the news: 'Before the rumours start, I want to say that Rich and Green asked for bonuses so high they would break our rules and traditions. They have separated. It's time to close ranks.'[37]

Six weeks later, on 3 April 1974, Rich walked into a law office in Zug to register his new company: Marc Rich + Co AG. That day, a new era in commodities trading began. Marc Rich would dominate the industry for the next twenty years, defining the popular image of a commodity trader in the 1980s and 1990s. The company he founded would also give birth to two other giants: Glencore and Trafigura. It was a corporate dynasty that had begun with Philipp Brothers, and continues to dominate the commodity markets today.

In some ways, Rich had been the ideal product of the Philipp Brothers machine. He was smart, imaginative, worldly, personable and hard-working. 'The secret of success in this business is to spot

trends,' one of his competitors said. 'Marc Rich spots trends quicker than anyone I know.'[38]

But in other ways the Philipp Brothers approach was too rigid and too conservative for him – and he was too driven, too much of a risk-taker for the venerable old firm and its managers. Years later, Rich shared his business philosophy with a young trader who was working for him. He took a knife and balanced his finger on the blade. 'As a trader,' he said, 'you will very often walk on the edge. Be careful and don't fall on the wrong side.'[39]

In April 1974, however, his first task was to ensure that his business didn't fail before it got started. Rich was suddenly bereft of the history, credit lines, clients and global network of offices of Philipp Brothers. Alongside him were Green and a few other Philipp Brothers traders who had jumped ship with them: John Trafford and Jacques Hachuel from the Madrid office, and Alexander 'Alec' Hackel from the Zug office. The five became the initial partners, putting together two million Swiss francs in capital (about $650,000). Rich borrowed from his family; others ploughed all their savings into the new company. Trafford, who until then had been Rich's assistant in Madrid, sold his car to raise the cash.[40]

The start of what would become the biggest and most powerful force in commodity markets was rather humble. It didn't help that Philipp Brothers, furious at the departure of the Marc Rich + Co traders, did its best to undermine it. For a commodity trading house in the 1970s, just as now, access to credit from banks was crucial. Philipp Brothers executives went around the banks and warned them about the newcomers: 'You can't trust these guys. They're not serious.'[41]

But the tactic failed. The bankers remembered that Jesselson had only a few months earlier been introducing Rich as his likely successor. Many banks – including Bankers Trust, Chase Manhattan and Banque de Paris et des Pays-Bas – lent to the fledgling company despite the warnings. At Paribas, Rich started a relationship with a senior banker, Christian Weyer, that would endure for decades.

Together, Rich and Weyer would popularise the use of letters of credit as the main way to finance oil trading. The instrument – effectively a guarantee from the bank that the trading house will pay – had been used for centuries, but applied to oil trading it allowed companies to buy and sell vast amounts of oil with a minimal deposit.[42] And Paribas – later, BNP Paribas – would become the largest financier of the commodity traders by far.

Rich's timing was once again faultless. He was back in business, and the oil market was still in the throes of its biggest ever upheaval. Marc Rich + Co made its first profits almost immediately, and thanks to the youngest member of the team: John Trafford engineered a deal to buy Nigerian oil from the French oil company Elf (a predecessor of Total) and sell it on to the American refiner Standard Oil of Ohio. This rather conservative, back-to-back deal was, ironically, exactly the style of trading preferred by the senior executives of Philipp Brothers. The first profit was a tidy $165,000. But Rich and Green would soon be doing riskier and more profitable deals. When the year closed, after barely eight months of operations, the accounts showed $28 million in earnings. The following year, their profits were $50 million. Already by 1976, in its third year of operations, Marc Rich + Co had overtaken Philipp Brothers in profitability, with earnings of $200 million.[43]

At Philipp Brothers, too, oil was driving record profits. After the initial shock of Rich's departure, the company quickly reorganised itself, putting Tom O'Malley in charge of oil trading. While metals remained important for Philipp Brothers, oil was increasingly the star. The company, which until 1973 had never made more than $35 million in pre-tax profits in a year, made over $125 million every year from 1974 until the end of the decade.[44] By 1977, oil accounted for more than a third of its revenues, dwarfing the other 150 commodities it traded.[45]

But Marc Rich + Co and Philipp Brothers weren't alone. The riches of the oil market attracted many other fortune-seekers, suddenly able to secure oil that was no longer in the grip of the Seven

Sisters, and wanting to profit from its new-found price volatility. Between 1975 and 1980, the number of independent oil trading companies proliferated to more than 300, although many went bankrupt as quickly as they entered the market.[46] It was a brave new world of daring gamblers and quick fortunes that would become known as the 'Rotterdam market'.

In the mid-1970s, Rotterdam became the centre of the oil trading industry. Its vast harbour, punctuated with rows of cranes arching into the sky like church spires, and dozens of squat, cylindrical oil-storage tanks, was the largest port in Europe. Strategically located between the Atlantic and the Baltic ports that were shipping ever greater volumes of Russian oil, Rotterdam was the focal point of the European oil market. In its heyday, huge tankers arrived every week from Saudi Arabia, Iran, Nigeria, Kuwait and elsewhere, navigating the deep canals that link the North Sea to Rotterdam, before discharging their crude oil in the outskirts of the city. Several large refineries converted the crude into refined products, which were sent on barges up the mighty river Rhine to buyers throughout much of northern Europe. The smell of oil hung over the whole area, as if it were an enormous filling station.

But Rotterdam in the 1970s was more than just a giant port. In the rapidly evolving oil industry of the time, it became the clearing-house for the global oil market. In previous decades, the Seven Sisters had exchanged cargoes of oil with one another when they found themselves with too much or too little; now the Rotterdam market performed the same service. The decline of the Seven Sisters continued apace, with their share of the international oil trade falling from 90% to 42% over the course of the 1970s – and much of that oil ended up being auctioned off in Rotterdam.[47]

When the Seven Sisters had lost control of the oil price in 1973, the ability to determine prices had passed to OPEC. But that position

continued to rely on the old, oligopolistic system of the Seven Sisters, where prices, once announced, would be respected. With the rise of the traders, the power to set prices now shifted firmly and irrevocably into the hands of the free market: soon oil was trading in Rotterdam at wildly different prices to the ones published by OPEC. And the price of oil in Rotterdam soon became the benchmark for the emerging 'spot' oil market – so known, because the oil was being bought and sold for immediate delivery (on the spot) rather than for some date in the future.

Few of the traders who dealt in Rotterdam oil were actually based in the Dutch town, instead negotiating from their offices in Zug, Geneva, London, Monaco or New York. That didn't matter. Rotterdam became infamous as the focal point of the new, untamed oil market, and a byword for wild speculation. The new breed of independent traders would buy and sell cargoes of crude oil and refined products as if they were casino chips.

They were ruthless in the pursuit of profit, and happy for it to come at their rivals' expense. 'It's a jungle … with a lot of people in it who are very tricky,' said BP's chief Rotterdam trader.[48] Another trader described the competition as a pack of sharks, waiting to pounce at the slightest sign a rival was getting into trouble. 'There are great noses in Rotterdam. The moment you're afraid, somebody smells it.'[49]

Oil prices, which had once been so low and so stable, were now anything but. In 1974–1978, oil traded between $10 and $15 a barrel, prices that would have been unthinkable a few years earlier. It was a heady set of circumstances for traders who had the nous to secure oil contracts and the guts to gamble on prices. Fortunes were made in days or weeks, and lost even more quickly. A group of Dutch trading companies that had started with fuel shipments on the Rhine grew to become important traders, including Vanol, Transol and Bulk Oil. Another Dutch company, Vitol, became a significant player in the market for refined products, though it barely touched crude oil until years later. Theodor Weisser's company, Mabanaft, used its

profits to build one of the world's largest oil storage businesses, called Oiltanking, which became a multi-billion dollar company with assets across five continents.

Other adventurers and businessmen soon elbowed themselves into the oil trading industry. Among them were Gerd Lutter of Marimpex; Oscar Wyatt of Coastal Corporation; David Chalmers of Bayoil; and the Koch brothers. Lutter would spend years courting Soviet and Iranian officials to secure oil deals, supplying South Africa with millions of barrels at the height of apartheid. Wyatt, an American oil tycoon who branched out into trading after his first gas business almost went bankrupt, would be a pioneer of the oil trade between China and the US. Later, he would befriend Saddam Hussein and Muammar Gaddafi. Chalmers would specialise in trading with Iraq. Charles and David Koch would transform their family's US-focused refining business into a global oil trader.

Large oil companies also started to flex their muscles in trading. Until this point, the oil majors had been handling their own crude and distributing their own refined products, but otherwise they had looked on oil trading with disdain. With the wave of nationalisations in the Middle East, however, their own supplies started to dry up and they were forced to start buying from others. Now they created subsidiaries in Rotterdam to challenge the traders: Shell created Petra; BP established Anro; and Elf founded CorElf.[50] The companies are still major oil traders today, over and above their activities in oil production and refining.

But foremost of all the fortune-seekers, gamblers and buccaneers who were drawn to the wilds of the Rotterdam market was Johannes Christiaan Martinus Augustinus Maria Deuss. Alongside Marc Rich, he would be one of the dominant figures in the oil market of the 1970s and 1980s, the epitome of the freewheeling trader. Deuss was the opposite of the conservative ideal of the Philipp Brothers school of trading. Unafraid to play politics, he mixed freely with Iranian ayatollahs, Arab sheikhs and Soviet bureaucrats, even becoming an adviser to the Sultan of Oman. He gambled on the price of oil with

abandon, making and losing hundreds of millions of dollars at a time. 'John Deuss is a mythical character,' says Bill Emmitt, a former executive at oil brokerage PVM, who dealt with him on numerous occasions. 'He always tried to play behind the scenes.'[51]

In contrast to Rich, Deuss somehow managed to avoid the limelight. He rarely spoke in public; he gave only a handful of interviews; and he managed to keep his profits and losses hidden from prying eyes. Despite his preference for discretion, he ended up making headlines a few times, such as when he inserted himself between the governments of Russia and Kazakhstan and the oil major Chevron to secure a decisive role in the construction of a key oil export pipeline from Central Asia worth billions of dollars. It was a classic Deuss operation, playing off several different governments against one another for maximum profit. In the end, US Vice President Al Gore personally intervened to eject Deuss from the project.

With his mop of sandy-coloured hair carefully parted on the side, and pinstriped suits with oversized lapels, Deuss looked like a character straight out of *Wall Street*, the film that chronicled the wild dealings of the finance industry in the 1980s. His lifestyle was more like that of a Bond villain, however. From his base in Bermuda, he entertained business contacts and friends on his 187-foot-long, three-mast yacht. His typical entourage included two English sheepdogs, and a troupe of bodyguards and striking female assistants. He crisscrossed the globe on one of his two Gulfstream private jets. 'He had this big villa where girls in bikinis were lounging around,' said Dutch journalist Friso Endt, of NRC Handelsblatt, who was one of the few to interview Deuss. 'A girl would bring him a telex about some deal and he would say "yes" or "no" and she would go away to carry out his orders.'[52]

Born in Nijmegen in the Netherlands in 1942, Deuss first dabbled in trading via a company called JOC Oil (the initials stood for 'John's Own Company') in the early 1970s.[53] He was soon successful in building a relationship with Soyuznefteexport, the Soviet export agency Theodor Weisser had successfully schmoozed two decades earlier.

In a meeting in Paris in November 1976, he won a coveted prize: a contract to export hundreds of millions of dollars' worth of Soviet crude in 1977. Between January and June, Moscow shipped thirty-nine cargoes to Deuss. JOC Oil paid for the first six shipments, but never paid for the other thirty-three cargoes, worth $101 million, despite having sold them to others at a profit.[54] Both sides claimed foul play, and a lengthy arbitration process ensued. Deuss would spend the next decade looking over his shoulder, fearful of a KGB assassin.[55]

The spat with Moscow didn't stop him, though. With JOC Oil entangled in the legal dispute and losing money, Deuss simply created a new company, called Transworld Oil.[56] By now he had perfected a business model designed for the freewheeling oil market of the 1970s and 1980s: use oil to get close to governments in the developing world, and use those relationships to make money trading oil. One day he would fly in to Malta[57] to negotiate a project to build an oil refinery, another he was in Botswana discussing a contract.[58] Then he'd appear in Turkey, offering to lend the government $200 million to buy oil.[59]

Deuss's oil deals took him to the darkest corners of global business, where commodity traders crossed paths with arms traffickers and spies.[60] Deuss was so at ease dealing with pariah countries that industry wags quipped that the acronym for Transworld Oil, TWO, ought to stand for Third World Oil. Unlike Marc Rich, who disavowed any interest in politics, Deuss positively relished using his oil-market power for political ends. For him, money was a proxy for political influence. When asked why money was so important to him, he replied: 'Don't you understand that it's a question of power, and money means power. It's as simple as that.'[61]

John Deuss personified a shift in the oil market's centre of gravity, away from the Seven Sisters and towards the traders. By the late

1970s, the likes of Rich and Deuss had been accumulating money and power for several years. But a new crisis in the Middle East was about to redraw the oil market, bringing them riches on a new scale – and catapulting them to a position of geopolitical significance that would catch the attention of governments around the world.

On 1 February 1979, a plane touched down in Tehran. From it emerged an elderly man with a white beard, dressed in long black robes. The man, walking gingerly and assisted by a steward, was Ayatollah Ruhollah Khomeini. His return to Iran after fifteen years of exile marked the culmination of the Iranian revolution and the beginning of a new era for the global oil market.

Speaking in a loud, firm voice, the septuagenarian told his supporters: 'We are succeeding, but this is only the first stage.'[62] A few weeks earlier, Mohammad Reza Pahlavi, the last Shah of Persia, who had been famous for his lavish parties fuelled by the petrodollars of the 1973–74 crisis, had left the country, ostensibly on holiday, never to return.

For the oil market, the Iranian revolution was a lightning bolt. Iran was the second-largest oil producer within OPEC, behind only Saudi Arabia. An oil crisis had already been brewing for several months when Ayatollah Khomeini landed in Tehran. Since early 1978, oil workers had been on strike in the south-east of Iran. At the beginning of the year, Iranian oil production had been around 5.5 million barrels a day; by the end of the year, production had fallen to a trickle.[63]

The Iranian revolution didn't affect everyone in the oil market equally. British Petroleum, which had grown out of the Anglo-Persian Oil Company, was hit hardest. Until the revolution, BP, thanks to its contracts with Tehran, had had enough crude not only to meet the needs of its own refineries but also to supply others. Suddenly, that supply was entirely cut off as BP's staff were forced to evacuate and then its assets were nationalised. The company suddenly needed to buy oil just to supply its own refineries. Japanese refiners, which relied heavily on Iranian crude supplied by BP and others, were also caught short. Some American refiners were in the same boat.

Despite an output hike by Saudi Arabia to compensate for the Iranian shortfall, official OPEC oil prices surged throughout 1979 and 1980, first to $18 a barrel, and then to $28. In reality, the market price went much higher. Oil changed hands in the spot market for $40 a barrel or more – there were rumours of deals at $50 a barrel. It was a price that would have sounded outlandish only a few years earlier, when prices had been anchored at $2 for a decade at a time.

The price of oil had been decisively freed from the grip of the Seven Sisters, and the lords of this new, volatile market were traders like Rich and Deuss. The world was thirsty for oil. Companies were desperate after being cut off from Iranian supplies overnight. It didn't matter where it came from or what it cost. 'What we had to do was to go out and buy that crude from somebody, somewhere,' said James Morrison, a senior executive at Atlantic Richfield Company.[64]

For the traders, the secret to an easy profit was a long-term contract to buy oil at the official prices. Then, with prices soaring in the spot market, they could resell the same oil for five or even ten dollars more per barrel. And how would a trader get hold of such a lucrative contract? 'What he had to do to get this contract was to pay a ridiculously small commission to the appropriate parties,' said an executive at a major oil company at the time. 'And sometimes the required brown envelopes would be passed.'[65]

No doubt brown envelopes or 'commissions' had always been part of doing business in far-flung parts of the world. But the oil crises of the 1970s created a new economy of corruption: the global oil industry was newly nationalised, and the people in charge of deciding who could secure a contract were no longer executives of large oil companies but badly paid government officials. And suddenly, thanks to the soaring oil price, they had the power to allot contracts that were worth many millions of dollars to a shrewd oil trader.

Rich was the kind of trader prepared to do what was necessary to get his hands on oil. The cost of securing a contract for Iranian oil those days was about $125,000 to the right man at the National

Iranian Oil Company.[66] 'The bribes were paid in order to be able to do the business,' Rich told his biographer. 'It's not a price which is disadvantageous for the government involved in the selling or buying.'[67] He saw nothing wrong with paying for access. While the US had introduced anti-corruption laws, some European nations hadn't. In Switzerland it was even possible to account for the 'facilitation fees', as the bribes were often called in corporate-speak, as tax deductible expenses.

The traders had done well in the first oil crisis of 1973. But this time the profits were truly extraordinary: in 1979, Marc Rich + Co made more than $1 billion in profit, according to four former executives (although the profit after tax that its official accounts showed was somewhat lower, at around $700 million, one of them said).

The rest of the oil trading industry was also making money hand over fist. Mabanaft, which hadn't built up the same global heft as Marc Rich + Co, nonetheless made profits of 200 million Deutschmark (a little over $100 million) that year.[68] And the pre-tax profits of Philipp Brothers, which had never before surpassed $200 million, hit $443 million in 1979 and $603 million in 1980.[69] Cargill made $178 million in 1979 and $269 million in 1980.[70]

To the modern eye, inured to figures in the billions of dollars, it's easy to forget quite how enormous those profits were. Philipp Brothers would plough its windfall profits into buying Salomon Brothers, one of Wall Street's most storied investment banks. Marc Rich + Co's 1979 profit made it one of the ten most profitable companies in America that year, on a par with giants such as General Electric and Ford Motors.

Yet, unlike those companies, Marc Rich + Co was owned by just a handful of people, reported nothing publicly about its activity, and was virtually unregulated. Politicians had begun to realise in the 1970s how little they knew about the commodity traders, who one year had sold a billion dollars' worth of grain to the Soviet Union and now seemed to control the oil price. But they did not know what to do about it.

The first response was to increase transparency. The US Department of Agriculture started publishing supply and demand estimates for global grain markets; the International Energy Agency did the same for oil. Their reports are still closely watched by traders today.

But when it came to actually controlling the traders, regulators drew a blank. At a meeting of the G7 in 1979, the leaders of France, West Germany, Italy, Japan, the United Kingdom, Canada and the United States urged oil companies and OPEC nations to 'moderate spot market transactions' and considered setting up a 'register of international oil transactions'.[71] It was a recognition, for the first time in history, of the commodity traders as a force to be reckoned with. But the push to regulate the market went nowhere, and the casino of Rotterdam continued to operate with glorious opacity.

In a decade, the oil market had undergone a fundamental change that redefined how the world would access its energy for decades to come.

The market no longer belonged to the oligopolistic Seven Sisters, with their almost colonial oil deals in the Middle East, Africa and Latin America. In their stead appeared traders like Marc Rich, hungry for risk and unburdened by history or, in some cases, ethics. Through their trading, they had facilitated one of the great geopolitical and economic revolutions of the modern era: the seizure of their natural resources by oil-rich nations, the rise of the petrodollar as a crucial element of international finance, and the rise of the petrostate as a force in global politics.

The price of oil was freed. No longer was it decided by a few large companies in boardrooms in London or New York, in consultation with American and European governments. From now on it would be left to the cut-throat world of the Rotterdam market to set the price of the world's most important commodity. It was a shift that went beyond oil. The collapse of the gold standard meant

the value of the dollar, too, was the preserve of the market. Everywhere, the grip of Western governments and institutions on the world economy was loosening, and a new era of more ruthless capitalism was born.

The commodity traders' moment had arrived.

THREE

THE LAST BANK IN TOWN

It was a Friday evening in the early 1980s when one of Jamaica's cabinet ministers found out that his country had run out of money.

Hugh Hart, the minister for mines and energy, was in parliament, and word reached him at around 6 p.m. that an official from the central bank was waiting to speak to him in a state of some distress. Hart stepped outside. The official's message was simple: Jamaica's coffers were empty. The central bank couldn't raise the money it needed to pay for a cargo of oil.

'And by the way,' the official added. 'We run out of oil on Sunday.'

'I just didn't know what the hell to do,' Hart recalls.[1]

Jamaica had been buying 300,000 barrels of oil every month for the Caribbean island's only refinery, located in Kingston, the capital. Each month, the central bank would provide a guarantee for $10 million to cover the cost of the oil. But this month, the central bank didn't have enough money, and so there would be no oil. Without the oil, Jamaica's refinery would stop producing gasoline and diesel, and the country's petrol stations would have to close.

Hart, a lawyer who had been coaxed into frontline politics by his brother-in-law, the prime minister, knew what that would mean. Jamaica's economy was still recovering from the ravages of the oil

crises of the 1970s, which had spilled over into political violence that had turned the streets of Kingston into a war zone. By the early 1980s, the worst of the violence had passed, but the economic and social fabric of the country was still fragile.

Hart called the only person he could think of who might be able to help avert the crisis: Willy Strothotte, the tall, statesmanlike German trader who ran Marc Rich + Co's affiliate in New York. The trading house was deeply invested in Jamaica: the scenic Caribbean island was one of the world's largest producers of bauxite and alumina, the minerals used to make aluminium.[2] And Marc Rich + Co was the world's top aluminium trader.

'Hugh, I'm really sorry, but I can't help you. I don't think anybody can help you,' Strothotte said. As a last resort, he offered Marc Rich's home phone number in Zug. 'But I warn you, it's something like two o'clock in the morning in Switzerland, so I'm not about to call him.'

Hart had never spoken to Rich before: his dealings up until that point had only been with Strothotte. With a little trepidation, he put in the call to Zug. A bleary Marc Rich answered the phone.

'Mr Rich, it's Hugh Hart,' he began. 'You probably don't know me.'

'Oh yes, I know all about you,' Rich replied. 'What the hell are you waking me up at two o'clock in the morning for?'

'Well,' Hart replied. 'It's just a small matter of life and death.' He explained Jamaica's predicament.

'What do you expect me to do about it? It's two o'clock on Friday night, and your central bank can't raise $10 million. What the hell?'

Hart pleaded. There was a moment of silence.

'Call Willy in an hour,' Rich instructed, and hung up the phone.

By the time Hart called Strothotte back in New York, a tanker full of oil was on its way to Jamaica. Rich had arranged for a shipment of Venezuelan crude he was delivering to the east coast of the US to stop off in Kingston on the way. On Saturday evening, less than 24 hours before Jamaica was due to run out, it unloaded 300,000 barrels of oil.

The trade was a demonstration of the massive power that Marc Rich now wielded thanks to his mastery of the oil market. The oil shocks of the 1970s had filled the coffers of the commodity traders, and they combined their new-found financial might with a chutzpah that few other investors could match. By the 1980s, staking their money where other companies wouldn't dare was the commodity traders' trademark.

Jamaica was a prime example: the country was on the brink of bankruptcy, shunned by its lenders, and Rich had just delivered the government oil worth $10 million without even signing a contract. The risk would be worth it, though. The Jamaican government would not forget how Rich had saved it from ruin. The Caribbean island would become a source of profits for Rich and his successors for decades to come.

'It was one of the most nerve-racking moments I've had,' Hart recalls. 'I think it would have brought the government down, quite frankly.'

Marc Rich's deals with Jamaica were emblematic of the shifts taking place in the world economy in the 1970s and 1980s. From Jamaica to Saudi Arabia and Guyana to Peru, the decades of global economic growth had spurred massive investments in commodity production around the world. Now, governments across the Middle East, Africa and Latin America had been seizing control of the commodities they produced in a wave of nationalisations. The shift in power from large American and European oil and mining companies to governments in what was known as the Third World opened a window of opportunity for the commodity traders that they exploited with gusto. In the process they became the connection between many newly assertive countries and the global financial system, helping to channel dollars to governments and leaders that had no other source of funding.

Nowhere was that clearer than in the aluminium industry. The economic boom that followed the Second World War had turned aluminium into the world's hottest metal. Cheaper than copper, lighter and more versatile than steel, aluminium consumption soared thanks to its wide array of uses in planes, cars and the white goods that were the symbols of the new age of consumerism.

Until the war, it had been a relatively niche material. But the military machine demanded an enormous quantity of aircraft, and so manufacturers needed an unprecedented quantity of aluminium. Americans were encouraged to collect aluminium items around their homes for scrap to help meet the military's needs. One New York radio station broadcast a programme called 'Aluminum for Defense', while children were offered free movie tickets in exchange for collecting balls of aluminium foil.[3]

By the time the war ended, the aluminium industry had the capacity to supply the consumer boom that was to come. Production rose from 1 million tonnes in 1945 to 10 million tonnes by 1970.[4] That, in turn, spurred a worldwide scramble for bauxite, the reddish-brown earth found in Guinea, Australia, and the famed blue mountains of Jamaica's interior. The bauxite was transformed first into white, powdery alumina, and then finally aluminium metal.

For decades the market for aluminium was dominated by a few large, mostly North American companies, much like the Seven Sisters had dominated the oil market. Alcoa, the company founded in 1888 by the man who had invented the process to extract aluminium, was so dominant that a US court in 1951 forced it to split entirely from its international assets, which were grouped under Alcan of Canada. By 1955, the six largest aluminium companies, led by Alcoa and Alcan, controlled 88% of the non-socialist world's bauxite supply, 91% of its alumina and 86% of the aluminium.[5] For much of the 1960s and 1970s, even aluminium from the Eastern Bloc was sold by the major producers under a restrictive 'gentlemen's agreement' that prevented it from flowing freely on to the market.[6]

As in the oil market, the large producers had also controlled the price, publishing the prices at which they would sell the metal in each region. But, just as in oil, that started to change in the 1970s. A trend of 'resource nationalism' swept the world, as newly-independent post-colonial states pushed for greater autonomy from their former rulers, and soaring prices made the commodity sector a lucrative target.

In the aluminium sector, the nationalisations began in Guyana, a state bordering Venezuela, which was the world's fifth-largest bauxite producer.[7] On 1 March 1971, Guyana's parliament legislated to allow the nationalisation of the country's bauxite industry, including a subsidiary of Canadian giant Alcan that was at that point the country's largest enterprise. The move sent a shockwave through Western boardrooms and capitals.

'Marketing patterns and investment plans of the world bauxite industry are being threatened by nationalist stirrings in the Caribbean area', the CIA warned.[8] But the US spy agency didn't rate Guyana's chances of making nationalisation a success: it predicted that the six big companies would shun the country's output, leaving it with no buyers for its bauxite and alumina. The CIA had not reckoned with Philipp Brothers, however. Two senior executives from the trading house flew to Guyana's capital and persuaded the government to allow them to sell its entire bauxite and alumina output.[9] A year later, the CIA noted that Guyana's efforts to sell its alumina had been aided by its 'aggressive new marketing agent, Philipp Brothers of New York'.[10]

Jamaica was a much bigger prize for the traders. By the 1960s the island was the world's largest producer of bauxite and one of the top suppliers of alumina, with investments from most of the large aluminium companies. Michael Manley, Jamaica's charismatic socialist prime minister, had opened the door to the trading companies with a dramatic move to increase the government's share of profits from bauxite and alumina in 1974. Much like the oil industry nationalisations in OPEC countries, his attempt to grab a larger share of the

industry's profits ended with the government owning shares of most of the country's bauxite mines and alumina refineries. So, by the end of the 1970s, the Jamaican government had bauxite and alumina to sell, but little expertise in selling or shipping it. For the traders, it was a dream scenario.

The Cold War was raging, and by the late 1970s, the battle for dominance between Moscow and Washington was playing out in microcosm on the streets of Kingston. Gangs loyal to the two main parties – one with ties to Moscow, the other close to the US – fought a bloody turf war in Jamaica's capital. A US ambassador at the time recalled stepping over a fresh dead body left each morning on the doorstep of the embassy.[11]

Left-wing revolutionaries were scoring victories across the region. The government of the Caribbean state of Grenada was toppled in a coup by a group who rapidly aligned themselves with Cuba and the Soviet Union. In Nicaragua, the Sandinistas seized power with the support of the Soviet Union.

Against this backdrop, Manley made the US nervous. He was friendly with Fidel Castro, and had struck deals with the Soviet Union. So when his party lost power in elections in 1980, the US was determined to support the new government of his rival, Edward Seaga.

The mechanism was bauxite. Ronald Reagan, recently elected US president, made Seaga the first foreign leader he invited to the White House. Convinced of the 'magic of the marketplace', Reagan directed the huge economic resources of the US to turn the political tide in the region, and Jamaica was the centrepiece of his policy.[12] He ordered the US stockpiling agency to buy a total of 3.6 million tonnes of Jamaican bauxite between 1982 and 1984, equivalent to a sixth of the country's production.[13] That was helpful, but Jamaica's need for cash was desperate. And so Marc Rich + Co stepped in, paying the Jamaican government in advance for the bauxite it would eventually sell to the US.[14]

'We didn't make a lot of money,' says Manny Weiss, one of the Marc Rich + Co traders who helped organise the deal. 'It was a way

of starting the relationship with Jamaica.' It was the beginning of a deep entanglement between the Jamaican government and the commodity traders that would include Hugh Hart's late-night call to Marc Rich in search of a cargo of oil.

But that was not the only way Marc Rich + Co helped the Caribbean country. For example, Jamaica, like many developing countries in the 1970s and 1980s, was heavily dependent on borrowing from the IMF. But the IMF imposed stringent conditions on it, which included meeting certain financial targets on a regular basis. Sometimes the government accounts would be short by a few million dollars.

And so, the government turned to Marc Rich + Co. On one occasion, Hart recalls calling Strothotte and telling him the Jamaican government was desperate for $5 million to meet its IMF requirements. The German trader immediately delivered. Again, Marc Rich + Co had saved the skin of the Jamaican government; and again, it had done so without even signing a contract. Such deals required some creative accounting: to satisfy the IMF, the money the trading house deposited in the government's accounts couldn't be shown as a debt. 'Of course it was a debt, but it was never shown as a debt,' Hart says. 'We didn't owe them anything on the books.'

That was not all. When the Jamaican government wanted to buy the country's oil refinery from an Exxon subsidiary, Marc Rich + Co lent it the money. The trading company even helped to fund Jamaica's team at the 1984 Olympics in Los Angeles, and paid for it to send a bobsled team to participate in the 1988 Winter Olympics – whose unlikely journey to the Games was chronicled in the Disney film *Cool Runnings*.[15]

For critics, Marc Rich was simply too dominant in Jamaica. 'He virtually hijacked Jamaica's economy,' one US official said.[16]

But Hart, who three decades later is still friendly with some former Marc Rich + Co traders, says the country would have been lost without the commodity trader.

'There is no doubt that Marc Rich helped us a tremendous amount,' he says. 'We had a great relationship. Sure, they made a lot of money.

They made a lot of money and so they should. But we did as well or better than we would have done if we'd just gone on the open market somewhere.'[17]

For Marc Rich + Co, the Jamaican relationship was the beginning of a dazzling series of deals, stretching from the Caribbean island to the industrial heartland of the US. They would give the trading house a towering position in the global aluminium market – and deliver it hundreds of millions of dollars in profits. What happened next was a masterful demonstration of how the traders at Marc Rich + Co could turn a relationship with an impoverished government to their own financial advantage.

By the mid-1980s, the aluminium industry had entered a punishing downturn. The reason was the cost of energy. While aluminium is one of the most common elements in the earth's crust, transforming it into pure metal is a costly two-step process – first, from bauxite to alumina, then from alumina to aluminium – that consumes huge amounts of energy.

Producing a tonne of aluminium uses the same amount of electricity as a US household consumes in a year. The energy consumption is so large that traders jokingly describe aluminium as 'congealed electricity'. It's why most smelters are built where electricity is cheap, such as Siberia with its hydropower, Iceland with its geothermal generation, or the Middle East with its natural gas.

Until 1973, aluminium companies hadn't worried too much about their electricity bills. But then the oil price soared, making energy costs exorbitant and plunging the industry into crisis.

At the same time, the pricing power of the industry was shifting from the big companies to the London Metal Exchange, where traders bought and sold the metal. Increasingly, the price of every element in the aluminium production chain, from alumina to kitchen foil, was benchmarked against LME quotes. And with consumption stagnating, LME prices fell.

Jamaica's industry was hard hit. The island's alumina plants had been built alongside oil-powered generators in the 1950s and 1960s, making them particularly exposed to the spike in oil prices. Alumina and bauxite production plunged.[18] One large aluminium company, Reynolds, announced it was closing its Jamaican bauxite operation in 1984. Then, in 1985, the manager of the Alcoa plant walked into Hart's office and informed him that the US company would be shutting down the plant within days.[19]

Alive to the potentially devastating consequences for the Jamaican economy, Hart quickly sketched a plan to save the alumina industry. He decided that the government would buy the plant. There was a catch: he didn't have the money to implement it. For the plan to work, he'd need to find someone willing to buy the alumina, and that did not promise to be easy. The market was oversupplied and prices were slumping. And to make matters worse, alumina can't be stored for a long time, since it absorbs moisture from the air. So Hart got on a plane to Switzerland to go and see the only people that could help: the traders at Marc Rich + Co.

Strothotte and Weiss didn't hesitate. They negotiated a ten-year contract to buy alumina from the Alcoa plant, Jamalco. They would also supply fuel oil and caustic soda, two of the plant's main input costs, as well as paying some of the money up front, helping to finance the government's acquisition of a share in the company from Alcoa.

In exchange for providing a cash advance and a certain market for Jamaica's alumina, they got a rock bottom price. The bulk of the supplies would be sold at a price calculated as 9.25% of the LME aluminium price.[20] It was a bargain: the World Bank, reviewing the deal years later, noted that the percentage was 'about 25% below typical contract terms'.[21]

It was the beginning of one of Marc Rich + Co's most profitable trades. The downturn had not just put Jamaican alumina producers under strain. Around the world, aluminium smelters – which transform alumina into aluminium – were also getting into financial

difficulty. And so Marc Rich + Co started offering the struggling smelters a deal: the trading house would supply them with alumina, and as payment take the aluminium they produced. This type of deal, exchanging a raw material for a finished product, was called 'tolling' and had been used before in oil and zinc, but Marc Rich + Co brought it to the aluminium sector.

'It caught on like wildfire,' Weiss says. The trading house became 'like a producer without the problems of owning production'.[22] In the space of a few months in 1986, Marc Rich + Co's US affiliate struck tolling deals with smelters in Oregon, Ohio and South Carolina.[23] The combination of the contract with the Jamaican government to buy alumina and these tolling deals for aluminium helped to make Marc Rich + Co the world's largest aluminium trader, competing with industrial giants like Alcoa and Alcan – all without actually running any smelters. In 1987, the company went further. At Mount Holly, just outside Charleston, the state capital of South Carolina, the trader bought a 27% stake in an aluminium smelter – its first major asset investment. It also struck a tolling deal for half the smelter's output.

It was propitious timing. In early 1987, Weiss had become convinced that aluminium prices were going to rise dramatically. Brazil had been seen as a major new source of supply, but its aluminium industry had been hit by power cuts.[24] Elsewhere, rising electricity prices had curtailed output. And, after the downturn in the early 1980s, the US economy was accelerating. Marc Rich + Co was already well positioned to profit thanks to its tolling deals, which guaranteed a steady flow of metal. But Weiss went further: he started buying aluminium directly on the LME, placing a big bet that prices would rise.

Aluminium prices didn't just rise, they skyrocketed. Burgeoning demand for the metal in cars and household appliances had drawn down inventories to dangerously low levels. Aluminium users rushed to buy metal, depleting the stocks held in warehouses linked to the LME. And Weiss joined them. At its peak, his position – which his bosses at Marc Rich + Co had limited to 100,000 tonnes – was larger than all the inventories left in LME warehouses.

It was a perfect storm. From a low point in 1985 to a peak in June 1988, the price of aluminium more than quadrupled. The impact was felt far and wide – even pushing up the cost of that kitchen staple, aluminium foil, by more than a third.[25]

Weiss had cornered the aluminium market. While he didn't own all the aluminium in the world – that would have been beyond even the financial means of Marc Rich + Co – he didn't need to. On the LME, and other futures exchanges, traders buy and sell contracts for delivery of a commodity on a specific date. When that date comes around, traders who have sold futures contracts must deliver the commodity to those who have bought. On the LME, that means handing over metal that's in an LME warehouse.

But in the aluminium market of the summer of 1988, there wasn't enough metal in LME warehouses to hand over. That put anyone who'd sold aluminium futures up against the wall. Without enough metal stocks to settle the contracts, the only way they could avoid defaulting was to buy back the contracts they had sold. And that, most likely, meant buying from Weiss.

The cost was eye-watering. The price of aluminium for immediate delivery soared to $4,290 a tonne – more than $1,000 higher than contracts for delivery in three months, an indication of the scale of the shortage. That price difference was so extreme that some rival traders started flying aluminium from the US into LME warehouses near Rotterdam on jumbo jets in order to get the metal in as soon as possible.[26] Weiss was counting his gains in the millions of dollars.

Then, as quickly as the market went up, it started to fall. Japanese traders started selling their inventories in an effort to deflate the squeeze. But Marc Rich + Co, which had found out about the Japanese sales through its contacts in Tokyo, had already sold its position. Weiss says he didn't set out to corner the market – he'd just foreseen that there wouldn't be enough aluminium to go round. 'It wasn't a corner that anybody could have conceived; it was luck.'[27]

Still, it made Marc Rich + Co even richer. By 1988, the metals division had overtaken oil as the company's main generator of profits.[28] Aluminium alone made more than $100 million that year.[29]

But as much as the trading house enjoyed the aluminium riches, in Jamaica opposition politicians argued that the government had been taken advantage of by the canny commodity trader. After the elections in 1989, former prime minister Michael Manley returned to power with a promise to investigate the previous government's deals with Marc Rich. But he was soon treated to a demonstration of the trader's power. Marc Rich was not to be done out of a profitable deal without a fight. And Jamaica still needed the trader's money.

Hugh Small, the new mining minister, had been one of the most public critics of the previous government's relationship with Rich. On a trip to Venezuela, Small was pulled aside by a Venezuelan minister, who extolled the virtues of Marc Rich + Co and suggested it might be 'in the best interests of Jamaica' to take a less unfriendly position towards the trading house. Soon afterwards, the minister was in Canada for negotiations with Alcan, the giant aluminium company. Again, the subject of Marc Rich was raised. This time, the Canadians showed Small a documentary film detailing the importance of the trader to the global aluminium industry.[30]

Small went to meet Willy Strothotte, who agreed to a small increase in the alumina price under Marc Rich + Co's contract.[31] But there was a catch. Strothotte wanted the Jamaican government to announce publicly that it was dropping any investigation into Marc Rich. The minister, offended at the quid pro quo, refused. Yet Jamaica had little choice: it still needed Rich's money. At the end of June, Manley stood up in parliament and announced that he'd taken a new $45 million loan from Marc Rich + Co to help the government meet its IMF target. 'If Marc Rich is good for Jamaica, Marc Rich is good for Jamaica,' he said. It was not quite the apology Strothotte had demanded, but it was close enough.[32]

For Marc Rich + Co, and later its successor company Glencore, Jamaica would be a source of sizeable profits for nearly three decades. In the mid-2000s, for example, as commodity prices soared, Glencore was paying the Jamaican government less than half the market price for its alumina, thanks to contracts signed years earlier. In just three years, from 2004 to 2006, the Jamaican government would have received $370 million in additional revenue if it had been selling its alumina on the spot market and not to Glencore.[33] It's fair to assume that the trading company's profits on the deal were similar in scale.

In return, over the course of nearly thirty years, Marc Rich + Co and Glencore would provide financing to Jamaica to the tune of close to $1 billion.[34] 'Glencore, and Marc Rich before, were really the last bank in town,' says Carlton Davis, a former head of the Jamaican civil service, who was involved in many negotiations with the trading house.[35]

The deals in Jamaica were a masterclass in the new-found clout of the commodity traders. Thanks to their unprecedented financial firepower and mastery of the commodity markets, traders such as Marc Rich were able to seize on the economic weakness of countries such as Jamaica. With the big Western oil and mining companies in retreat, almost no regulatory scrutiny, and with Wall Street banks yet to discover emerging markets, the traders had a free rein.

Marc Rich wasn't the only commodity trader in the ascendant in the early 1980s. The era became a byword for the excesses of Wall Street, but the commodity traders were no less expansive in their paycheques or their tastes. Marc Rich + Co traders turned up to their office in Mayfair wearing expensive ties from Hermès; some also had expensive cocaine habits; at its Christmas parties, the company handed out sports cars.

To a large degree, the traders had the changing global political landscape to thank for their fortune. Jamaica's financial distress was far from unique. The spike in oil prices in the 1970s had plunged

many importing countries into chaos. Across Latin America, nations were on their knees due to a debt crisis that wiped out the continent's middle class and sent millions into poverty. Meanwhile, Moscow and Washington were waging proxy wars around the globe, from Nicaragua to Angola. Trade embargoes proliferated.

It wasn't just the bauxite industry that the governments of the developing world were nationalising. Everywhere, control of commodity markets was being wrested from the hands of large American corporates. Four of the world's largest copper exporters – Chile, Peru, the Democratic Republic of Congo and Zambia – nationalised some or all of their mining industries in the 1960s and 1970s.[36] The Eastern Bloc of Communist states became an ever more important source of supplies of lead, zinc and oil for those willing to trade with them. Everywhere, commodity markets were opening up. Supply chains were becoming more fragmented, and the power of the large oil and mining companies dissipated. Prices were being set by the market rather than dictated by a few dominant companies – and into the vacuum stepped the commodity traders.

As the commodity traders got involved with what others saw as difficult nations, they found a world short of money, where the risks were numerous but the rewards were enormous. In 1981, an economist at the World Bank coined the term 'emerging markets' to describe a set of fast-developing Third World nations rapidly being incorporated into the global economy – and the traders were discovering these nations before anyone else.[37] Countries such as Brazil, Indonesia or India that today are must-go destinations for even mainstream investors were the frontiers of the capitalist world.

In emerging markets, the commodity traders didn't just buy and sell raw materials. Instead, they expanded into merchant banking and private equity, one day lending money to the government of Nigeria, the next investing in Peruvian anchovy factories. The commodity traders were, effectively, engaging in capital arbitrage: raising funds in the industrialised world, and investing them in emerging markets, where they enjoyed fatter returns.

It was a risky world, however, besieged by political crisis, encumbered by foreign exchange controls, and handicapped by red tape. But if they got the timing right, the traders could hit the jackpot. In Brazil and Argentina, for example, investments paid for themselves in as little as two or three years, compared with ten years or longer in developed nations.[38] The trading houses were confident they would get paid: without them, countries couldn't export their goods and earn precious hard currencies.

For commodity traders like Rich, with an appetite for taking risks and a willingness to do business with anyone and everyone, it was an ideal environment. A left-wing government nationalises its resources industry? The traders were on hand to help them sell the commodities. A right-wing government seizes power in a military coup? Well, they would need help selling commodities too.

That's exactly how it had played out in Jamaica. When the country's left-wing government did a deal with Moscow to exchange bauxite for Soviet-made Lada cars, Marc Rich + Co helped handle the logistics; when the next government swapped bauxite with the US government for American grain and milk powder, Marc Rich + Co acted as intermediary.

'It's almost unfair competition,' complained one rival trader at a large French company. 'In most companies, if you asked to lend money to Jamaica, they'd throw you out the window.'[39]

In the 1980s, the list of countries that 'most companies' wouldn't dream of dealing with grew longer and longer. Exactly where to draw the line was a question of personal taste. Some traders were happy to do business in tricky countries such as India or the Philippines, but drew the line at war zones and pariah states. For others, any corner of the world was fair game.

Marc Rich was among those who didn't have any qualms about dealing with anyone, including those under economic sanctions. 'In an embargo, only the small people suffer,' said Eddie Egloff, a senior partner at Marc Rich + Co. 'We did business according to our own laws and not those of others.'[40] So Rich traded just as happily with

the right-wing Chilean government of Augusto Pinochet as with Nicaragua's left-wing Daniel Ortega. His lodestar was money, not politics.

Of all the difficult places that became playgrounds for commodity traders in the 1980s, it was apartheid South Africa where the traders' amoral approach to business was most clearly on show. And the rewards for putting morality to one side were significant. 'Everybody was trading with South Africa,' Eric de Turckheim, head of finance of Marc Rich + Co and later a founding partner of Trafigura, recalls.[41] Rich himself said the trade with South Africa had been his 'most important and most profitable'.[42]

Yet the fortunes of a handful of oil trading houses and executives were built in no small part by prolonging the suffering of black South Africans. Oil was the Achilles heel of South Africa. The rest of the continent was blessed with significant oil riches, but geology hadn't been so kind to South Africa. For years, its only domestic source of gasoline involved making it from coal using an expensive process that had been pioneered by Nazi Germany during the Second World War. If South Africa wanted oil, it would need to be imported.

For a handful of years after the imposition of white-only rule in 1948, South Africa had been able to trade freely with the world. Its segregation laws didn't yet look out of place in the eyes of many in Washington and London, who were happy to support a Cold War ally.

But, over time, the racist South African government came under increasing pressure. The change in attitudes was reflected in a speech by British Prime Minister Harold Macmillan in Cape Town in 1960. 'The wind of change is blowing through this continent. Whether we like it or not, this growth of national consciousness is a political fact. We must all accept it as a fact,' he said.[43] The world's outrage was heightened by news of massacres perpetrated by the white-only South African police. The country was excluded from the 1964 Tokyo

summer Olympic Games, the first of many such bans.[44] But while South Africa was boycotted on the world stage in sporting and cultural events, its economy wasn't yet much affected. Oil was still flowing freely.

That began to change in 1973, when the Arab members of OPEC imposed a petroleum embargo on South Africa due to its perceived friendliness with Israel. Soon after, in 1977, the United Nations General Assembly called for an oil embargo in response to Pretoria's violent repression of the Soweto uprising a year earlier. And yet South Africa could rely on the Shah of Iran, who ensured that his oil continued to flow, regardless of what the rest of the world might think. Iran came to account for roughly 80% of South Africa's petroleum supply, with some of its refineries configured to run exclusively on a diet of Persian crude. The Islamic revolution in 1979 ended the trade overnight, however, at least officially. With Ayatollah Khomeini in power, Iran stopped selling oil directly to South Africa.

Pretoria had to turn to the commodity traders. They helped to secure oil from Iran, the Soviet Union, Saudi Arabia and Brunei – for a price. The trade was shrouded in secrecy, since few oil-producing countries permitted oil sales to South Africa. At least, not officially. In many cases government officials turned a blind eye, happy to secure foreign exchange earnings and, sometimes, bribes. It was an era before satellites were tracking every ship on the water, and the traders could easily hide their manoeuvres. On one occasion, the captain of the *Dagli*, a tanker contracted by Marc Rich + Co, was told simply to erase the name of the vessel. The captain was taken aback by the request, replying via telex: 'under no circumstances will the name be painted over under my command stop but i will cover the name with canvas if the weather permits. regards'.[45]

The traders also used secret codes to refer to unsavoury countries in their internal communications. In Vitol's telexes, South Africa was 'Tulip'.[46] Inside Marc Rich + Co, South Africa was known as 'Udo', after Udo Horstmann, the trader in charge of the country. Iranian Light oil was 'crude number three'. Mark Crandall, who became head

of oil at the company in the early 1990s, before co-founding Trafigura, recalls meetings in Texas in the late 1980s with executives of Caltex, a subsidiary of Chevron, which owned a refinery in South Africa. Everyone talked in code to avoid problems with the US authorities. 'So here we are sitting in Dallas with a bunch of white boys, who are American, saying, "Well, do you think next year you would have better availability of crude number three than you have this year?"'[47] The oil business at the offices of Marc Rich + Co in Johannesburg was done from a special room, with its own telex line and a door fitted with a padlock.[48]

Despite all the tricks, a network of informants and the use of insurance reports allowed many of the trades to be tracked by the Shipping Research Bureau, a non-governmental organisation. The SRB tracked more than 850 oil tankers discharging in South Africa between January 1979 and December 1993. The list is a who's who of oil trading at the time, with Marc Rich + Co, Transworld Oil and Marimpex responsible for the bulk of the cargoes. But they were far from alone: other shippers included oil companies such as BP, Total and Royal Dutch Shell, and, to a lesser extent, other commodity traders, including Vitol.

More insight came when South Africa declassified documents relating to the oil deals after the end of apartheid. In the early days of the South African oil trade, it was Deuss and Transworld Oil that were dominant. In 1982, for example, Deuss accounted for more than half of South Africa's purchases, according to a memo from an official from the Strategic Fuel Fund, which managed the country's oil storage.[49] The Dutchman had such a stronghold on South Africa in the early 1980s that senior officials made a concerted effort to diversify their sources of supply, travelling from Pretoria to New York to meet Marc Rich + Co and to Hamburg to see Marimpex.

Without the traders, the economy of apartheid South Africa would almost certainly have collapsed many years earlier than it did. Chris Heunis, a South African minister, admitted that Pretoria had more difficulties buying oil than arms, and that the oil embargo

'could have destroyed' the apartheid regime.[50] For the traders, it was a hugely profitable business. P. W. Botha, the leader of South Africa from 1978 to 1989, said that buying crude oil from the traders had cost the country an additional 22 billion rand (more than $10 billion) over a decade.[51] In one single contract in 1979, Rich was able to sell South Africa millions of barrels of crude at $33 a barrel that he had bought at the official price of $14.55 a barrel, charging a 126% premium.[52] 'We had to spend it because we couldn't bring our motor cars and our diesel locomotives to a standstill as our economic life would have collapsed,' Botha, who was known as 'the big crocodile', told a local newspaper. 'We paid a price, which we are still suffering from today.'[53]

The traders weren't making money through a brilliant understanding of the market. They were simply willing to put aside any ethical principles to make more money. When challenged on their dealings with South Africa, the traders would reply that everything they were doing was legal. The BBC managed to corner Deuss in 1986 at a conference in London, in what is his only known television interview. Asked about his trade with South Africa, the Dutchman was evasive, but insisted that whatever he was doing, there was nothing wrong with it. 'We do not break any laws in any of the countries in which we operate,' he said. 'Using false documents? That I call illegal. But covering up a ship's name? Well, I'm not so sure ... I mean, if you have a boat in your backyard and you cover up its name, is that illegal?'[54]

Rich's response was even more contorted. 'I was fundamentally against apartheid. We were all against apartheid,' he said. And then, in the same breath, added: 'The South Africans needed oil, and people were reluctant to sell it to them because of the embargo. We agreed to do it because we felt it was nothing illegal.'[55]

In the world of embargoes and political favours of the 1980s, the traders learnt to be masters of disguise and deception. Trade was

divided along political lines: many countries refused to allow their products to be sold to South Africa; others refused to buy from certain countries; some sold to their allies at discounted prices.

The restrictions opened up opportunities for profit to traders who could get around them. Often, this meant being able to produce documentation to show that oil or metals had come from a different place than they actually had done. Marc Rich + Co, according to one senior trader at the time, had a whole cabinet filled with stamps and customs forms from every country in the world.[56] A trader needed to prove that their oil had loaded in Puerto Rico? No problem. Or that it had been delivered to Singapore? Easy.

For Marc Rich + Co, one of the most profitable disguises of the era was called Cobuco. It involved the world's wealthiest commodity traders disguising themselves as bureaucrats from the poorest nation on the planet.[57]

Established in the early 1980s, Cobuco was the *Compagnie Burundaise de Commerce*, headquartered in a chic neighbourhood of Brussels. Ostensibly, Cobuco was a trading company buying crude in the international market to supply Burundi, a tiny landlocked and poverty-stricken African nation in the Great Lakes region bordering Rwanda, Tanzania and the Democratic Republic of Congo. With little more than coffee, tea and subsistence agriculture for its economy, Burundi, which only won independence from Belgium in 1962, is the world's poorest country.[58] Its ten million or so inhabitants live on the equivalent of just $275 per capita a year, about half as much as people in Afghanistan.

A casual observer might assume that Cobuco was a bureaucratic outpost of the Burundian government. Call the company's office at Marie Depage 7 in Brussels and a Monsieur Ndolo would answer the phone.

In reality, however, the company was a front for Marc Rich + Co – a demonstration of the trading house's willingness to engage in deception in its pursuit of profit. And Monsieur Ndolo was not a

Burundian functionary, but a European trader for Marc Rich + Co whose name, needless to say, was not actually Monsieur Ndolo. He was not even based in Brussels – he had his calls routed from whichever European or African city he happened to be in to make them look like they had originated from the Belgian capital.

According to Monsieur Ndolo himself – who agreed to tell this story only if he was referred to by his pseudonym – the story of Cobuco began when he read a newspaper article about an African nation sending a delegation to oil-rich Libya to secure crude supplies at preferential terms. It was the early 1980s, and the world was still weathering the second oil crisis, with prices hovering around $30 a barrel. For many African nations, fuel became prohibitively expensive, so they turned to neighbouring oil producers for help. The Non-Aligned Movement, a group of countries that tried to keep their distance from both Washington and Moscow during the Cold War, was still relatively cohesive, and the very poorest nations in the group could count on the richer members to help them out. OPEC nations, in particular, were willing to sell crude at a discount to African nations. US dollar interest rates were approaching 20%,[59] and for many African countries securing soft loans to finance their oil purchases was just as important as getting access to cheap barrels.

The Marc Rich + Co trader hit on an idea: use a poor African or Latin American nation as a front for the trading house to get its hands on cheap barrels and even cheaper finance. And so Cobuco was born. Officially, the company was a joint venture half owned by Rich and half by the government of Burundi. On paper, it was perfectly aboveboard: its constitution was even formally approved by the African nation's parliament. In reality, the trader's scheme amounted to an absurdist joke. Tiny Burundi was as unlikely a candidate as any for an international oil-trading venture. For one thing, it was landlocked. For another, its oil consumption was so small that even one tanker of crude would be enough to meet its needs for more than six years.[60] In the end, Cobuco didn't supply the country with a single barrel of

oil – although it helped to line the pockets of a number of Burundian officials.

The young trader who had organised the venture took over the running of Cobuco, and began to go by the pseudonym of Monsieur Ndolo. He chose Iran as the potential source of the oil for Burundi. Through the contacts that Marc Rich + Co already had in Tehran, he organised a trip for Burundi's president to the Iranian capital. Monsieur Ndolo gave his African partners precise instructions. The trader wanted to buy crude at official OPEC prices (about $27–$28 a barrel), significantly below the spot market at the time ($30–$35 a barrel). Payment conditions were unusually advantageous: as Burundi was a non-aligned nation, it wouldn't need to pay for the oil for two years. Effectively, that amounted to a two-year interest-free loan. Cobuco told the Iranians that Marc Rich + Co would handle all the details of the shipments, and that the crude would be processed in a refinery at the Kenyan port of Mombasa and from there trucked up to the highlands of Burundi.

The revolutionary Islamic government of Iran agreed.

Over the next few months, Marc Rich + Co sent tankers to the Persian Gulf to pick up the crude. Officially, all the barrels made it to Mombasa. And actually? Of course not, says Monsieur Ndolo. 'But we had all the paperwork saying that the barrels have been discharged in Mombasa,' he added. Instead, Marc Rich + Co diverted the oil into the global market, re-selling the barrels at large mark-ups. A portion of the crude went into South Africa, whose apartheid regime was ready to pay a premium above even the spot price.

Rich made a fortune. The price difference between the official price Cobuco paid to the Iranians and the spot price, equal to $5–$8 a barrel, yielded somewhere between $40 and $70 million in profits, although Monsieur Ndolo isn't sure of the exact figure any more. What he remembers clearly is the profit from the exceptionally generous payment terms. Cobuco didn't have to pay the Iranians for two years, but whoever bought the crude from it would pay within thirty to sixty days. That gave Marc Rich + Co the opportunity to invest

the cash for a year or more in the money market, and to pocket interest rates of close to 20%. Monsieur Ndolo remembers exactly how lucrative the two-year loan was: the company made an additional $42 million in profits, or nearly as much as it did re-selling the crude in the spot market.

Burundi was paid a fee for its services: 20 cents per barrel, a small fortune for the country – although Monsieur Ndolo won't say whether the money ever made it into the state coffers – but a pittance compared with the millions of dollars that Marc Rich + Co made.

Rich was delighted. He sent a telex to every office in his sprawling commodity empire: 'We want more Cobucos'. And he got them. By the end of the 1980s, Marc Rich + Co had established four or five such ventures across Africa, according to another senior oil trader at the company at the time.[61]

For all of Marc Rich's dominance in the 1980s, there were limits to what even he could do without attracting unwanted attention.

Rich had made Iran the linchpin of his empire – but it was also, in some ways, his undoing. The country had been the source of his lucrative deals on the Eilat–Ashkelon pipeline in the 1970s. It had underpinned the fantastic profitability of the Cobuco arrangement. And it was the source of much of the oil he shipped to South Africa. The revolution of 1979 hadn't deterred him: Pinky Green flew in to Tehran the very day that Ayatollah Khomeini returned to persuade the Iranians to continue selling oil to Marc Rich + Co.[62]

A few months later a mob stormed the US embassy in Tehran and kidnapped dozens of American diplomats, holding them captive for more than a year. In response to the kidnapping, President Jimmy Carter issued several executive orders freezing Iranian assets in the US, imposing a general trade embargo and specifically banning oil trading with the country.[63]

Many Americans may have put an end to their dealings with Tehran at this point – for legal or for ethical reasons. Rich, however, wasn't deterred. He had, after all, built an enormously successful business in part through his willingness to circumvent embargoes. The international nature of the commodity trading business meant that no one government could effectively regulate it. If the US government banned oil trading with Iran, that didn't stop a Swiss company, such as the Zug branch of Marc Rich + Co, from doing it. 'I feel comfortable,' he replied, when asked if he felt any guilt about buying Iranian oil during the hostage crisis.[64]

And so, it was nothing unusual for Rich when, in spring 1980, John Deuss stepped into his Manhattan office with an offer to buy some Iranian oil.[65] Deuss and Rich were the two oil-trading titans of the era – they handled the biggest volumes, took the biggest risks, and paid no heed to political scruples. It didn't matter that at that very moment fifty-two Americans were being held hostage in Tehran; there was a deal to be done. And Deuss had come to Rich seeking a massive deal: the sale of more than $200 million of Iranian oil.

From July to September, Rich's trading house would deliver eight cargoes of crude oil and fuel oil to Deuss's Transworld Oil, culminating in a cargo of 1,607,887 barrels of Iranian crude worth $56,463,649, delivered on 30 September. The money flowed from Transworld's account at Société Générale in Paris to Rich's account in New York, and from there back again to Paris to an account that the Iranian central bank kept at the Banque Nationale de Paris.[66]

The deal would change the course of Marc Rich's life, and probably the history of the trading industry. It would mark the beginning of a twenty-year legal battle that put Rich's photograph on the FBI 'Ten Most Wanted' list.

Around the same time as he was trading Iranian oil with Deuss, US prosecutors were building a case against Rich for tax fraud. When they discovered the deals with Iran, the prosecutors knew they'd hit the jackpot. What had started as a complex tax case became a tale of the amorality of the commodity traders that would stir the

fury of the American establishment and condemn Rich in the eyes of the public.

In 1983, when Rich was indicted by a grand jury, he was transformed into a celebrity overnight. His story read like the plot of a Hollywood thriller: a billionaire commodity trader evading taxes; oil trading with the cronies of Ayatollah Khomeini of Iran; and prosecutors stopping a Swiss Air flight on the runway of John F. Kennedy airport late at night to prevent documents being smuggled out of the country.

The case captivated the imagination of the world. Reporters flew in to Zug to stalk the streets of the small Swiss town in the hope of catching a glimpse of him; he snuck from his office to the restaurant he owned across the road in the company of bodyguards. The image of him beamed around the globe was that of a pantomime villain: his dark hair slicked back and a long cigar smoking in his hand. Rich, ever the outsider, maintained he had been wronged. 'I've been portrayed in a horrible way, as a workaholic, a loner, a money machine. It's not a true picture. I'm a modest, quiet person who has never done anything illegal,' he said.[67]

The American people, suffering from high gasoline prices, cared little for his protestations. Thanks to the acres of newspaper copy written about Marc Rich and his band of traders, they had discovered the vast profits that the commodity traders had been making. To add to the aura of Hollywood drama, Rich emerged as the mysterious owner of a 50% stake in the film studio 20th Century Fox. The popular image of a commodity trader was born. Within the trading industry, the case of Marc Rich would be internalised as a cautionary tale of why commodity traders should stay out of the public eye.

Of all the prosecutors' charges, the one that condemned Rich in the court of public opinion was his deals with Iran at the very moment when the revolutionary government was holding American citizens hostage. But the heart of the case involved deals that had nothing to do with Iran. It focused on the byzantine regulations of the US oil sector, under which oil from new fields could be sold at higher prices

than oil from older fields. Through a complex series of transactions, Rich and his companies avoided paying tax on more than $100 million of income, the indictment alleged. The federal prosecutors – first Sandy Weinberg and later Rudy Giuliani, who would later become mayor of New York and then the personal attorney to President Donald Trump – called the indictment the largest tax fraud case in US history. Rich faced up to 300 years in jail if he was convicted on all counts.

Rich's lawyers challenged the indictment, arguing it was a civil tax case rather than a criminal matter. Many other companies had engaged in similar activity and paid hefty fines, but weren't accused of criminal offences. Exxon, for example, was fined $895 million in 1983 for charging 'new oil' prices for what was in fact 'old oil'.[68] Atlantic Richfield, which had been on the other side of some of Marc Rich's trades, settled for $315 million in 1986.[69] Rich's lawyers also argued that while he did indeed trade with Iran, he was doing so on behalf of a Swiss company, something that, they believed, was permitted.

But their protestations mattered little. Marc Rich + Co, the company, ended up paying about $200 million to settle the accusations against it. But Rich and Green, as individuals, never settled. Rather than face trial, they had fled the country, never to return. By the time they were indicted in 1983, they'd abandoned New York and relocated to Zug, where the Swiss government protected them.

Rich renounced his US nationality and obtained Spanish and Israeli passports. For many Americans, that alone was an act of treachery. Rich's own lawyer, Edward Bennett Williams, was shocked when he heard that Rich was on the run. 'You know something, Marc? You spit on the American flag. You spit on the jury system. Whatever you get, you deserve. We could have gotten the minimum. Now you're going to sink,' he said.[70]

Ultimately, Rich and Green never faced jail time or any financial penalty. After nearly two decades as fugitives hunted around the world by US marshals, they were pardoned by President Clinton in

his last act before leaving office in January 2001, thanks to a careful lobbying campaign that included the prime minister of Israel and the king of Spain. The pardon triggered a rare show of consensus in Washington, with Democrats and Republicans uniting in condemnation. It emerged that Rich's former wife, Denise, had been a top donor to both the Democrats and the Clinton Presidential Library. Congressman Henry Waxman, a Democrat from California and traditionally a Clinton supporter, called the pardon a 'shameful lapse of judgement that must be acknowledged because to ignore it would betray a basic principle of justice'.[71]

Rich emerged a free man, but two decades as a fugitive from US justice had left their mark. The trader who'd relished conquering the world had for years been confined to just a handful of countries, and spent his time jetting back and forth between houses in Switzerland, Spain and Israel. Rich, ever the outsider, had become defensive, embittered and suspicious.

His business, however, thrived – as the deals in Jamaica, South Africa, Burundi and Angola show. In a world of Cold War divisions and political embargoes, he had taken the model for commodity trading that he'd learnt at Philipp Brothers and made it more aggressive and more global, and had become more willing to risk falling off the edge of the knife. He had been prepared to put more of his company's money to work in difficult, corrupt and economically fragile countries – in the process becoming a pioneer for investment in emerging markets. Marc Rich + Co had added agriculture to metals and oil and become the clear leader in global commodity trading. It had even continued to do business in the US, through the affiliate run by Willy Strothotte and officially owned by Rich's partner, Alec Hackel.

The rest of the commodity traders were forced either to follow his style or to give up trying to do business in countries where Marc Rich + Co was dominant. Such was the shift that even Rich's alma mater, Philipp Brothers, fell on hard times.

More changes were coming to the industry, however. And this time they wouldn't be driven by Marc Rich. As control of natural

resources was freed from the grip of big producers, financial markets for commodities expanded and became more frenetic. And as the financial side of the markets grew more important, so a different kind of trader began to dominate the commodities industry – one that looked nothing like Marc Rich and his generation.

FOUR

PAPER BARRELS

Andy Hall was jolted from sleep by a Japanese voice on the phone.

It was one o'clock in the morning, and Hall was in bed at his home in Greenwich, Connecticut, a moneyed suburb an hour from New York, when the phone rang.

'Iraqi tanks in Kuwait City!' the voice said.

Now Hall was wide awake. As head of one of the world's largest oil traders, he had staked millions of dollars of his company's money – and possibly his career – on a prediction that oil prices would rise. War between Iraq and Kuwait, between them controlling 20% of the world's oil reserves, would almost certainly vindicate his bet.

On the end of the phone was one of his underlings in the Tokyo office, charged with keeping an eye on the oil market while the boss slept.

'And what is the market doing?' Hall asked.

The answer came: 'All buyers. No sellers.'[1]

Hall put down the phone. Tall, thin and exuding a Zen-like calm, Hall was not given to displays of emotion. But the significance of the news was not lost on him. At a stroke, his trade would deliver hundreds of millions of dollars in profits for Phibro Energy, the oil trading unit of Philipp Brothers, which he ran.

It was the early hours of 2 August 1990. Four divisions of the Iraqi Republican Guard, the country's elite forces, which reported directly to Saddam Hussein, had invaded neighbouring Kuwait. Two days later, they won control of the emirate.

In less than 48 hours, Saddam Hussein had seized control of the world's fourth-largest oil reserves and a significant chunk of its production.[2] The UN Security Council responded by imposing an 'all commodities' embargo on Iraq.[3]

The oil market reacted just as Hall had anticipated. By early morning in New York, the price of one widely-used oil benchmark, Brent crude, had jumped 15%. Within three months, it had doubled, hitting a peak above $40 a barrel. It was the biggest oil crisis since 1979.

For Phibro Energy and Andy Hall, the Gulf War was a major payday. In the space of a few weeks, Hall's oil price bet delivered profits of between $600 and $800 million.[4] It was a trade that combined geopolitical insight and market savvy, taking advantage of a host of new financial instruments being used in the oil market. After costs, Phibro Energy reported a stunning $492 million in earnings for the year.[5]

The oil market had evolved since the crises of the 1970s, and traders like Andy Hall were in the ascendant. Intense and thoughtful, Hall preferred carefully analysing the market from his base in Connecticut to jetting from one African country to another. He turned his nose up at the trading styles of the likes of Marc Rich and John Deuss, who had made a killing through their networks of relationships in oil-rich nations.

In the late 1980s and early 1990s, the world of energy trading was undergoing another revolution. In its way, it was just as significant as decades earlier, when Theodor Weisser and other pioneers of the oil trade had changed the way the oil price was set by breaking the Seven Sisters' grip on the market. Now, a second shift was occurring in the way the price of oil was set. This time it was Hall and his cohort who were driving the change, thanks to the brave new world of futures and options.

These new financial products served to reduce risk, allowing traders to bet on the price of virtual barrels of oil. Now traders could lock in prices for their physical oil deals and so chase much larger contracts without having to worry that an adverse price move could bankrupt them. But futures and options also enabled speculation: never had it been easier to play roulette on the direction of the oil market.

'It was really the creation of the derivatives markets by the Wall Streeters going and selling to end users, airlines, marine fuel consumers, etcetera, that then started to add the extra drive to the markets,' says Colin Bryce, an oil trader at Morgan Stanley from 1987 onwards, who went on to run the bank's commodities business. 'That was the game of the 1990s.'[6]

This financialisation of the oil market opened up a whole new way of doing business. The hot shots of Wall Street had already revolutionised markets for mortgages and junk bonds, and, in the late 1980s, they were turning their attention to the oil market. With new financial instruments at their disposal, they opened the market to an array of new participants, who had no intention of ever seeing a barrel of actual crude oil, and instead were happy to buy and sell notional quantities of what were soon dubbed 'paper barrels'. That included financial investors, such as pension funds, as well as oil users, such as airlines and shipping companies, that were looking to insure against a rise in oil prices.

That's where futures, options and other similar financial products came in. In reality, there was very little new about them. Copper and tin traders had been buying and selling futures on the London Metal Exchange for a century. So had grain traders on the Chicago Board of Trade and elsewhere. Rice brokers in Japan had been trading futures since as early as 1697, starting what is believed to be the world's first futures exchange.[7] For oil, though, no such market existed until the 1980s.

A commodity futures contract is, as its name suggests, a contract for delivery of a commodity at some point in the future. The creation of futures markets opened a new range of possibilities for oil traders: they were no longer restricted to buying and selling oil on the spot, but could also buy and sell oil for delivery in a few weeks, months or years.

Anyone who buys a futures contract and holds it until its expiry date will receive a parcel of commodities; on the other hand, someone who sells a futures contract must, at expiry, deliver the commodities. Once the oil futures market came into being, traders could use futures contracts to buy or sell their oil many months in advance. But the usage of the new instruments was much broader than that. Most people didn't hold them until expiry – instead, they bought and sold futures much as they would buy and sell the barrels of oil themselves. The futures allowed traders (and anyone else) to bet on the direction of the market without having to touch a physical barrel of oil. Hence the talk about 'paper barrels'.

Futures served multiple roles: some used them to speculate, others used them to insure – or 'hedge' – their exposure to the price of oil. Say a trader bought a cargo of oil and planned to sell it a month later. Rather than endure an agonising wait over the course of the month, hoping that the oil price would go up, the trader could immediately lock in a known price by selling futures contracts. Now, if the price of oil went down, the value of the futures contracts the trader had sold would also go down, and the trader would be able to buy them back at a lower price. If the price of oil went up, the trader would lose money on the futures contracts but make the same amount of money on the increased value of the physical cargo of oil. Either way, the use of the futures market allowed the trader to lock in the price of oil, reducing risk.

Options offered even more flexibility. For a fee – a 'premium' – they gave a trader the choice, but not the obligation, to buy or sell a futures contract at a predetermined price and time. Together, futures and options are called derivatives, because their value derives from that of an underlying commodity.

For the oil market, the advent of derivatives was a radical transformation. Early oil traders, such as Theodor Weisser and Marc Rich, hadn't been able to insure their trades against moves in prices. If they bought oil one day and the price collapsed the next, they would be on the hook for the entire loss. Of course, that hadn't been a problem when prices were fixed. But the oil crises of the 1970s had made oil trading a perilous business.

That changed in the 1980s, and it was all thanks to another commodity: the humble American potato. For more than a century, commodity derivatives had been traded at the New York Mercantile Exchange (Nymex), where trading pits erupted in frenzied shouting matches, and traders had a reputation for sleazy behaviour. In the 1970s, while traders such as Marc Rich and John Deuss were making a killing buying and selling oil, the traders on the Nymex were obsessed with potato futures. The tuber was by far the exchange's most popular contract. But in May 1976, Nymex traders defaulted on their obligations in what was, at the time, the largest ever default in commodity futures. For Nymex it was a disaster; the exchange was bordering on ruin. Desperate to stay afloat, the exchange's board of directors looked at other commodities to replace potatoes as their star derivatives contract. After much debate, they decided to try their luck with petroleum.

Oil derivatives weren't a complete novelty: futures and options had existed a century earlier, in the years after commercial oil production began in the US in 1859. For a brief period, oil futures were traded on at least twenty exchanges across the US.[8] But the primitive market for oil derivatives – like the spot trade in physical oil – came to an end when Rockefeller won control of the industry.

On 30 March 1983, Nymex reinvented the market with the launch of its futures contract for light, sweet oil – that is, low density oil with low levels of sulphur – based on West Texas Intermediate crude delivered at Cushing, Oklahoma, where Atlantic Richfield (today part of BP) had a major storage hub.

For the first time in the modern era, oil traders were able to hedge their transactions. The impact was huge: suddenly, traders could handle much larger volumes without risking everything. And the existence of futures markets opened up a whole new set of possible plays, particularly for those with a foot in both the physical and the financial worlds. The casino of Wall Street had penetrated the world of oil. And there was nobody better equipped to profit from this collision of cultures than Andy Hall.

Hall had learnt his trade at the giant oil company British Petroleum, just as the power of it and its fellow Seven Sisters was waning. He joined the company on an apprenticeship scheme while he was still at school. BP sponsored him to go to Oxford University, and then offered him a job when he graduated, just as the first oil crisis hit in 1973.

He was soon working in the nerve centre of the company: the scheduling unit, which decided where every barrel BP pumped would end up. It was a gigantic operation: BP, the former Anglo-Persian Oil Company, was pumping about five million barrels a day, much of it from the fields it controlled in Iran. But there was no trading. The job of the scheduling department was to organise for BP oil to be refined in BP refineries and from there to be sold at BP fuel stations.

The British oil company would soon be forced to change, however, when the Iranian revolution of 1979 dispossessed it of much of its oil production. Hall was dispatched to New York to start buying and selling oil for the company. Initially, he was just dealing in oil for BP's own supply chain. But he soon developed a taste for trading. If he saw a cargo of oil that looked cheap, he would buy it, regardless of whether BP needed it or not, and try to resell it to someone else at a profit. Until then, trading with third parties had been regarded within BP and other integrated oil companies as beneath them. But

Hall had no time for that orthodoxy. 'We basically started trading oil like crazy,' he recalls.[9]

The young British trader's risk appetite soon caught the attention of the leading trading houses of the day, and Philipp Brothers and Marc Rich + Co offered him a job almost simultaneously. In 1982, he joined Philipp Brothers, and in less than five years he was running its oil division, by then rebranded Phibro Energy. The first Gulf War would cement his reputation as the most successful oil trader of his generation. From there, he would go on to make hundreds of millions of dollars after correctly calling the rise of China, earning a personal pay packet of more than $100 million in 2008 and the nickname 'God'.

At BP and later Phibro, Hall developed the trading style that he would become famous for: assiduously calculating the political and economic factors that would drive the oil market, placing a high-stakes bet, and waiting with nerves of steel to be proved right. 'We're not like other Wall Street firms that grub around for pennies and nickels, trying to chisel and scalp people,' Hall told an interviewer in 1991. 'As long as our analysis is valid, we will stick with our positions.'[10]

Hall had approached his blowout trade in 1990 with characteristic conviction. Although he was already known among other oil traders as an inveterate market bull, always preferring to bet on a rising oil price, in early 1990 Hall was convinced that the oil market was over-supplied. That was hardly a revelation to anyone following the intricacies of the market: crude was going unsold, and storage tanks were filling up. At the beginning of the year, stocks of crude oil in the wealthy countries that were members of the Organisation for Economic Co-operation and Development (OECD) hit their highest level since 1982.[11]

By now oil prices, which in the first half of the 1980s had averaged more than $30 a barrel, were less than $20 (see graph on page 334), and the oil-rich nations of OPEC were feeling the pinch. One by one, they began to cheat on production quotas they had agreed with the rest of

OPEC, hoping to sneak out a few extra barrels of production and earn a few extra dollars of revenue. The effect was to push prices even lower.

Among all OPEC members, few needed higher oil prices more than Iraq. Baghdad had just emerged from a long war against Iran all but bankrupt. The country faced a costly reconstruction and the repayment of roughly $40 billion in loans, with a significant chunk due to neighbours such as Kuwait, Saudi Arabia and the United Arab Emirates.[12] With oil below $20 a barrel, Saddam Hussein had little way to pay his country's debts. In mid-1990, he told diplomats he might be forced to stop paying pensions to Iraqi war veterans.

If Iraq was the country in direst need of higher prices, Kuwait was the most notorious cheater among the members of OPEC. At the beginning of the year, the emirate had quietly started to offer discounts to some refineries if they would buy extra barrels. Kuwait, ignoring its OPEC commitments, was hoping to make up for the drop in oil revenues by increasing production. Phibro Energy, which owned four refineries, soon got word of what Kuwait was doing: it only reinforced Hall's conviction that oil prices were headed lower.

The oversupply had pushed down oil prices. But futures contracts for delivery of oil in six months' time had not fallen as fast. The price divergence created an opportunity for a creative trader, and Phibro Energy had for years been one of the leading innovators of the growing universe of financial oil contracts. Hall realised he could make a profit by simply buying a barrel of oil, storing it, and reselling it six months later. In the past, a trade like that would have been a risky bet entailing six months of nervously hoping that the oil price would go the right way. But the arrival of the futures market in the mid-1980s had changed the landscape. In the spring of 1990, Hall could buy a barrel of oil and the very same day fix the price at which it would be sold in six months' time using a futures contract. The profit would be locked in.

The only issue was finding a place to store the oil. Onshore tanks were brimming. So Hall decided to hire a flotilla of oil tankers – called 'very large crude carriers', or VLCCs – and turn them into a

floating oil-storage facility. Rather than ship crude from one port to another, he would fill up the tankers and let them sit idle on the high seas, paying a demurrage fee for every day they were at anchor. The idea of storing oil at sea wasn't entirely new, but never before had it been done at such scale as part of a play by an independent trader. 'We were big charterers of crude tankers,' Hall recalls. 'So I said to our chartering guys: "Hey, could you charter a VLCC and get an option to put it on demurrage for six months?" The guy replied to me something like, "Why would you want to do that?" And I told him just to ask the question. "Sure," he came back, "We can do this."'[13]

Hall began to put the trade into effect on an enormous scale. He hired more than a dozen VLCCs, each capable of holding about 2 million barrels of oil. As he was buying crude, he sold more expensive futures contracts, in effect locking in his profit. All he needed was enough credit to be able to buy the oil and hold on to it for at least six months. But that was no problem – Phibro Energy had, since 1981, been part of Salomon Brothers, the result of a traumatic merger that had defined the business for much of the 1980s. As a result, Hall had access to one of the biggest credit lines on Wall Street. At the peak, he was sitting on oil worth some $600 million – more than 37 million barrels at the price of the day. Hall was using so much money for the trade that John Gutfreund, the head of Salomon Brothers, who traditionally took little interest in the day-to-day of the oil business, phoned to ask what was going on.[14]

He was soon reassured. It was a perfect deal: with the price locked in on the futures market, Phibro Energy would make money on the trade whatever happened to the price of oil.

The oil price didn't stay in the doldrums for much longer. In late June, Saddam Hussein openly accused Kuwait of pumping too much crude and threatened to resolve the matter one way or another. Over the next few weeks, his rhetoric became more bellicose. 'Iraqis will not forget the saying that cutting necks is better than cutting means of living,' he said in mid-July. 'O God Almighty, be witness that we

have warned them. If words fail to protect Iraqis, something effective must be done to return things to their natural course and to return usurped rights to their owners.'[15]

In Connecticut, Hall was reading the Iraqi leader's words in the *New York Times*. He soon decided that the risk of war in the Middle East was too big to ignore. In a daring move, he decided to buy back a portion of his hedges on the oil he had stored on tankers. In doing so, he took a big risk. From that point onwards, Phibro Energy was unhedged – 'naked' in trader-speak – and exposed to whatever might happen next on the oil market. It was an old-fashioned gamble, but it wouldn't have been possible without the new world of futures. Hall had used the derivatives market to amass a vast quantity of oil without taking any risk, and then transformed it in the blink of an eye into a huge bet that prices would rise. If oil prices fell, the losses would be sizeable.

But events in the Persian Gulf were heading inexorably towards war. On 1 August, Saudi-mediated talks between Iraq and Kuwait failed, with Kuwait refusing to accept a long list of demands from Baghdad.[16] The following day, Iraq's Republican Guard crossed the border into Kuwait, supported by dozens of helicopters and tanks.

Hall's oil tankers turned into cash machines. He had bought the oil at less than $20 a barrel. Three months later, the same barrels were changing hands at more than $40 a barrel as both Kuwaiti and Iraqi oil supplies to the world market stopped. Hall's punt on the price had paid off handsomely. But that was not all: even the rest of his flotilla of oil, the part that remained hedged, delivered vast profits. While the spot price of oil had soared on the invasion of Kuwait, the price of futures for delivery in six months rose less. In June, the spot price of a barrel of oil had been trading $2 below the price of futures for delivery in six months; by October it was trading $8 above the futures. Hall had locked in a modest profit using futures to hedge the price; now he could unlock a much bigger gain by selling his oil on the spot market and buying back the lower-priced hedges. Cash was flowing in.

'We made six, seven, eight hundred million dollars,' Hall says.

The trade wasn't over, however. The conflict dragged on throughout 1990, and the world's oil traders followed every twist and turn in real time on CNN. One trader, Oscar Wyatt of Coastal Petroleum, got significantly closer to the action, using his personal relationship with Saddam Hussein to secure the release of two dozen American hostages. Wyatt, a hard-bitten Texan, who had been buying Iraqi oil since 1972, flew in to Baghdad in December 1990 – despite a direct request from the White House not to – and persuaded Saddam to allow him to take back to the US a group of Americans who had been held in Iraq as human shields.[17]

The US was edging closer to entering the war, and Hall remained bullish. In January 1991, the US finally launched Operation Desert Storm with an overwhelming bombing campaign to free Kuwait.

For the oil market, it was an anticlimax. The market had been braced for a prolonged war and further disruptions to global oil supplies. But as oil traders watched Baghdad respond to the US assault with a few Scud missiles, which caused limited damage, they realised the US would quickly overpower Iraq. At the same time, Washington opened its strategic petroleum reserves, selling millions of barrels.

The market reaction was immediate and brutal. In less than 24 hours, Brent crude plunged nearly 35%. It was the biggest one-day selloff the oil market had ever seen. In one single night of January 1991, Hall lost $100 million. After a bonanza the previous year, Phibro Energy ended 1991 in the red.[18]

The financialisation of the oil market, with the arrival of futures, options and other derivative contracts that Hall had exploited masterfully during the first Gulf War, opened all sorts of new possibilities for the traders. It soon prompted a changing of the guard in the commodities industry. Some old-school energy traders stuck to the oil business they knew, buying and selling physical cargoes of oil and

trying to make a profit on the difference. But others saw better opportunities trading in the newly-created financial markets. Never had it been easier to gamble on the oil market's next move. Losing $100 million in a single night was something unthinkable in the 1970s. Two decades later, it was a real possibility.

The traders of the 1960s and 1970s, who had learnt the business in the mailroom and grown up imitating the buccaneering ways of Marc Rich and John Deuss, were now joined by a new generation of maths whizz-kids fluent in the language of Wall Street. Trading houses were increasingly divided between those who specialised in 'business development', who would fly to far-flung countries to wine and dine powerful local oil barons, and those who called themselves 'traders', glued to their phones and computer screens, buying and selling financial contracts to make money from the physical deals brought in by the business developers.

It wasn't just the tools of Wall Street that arrived in the oil market: Wall Street banks also began trading oil. With cheap funding and fluency in the new financial language of oil, banks such as Goldman Sachs and Morgan Stanley quickly became major oil traders, nick-named the 'Wall Street refiners'. The new breed of oil traders used the information they acquired in the physical markets to make out-sized financial bets, or the financial markets to enable new kinds of physical market plays. Traders such as Andy Hall at Phibro Energy, Stephen Semlitz and Stephen Hendel at Goldman Sachs, and Neal Shear and John Shapiro at Morgan Stanley became specialists in dancing between the physical and financial worlds to profitable effect.

The old-school trading houses struggled to adapt to the changing times. The easy money of the 1970s had attracted a wave of new players to the markets. Now the competition among traders was intense, and few of the older companies could compete for scale with the newcomers from Wall Street, who could draw on vast sums of money for their traders.

It was a dynamic that played out in microcosm at one of the most storied commodity trading houses of all, and, ironically, the one

where Andy Hall was working – Philipp Brothers. Over the course of the 1980s, the venerable old company was eaten and spat out by a bank that epitomised the freewheeling culture of Wall Street.

Philipp Brothers had reached its zenith in 1979 and 1980, riding the oil market rollercoaster on the back of the Iranian revolution.[19] The company's profits in 1979 and 1980 totalled more than $1 billion.[20] *BusinessWeek* profiled the company in September 1979, with a photo of Jesselson on the magazine's cover next to the headline: 'A $9 billion supertrader most people don't know'. In the article, Jesselson, now chairman, and David Tendler, his anointed successor and the company's president, boasted of the company's global reach and unmatched prowess.

The supersized profits masked a dilemma, however. 'The concern we started to have, and I started to have, was that the good days can't go on. We needed something else,' recalls Tendler. High energy prices had plunged the US and most of Europe into recession. 'The oil crisis was good for the oil business. But what about everything else?'[21]

Tendler and Jesselson decided that Philipp Brothers should diversify into a new commodity: money. Tendler learnt that the partners of Salomon Brothers, the largest private investment bank in America, were looking to raise capital. Quickly the two sides agreed that Philipp Brothers would take over Salomon and create a new powerhouse called Phibro-Salomon.[22] The merger, announced on 3 August 1981, took the financial world by storm. The *Financial Times* called the company 'Wall Street's new world force'.[23] Tendler would run the new company, with John Gutfreund, the abrasive and ambitious boss of Salomon, as number two.

Corporate marriages often end unhappily, and the honeymoon period for the commodity traders of Philipp Brothers and the bond traders of Salomon was pitifully short. Already at the time of the merger, the traditional metal trading business of Philipp Brothers had been struggling with a drop in profitability. On the other hand, the Salomon bankers were raking in profits thanks to a boom in bond trading. In an era when all markets, commodities included, were

being transformed by the development of new financial instruments, the Philipp Brothers traders could not keep pace with their Salomon counterparts.

By the end of 1983, Gutfreund had been elevated to co-CEO. A few months later, Phibro-Salomon split the commodity trading business in two: the old Philipp Brothers would handle metals, and a new division called Phibro Energy would focus on oil. Tom O'Malley, the man who had replaced Marc Rich in 1974 as head of oil, became the boss of the new unit, which moved out of New York, where the other commodity traders were based, to Greenwich, Connecticut. Tendler was technically the boss, but in reality O'Malley could do whatever he pleased.[24]

The metals business of Philipp Brothers continued to decline. After an abortive attempt to spin off the metals unit, Tendler left the company in October 1984.[25] Soon after, Phibro-Salomon was renamed simply Salomon. Unable to evolve with the markets, the metals division where Marc Rich had cut his teeth became an ever less potent force in the market. In 1990 it finally died an ignominious death, when Marc Rich + Co bought what remained of its metals contracts.

The oil business, however, thrived. When O'Malley left in 1986, Hall, after a brief interlude, became the head of Phibro Energy. He expanded the company's reach, trading in excess of one million barrels a day in the physical market, investing in refineries and oilfields, and, above all, embracing futures and options. In doing so, he straddled the worlds of physical trading and high finance – not only shipping oil around the world but also executing derivatives trades on behalf of airlines and investors – and thereby ensured that one part of the historic trading house, at least, would prosper in the transformed landscape of oil trading.

Philipp Brothers wasn't alone in struggling in the markets of the late 1980s and early 1990s. The financialisation of the oil market had made

life harder for all the trading houses that had grown up in an earlier era. It was no longer enough to have good connections with a few OPEC ministers or some officials at a state oil company. Succeeding in the new environment required a combination of relationships, deep pockets, geographical reach and the financial know-how required to use the newfangled derivatives markets. The arrival of well-capitalised Wall Street banks meant that those traders who had dominated the market in the 1970s found they were no longer able to do so. Some failed to adapt, and went out of business. Others tried to embrace futures and options with catastrophic consequences.

Commodity trading, which had attracted all comers in the 1970s as a route to a quick fortune, now became known for scandals and collapses. Voest-Alpine, the largest state-owned company in Austria, had to be bailed out by the government after its in-house trading arm lost nearly $100 million speculating in the oil market in 1985.[26] Klöckner & Co, a German conglomerate with interests in steel and metals trading, lost about $400 million on oil bets.[27] Italian trader Ferruzzi reported a $100 million loss in 1989 trading soybeans. The company ended in bankruptcy and its president committed suicide.[28] Sucres et Denrées, a French trading house best known as a sugar specialist, suffered losses of $250 million, in part in the oil market.[29] And Metallgesellschaft, the historic German metal trader, lost $1.4 billion on a massive oil trade that went wrong.

None of the collapses marked the end of an era more than that of Transworld Oil, the company owned by John Deuss, who along with Marc Rich was one of the poster boys of the 1970s. Between 1987 and 1988, the Dutchman tried to pull off one of the most audacious deals the oil market had ever seen. It was a trademark Deuss plan, combining his unmatched political connections with his financial firepower in the oil market.

The venue for Deuss's trade was the Brent market.

The Brent oilfield, about 190 kilometres off the Shetland Islands at a depth of roughly 140 metres, started pumping crude in 1976 and quickly became the gold standard for oil traders. In its early days,

Brent served as a clever way for North Sea-oil producers, such as BP and Shell, to reduce their tax bill. The companies timed when to buy and sell cargoes in such a way as to show the British authorities lower sales prices than they otherwise would have, a process that became known as 'tax spinning'.

By the mid-1980s, the Brent field, operated by Shell, together with several others that fed into its pipeline system, was pumping enough crude each month to fill about forty-five tankers, each carrying about 600,000 barrels. By now, Brent had also become a global benchmark: crude varieties from the Middle East, Russia, Africa and Latin America were priced by reference to the cost of oil in the North Sea. On top of that, the physical market underpinned several layers of financial derivatives, including, from 1988, an oil futures contract at the International Petroleum Exchange in London. If a trader was able to influence the price of Brent, the effect would be felt across the world.

And the price of Brent was particularly vulnerable to a squeeze. The relatively small number of cargoes each month meant any party that won control of most of them could dictate terms to the rest of the market. The physical market was – and still is – almost entirely unregulated, and there was no legal limit to how many cargoes a trader could buy.

Starting in the summer of 1987, when North Sea production fell as oil companies performed maintenance on their offshore platforms, Deuss set about buying every cargo he could get his hands on. Mike Loya, one of Deuss's top traders in London, scooped up all but one of the forty-two contracts for January delivery of Brent oil, driving prices higher.[30] It was a bold play, even by the standards of the take-no-prisoners North Sea market in the 1980s. One of his lieutenants recalls that Deuss wasn't satisfied with simply cornering the Brent market – he wanted to corner the entire global oil market.[31]

Next, Deuss attempted to engineer an unprecedented geopolitical deal: an agreement between OPEC and non-OPEC producers to cut production. The pact would have sent prices skyrocketing – making Deuss even more fabulously wealthy. The OPEC and non-OPEC

talks were spearheaded by Oman and the United Arab Emirates – both nations where Deuss had deep contacts. Deuss was also on the phone with OPEC ministers, advising them what to do, and when and how to leak their intentions to the market.[32]

But the plan for a 'World OPEC', as the *Wall Street Journal* called the project, crashed after Saudi Arabia vetoed it. In the Brent market, Shell and others traders joined forces to break Deuss's corner. Instead of rising prices and vast profits, Deuss was forced to retreat, losing around $600 million when oil prices fell.[33] Transworld Oil only survived by selling its prized American refining empire to Sun (today's Sunoco) for $513 million.[34]

The failed corner was a turning point for Deuss, and the oil market. The most outrageous oil trader of his generation would continue trading throughout the 1990s, but Transworld Oil would never recover the swagger and dominance it had once enjoyed. One by one, the old guard of the commodity trading industry was being replaced by a new generation of traders, such as Andy Hall, able to hold their own in the physical oil market but also versed in the new world of futures and options.

Soon, trouble would also arrive at the door of Deuss's arch rival, Marc Rich.

FIVE

THE FALL OF MARC RICH

The Swiss town of Zug is a picture of calm. From its mediaeval old town, cobblestone streets lead down to the peaceful waters of an alpine lake. The town, which boasts some of the lowest corporate tax rates in the world, has been drawing commodity traders since the 1950s, when Philipp Brothers first opened an office here. But between the boxy offices you can still catch a glimpse of rolling farmland, a legacy of the cherry orchards for which the town was known before the commodity traders arrived.

By the end of 1992, however, all was not calm at Marc Rich + Co. Within the steel-and-glass cube in the centre of Zug that was the headquarters of Marc Rich's trading empire, a storm was raging. The world's pre-eminent commodity trading house was running out of money. Each day, the executives in charge of the finance department held emergency calls to try to stave off the company's collapse.

At the centre of the storm was the desk of Zbynek Zak, a tall, upright man with a bushy moustache, who was responsible for making sure Rich's metals traders had enough financing to trade. 'Where else can we get money from?' Zak would ask, with growing desperation. 'How do we pay the bills tomorrow?'[1]

Born in what was then Czechoslovakia, Zak had moved to Germany as a refugee after the Soviet invasion of 1968. After a career as an engineer, consultant and banker, he'd joined the trading house to help it with its finances. And by 1992, for all Marc Rich + Co's power as the world's dominant trader of natural resources, its finances were in an increasingly fragile state.

The operations of a commodity trader are enormously dependent on banks, which provide guarantees and loans that allow the company to buy and sell using borrowed money. Every day, its requirements change depending on moves in commodity prices: if prices rise, the same cargo of oil or metals costs more; if they fall, it costs less. The job of the three finance specialists at Marc Rich + Co was to make sure that no trader was ever forced to sell a cargo of oil, metals or grains earlier than was desirable because the company couldn't afford to finance it.

Each of them had relationships with banks in Switzerland, London and New York. Each day the calls would go round. Did one of them have some unused credit with one of their banks? Perhaps a customer was about to pay for a cargo, freeing up some cash? Maybe they had overlooked some inventory of oil that they could mortgage?

'Being a finance guy in a situation like this, it's a nightmare,' Zak recalls.

Despite the company's total reliance on its banks, the financiers were seen as dowdy suits. The traders were the queen bees of the organisation: it was they who took hair-raising flights to scary places to negotiate big deals; they who bet the company's money on the commodity markets; and they who took home the biggest bonuses. Throughout its existence, Marc Rich + Co never had a finance specialist on its executive committee. For the first few years of its life, it had not even had a finance director – Pinky Green had handled the relations with banks personally.[2]

But by the early 1990s, the traders at Marc Rich + Co were failing to deliver. The world-beating profits of the 1970s and 1980s were a distant memory, and the world's most powerful commodity trading company had been overrun by paranoia and backstabbing.

Over the course of 1992 and 1993, the battle for the future of the company would reach a climax that would change the landscape of commodity trading for ever. It would be the latest bitter family feud in the dynasty of dominant commodity traders that began with Philipp Brothers and continued with Marc Rich + Co. By the time the dust had settled over the boardroom squabbles at Marc Rich + Co, two new members of the corporate dynasty would have been born: Glencore and Trafigura.

The crisis effectively ended the career of Marc Rich himself, capping decades at the pinnacle of the global commodity trading industry. The end of his period of dominance drew the curtain on a whole era of commodity trading: the buccaneering years of the 1970s and 1980s, when a commodity trader with enough money and chutzpah could get away with ignoring all rules and standards of decency. While later generations of commodity traders would continue to trade in the Marc Rich mould, the industry would never again have quite the same feeling of untouchability.

For the founders of Glencore and Trafigura who emerged from it, the crisis that engulfed Marc Rich + Co in 1992 was a formative experience that would shape their approach to trading – and, thanks to the influence of their companies, the entire industry. They remained graduates of the Rich school, but, scarred by the megalomania of Rich's final days, they sought to share out ownership and control of their companies, forging tight-knit groups that endured through generations.

And, with the most notorious commodity trader in the world now in semi-retirement, his successors took the opportunity presented by his departure to retreat into the shadows, turning the commodity trading industry into a bastion of secrecy. By freeing themselves from the toxic name of their fugitive founder, they were able to integrate further into the wider financial industry – laying the foundations for a future in which they would combine the adventurous spirit of Marc Rich with the economic firepower of Wall Street.

★

By the early 1990s, Marc Rich's original partners had all retired – even Pinky Green. Rich's soon to be ex-wife, Denise, whose family had helped bankroll the company in its earliest days, had also sold her shares.[3] In every case, Rich organised to buy out the shares of the departing shareholder, and as a result, for the first time since it was founded, Rich had a controlling stake in the trading house that bore his name.

Rich, by now in his late fifties, remained at the helm of his company. Beneath him was a quartet of four younger traders in their thirties and forties. There was Willy Strothotte, the imposing German who had steered the company's US unit through the crisis of the indictment, and was now in charge of metals and minerals trading. In London there was Manny Weiss, the fast-talking Brooklynite, who, together with Strothotte, had masterminded Marc Rich + Co's dominance of the aluminium market, and Claude Dauphin, a charming, exquisitely tailored Frenchman, who had taken charge of oil trading. And in the Netherlands was Danny Dreyfuss, a wily, old-school trader, who ran grain trading.

Rich was under pressure, professionally and personally. His marriage to Denise had collapsed into an acrimonious divorce, and his family had moved out. His daughter had been diagnosed with cancer. US officials continued to pursue his arrest. And after a West Virginia aluminium smelter linked to Rich got into a dispute with its workers, the unions launched a publicity campaign against him, travelling the world and handing out 'Wanted: Marc Rich' posters as they went.[4]

Rich, with none of his old partners to lean on for advice, was an increasingly embattled figure. Danny Posen, then head of the Moscow office of Marc Rich + Co and the son of one of Rich's earliest partners, says: 'I don't think he went nuts, but I think something happened to him.'[5]

In early 1991, Rich brought his personal lawyer over from the US to help him run the company. The lawyer, Bob Thomajan, was a bon viveur from Austin, Texas, more at home on his jet skis than dealing with the logistical details of a shipment of copper ore. But

Rich, now alone at the top and suspicious that the traders were scheming to depose him, made Thomajan his gatekeeper. Suddenly, the traders, many of whom had proved themselves through a series of menial jobs at Philipp Brothers or Marc Rich over years or decades, found themselves taking orders from him.

'He installed Thomajan in the office outside his office,' recalls Mark Crandall, a senior oil trader. 'When you wanted to speak to Marc, Marc would tell you to meet with Thomajan instead.'[6]

The mood of the company changed. Marc Rich + Co was still on top of the world, but it no longer felt that way. The traders who in previous years had executed deals at turns brilliant, risky or shady, were now consumed by office politics. Weiss, Strothotte and others urged Rich to distribute the shares more widely to the employees, but Rich stood firm. He gave no indication that he would ever make way for the younger generation.

'I love the business and this is what I want to continue to do,' he told an interviewer. 'I like to delegate but, at the same time, on major decisions and special exposures, I have the final say.'[7]

The traders no longer felt like they were partners in a thrilling business venture with a chance to take over the company one day, but indentured servants doing the bidding of their distant master. Rich, the Philipp Brothers prodigy who had left because Jesselson wouldn't give him his fair share of the company's earnings or allow him the freedom to trade the way he wanted, was repeating the same mistakes at his own company.

'It isn't just about money ... it's about money, it's about a sense of belonging, it's about a sense of having some say in how the company is organised,' says Crandall. 'And Marc, by walling himself behind Thomajan, he made everybody into vassals. He made everybody feel like a bunch of hookers.'[8]

A showdown was inevitable. The first clash came between Rich and Strothotte. The German trader had given a speech at a university in Zurich in which he'd discussed the company's business. Rich, increasingly paranoid, took this as a sign of insubordination.

The entreaties for him to reduce his stake had already aroused his suspicions. So he told Strothotte to leave.[9]

More were to follow. Claude Dauphin, the head of oil trading, had been chafing under Rich's rule for years. Then, in the summer of 1992, his father died. Dauphin decided he'd had enough: in early July he resigned, telling Rich he planned to return to France to run his family scrap metal business.

Rich telephoned Weiss, by now the only senior trader left in London. Come back to Zug and take over the presidency of the company, Rich implored. Weiss said no.[10] He was about to turn forty, he was already wealthy, his family was settled in London, and he wanted to spend more time with them. He told Rich that, whatever happened, he wanted to take a lengthy sabbatical.

'If you're going to leave, you might as well leave now,' Rich snapped.[11] And so Weiss resigned on 8 July, just a few days after Dauphin had.

By now Marc Rich + Co was in the throes of a full-blown crisis. But it was about to get much worse.

The late 1980s and early 1990s had not been a happy time for many in the commodity trading industry. Markets were tough, the US tipped into recession, and the industry became known for its spectacular collapses – such as John Deuss's disastrous attempt to corner the Brent oil market. Marc Rich + Co, thanks to its oil deals with South Africa, its aluminium trading and its growing business in Russia, had ridden out the period without a crisis. But that was about to change.

While the most senior traders at the company had been absorbed in internecine squabbles, Marc Rich himself had been embarking on an enormous and extremely risky trade.

It had begun in 1991, when David Rosenberg, a metals trader in London, had convinced Rich to back his plan to corner the market for zinc. It was nothing new for Rich's traders to take big positions or even corner a market by controlling a large share of the available supply. Weiss had done it to great effect in aluminium in 1988. But

there were many ways the tactic could backfire, as John Deuss had discovered in the Brent market. By artificially pushing up prices, a trader who cornered a market risked encouraging consumers to defer their buying and suppliers to sell more. And while acquiring a large share of the market might be easy enough, selling the material and still making a profit required skill and experience.

For his zinc play, Rosenberg had lined up outside support in the form of Spain's Asturiana de Zinc and Germany's Metallgesellschaft, two of the world's largest zinc producers. Between them, the three set about buying up much of the available zinc. Rosenberg bought large quantities of options contracts, and used them to terrorise other traders. At one point, the three companies held more than 90% of the LME stocks of zinc.[12]

By June 1992, the LME's board, a group of metals market grandees charged with ensuring things didn't get too far out of hand, felt it had no choice but to intervene. The exchange ruled that any company that had sold zinc but was unable to deliver to the exchange could pay a fixed fee to defer delivery – effectively capping the potential profits for Rosenberg and his fellow travellers.

The other senior traders tried to persuade Rich that the scheme was doomed. But Rich, already suspicious of a coup attempt, wouldn't listen. He seemed determined to prove to the traders that he still had the chops to pull off a spectacular manoeuvre.

In mid-July, Isaac Querub, the Madrid office manager and point man for the relationship with Asturiana de Zinc, flew to Rich's house in Marbella to try to persuade him otherwise. Rich, about to set sail on his yacht, handed him a swimming costume and a beer and told him to climb aboard. But he was not in the mood to listen.

'What do you want?' he asked. When Querub explained, Rich exploded.

'Mind your own business,' he barked.[13]

In September, the zinc price rallied again, touching a two-year high. But it was to be a last hurrah. Metallgesellschaft decided it wanted no more part in the attempted corner, and started selling.

The zinc price tumbled. In two months, it fell by more than a quarter.[14]

Rosenberg's zinc position became an enormous liability. Like all traders on futures markets, Marc Rich + Co hadn't paid in full for its zinc contracts, but had bought them 'on margin'. That meant that the trading house had paid a deposit to its banks and brokers, and they had bought the contracts on its behalf. As long as the price went up, everyone was happy. But each time the price went down the banks and brokers asked Marc Rich + Co to top up its deposits – a procedure known as a 'margin call'.

That was how Zak and the other finance specialists found themselves running out of money. Each day the banks would demand millions of dollars in margin calls, and Zak would have to come up with the cash. 'We said: look, guys, we can't run the business like this. We're basically running out of cash here,' Zak recalls.[15]

The traders eventually persuaded Rich to sell the massive zinc position – a task that took several months. But Rich had been wounded. His attempt to recreate the glorious trades of his youth had failed. His trading house had lost $172 million thanks to the disastrous zinc trade.[16] It was a sign of the changing nature of the markets – by the 1990s, succeeding in commodity trading didn't just require gumption and a wide network of contacts. It also rested on an understanding of the evolving world of derivatives, and the ability to manage risk rather than betting the house on one trade. That was a world in which Marc Rich looked increasingly out of place.

The mood at Marc Rich + Co was gloomy. The traders who had remained at the company started putting pressure on Rich. Individually and in groups, they told him he needed to set out a path to reduce his stake in the company, and to bring back Strothotte.

Simultaneously, they started preparing for the company's collapse. In Zug, Strothotte, Zak and Craig Davis, who was in charge of the

company's aluminium assets, had hatched a plan to start a new company and had even found an office for the new venture. In London, Dauphin had begun to call around some of his old colleagues on the oil team to ask if they would want to join him in a new company.

The oil team resigned en masse in February 1993. For the company's banks, this was the last straw. They told Rich to do something to stop the crisis. He called on Alec Hackel, a universally popular figure, who had been one of his original partners and who had hired many of the younger traders, to act as a go-between.

And so, on a winter's day in early 1993, a group of traders gathered in London. They were led by Dauphin, the former head of oil. He was joined by his former team: Crandall, who, after Dauphin had left, had been elevated to run oil trading at Marc Rich + Co, as well as Graham Sharp and Eric de Turckheim. Strothotte and Weiss, the two other senior traders who'd left the previous summer, were also involved in the discussion. Hackel, the mediator, completed the group.

Dauphin and his team wrote a one-page manifesto setting out the terms under which they would return. It boiled down to a total coup: Rich should sell all his shares over time, he should step down from the management, and the company would change its name.

'I thought it was brutal in the way they wrote it,' Weiss says.[17]

Rich initially agreed to the demands of the renegade traders, but his pride had been wounded. And after all, he was still a trader. 'Marc doesn't know how to do a deal and not try and renegotiate,' Crandall says. 'Marc would renegotiate his children, that was his DNA.'[18]

A few days later, he called Dauphin in France. 'You guys were a little too harsh, and I think it's all happening slightly too quickly,' Rich began, according to Crandall, who was listening in on the call. And so he started trying to renegotiate. Perhaps the buyout would happen over several years, during which time he would remain at the company, he suggested. Dauphin lost his temper. 'We are going to be negotiating with Rich until we are dead!' he fumed.[19] He told Rich the deal was off and prepared to go it alone.

A few days later Strothotte called Dauphin and Crandall to ask if they would mind if he tried again with Rich. Where Dauphin had lost patience, Strothotte pressed forward. Ever the canny negotiator, Strothotte managed to swallow his ego and agree to some of Rich's terms. A few weeks later, on 8 March 1993, the deal was announced. It looked very much like the one Dauphin had been negotiating, with a few small tweaks: within months, Marc Rich would sell enough shares so that he no longer had a controlling stake in the company; Strothotte would return as chief executive, but Rich would remain as chairman; and the company would keep the name Marc Rich + Co.[20]

'There is nothing exceptional in the timing of the moves,' Strothotte told journalists, understating the significance of the moment. 'There has been a long-term plan to pass control of the company to minority shareholders.'

The atmosphere was frosty when Strothotte and Rich met at a private room at the Glashof, the restaurant across the street from the company's offices, to sign the contracts.[21] There were no handshakes. Once the lawyers were satisfied, Rich simply stood up and walked out. As he left, he turned to Strothotte and snarled a warning: 'I still own a good piece of the company – keep it in mind.'[22]

On Monday 29 November, the sale was complete, and Marc Rich formally cut his stake to just 27.5%.[23] The remainder was owned by around 200 employees. The employees had an option to buy Rich's remaining stake, but they'd have to do so in cash. 'Rich never imagined that we would have the money,' says Querub, the head of the office in Madrid and perhaps the closest executive to Rich at the time.[24] Perhaps he had hoped that, after a few years, the minority stake would give him a way back in to his company.

But Strothotte, mindful of Rich's parting shot, was determined to sever all ties. He set about hunting for sources of funding to buy out Rich's remaining stake. After a tough few years for the company, its traditional banks were unwilling to hand it more money. Strothotte and his traders discussed bringing in as an investor Martin Ebner, a

bow-tie-wearing billionaire known as Switzerland's leading corporate raider. But Ebner, who had made his name buying up stakes in Swiss companies and agitating for change, would have wanted a say in how the company was run, and Strothotte, still smarting from his run-in with Rich, didn't like that idea.[25]

What followed was an outlandish corporate coup, of the kind that could only have been executed in the clubby world of Swiss business in the 1990s. Strothotte's saviour was not a sharp-elbowed fund manager or a Wall Street bank, but one of the largest fortunes in Switzerland. The newest investor in Marc Rich + Co, the world's largest commodity trader, was Roche, the pharmaceutical company. And it arrived at Strothotte's doorstep thanks to Valium.

Roche had introduced the little yellow pill in 1963 and it soon became the world's most prescribed drug, immortalised in the 1966 Rolling Stones hit 'Mother's Little Helper'. For Roche, it was a cash machine that transformed the family-owned company into a global giant. But in 1985, the patent for Valium expired in the US, and profits from its pharmaceutical business tumbled.

But what Roche did have was cash, and lots of it, accumulated from selling Valium during the bonanza years. By the early 1990s it had some $9 billion.[26] And so, under the watch of chief financial officer Henri B. Meier, Roche set about putting its cash pile in an array of investments that had nothing to do with pharmaceuticals. That was how, in 1994, thanks to an introduction by Marc Rich's financial adviser Heinz Pauli, the pharmaceutical company came to Strothotte's rescue. Unlike Ebner, Roche had no interest in how the company was run – it just wanted to make money. Strothotte agreed to sell 15% of the company's shares for about $150 million, with a promise to buy them back at a later date and a guarantee that Roche would receive a certain return on its investment.

Finally, Marc Rich could be ejected once and for all. Within the trading house, there was a hunt to find a new name for the company. Traders walked the corridors browsing Greek dictionaries for the name of an appropriate god. Eventually, a consultant came up

with the name Glencore, a contraction of the words global, energy, commodities and resources. On 1 September 1994, Marc Rich + Co officially became Glencore International, and, two months later, the company announced it had severed all ties with its fugitive founder.

Rich was shocked. In just a year and a half, his former employees had secured full ownership of the company, and removed his name from the door. And they had done so at a bargain basement price, funded in part by the firm's own resources and trading profits. The company's book value, shrunken by the departures of its founders and its zinc loss, was a little under $1 billion, according to several former partners. That meant that Rich, for his share of around 70%, received about $700 million.[27]

'I was weak and the others could sense it, so they took advantage,' he later told his biographer. 'They held the knife to my throat.'[28]

The dominant commodity trader of his era had been toppled. But his successors were lining up to take his place, all of them imbued with the Marc Rich philosophy – go anywhere, take risks and leave any squeamishness at home.

Dauphin, the former head of oil, didn't waste any time after breaking off negotiations with Rich.

The very next evening he gathered all his closest allies at his house on Redington Road, a quiet, leafy street in north London. Dauphin told them he wouldn't work with Rich any longer. 'So you guys all have to make your decision,' he said.[29]

It was a quick debate. Five others joined Dauphin. The group included the oil team of Crandall, Sharp and de Turckheim, who had been negotiating with him for a return to Marc Rich + Co. They were joined by Danny Posen and Antonio Cometti, who would run metals at the new company. Striking out on their own entailed risks. They'd leave behind the comfort of Rich's long-established

relationships with buyers and sellers of commodities around the world, as well as his banking lines.

The six men, most of them in their thirties and forties at the time, decided to set up a new trading venture. They pooled their savings, of which the largest were Dauphin's, for the company's capital, and also invested in Dauphin's family business in France. 'We started out with equity capital of about $12 million, which in those days was quite a lot,' recalled de Turckheim.[30]

By then, Sharp, the oil trader, had secured the company's first deal: buying a cargo of gasoline from the Romanian state-owned petroleum company. Bucharest wanted to sell, but it needed to know to whom. The new company needed a name.

Dauphin, wary of repeating Marc Rich's errors, refused to put his name to the new ventures. The group was offered a choice of dormant Dutch-registered companies to buy in order to speed up the process of starting. Now they were forced to choose quickly which name they would use. The options were Skydiver, Blackheart and Trafigura.[31] Everyone agreed Skydiver was not an ideal name for a highflying commodities trader; and Blackheart sounded a little too buccaneering, even for the trading industry. So Trafigura it was.

The new company became the life project of its founder. Dauphin had been born into the world of commodities, the son of a scrap dealer in Normandy in northern France. He joined Marc Rich + Co in 1977, when he was in his twenties, heading to Bolivia to run the company's office there, and rapidly rising through the ranks as head of lead and zinc and then oil. He was a trader in the old school, with a tireless work ethic and a relentless travel schedule. At Trafigura, he ensured that the company had permanent access to the earliest landing slot at Geneva airport on a Sunday morning, in order to be able to squeeze a few extra working hours out of the week.

He'd also picked up from the old-school traders the ability to charm anyone from small-time Bolivian miners to the presidents of African countries. Edmundo Vidal, who was Trafigura's man in Mexico City before taking over its business across Latin America,

remembers Dauphin's uncanny memory for which little gifts would best please each of the Mexican mining magnates they were meeting. For one, it was a bottle of Cognac; for another, a box of chocolates. 'This guy was amazing, the touch he had,' Vidal recalls.[32] Over the course of his career, Dauphin forged relationships with oil suppliers in Angola and Nigeria and buyers in Latin America; he bought minerals from dozens of small mines in Peru and Mexico and shipped them to ravenous Chinese buyers.

Dauphin was an exacting boss who could blow up at anyone who didn't keep up with his pace and exacting standards of dress, hospitality and punctuality. But he had an impish sense of fun. One former employee remembers a long plane journey where, after hours of intense work, Dauphin suddenly stood up and announced: 'Gentlemen, the bar is open.'[33] Over twenty-five years at the helm of Trafigura, he became a mentor for a whole generation of traders, a master of the swashbuckling school of commodity traders that valued hard work and personal relationships above all else.

In spite of all his charm, however, it would take years for Dauphin and his band of traders to build up Trafigura from scratch. For Glencore, on the other hand, it was an easier process. From day one, business boomed. Freed from the controversy of the Marc Rich name, the company could take advantage of new opportunities. Since 1983, when Marc Rich had become a fugitive from US justice, American banks hadn't lent to the company. Even some European banks had held back.

Then, just a few days after the buyout had been completed and the company had changed its name, Zak got a call from J.P. Morgan. The US bank wanted to see how it could be of assistance. Then Deutsche Bank called. Then Goldman Sachs. 'For a finance guy like myself, it was heaven,' Zak says.[34]

A whole range of new possibilities opened up. Glencore got a credit rating, a seal of approval from the gatekeepers of Wall Street.

It started raising all sorts of new forms of financing from new groups of investors: short-term funding from the US commercial paper market; its first syndicated loan in 1995; and, the next year, its first private placement, through which the company sold its debt to American pension funds and insurers.

The trading house had already begun to invest in assets such as smelters and mines in the late 1980s. But it hadn't been able to raise longer-term debt to fund the investments. Now, with the debt markets open to it, Strothotte and his team were free to invest in assets in Australia, Colombia, Kazakhstan and Russia.

The Glencore traders maintained the culture they'd inherited from Rich (and which he, in turn, had learnt at Philipp Brothers) of hard work and high expectations. 'In Glencore it's like a jungle,' says Lucio Genovese, who joined the company in the late 1980s and rose to run the Moscow office. 'You've got to perform and you've got to perform highly, every day and every year, otherwise you're in trouble. It's either perform or die.'[35]

A new group of a dozen senior traders was now at the helm of the company, nicknamed by some the 'G12' or the 'twelve apostles'. Strothotte was their leader, now in his element as the commander-in-chief of a global empire. He would jet around the world, bear-hunting with a Siberian aluminium magnate one day, wining and dining customers on his yacht in the Caribbean the next. Among the group of rising stars was a man who would go on to run the whole company: Ivan Glasenberg.

Marc Rich + Co had always generated enormous wealth for its partners, but now Glencore became a millionaire factory without precedent. The shares were rapidly distributed to around 350 traders, although Strothotte, Dreyfuss and the rest of the G12 kept a significant chunk of them. (In the first half of the 2000s, the years for which data is available, the top dozen executives owned between 26.7 and 44.4% of the company.) Each year, a trader would receive a salary; a cash bonus calculated as 10% of their trading profits; and, on paper, a share of the company's net profits in proportion to their

shareholding. When the trader left the company, their accumulated profits would be paid out over a period of five years.

The bonuses alone were enough to make most traders extremely wealthy. Between 1998 and 2001, the final four years of Strothotte's reign, the company paid an average of $110 million a year in bonuses to a few hundred traders.[36] The shares were even more remunerative. The company was averaging profits of $150–$200 million a year in the 1990s, a figure which rose into the billions in the 2000s.[37] Strothotte alone was in line to receive about 10–15% of that. And the multimillionaires continued a long way down the shareholder register. In just one example, public because of a tax dispute, an Australian coal trader who worked for Glencore for fifteen years without ever rising to a senior management position received a payout of $160 million when he left the company in 2006.[38] It's not outlandish to speculate that the company has turned more than 100 people into $100-millionaires over the course of its history.

The battle for Marc Rich + Co had reshaped the commodity trading industry, and not just by forcing Rich into semi-retirement. The approach to trading that Rich had pioneered would live on in Glencore and Trafigura, but by dropping his tarnished name and keeping their own names out of the headlines, they would be able to become more deeply entwined in the global financial system. The two companies would not only go on to dominate global oil and metals markets, but also to become financiers of resources the world over, marshalling sums of money that Marc Rich could only have dreamed of.

For Strothotte and his partners, dreams were already coming true. Their acquisition of Marc Rich's shares at a relative pittance had been an enormous coup. 'Buying Marc out was the best deal he ever did in his life,' says Crandall. 'It was a money avalanche. Once they bought out Marc they just stood under the avalanche with buckets.'[39]

SIX

THE BIGGEST CLOSING-DOWN
SALE IN HISTORY

David Reuben was sitting in his office when a man limped in who would change his life.

The setting was Moscow, May 1992, a few months after the Soviet Union had collapsed. For an aluminium trader like Reuben, it was chaos. For years he had been dealing with just one supplier: the Soviet state. Now it didn't exist.

All he knew was that aluminium could be bought much cheaper inside Russia than anywhere else on the planet. Anyone who could get his hands on a reliable supply and sell it on the world market would become rich.

The man sitting in front of him was such a person. Born in Central Asia and disabled by polio as a boy, with intense blue eyes and a quick temper, Lev Chernoy was one of many sharp-elbowed wheelers and dealers who were thriving as the planned Soviet economy gave way to a free-for-all.

As Reuben and Chernoy sat and talked, an entire world was imploding around them. The enormous Soviet manufacturing industry had ground to a halt, as demand from the only buyer – the state – had disappeared. The Russian government had removed

controls on the price of everyday goods, and the cost of bread, milk and cheese skyrocketed as the value of the rouble plummeted. Ordinary Russians' savings, painstakingly accrued over lifetimes, were wiped out overnight. Pensioners huddled on freezing street corners selling whatever they could to scrape together enough money to buy food.

The reason why Chernoy had arrived in Reuben's office was in keeping with the anarchy of those times. Chernoy had agreed to sell a small quantity of aluminium to Reuben's company, Trans-World, and then never delivered it. That was fairly normal in Russia in those days; what was unusual was that Chernoy had come to apologise.

Reuben's company, Trans-World (which had no connection to John Deuss's Transworld Oil), was already an established player in the small clique of metal traders. With a round, open face and a manner that led some to think of him as naïve, Reuben was a man with big visions for his business, willing to take large risks but uninterested in details. He didn't want to hear Chernoy's apologies for not delivering his aluminium. What did interest him was that Chernoy appeared to know where in this brave new world of post-Soviet Russia it was possible to buy aluminium.

Chernoy started to explain. But Reuben cut him short.

'Show me,' Reuben instructed his visitor, 'and I'll make you a billionaire.'[1]

The collapse of the Soviet Union was a seismic event for the commodity traders, the most significant development in the history of the industry since the oil market had been freed from the grip of the Seven Sisters in the 1970s. At the time of its break-up, the Soviet Union pumped more oil than any other country in the world and was also one of the biggest producers of metals and grain. Now, at a stroke, it was transformed from a closed system into a shambolically integrated part of the world economy.

Until the early 1990s, the Soviet Union's trade with the outside world had been tightly controlled by the State. Suddenly Russian aluminium, copper, zinc, oil and coal flooded on to global markets. For a while, Russia and the other former Soviet states had little infrastructure to export their commodities, no expertise on how to sell internationally, and no connection to the world of finance.

Commodity traders like Reuben stepped into the void, connecting Russia's enormous natural resources industry to the rest of the world, and so funnelling precious foreign currency earnings into Russia. That made the traders extraordinarily important – to the survival of whole industries, to the health of national economies, and to the question of who would get rich from the spoils of all this economic chaos.

By the time the Soviet Union collapsed, the commodity traders had been doing business in Moscow for decades. Theodor Weisser had travelled there to buy oil in 1954. Cargill and the other grain traders had made regular visits through the 1960s and 1970s. Philipp Brothers had been one of the first American companies to open an office in Moscow in 1973.

Through all this time, the traders' dealings in the Soviet Union were highly centralised. The entire country's foreign trade was conducted by just a handful of state agencies. For metals, there was Raznoimport (which also handled exports); for grain, there was Exportkhleb (which also negotiated imports, as it had during the Great Grain Robbery); and for oil, there was Soyuznefteexport.

The traders had focused their efforts on wooing the Soviet bureaucrats who ran these agencies. In metals, Felix Posen, a partner at Marc Rich + Co in the 1970s and 1980s, had established a close relationship with the bosses of Raznoimport that helped make his firm the major counterparty for the Soviet Union's international metals trade. Posen remembers that the Raznoimport bosses 'loved to be invited for dinner and drinks'.[2]

The centralised system began to change in the late 1980s. Under Gorbachev's programme of *perestroika* (restructuring) and *glasnost*

(openness), the creaking Soviet system slowly started opening up to private enterprise. In 1987, young Soviet citizens with an entrepreneurial flair were for the first time allowed to operate small businesses, called cooperatives. Among them were many of the country's future oligarchs. The cooperatives would cater to needs unmet by the organs of Soviet government – importing computers, running lotteries, or trading theatre tickets. And they would exploit the inefficiencies of the crumbling Soviet system, buying surplus materials on the cheap or offering services to bureaucrats who needed to find a way to spend their budgets. Sometimes, the young entrepreneurs managed to get their hands on commodities, and sometimes they could find a way to export them. And so they crossed paths with the commodity traders.

Once again, the traders employed their best skills of persuasion. Among the new breed of Soviet entrepreneurs was Artem Tarasov, who shot to fame in the late 1980s after proclaiming himself the Soviet Union's first legal millionaire. Like many others, he was making his fortune wheeling and dealing in the shadows of the Soviet economy. One day, he struck on an opportunity to buy some fuel oil. The situation was a microcosm of the inefficiencies of the Soviet system: an oil refinery in Ukraine was producing fuel oil to supply local power stations. When a mild winter came, the power stations used less, and so the refinery had excess supplies. With no other instructions on where to deliver it, the director of the refinery simply told his employees to dig holes in a nearby forest and pour the fuel oil into them.

From situations like that one, Tarasov soon found himself with meaningful quantities of Soviet fuel oil to sell. And so he attracted the attention of the traders at Marc Rich + Co, who were looking for ways to deal outside the confines of the state trading agencies. In his memoirs, Tarasov recalls his 'unforgettable' first visit to the UK.

'Rich's people who were in charge of buying oil and oil products immediately understood: finally a wonderful loophole had opened

up, which would allow them to bypass the state and to trade without any limits or reporting! So they decided to treat me well, to make sure their number one client wouldn't go astray,' he wrote.[3]

The team at Marc Rich + Co went to great lengths to make sure Tarasov would return to the Soviet Union a happy man. They put him in a suite at the Meridien hotel in Piccadilly. They hired a boat on the Thames with an orchestra to entertain him. And in the evenings, they made sure his every need was catered for. 'They hired several nightclubs, where they told me to take any dancer I wanted back to my room: everything had already been paid for on the company account,' recalled Tarasov. 'Of course, this had a great effect on my delicate Soviet psyche, and soon I unquestioningly considered Marc Rich to be the best foreign company in the world. For several days, I ate and drank well, travelled, went fishing, listened to the orchestra playing in my honour, and in the end, of course, I signed a contract.'[4]

A motley assortment of characters flourished in those dying days of the Soviet Union. The country's economy was in freefall. All kinds of wild deals were struck. PepsiCo briefly became one of the world's largest naval powers when it agreed that, in exchange for the Pepsi it was selling to the Soviet Union, it would be paid with 17 Soviet submarines, a cruiser, a frigate and a destroyer. The naval fleet was sold for scrap, leading PepsiCo's chairman to joke to the White House: 'We're disarming the Soviet Union faster than you are.'[5]

For years, Marc Rich + Co had been a dominant force in the Soviet metals trade thanks to Felix Posen's cultivation of the Raznoimport bosses. But then the KGB started investigating the relationship, and Marc Rich + Co fell out of favour.[6] Other metals traders didn't hesitate to pounce. Philipp Brothers struck a deal to buy Soviet nickel, a coup as the country accounted for a quarter of the world's nickel production. When it came to specify the quantity that Raznoimport would sell to Philipp Brothers, the contract simply read: 'Total Soviet exports'.[7]

And then there was David Reuben's Trans-World.

Reuben, who was born in India in 1938 to a family of Iraqi origin, had moved to London as a teenager in the 1950s with very little money.[8] Almost immediately, he started working in the metals trade, joining a scrap metal dealer called Mountstar Metals in 1958. Determined to establish himself in the UK, he threw himself into business along with his brother Simon, his closest friend and confidant, who had started investing in property. Speaking English with a faint accent, David Reuben had an immigrant's love for the trappings of English high society and of the English language, with a particular passion for crosswords and the word game Scrabble.

While Simon was a micromanager who liked to know every detail of his business, David was a visionary uninterested in the nitty-gritty. According to his son: 'My father is very big picture. He's not a details man. If he says something in one line, he expects people to translate that into whole business plans.'[9]

Even in the early days of his metal trading career, David Reuben travelled widely in search of metal to buy, visiting the Soviet Union, China and North Korea.[10] In 1974, he joined a metal trading venture part-owned by Merrill Lynch, and three years later left with his team to start out for himself.

And so Trans-World was born in March 1977. The company started small, with just $2 million in capital and offices in London and New York, but Reuben soon made a niche for himself trading aluminium and tin. By the late 1980s, however, Reuben was falling out of love with the metals business. He'd been wrangling for months over a crisis on the London Metal Exchange after the collapse of an intergovernmental scheme to control the tin price. His brother Simon had been diagnosed with cancer. Exhausted, he took a step back from business.

Reuben was jolted out of his absence by trouble in the Soviet Union. Trans-World had been a significant presence in the Communist nation

since the 1970s, selling tin to Raznoimport and buying aluminium in exchange. But when Chernoy walked in to Reuben's Moscow office in 1992, the whole system was collapsing. Men like Artem Tarasov, the fuel oil trader, had been chipping away at the centralised Soviet agencies' dominance over commodity exports since the late 1980s. When the entire country disintegrated in 1991, what had been a trickle became a tidal wave.

The collapsing Soviet Union was like a closing-down sale for commodities. Valuable resources, such as oil, aluminium and chrome, could be bought for as little as a quarter of their international market price.[11] For the traders, it was a prize too mouth-watering to turn down. As they dived in, they also helped to forge a new economic system. Where once Soviet economic planners had determined how resources and cash would flow around the country, now it was West-ern commodity traders who played that role.

The Soviet Union's enormous industrial enterprises were in shock. The system which had instructed them what to produce and where to send it, that had supplied them with raw materials and delivered them cash to pay their workers, suddenly stopped working. Mines, oilfields, refineries, smelters, even government ministries ran out of money to pay salaries and to buy the supplies they needed to keep operating. In desperation, they started striking deals directly with local wheeler-dealers or foreign commodity traders, ending the domin-ance of government agencies such as Raznoimport once and for all.

What's more, the economy's freefall meant that domestic demand had collapsed, adding to the quantities of commodities available for export. Some traders who had sold metals to Raznoimport found themselves buying back the same metals a few months later, still in the same packaging, as the focus shifted from feeding the Soviet industrial machine to raising cash by any means.

For citizens of the countries of the former Soviet Union, this was a time of brutal hardship. In the once mighty Soviet empire, there were now shortages of food, clothes, and of money itself. A torrent of capital had flowed out of the Soviet Union in its dying years, and,

in the newly independent Russia, inflation skyrocketed and the rouble collapsed.

For Western commodity traders, though, opportunities for enormous profits were everywhere. As David Issroff, a trader at Glencore who went on to be head of ferroalloys, explained: 'You had these huge production facilities [with] no outlets. And along came these couple of Western traders who were nice guys and said: "We'll take all your product, we'll help you get it to the ports." So that's how we started.'[12]

Doing business in a collapsing economy forced the traders to improvise. They would hire whole jets for $20 an hour, loading up with cases of cigarettes and Johnnie Walker whisky, the only currency they could use to buy fuel at remote airports in struggling Siberian towns.[13] They'd arrive at vast mines and smelters where the Soviet-era bosses – known as 'red directors' – would start morning meetings with a glass of vodka, or several.

Reuben had travelled to Moscow in May 1992 to try to understand this new order and work out what role there would be for him in it. Now faced with the reordering of the entire Soviet economic system, he realised it could be a huge opportunity.

What stood in his way was the complex, secretive and counterintuitive way in which Soviet industry had been organised. In aluminium, for example, a metal whose widespread use in the aerospace industry made it strategically important for both Cold War powers, the Soviet Union was the world's second largest producer after the US. But different parts of the Soviet aluminium industry were spread out across the country. Some of its most important alumina refineries were located in the far west in Ukraine and in the east in Kazakhstan, near the border with Mongolia. The biggest smelters, which turn alumina into aluminium, were located in Russian Siberia, thousands of kilometres from the ports and cut off from the supply of alumina by vast distances and newly erected international borders.

Into this disorder arrived men like Lev Chernoy. Born in 1954, Chernoy had grown up in Tashkent, a bustling metropolis with rough

edges that befitted its status as the capital of Soviet Central Asia. As with the other early Soviet entrepreneurs, Chernoy started operating in the shadows of the creaking system, exploiting its inefficiencies for profit. Along with his older brother, Mikhail (who transliterates his name Michael Cherney), he made his first fortune running a cooperative making shoes. They rented space and equipment from a factory that wasn't using it, and bought scraps of leather and PVC that were surplus to the requirements of the Soviet system.[14] It was a world that required the Chernoy brothers to maintain a network of relationships with everyone from bureaucrats in Moscow to the local powerbrokers on the streets of Tashkent.[15]

As the Soviet system crumbled, it was a short step for the Chernoy brothers to graduate from shoes to commodities such as timber and aluminium. Lev Chernoy had been selling goods to the managers of an alumina plant in northern Kazakhstan. But they, like every other business in the former Soviet Union, had no cash. So they were paying him in alumina. The alumina would be processed at an aluminium plant at Krasnoyarsk, in Russian Siberia. The aluminium plant didn't have money to pay either, so it paid him in aluminium.

That was how, he explained to Reuben that day in Moscow in May 1992, he had got his hands on aluminium. But it wasn't enough for Reuben to hear the explanation – he wanted to see it. Chernoy didn't hesitate: the two men should board the next plane for Siberia, he proposed.

It was a Friday. Reuben demurred. He had been planning to go back to London for the weekend. He wasn't prepared for a journey to Siberia. For one thing, he didn't have any clean shirts.

But now Chernoy insisted.

That was how Reuben first arrived in Krasnoyarsk. Founded by a military detachment of Cossacks in the seventeenth century, the town of Krasnoyarsk had since become one of the Soviet Union's major industrial hubs. It had been home to a secret, sprawling Soviet base, not to be found on any map, where the USSR had produced nuclear fuel for the atomic bomb.

Now aluminium was the main industry of this city of one million inhabitants, with its endless identikit apartment blocks interspersed with older, elaborately carved wooden houses. Located on a bend in the Yenisei river, the aluminium smelter consisted of row upon row of vast halls, each half a kilometre long, filled with pots for molten metal. Together with its sister-plant at Bratsk, a few hundred kilometres away, it was the largest aluminium smelter on the planet.

For Reuben it was an eye-opening experience. The manager of the Krasnoyarsk smelter was worried because he didn't have enough money to pay for the town's food supply. On the spot, Reuben agreed to advance him money, to be repaid in aluminium.

Convinced that he had stumbled on a once-in-a-lifetime opportunity, Reuben flew back to London and set about persuading his brother to invest in Russia. They gathered together much of their wealth and borrowed money on top of that, all to be invested in the aluminium industry in the former Soviet Union. They would build a relationship with Lev Chernoy.

'Lev gave me the blueprint for how to do business in the former Soviet Union,' David Reuben said later.[16]

In Krasnoyarsk, the Trans-World partners struck a deal to deliver the alumina the plant needed and receive payment in aluminium. It was the same type of arrangement that Willy Strothotte and Manny Weiss, the traders at Marc Rich + Co, had pioneered in Jamaica and the US in the 1980s. This kind of 'tolling' deal soon swept through the Russian aluminium industry, spearheaded by traders like Trans-World.

David Reuben handled the sales of the Russian aluminium around the world, while Chernoy looked after things on the ground. 'Lev promised that his people would literally live in the plants and follow the trains around to make sure that the aluminium was delivered on time,' Reuben said.[17]

The combination of the Reubens' money and Chernoy's local presence proved effective, and soon Trans-World was the dominant player in the Russian aluminium industry. It didn't just strike tolling

deals. When the Russian government started selling off shares in its major industrial companies, Trans-World didn't hesitate, buying up stakes in Russia's three largest aluminium smelters. And it built new infrastructure too, such as a port in the Far East of Russia for imports of alumina from Australia.

It didn't hurt that Trans-World's largest potential rival, Marc Rich + Co, was consumed by in-fighting as the Soviet Union collapsed. The hesitation was fateful. The company, by then renamed Glencore, would in later years return to become Trans-World's toughest and most resilient competitor in Russia. But, for a critical window in 1992–93, it was weakened and unfocused. That meant that Trans-World's only real competition came from smaller companies, such as AIOC, an upstart trading house, Gerald Metals, and Euromin, a joint venture between a group of former Marc Rich + Co traders and Vitol.

The risks of doing business in the new Russia were substantial. The rules on private ownership of property were still being written, and there was no guarantee that a trader like Trans-World would be allowed to hold on to its share of Russia's natural resources industry. But of all the traders, it was Reuben, encouraged by Chernoy, who was most willing to take the risk. 'We were risk-takers. That's why we went into Russia, and that's why you don't see any of the big producers, the Alcoas, the Alcans, in Russia,' David Reuben said, referring to the largest US and Canadian aluminium producers. 'They are not risk-takers. It was only people like us.'[18]

Out of the chaos of the Soviet collapse, a semblance of order had once again been imposed on the industry – only in the new capitalist Russia, it was traders like the Reubens rather than the Soviet planning committee that were directing the flow of commodities.

'Our work with TWG [Trans-World Group] made a key contribution, in our country's most difficult years, to the revival of the Russian aluminium industry, to the renovation of its infrastructure, to the provision of working capital to its plants and the expansion of its production capacity,' says Lev Chernoy. 'Thanks to these efforts, our

country's aluminium industry was saved from collapse, allowing Russia to maintain its position and become one of the leaders on the world aluminium market.'[19]

By the end of the first wave of privatisations in 1994, Trans-World had ownership and trading links to all of Russia's largest aluminium smelters, making the group, in the estimation of one investment bank, the world's second-largest aluminium company after Alcoa of the US.[20] Together with its tolling deals, it controlled around half of Russia's aluminium output, and at times possibly more – making it the supplier of somewhere between 5% and 10% of global production of the metal.[21]

The Reubens' big bet on Russia had paid off in spectacular fashion. The Trans-World group, which was a collection of dozens or even hundreds of entities in jurisdictions from Monte Carlo[22] to Samoa,[23] never published any financial information. But rivals and former employees estimate that, at its peak, it was making hundreds of millions of dollars a year. The tolling business was 'extraordinarily profitable', says Gary Busch, who handled the Trans-World group's logistics from 1992 to 1997, estimating that the Trans-World group made about $3 billion from its business in Russia over the course of the 1990s.[24]

In the early days, the price of aluminium inside Russia traded at a fraction of the global price, particularly as the rouble tumbled. The profit margin for trading aluminium in the Western world at the time was as little as $5 a tonne. In Russia, a trader could make $200 a tonne or more. The smelters' need for alumina gave the traders the upper hand in negotiating the tolling deals. And then, when the industry opened up to privatisation, the traders were able to buy up major industrial assets on the cheap. 'We hit on a bonanza market,' Reuben said.[25]

The tidal wave of aluminium flowing out of Russia rippled across the global market. Between 1990 and 1994, more than 2.5 million

tonnes of aluminium flooded on to the London Metal Exchange.[26] The price of aluminium, which had touched $4,000 a tonne during Manny Weiss's squeeze in 1988, slumped to $1,000. So much metal flowed into the port of Rotterdam, the key delivery point for the exchange, that the warehouses there could no longer store it all and started stacking it outside.

For the traders, it was a lucrative but dangerous industry.[27] International businessmen like the Reubens were not alone in seeing opportunity in the ruins of the Soviet Union – the riches of the resources industry attracted all kinds of local fortune-seekers, including the criminal kind. Soon, traders like Trans-World found themselves in competition with local tycoons and gangsters.

Across the world of metals trading, the former Soviet Union became known as the 'wild east' – a high-risk frontier where only the brave or the foolhardy would dare to venture. 'Every three days somebody was murdered in that business,' Roman Abramovich, a prominent Russian oligarch, later told a London court.[28]

In 1995, the violence spilled into the streets of Moscow. Felix Lvov, the confident and charming representative of commodity trading house AIOC in Moscow, had been pushing to do more business with the Krasnoyarsk smelter. But even this buccaneering trader was afraid for his life. By the autumn of that year, when he set off for Moscow's Sheremetyevo airport to fly to Kazakhstan, he was travelling with bodyguards.

Lvov's hired muscle accompanied him to airport security, and, having watched him go through the metal detectors, returned to Moscow. But Lvov never boarded the plane. Somewhere between security and the gate, Lvov was approached by two men in uniform who told him to follow them. A day later, his body was found, riddled with bullets.[29]

For AIOC, the murder was a shock too big to weather. Within months, it collapsed into bankruptcy.

With AIOC no longer, Glencore became the main competitor to Trans-World among the international commodity traders. At

Krasnoyarsk, the director of the aluminium smelter hit it off with Willy Strothotte and invited him and his team on a three-day bear-hunting trip in the taiga, the swampy, coniferous forest that surrounds the region.[30]

Bears were not the only danger facing the Glencore traders, however. David Issroff, the Glencore ferroalloys trader, was about to get on a plane to Almaty in Kazakhstan to close a business deal when the Glencore representative there told him not to board the plane. The person he was going to meet had just been found dead, hanged in a hotel room on the outskirts of the city. 'When I go into restaurants, I still sit facing the door – just from those times,' says Issroff.[31]

Krasnoyarsk was the focus of the most bitterly fought battle for control, something that David Reuben attributed to Trans-World's forced exit from the plant in the mid-1990s. 'In 1994 they seized our shares in Krasnoyarsk,' said Reuben.[32] 'A vacuum was created and this attracted a lot of competitors, each one vying to gain power over the others.'[33]

The Russian press counted dozens of murders connected to the metal trade, and dubbed the struggle the 'Great Patriotic Aluminium War'. The victims included both allies and competitors of Trans-World, though Reuben has always denied any hint that he or his partners had any role in the violence. 'There is absolutely no truth to any of the allegations that Trans-World has been involved in any illegal activity in Russia,' he said in 2000. 'Let me be clear. Trans-World has one unshakeable principle – that is a commitment to follow legal principles and norms wherever we work. On more than one occasion we have been on the receiving end of actions that have lacked any legality.'[34]

By the late 1990s, however, troubles were mounting for Trans-World. The group had run into difficulty in Kazakhstan, where its local partners seized its assets after a dispute about non-payment of

taxes.[35] And a political shift was taking place in Russia, where ageing leader Boris Yeltsin's power was waning and Vladimir Putin was waiting in the wings to become the next president. Around him were people who argued in favour of a stronger Russian state, and against foreign ownership of Russia's natural resource wealth. At the same time, Oleg Deripaska, a local aluminium tycoon who'd worked with Trans-World in the early 1990s but now was working for himself, had emerged as the force to be reckoned with in the aluminium industry.

With little ceremony, the Reubens decided to cash out. They settled their lawsuits in Kazakhstan, receiving a payout of around $200m–$250m.[36] With their partners, they struck a deal to sell their Russian aluminium assets to a group headed by Roman Abramovich for $575 million. Together with the profits they'd made over the years, it amounted to a 'very significant cash sum', according to the Reubens' own account of those years.[37] 'Structures in the industry have changed in recent years,' Simon Reuben said in 2000. 'New players are appearing on the scene. We saw an opportunity to divest ourselves of some of our interest on favourable terms and therefore pursued them.'[38]

The Reuben brothers didn't sit on their laurels. They took the proceeds from their adventure in the former Soviet Union and invested them into the London property market, buying up large swathes of Mayfair. If anything, it was an even more lucrative decision than their all-in bet on Russia at the start of the 1990s. As of 2020, they were the fourth- and fifth-richest people in the UK, with an estimated wealth of $6.8 billion each, according to *Forbes*. They became major donors to the Conservative Party, rubbing shoulders with prime ministers.[39] And, in 2020, Oxford University announced it would open its first new college in thirty years, to be named Reuben College following an £80 million donation from the brothers' family foundation.[40]

For Glencore, it was a different story. Trans-World's exit removed the trading house's great competitor in the Russian metals industry.

Deripaska, who had started out grabbing a stake in the Sayanogorsk aluminium smelter a few hundred kilometres from Krasnoyarsk, had been aggressively buying up control of other parts of the Russian aluminium industry. Now Glencore became his closest ally. When, in 2000, Deripaska struck a deal to put together a large chunk of Russia's aluminium assets to create a company called Rusal, his smelters once again needed alumina and cash. And Glencore stepped in. The commodity trader organised $100 million in financing for Rusal, as well as supplying it with alumina, according to Igor Vishnevskiy, the former head of Glencore's Moscow office. 'We saved Rusal, because we gave them [their] first financing, and we gave them alumina,' he says.[41]

Realising that Deripaska was the rising king of Russian aluminium, Ivan Glasenberg, by then Glencore's chief executive, courted him as a friend. Together, they would go to a VIP box at Stamford Bridge to watch Chelsea, the football team that Deripaska's fellow aluminium magnate Roman Abramovich had bought in 2003.[42] There, they brushed shoulders with members of the British establishment and celebrities. In 2007, Glencore, Deripaska and another group of Russian investors agreed to merge their aluminium assets. The deal gave Rusal an effective monopoly in the Russian aluminium market. And Glencore was its connection to the world.

The collapse of the Soviet Union had redrawn the world map, replacing a crumbling empire with new nations and creating a new set of billionaire oligarchs whose money would flow around the world over the coming decades. Reuben had kept his promise to Chernoy – both men became spectacularly rich.

But Reuben's impact was felt far beyond his own bank balance: the loose conglomerate of Trans-World companies would be the finishing school for a new generation of Russia's elites – the future oligarchs. As Chernoy boasted in an interview in 2004: 'Almost half of the business elite of the country are my protégés.'[43]

And it was not just Trans-World. 'We sponsored a number of oligarchs,' says Lucio Genovese, who was head of Glencore's Moscow office in the 1990s, counting off a list of men who are now among Russia's wealthiest. 'They started to become owners of some of these operations and we were funding them.'[44]

This partnering-up of the commodity traders and the men who would become Russia's new elite had wide-ranging consequences. The commodity traders were on hand to show the early oligarchs how to export their goods, helping them earn the seed capital that allowed them to buy up large swathes of the Russian economy as it was privatised. They linked the Russians to the world of Western finance, helping in some cases to teach them the tricks of tax havens and offshore shells that commodity traders had been employing for decades.

For example, traders at the Lausanne-based grain trader André struck up a relationship with the most powerful oligarch of that era, Boris Berezovsky. Intelligent, mercurial and arrogant, Berezovsky was, for a time in the 1990s, Russia's richest and most influential man – the 'godfather of the Kremlin', in the words of Paul Klebnikov, a prominent American journalist who was assassinated in Moscow in 2004. The traders at André showed Berezovsky how to structure his companies as Swiss entities owned on the basis of bearer shares – meaning the owners were not identified on any shareholder register.[45] Berezovsky established a whole series of entities in Lausanne, the lakeside town where André was based. In exchange, the Swiss trading house became a partner in many of Berezovsky's ventures. One of them, for several years, handled almost all of the foreign currency earnings of Aeroflot, the Russian national airline in which Berezovsky owned a stake, including the hefty payments it received from foreign airlines using Russia's airspace.[46]

The personalised nature of power in Russian politics and business suited the commodity traders perfectly. 'Everybody tried to choose a partner. Who's going to work? Who will bring money? Who will give financial strength?' explains Vishnevskiy, the former head of

Glencore in Moscow. 'The situation was win-win for all sides who survived.'[47]

For the traders, it was a Klondike. Those willing to throw themselves and their money into the 'wild east' of the former Soviet Union were rewarded with enormous profits. And it was not just in the Russian metals industry that the traders thrived. The fall of the Soviet Union redrew the economic landscape for dozens of nations that had been operating under Moscow's patronage, from Latin America to East Asia. Everywhere, there was a role for the commodity traders.

SEVEN

COMMUNISM WITH CAPITALIST INFLUENCES

The Cuban revolution was in trouble. The Caribbean island nation had relied on handouts from Moscow since Fidel Castro swept to power in 1959. But now the Soviet Union had ceased to exist, so had Cuba's economic support. The island, an outpost of Communism in America's backyard, was facing shortages of everything from gasoline to food and medicine.

Cats disappeared from the streets and reappeared on dinner tables. The roads emptied of traffic, as there simply wasn't any fuel for cars. The historic seafront centre of Havana was quite literally crumbling.

But in the mid-1990s, a gleaming modern edifice sprouted up from the rubble in Cuba's capital. This mass of glass and Italian marble, complete with a palm-lined pool on its roof, was the Parque Central hotel. It was a jarring mix of glitzy pleasure palace and Communist propaganda piece. Behind its arched neo-colonial façade, the hotel boasted four restaurants, a parade of shops and a cigar lounge. In the expansive lobby, lush with tropical plants, American tourists and European businessmen rubbed shoulders under the watchful eyes of the heroes of the Cuban revolution, whose portraits lined the walls.

The hotel represented Castro's last hope to save his country's economy, a desperate bid to keep the revolution alive by relaxing

restrictions on foreign investment and opening up Cuba's white sandy beaches and colonial cities to throngs of wealthy tourists. At the 281-room hotel's grand opening in 1999, Carlos Lage, one of Castro's closest advisers and the country's de facto prime minister, praised the $31 million development as a model for the Cuban tourism industry. Over the coming years, it would be officially recognised as the country's first five-star hotel, playing host to a diverse array of world leaders and celebrities, including a delegation from the US House of Representatives, Argentine footballer Diego Maradona, and, most recently, Kanye West and Kim Kardashian.[1]

Who had paid for this luxury hotel in one of the planet's last outposts of Communism? Who had been willing to invest their money in Havana in the throes of an economic crisis, ignoring the risk of US sanctions? It was not a canny European hotel developer; nor was it one of Castro's socialist allies. The first investor in Cuba's first five-star hotel was none other than Vitol.

The commodity trader had embarked on the project in 1994, taking the rather unconventional decision to move beyond its traditional business of buying and selling commodities and venture into the hospitality industry. Spurred on by its ambitious crude oil trader, Ian Taylor, Vitol had been selling fuel to Cuba for several years, and the cash-strapped nation had racked up a sizeable debt. The trading house was looking for a way to get its money back – and tourism seemed like the best chance it had. 'Cuban growth will be through tourism,' explained Enrique Castaño, Vitol's man in Havana, as he announced plans to spend $100 million building six hotels on the island.[2]

Vitol's hotel gambit revealed quite how globally the fallout of the collapse of the Soviet Union was being felt. At a stroke, deeply rooted networks of trade and economic dependence were ripped up. Many foreign investors hesitated to put their cash and their reputations on the line in places that had, until recently, been part of the Soviet Union's sphere of influence. But not the commodity traders: they propped up cash-strapped countries, supplying oil and food on credit; they plunged their money into projects across the countries

of the erstwhile Communist Bloc; and they redirected flows of natural resources from the politically expedient supply chains favoured by central planners to wherever the price was highest.

This was how Vitol found itself building a luxury resort in Cuba. From now on, only the logic of the market would apply. It was a masterclass in how the commodity traders could transcend politics like no one else: they were stepping in to replace the old Soviet system and, in the process, helping to keep Communist regimes such as Castro's afloat; and they were doing it all by connecting them to financial markets in London and New York.

The re-carving of such a large swathe of the global economy was a gift to the traders, opening up a huge new region to play in and many more opportunities to buy and sell commodities. The traders who had thrown themselves into Russia in the early 1990s had made fortunes; but across the Communist world there were even more opportunities for profit – from Angola, with its large oil resources, to Romania, a key oil-refining hub on the Black Sea, to Kazakhstan, with its vast mineral wealth. It was an era when ideological divisions forged in the Cold War fell away, and the only thing that mattered was money. Of course, that had been the central tenet of the traders' philosophy since at least the 1950s, and they embraced their role in the new economic order with relish.

If there was one trader who embodied the spirit of the era, it was Ian Taylor. He had all the buccaneering verve of his predecessors, ready at a moment's notice to jet to Havana to meet Fidel Castro or to Muscat to see the Sultan of Oman – or to fly into war-torn Benghazi to strike a deal with Libya's rebels. But he was smoother and more politically adept than traders like Marc Rich and John Deuss. Even as he led Vitol to all corners of the earth in search of oil to trade, he ensured that its name would be smiled upon in the corridors of power of the West.

Born in 1956 in southwest London to a family with Scottish roots, Ian Roper Taylor grew up in Manchester, where his father was an executive at chemicals giant ICI. He became an oil trader by chance: he studied philosophy, politics and economics at Oxford University, a course that is famous as a fast-track to a career in politics. But Taylor, looking to earn more serious money, applied for several corporate jobs. When the offers came in, one job came with a salary that was £200 a year higher than the others. And so he accepted it. The job was at Shell.

Already, at an early age, Taylor had shown a taste for adventure that would serve him well in the world of oil trading. When his parents moved to pre-revolution Iran, Taylor took to spending his school holidays in Tehran. As a young man, he once hitchhiked from Iran to Kabul. And so, when a job became available at Shell for someone to represent the oil company in Caracas, Taylor jumped at the opportunity.

Speaking not a word of Spanish but full of youthful wanderlust, Taylor arrived in Caracas at a time of upheaval for the oil markets: 1979. He soon found himself drinking beers at the swimming pool of an upmarket Caracas hotel with ministers from OPEC, who were meeting in the Venezuelan capital. It was a thrilling time for the young oil trader. He travelled throughout Central America, buying and selling refined products in Haiti, Dominican Republic and Barbados. He was in Suriname when a coup broke out, and had to stay the night in a brothel, as it was the only two-storey building in town and so afforded slightly more protection from the situation on the street. When he travelled to Jamaica, Shell equipped him with a gun (but didn't teach him how to use it).

'It was wonderful. It was great fun,' Taylor said of his time in Caracas.[3] It was also where he met his wife, Cristina, proposing to her in the early hours of the morning after a night of partying.

Taylor's next stop was Singapore, the frontier for the developing Asian oil market. He quickly stood out. He had a boundless energy and enthusiasm that he applied equally to both his business and social

lives. And he combined a sharp intellect with a personal magnetism that won him friends wherever he travelled.

'The key to Ian's success is that he was one of these rare people who was a schmoozer and networker and contacter, but he had the commercial nous to monetise that,' says Colin Bryce, an oil market veteran, who, as the boss of Morgan Stanley's oil business, was for many years one of Taylor's toughest competitors.[4]

It was this commercial nous that first caught Vitol's attention. David Jamison, one of Vitol's early partners, who was then heading its Asian operations, had shipped a large cargo of fuel oil to Singapore to sell on to other distributors. Of all the people he sold to, Ian Taylor was the only one who had correctly worked out Jamison's costs on the trade.

'I made very little money out of him,' Jamison recalls. 'And I didn't forget that, so I invited him out to lunch and told him he had to come and work for Vitol.'[5]

Without the rough edges and bullying style of some other top traders, Taylor had the social skills to succeed in an industry where personal relationships are crucial. He could work a room as well as any politician, instinctively knowing how to win over each person, remembering details of people's family lives, and always following through on his promises. And he had the charisma of a born performer. One colleague remembers being told by Taylor that, if he could swap places with anyone else in the world, it would be with Prince, the musician, who, at the time, was one of the world's biggest stars. 'He always did enjoy the limelight and was never one to shuffle quietly on the dance floor,' his fellow oil trader remembered.[6]

Taylor's personal style was well suited to the era. The end of the Cold War marked the beginning of a period of US hegemony, in which it would be impossible for a fugitive from American justice to lead a major commodity trader, as Marc Rich had done. With global commodity trade expanding and the rise of futures and options making markets more efficient, a trading house increasingly needed

scale to succeed. For that, it needed unfettered access to financial markets and credit lines from American and European banks – it needed, above all, to be respectable. And Taylor was just the man to ensure that Vitol had a network of friends and connections within the establishment in London and Washington. The company would continue to walk the edge of Marc Rich's proverbial knife in the decades to come, but Taylor's easy charm and bulging contact book gave it the veneer of respectability that the times demanded.

Decades of riches from trading oil meant that Taylor was able to afford to splash out on some personal indulgences – a silver Aston Martin and an extensive art collection. But his true passion was always trading. When, battling throat cancer many years later, he slipped into a coma, his hallucinations were those of a born trader. 'I thought I was ... floating in space negotiating deals for the planet,' he recalled.[7] And it surprised few of his colleagues within Vitol when, a few days after undergoing surgery, he was back on the trading floor.

In the early 1990s, Cuba was a hot destination for anyone with a passion for commodity trading. And Taylor, a rising star who was on his way to the top job at Vitol, didn't need to think twice before diving in. Fidel Castro would soon count Taylor as a loyal comrade, and Vitol would become a crucial creditor to the struggling Cuban economy.

Vitol had not been the first trading house to discover the potential profits on offer in Cuba: that honour belonged to Marc Rich + Co. Since the 1960s, the Soviet Union had supported Cuba through a massive deal to swap oil for sugar. Moscow supplied 90% or more of Cuba's imports, largely at subsidised prices. And the Caribbean island, then the world's largest sugar exporter, in turn sent the large majority of its enormous sugar crop to Russia.[8] This system made perfect political sense, but commercially, it was illogical: the Soviet oil was located much closer to refineries in Europe, while oil from other

countries nearer Cuba could easily supply the Caribbean island. The same logic applied to sugar.

In the late 1980s, the traders at Marc Rich + Co cooked up a plan to address the inefficiency: they would deliver Venezuelan and Mexican oil to Cuba, and in exchange the Soviet oil would be shipped to refineries in Italy and elsewhere in the Mediterranean. Similarly, Cuba's sugar could be sold to other countries in the Americas, while suppliers closer by could meet the needs of Russia and Eastern Europe. The arrangement was beneficial for both sides. For the Cubans and the Soviets, it saved millions of dollars in shipping costs. And for Marc Rich + Co, it was 'very substantially profitable', according to one person directly involved in it.[9]

When the Soviet Union began to disintegrate, Cuba suddenly had much more need of the traders. Without support from Moscow, Castro was forced to accept the prices of oil and sugar on the international markets. When Saddam Hussein invaded Kuwait in August 1990, Cuba felt the full force of the spike in oil prices. When sugar prices also tumbled, it seemed that the markets were conspiring against Cuba.

The shock was almost too much to bear. The island's economy plunged into a period of hardship, known in Cuba as 'the special period in time of peace'. Without the assistance of Moscow, the island faced shortages of all kinds of basic products. Castro told Cubans to prepare for the worst. 'We cannot deceive ourselves. We do not have large oil or gas pipelines, power lines, or railway communications. We export some raw material. We export some food. I do not think that they are worthless in any sense, but they do not have the same kind of power that energy has,' he said in January 1990.[10]

For Castro, short of cash and desperately in need of oil, options were running out. So he turned to the commodity traders. Marc Rich + Co had been the first to insert itself into the Cuba oil-for-sugar deals, but it was not long before rival traders were jetting to the island in search of their own deals.

Taylor was quick to spot the opportunity. Part of his remit when he joined Vitol a few years earlier had been to challenge the likes of Marc Rich + Co and Phibro Energy in crude oil trading, and Cuba had the potential to be a sizeable customer. Helped by the internal squabbles that were engulfing Marc Rich + Co around this time, Taylor soon made Vitol a leading player in the commodity trade with Cuba. He became a regular at Fidel Castro's marathon dinner parties, sitting late into the night in Havana's Palace of the Revolution as the cigar-chomping Cuban leader lectured on everything from geopolitics to the intricacies of the commodity markets, occasionally firing a question at his audience to check they had not fallen asleep. It was an incongruous relationship between one of the world's last surviving Communist leaders and one of its most ardent capitalists. And yet, it was a crucial one: the traders would provide Castro with a solution to his economic troubles just as the situation seemed all but hopeless.

The plan dreamt up by Taylor and the other traders was to update the Soviet-era sugar-for-oil deal for the capitalist age. The traders would, in effect, take on the role that had previously been played by Moscow. They would agree to buy Cuba's sugar months in advance of the harvest, providing desperately needed financing to the Cuban government. And Havana, in turn, would use that credit to buy oil and fuel from the traders. Then Cuba would pay the traders with the sugar, closing the loop. On one side of the deal stood the commodity traders and a group of European banks willing to finance the operation; on the other were Cubazucar and Cubametales, the two state-owned companies in charge of sugar, metals and oil trading.

Vitol was among the most aggressive of the commodity traders drawn to post-Cold War Cuba. In 1992, it opened a sugar trading operation, a Swiss unit called Vitol Sugar SA, which was a joint venture between the trader and the Cuban state.[11] At its peak the unit handled 5% of the world's freely traded sugar.[12] Vitol even briefly invested in a sugar refinery in Kyrgyzstan, where it shipped some of this Cuban harvest.[13] By 1993, it was delivering $300 million of fuel to Cubametales.[14]

For Castro, the traders represented a financial lifeline at his country's moment of greatest need. His own ministers were struggling to raise money for Cuba, but this band of capitalist traders seemed to have no difficulty. After a meeting with Serge Varsano, the head of sugar trading house Sucres et Denrées, Castro said: 'I don't know how you have borrowed over one billion dollars, but we will make it a priority to repay them.'[15]

The funding the Cuban government received in the early 1990s would have been impossible without the traders. It relied upon the willingness of companies such as Vitol to take an enormous risk on the creditworthiness of the Cuban government. In the process, Vitol racked up a large financial exposure to the struggling Cuban economy. It was a bet that, relative to the trading house's size at the time, was every bit as daring as its deals with the Libyan rebels two decades later. 'It was a silly exposure versus the size of our company,' recalls David Fransen, who, as Vitol's representative in Bermuda, took responsibility for many of its Cuban investments.[16]

Vitol was not alone in seeing potential in Cuba. Claude Dauphin, the former head of oil at Marc Rich + Co, had not forgotten the profits during the early days of the Cuban oil trade. After founding Trafigura, he was soon travelling to the island in search of business. Among the deals he struck was one that involved Trafigura helping to finance the country's inventories of oil and refined products.

But it was not all easy money for the traders. Cuba's ability to pay back its lenders depended largely on a tricky balance between the price of sugar, the size of the crops and the price of oil on the international market. Lacking imported fertilisers and pesticides, Cuba's sugar output plunged in the early 1990s, making the situation even worse.[17] From 8 million tonnes in the 1989–90 season, the island's production more than halved to 3.3 million tonnes in 1994–95.[18]

For the traders who had sold oil to Cuba against the promise of future sugar deliveries, that meant a wait of years or even decades to get their money back. More and more often, the traders found themselves in Havana to try to save old deals rather than to sign new ones.

With the sugar crop in decline, the traders came up with ever more inventive ways to get paid.

For Vitol, the way to recoup its investment in Cuba involved getting into the hotel business. By the mid-1990s, Castro had recognised the need to open up the country to foreign investment and to find a source of foreign earnings other than sugar. And tourism seemed like the natural solution. The Cuban leader, determined to find suitable investments for his commodity trader friends, ferried Taylor and the rest of the Vitol team around the island to scope out locations for further hotel investments in addition to the Parque Central. On one occasion, they flew between white-sand beaches on Castro's personal helicopter, a Soviet Mi-8 fitted out with large leather armchairs on which the commodity traders sweated in the Caribbean heat. 'We were trying to deliver oil and somehow get paid,' Fransen says.[19]

Already in the early 1990s, the US government was asking questions about the traders' activities in Cuba. There had been a US embargo against Cuba ever since the revolution, and in 1996, Congress passed the Helms–Burton Act, strengthening the blockade and penalising non-US companies that did business on the island.

Cognisant of the risks of antagonising Washington, Vitol created a web of companies from Switzerland to Bermuda to keep its dealings in Cuba away from the reach of American regulators. The hotel investments were made, in conjunction with the Cuban state tourism company, through an entity called Amanecer Holding ('amanecer' is Spanish for sunrise). Vitol's share was owned through a series of shells in Bermuda and Switzerland: Sunrise (Bermuda) Ltd, which in turn was owned by Vitol Energy (Bermuda) Ltd, which in turn was owned by Vitol Holding Sarl, a Swiss holding company for the trading house.[20]

Traders talked in code when discussing the Cuban business, referring to it as 'The Island Exchange'.[21] And Vitol was careful not to involve anyone from its Houston or New York offices in the deals. 'It was no US person, no US entity, no dollars, nothing,' Fransen recalls.

For all the fanfare, Vitol's heart wasn't entirely in the hotel business. Only a few years after announcing its foray into Cuban hospitality, the trading house quietly sold its hotel venture. But it assiduously maintained its relationships in Cuba. Taylor, by now Vitol's chief executive, visited the island every year to make sure the Cubans never forgot who had supported them in their hour of need. On one occasion he encountered the UK's trade minister in Havana, and the two Brits found themselves sitting up with Castro until 4 a.m., drinking the last two bottles of 1956 Bordeaux from the Cuban cellars, a gift from French president François Mitterrand.[22]

They made for a strange party – the oil trading tycoon, a British politician, and the guerrilla leader of a Marxist revolution. Yet it somehow fitted the age: an era in which money mattered more than ideology, and in which the commodity traders' influence stretched into ever-more presidential palaces around the world.

As the first manager of the Parque Central hotel put it: 'The revolution that began in 1959 is being adapted to modern times with capitalist influences.'[23]

As the collapse of the Soviet Union reverberated around the world, the commodity traders were on hand to exploit the changed political landscape. It offered up new opportunities to grow, buying and selling commodities in more countries and on a larger scale. The disintegration of the Soviet Union gave birth to fifteen new countries, from Lithuania in the Baltic to Turkmenistan in Central Asia. And the end of the Cold War helped end many conflicts around the world that had been fuelled by American and Soviet money and arms. Long-running civil wars in Mozambique and Angola, as well as in Nicaragua, El Salvador and Guatemala, finally came to an end.

In some ways, the transition was harder outside Russia. Not only had other countries of the former Communist Bloc had to deal with the transformation to more or less capitalistic systems, but they had

also lost the Russian handouts that many depended on. From Central America to Central Asia, countries had to engage with the market where previously they had depended on the deep pockets of Moscow. And in almost every case, the commodity traders came to the rescue.

To thrive at the frontiers of capitalism in the 1990s required a willingness to do business in all kinds of hairy places. In Tajikistan, bordering Afghanistan in Central Asia, Marc Rich + Co and then Glencore financed the government in the midst of the bloodiest conflict of the disintegration of the Soviet Union, buying aluminium, its main export. 'It was a stunning business, actually, because it was a civil war,' recalls Igor Vishnevskiy, the Glencore aluminium trader who went on to lead the company's Moscow office. 'A little bit risky — because nobody knew exactly what will happen with this power struggle.'[24]

It also required the traders to be creative, finding ways to turn a profit from countries that had little ability to pay them for their services or their commodities. It was a time of furious bartering — few countries or companies had cash on hand, and so the traders became experts in exchanging one good for another.

'There were people that were desperate to sell things they didn't know how to sell because Raznoimport was falling apart and nobody knew how to pay,' says Danny Posen, who was head of Marc Rich + Co's Moscow office in 1992, before leaving to co-found Trafigura. 'And then we realised you didn't have to pay with money; you could pay with things that other people needed.'[25]

Marc Rich + Co was far from alone. In Uzbekistan, Cargill agreed a barter deal to buy cotton, paying for it with corn from another former Soviet Republic, Ukraine.[26] André, the Swiss trader that was the world's fifth-largest grain merchant, became a master of barter deals. It supplied milk powder to Cuba and took cigars as payment. And it swapped grain for metals with North Korea.[27]

But of all the trading houses that sought to profit from the chaotic post-Communist world, it was Vitol whose transformation was most

dramatic. At the start of the 1990s, the company had been a medium-sized player focusing mostly on refined products; by the end of the decade it was the world's largest oil trader. Between 1990 and 1999, its trading volumes tripled.[28]

'The Vitol Group is the world's largest independent oil distributor,' the company was able to boast by the end of the decade. 'No other single company covers all the global markets with the physical trading coverage of Vitol.'[29]

Vitol's beginnings were rather more modest. In August 1966, two Dutchmen in their early thirties, Henk Viëtor and Jacques Detiger, started the company to try their luck buying and selling barges of refined products up and down the Rhine. They crunched Viëtor and 'oil' to make the new company's name. Their initial capital was 10,000 Dutch guilders (about $2,800 at the time) – a loan from Viëtor's father. Detiger remembers Viëtor senior warning the pair: 'You have 6 months – if it doesn't work, you're out.'[30]

The two traders got lucky. They were taking their first steps in oil trading just as the market was about to boom. And Rotterdam, the base of their business, was about to become the capital of the global oil market. At the end of 1967, after just seventeen months of operations, the company's first profit was a respectable 2.4 million guilders (about $670,000).[31]

More profits followed, and Vitol expanded beyond the Netherlands, with offices in Switzerland, London and the Bahamas. In 1973, the year of the first oil crisis, Vitol made roughly $20 million[32] (the same year, Philipp Brothers' pre-tax profits were $55 million).[33] It began to look around for new places to put its profits, even creating a subsidiary to invest in art. The subsidiary, the company noted in an annual report, 'has the attraction of combining investment sense and collectors' hobby'.[34] It invested in modern paintings, Russian icons and Chinese miniatures.

In 1976, a decade after they had begun working together, Detiger and Viëtor split. They had clashed over their appetite for risk: Viëtor wanted to plunge their trading profits into investments in oilfields;

Detiger was more conservative, preferring to stick to trading. Viëtor, who had controlled 90% of the shares, left the company and Detiger took over as president. The bulk of the shares – 72% – were split between him and three other senior employees.[35] From a discreet glass-fronted building on one of Rotterdam's canals, Detiger ran what was becoming a significant player in the market for refined oil products. With his well-tailored suits and expensive cigars, the Dutchman was a consummate relationships man, taking the great and good of the Rotterdam oil industry out to lunch on a rotating basis.[36]

But at the heart of the company was a tug-of-war between the Dutch traders in Rotterdam and their British counterparts in London that would define Vitol for the next two decades. As the world of oil trading evolved into the casino of the Rotterdam market, risk-taking and speculation were the order of the day. David Jamison, who would later talent-spot Ian Taylor and was then running the company's office in London, was 'speculating more and more', he remembers.[37] But Detiger was still uncomfortable with the potential for an adverse price move to wipe out his company overnight. Detiger's caution paid off: while many of the early traders disappeared within a few years of starting, Vitol persisted.

By the mid-1980s, the company was handling about 450,000 barrels a day of refined products. That made it a significant player in certain niches, such as supplying fuel oil to power stations or shipping diesel on barges around Continental Europe. But it had yet to make its mark in the biggest market of all: crude oil. Vitol had dabbled in crude in the early 1970s, setting up a subsidiary called Crude Oil Trading in Switzerland. But it had struggled to gain traction, noting in its 1970 annual report: 'To say that C.O.T.'s arrival on the market has been greeted with enthusiasm is exaggerated because, it is an open secret, majors never look favourably at an intermediary to creep among producers and consumers.'[38]

The misadventure put Vitol off crude until the mid-1980s. But it had established good relations with the various state trading agencies of the Eastern Bloc. Then, with Russian oil production rising sharply,

the Soviets offered to sell crude oil to Vitol in addition to the usual refined products. After losing money on the first few cargoes, the Vitol managers decided they ought to hire someone who knew something about crude oil. And so they approached a young trader from Shell by the name of Ian Taylor. It was a prescient decision: crude oil would be the company's future, as the collapse of the Communist order opened up a vast array of new supplies for traders like Vitol.

After joining Vitol in 1985, Taylor had risen rapidly through the ranks. In 1990, he was one of around forty traders who bought out Detiger and the older partners for 250 million guilders (about $140 million). The management buy-out, financed by the bank ABN, saw Ton Vonk, one of the company's Dutch traders, take over as chief executive.

In those years, Taylor criss-crossed the world building Vitol's presence in the crude oil market. The collapse of the Soviet Union unleashed a wave of new flows on to the international markets, creating the perfect opportunity for Vitol. It was not just Cuba where Taylor saw potential. Vitol opened an outpost in Moscow, which attracted traders with a taste for adrenaline, including one who would drive visiting executives around Red Square in his ex-Russian military jeep, while wearing night-vision goggles, with the headlights switched off.[39] The company also pushed into the other former Soviet republics, striking deals everywhere from Kazakhstan to Turkmenistan.

Not everything went right for Vitol in the 'wild east' of the former Soviet Union, though. The company's biggest misstep involved an ill-fated attempt to get into the metals market, aping the aluminium deals that were delivering such eye-popping profits for the likes of Trans-World and Marc Rich + Co. In 1991, Vitol created a joint venture with a group of former Marc Rich + Co employees to trade metals, called Euromin. The company started well, striking tolling deals with Russian aluminium smelters and buying a Russian zinc plant. It even invested in a hotel in the grim industrial city of Chely-abinsk – a Russian parallel of its Cuban bet.

But, in 1995, Euromin started haemorrhaging money. The biggest problem was what the company described as 'receipt of a significant tonnage of substandard aluminium sheet'.[40] The reality was that the company had been ripped off. It had bought tens of millions of dollars' worth of what it thought was aluminium, and then the metal had started to rust – a sure sign that it wasn't aluminium. Vitol had to spend 96 million Swiss francs (about $85 million) to keep Euromin afloat.[41]

It wasn't only in the former Communist world where Taylor struck oil deals. He returned to his childhood stomping ground of Iran, building on a relationship that had already been established by Vitol's Dutch partners. He bought oil from Colonel Gaddafi of Libya and the Sultan of Oman. And he ventured into the kleptocratic heart of Africa's growing oil industry, Nigeria.

In 1995, Vonk retired, and Taylor became Vitol's chief executive. It was the triumph of the London office in the tug-of-war with Rotterdam. Vitol was now thoroughly British in feel, and the conservatism of the Dutch managers was gone. 'London was the driving office of the company; it became less Dutch,' Taylor said. 'The Dutch were wonderful but they didn't want to work outside nine to five. That ruled them out quite quickly.'[42]

Vitol became a harder-working and harder-charging company, with a greater appetite for the risks inherent in buying and selling oil in some of the world's trickiest corners. It was the perfect moment to build Vitol into a truly global trading company: the integration of the former Communist Bloc into the rest of the global economy provided a rare opportunity for a trader to expand, and the growing ubiquity of technologies like mobile phones and the internet were making it easier to trade across large distances and time zones. By the end of the decade, Vitol had just about overtaken Glencore to become the world's largest oil trader,[43] and Taylor was on his way to securing his place in the history books of the trading industry.

★

The chaotic landscape of the former Communist world was a boon for the commodity traders who could successfully navigate it. But it was also a challenging place to operate in the early 1990s – full of ever-changing rules that were sometimes in direct conflict with one another; deeply corrupt, at every level from the factory floor to the presidential palace; and full of bloody conflicts and brutal power-brokers. It was for exactly these reasons that many Western companies avoided the region. Some of the commodity traders who pushed into it regardless emerged with their bank accounts overflowing but their reputations sullied.

Vitol, for example, supplied fuel to Yugoslavia even as the country was splitting apart in a series of brutal wars. The UN had imposed sanctions on the regime of Slobodan Milosevic, the Serbian leader involved in a bloody conflict in Bosnia. Then, after a peace deal in late 1995, the sanctions were lifted. Vitol lost no time in starting to ship fuel to Milosevic's country. When it got into a dispute with its customers, Vitol paid a notorious Serbian warlord to help resolve the situation. Bob Finch, Taylor's right-hand man at Vitol, flew into Belgrade for a meeting with the person who had failed to pay Vitol. The warlord, known by his *nom de guerre* Arkan, sat in – a service for which Vitol paid him $1 million. Coincidentally or not, Vitol's debt was quickly paid. A year later, Arkan was indicted for crimes against humanity, including the ethnic cleansing of dozens of Bosnians.[44] 'I have met Arkan once,' Finch said, when the matter became public. 'It does not look good, I agree.'[45] (Vitol says its employees had not known who Arkan was before the meeting took place, and that they paid him because they feared for their safety.)[46]

Glencore did not always behave entirely admirably in the region either. Marc Rich had left, but Glencore remained very much the company that he had built: adventurous, innovative, and willing to bend the rules.

On 28 April 1995, a few months after Rich had left the company for ever, Glencore signed a deal with a government agency in Romania to supply the country with oil. There was nothing particularly

remarkable about the contract. But when it surfaced several years later as part of a legal battle, it provided a window on to Glencore's inner workings – and the types of unethical behaviour that the commodity traders indulged in amid the chaos of the post-Soviet world.

For oil traders, Romania was an important client. The port of Constanta on the shores of the Black Sea made it a key regional hub. With 500,000 barrels a day of refining capacity, Romania could meet its own consumption and export a significant surplus of gasoline, diesel and other petroleum products to its landlocked neighbours.

Glencore had been doing business in Romania since the days of Marc Rich, and the contracts signed in 1995 were a continuation of the relationship. Under them, Glencore agreed to supply Romania with crude oil of certain pre-agreed varieties – Iranian Heavy, Gulf of Suez Mix from Egypt, and Urals from Russia.

Not all oil is equal. A refinery normally processes up to forty or fifty different varieties. Each has its own chemical fingerprint: there's heavy crude, which looks like marmalade and when refined yields lots of fuel oil, but little diesel and gasoline; there's light crude, akin to cooking oil, which yields more gasoline and petrochemical products. And each variety has differing levels of sulphur, heavy metals and other impurities. Each variety also has its own price. The three varieties which Glencore agreed to deliver to Romania were popular grades of oil, whose market prices were well known.

But Glencore did not deliver the grades of oil it had promised. Instead, over a period of several years, Glencore delivered a range of other, significantly cheaper varieties of oil, and falsified documents so that the Romanians wouldn't realise. Once again using the Eilat–Ashkelon pipeline that Marc Rich had pioneered, Glencore created blends of different oils at the port of Ashkelon that looked similar to the grades it had agreed to supply, but in reality were cocktails of other varieties of crude oils from Yemen, Kazakhstan, Nigeria and elsewhere. The blends were never identical, instead being made up of whatever Glencore had on hand. But the objective was always the same: mimic the chemical makeup of the grades of oil named in

Glencore's contract, but at a lower cost for the trading house. At one point, Glencore went as far as mixing crude with much cheaper refined fuel oil, and supplying the new blend as if it were crude.

It was a testament to how easy it could be to take advantage of the former Communist nations, where few officials understood the intricacies of commodity trading, and those who did understand could often be paid off cheaply. In a ruling in the UK's High Court, Lord Justice Flaux concluded that Glencore created 'a suite of false documents', including shipping manifests, commercial invoices and insurance agreements. The judge finished his ruling by expressing his 'outrage and displeasure at Glencore's fraud', and ordering the company to pay $89 million to the Romanians in compensation.[47]

Despite all the opportunities for inventive traders that had been thrown up by the collapse of the Soviet Union, the 1990s was a challenging time for the industry. The global economy was on a bumpy path that kept commodity prices low and made it hard to turn big profits. Successive economic crises hit several countries where the commodity traders had invested heavily: first Mexico in 1994; then South-East Asia, starting in 1997; followed by the Russian sovereign debt default in 1998 and the Brazilian financial crisis the following year.

And costs were also rising. In the ever more connected and financialised markets of the 1990s, it was no longer enough for a commodity trader to ply a particular market niche. Increasingly, it was necessary to have a presence in every corner of the world. That meant financing an expensive network of offices, and more employees.

To make matters worse, the investments traders had made in assets, such as oilfields, refineries, feedlots, mines and smelters, struggled as the crisis in emerging markets hit demand for commodities. Oil prices averaged just $12 a barrel in 1998, the lowest since before the Iranian revolution.

For the trading industry, it was a Darwinian period of consolidation which only the strongest survived. Trafigura, which had started business in the midst of all these upheavals in 1993, struggled in its first few years. 'We underestimated the value of scale, how hard it is to build a business from scratch,' says Graham Sharp, one of Trafigura's founders.[48] The company's first accounts showed a profit of $3.6 million, and from 1993 to 2000 it registered modest earnings of $20 million to $30 million a year. Glencore recovered from its zinc loss in 1992, but profits remained far below the heydays, reaching just $192 million in 1998. Symbolically, the company left the office it had occupied in its Marc Rich + Co days, moving a few miles up the road to Baar, a village that begins where Zug ends. Even Vitol, on its way to dominance of the oil market, had a few scary moments: in 1997, it barely broke even due to trouble at an oil refinery it had bought in Newfoundland, Canada.[49]

The agricultural traders ran into even bigger difficulties. André collapsed in 2001. Continental's asset securitisation unit, Conti-Financial, was wrongfooted by the emerging market debt crisis in 1998, and the unit went out of business. Continental sold its grain trading business to its arch-rival Cargill for approximately $450 million, plus the market value of the inventories on hand.[50]

Just as important as the consolidation in the trading industry, there was a parallel consolidation taking place among the major producers of commodities – a process which further narrowed the competitive landscape for the traders.

The oil companies had been significant traders since the early 1980s, when the Seven Sisters realised they couldn't keep ignoring the burgeoning spot oil market. But now many stepped back. Exxon bought Mobil in 1998, and Chevron took over Texaco in 2000. Neither Exxon nor Chevron possessed the deep-rooted trading culture of the companies they acquired, and so the once-mighty trading arms of Mobil and Texaco rapidly withered. Total, the French oil giant, merged with rivals Fina and Elf Aquitaine in 1998 and 1999, consolidating three trading operations in one. Something similar happened in

mining. Companies such as Billiton and Pechiney, which had run major trading operations alongside their mining and smelting businesses, largely stepped back from the market as a result of mergers and acquisitions.

Out of this manic dealmaking, two big oil companies emerged that not only kept their in-house trading businesses, but expanded them. Around the turn of the millennium, both BP and Shell reorganised and centralised their trading operations, becoming formidable competitors to trading houses like Vitol, Glencore and Trafigura.

The two companies have kept extremely quiet about their trading businesses for years, and few details about their activity have ever been reported. But, according to people with direct knowledge of the companies' trading businesses, each of them handles more than 10 million barrels of oil a day, several times what they produce. Just as for the independent traders, it has been a magnificently profitable business for BP and Shell: BP typically records pre-tax profits from trading of between $2 billion and $3 billion a year; Shell targets trading profits of $4 billion.

In the realm of financial derivatives, their trading units are as innovative as the trading houses. In the late 1990s, for example, BP allocated a pot of money to be traded, in effect, by a computer – long before algorithmic trading became a dominant force in financial markets. BP's trading strategy, devised by an in-house maths whizz and known as the 'Q book', traded dozens of commodity futures including gold and corn.

And their market intelligence is every bit as sharp as that of the trading houses. From the days of Andy Hall onwards, BP's traders have never been afraid to bet big – and they've maintained that fearlessness up to the modern day. When oil tumbled to lows of less than $30 a barrel in 2016, for example, BP's traders placed a large bet on the futures market that prices would rise. It was a risky move: the company was already enormously exposed to moves in the oil price thanks to its ownership of oilfields around the world. The traders, however, argued that the price had fallen so far that it could only go

up. They were proved right, and the bet delivered profits in the hundreds of millions of dollars.

But while BP and Shell used the consolidation of the 1990s to build up huge trading businesses, they weren't prepared to match the trading houses blow-for-blow in the riskiest markets, such as the countries of the former Communist Bloc. And so, despite their size, they left many of the juiciest – and most politically influential – deals to the traders. Brian Gilvary, who was BP's chief financial officer until 2020, says there are countries where the British oil major will not trade because of the risks involved. 'Is there value available to us that could be captured over and above what we capture today? Absolutely. Are we prepared to take the risk associated with that? Definitely not. I can give you a list of countries, but you know where they are.'[51]

For some traders, surviving the 1990s meant going to ever more adventurous corners of the globe; for others it meant taking more dubious steps. The era's single most aggressive driver of consolidation was neither a trader nor an oil major. It was a company that had started life as a staid pipeline company, but went on to surf the liberalisation of gas and electricity markets to become one of the world's largest commodity traders: Enron.

Throughout the 1990s, Enron had been an all-consuming force in the trading industry, hoovering up bright young traders and buying up rival trading companies, redefining how a trading company could behave, and redrawing the commodity markets themselves. Just as financial innovations had begun to revolutionise the oil market, Enron, with its army of bright young traders and its hefty lobbying budget, helped to turn electricity and natural gas from a boring regulated industry into a casino where fortunes could be made or lost in the blink of an eye.[52]

From its origins in gas and electricity, Enron looked to conquer the rest of the commodity trading industry. In early 2000, it bought MG, the venerable metals trading business of Metallgesellschaft, which was the world's largest copper trader at the time, paying

$445 million plus more in debt.[53] It tried to expand into oil trading too, making a bid to buy Vitol. Ian Taylor and his partners turned down the offer, thereby staving off a disaster: Enron was offering to pay the owners of Vitol with its own shares, which soon turned out to be worthless.[54]

In the days of the dot-com bubble, Enron was the darling of Wall Street. It had no need to compete in the oil market with the likes of Marc Rich and John Deuss, or even Andy Hall – it would just invent new markets. After it had mastered gas and electricity, it would start buying and selling access to fibre-optic cables used to transmit data. Everything would be bought and sold on Enron's internet platform. 'We almost believed that you could create a market by sheer force of will,' a former Enron trader said.[55]

The reality was more prosaic, however. The company was simply a house of cards. Debt was hidden from investors and regulators. Profits were vastly inflated. Enron had created a culture that encouraged traders to push markets around, using their dominance to gouge customers.[56] Enron went out of business in December 2001, filing for bankruptcy in a massive accounting fraud.[57] CEO Jeffrey Skilling and chairman Kenneth Lay were both found guilty of multiple counts of conspiracy and fraud. Its collapse was one of the largest ever in corporate America, transforming the crooked Enron logo into a symbol of impropriety, and it marked the culmination of one of the commodity trading industry's most challenging periods, in which only the toughest survived.

Out of the wreckage of the former Communist Bloc emerged the contours of the present-day commodity trading industry. By the early 2000s, a few giant traders had accumulated a large share of the flow in oil, metals and agriculture – a formation that has remained remarkably constant up to the present day. In agriculture, Cargill, by absorbing Continental, accounted for approximately 40% of all

US exports.[58] In oil, Vitol had expanded to become the leading trader; Glencore was the dominant force in metals. Behind them, Trafigura was growing rapidly. Only in the North American gas and power market was there still fierce competition, as Wall Street banks and trading houses scrambled to fill the gap left by Enron.

The commodity traders had emerged from wild and dangerous deals of the 1990s with businesses stretched across the world, from Communist Cuba to the rapidly growing capitalist nations of Eastern Europe, with a whole array of dictatorships and failed states in between. Above all, the survivors of the decade's brutal consolidation had grown to become mighty merchants of natural resources, larger in scale and more global than ever before.

The traders may not have realised it yet, but that would soon be their ticket to a new era of riches. A major new source of demand for natural resources was just about to emerge that would revolutionise their business: China.

EIGHT

BIG BANG

It was a hot and humid morning in late June 2001, and Mick Davis was sitting at his desk in his home in north London overlooking the leafy expanse of Hampstead Heath.

'XSTRATA,' he typed. 'A Leap Upwards.'

In a six-page memo to his closest lieutenants, he set out his plans for Xstrata, a small, struggling Switzerland-listed holding company. He instructed them to scour the globe for mining companies to buy.[1]

At forty-three years old, with a stubbly beard and a paunch, Davis looked more like a teddy bear than an uncompromising corporate raider. But the South African's cuddly-looking exterior belied his confidence and ambition.

A few months earlier, he'd received a call from an old acquaintance, Ivan Glasenberg, the CEO-designate of Glencore, with an intriguing offer: would he like to run Xstrata, in which Glencore had a 39% stake, and try to turn it around?

Davis had jumped at the suggestion. In a whirlwind career, he'd risen from an accounting job in his native South Africa to spearheading the mining industry's biggest ever deal up to that point: the combination of a big Australian iron ore producer called BHP, and London-listed Billiton. With little prospect of

getting the top job at the new BHP Billiton, he gladly took up Glasenberg's offer.

So by the end of June, he was at leisure, in the middle of a period of enforced time off, with plenty of space to plan his strategy to turn Xstrata into one of the world's largest mining companies.

At the heart of his plan was a bet on commodity prices. The world was emerging from a period of brutally low prices that had humbled the mining companies and their investors. Davis became convinced that commodity prices were about to rise. He'd visited China a few months earlier in his previous job as Billiton's finance director, and had begun to believe that the country was about to go through a major phase of industrialisation, driving demand for natural resources.

'Commodity prices must be at or near their lows,' he wrote in the memo, sent at 11.42 a.m. on 27 June 2001. 'Supply side constraints are growing, demand from China must see margin expansion in the next few years – so now is the time to act!'

Davis's predictions would be proved right beyond his wildest expectations. Over the next decade, China would undergo an astonishing period of growth that would transform the natural resources industry. It became by far the world's largest consumer of raw materials as varied as steel, nickel, soybeans, wool and rubber, causing prices to triple or quadruple. It would make Xstrata the most valuable part of Glencore, turning the trading house that had inherited the mantle of Philipp Brothers and Marc Rich + Co into a hybrid of trader and miner. It was a bonanza for the commodity traders like none since the 1970s. And very few of them saw it coming.

China is the world's most populous country, but until the late 1990s, it had been an afterthought for the commodity traders. For years, companies such as Philipp Brothers, Cargill and Marc Rich + Co ran their Asian operations from Tokyo, rather than Hong Kong, Beijing or Shanghai.

The industry was accustomed to seeing China as an exporter of raw materials to the rest of the world. Chinese crude oil fuelled cars in California. Chinese coal powered electricity plants in Japan. And Chinese rice filled stomachs across the rest of Asia. Few doubted that China would one day be a major buyer of raw materials. The sheer size of its population meant it could only be a matter of time before the country would become one of the most important factors in the global supply and demand of commodities. But no one knew when that would happen.

The shift in the Chinese economy began in 1978, while Davis was still a student at Rhodes University in South Africa. At the Communist Party gathering that year in Beijing, Deng Xiaoping, the Chinese leader who came to power after the death of Mao Zedong, set out a new direction for the country. Deng rejected the chaos and terror of Mao's Cultural Revolution, and called for a new economic era under the rubric of reform and opening: a limited embrace of capitalism and growing engagement with the outside world. 'Under our present system of economic management, power is over-concentrated, so it is necessary to devolve some of it to the lower levels,' he said. 'Otherwise, we won't be able to rid our country of poverty and backwardness or to catch up with – still less surpass – the advanced countries.'[2]

The transformation unleashed three decades of spectacular growth in China, with the economy expanding by an average of 10% each year between 1980 and 2010. In the biggest economic metamorphosis since the industrial revolution in Europe and America in the nineteenth century, China became the world's factory, producing everything from household appliances to iPhones. By 2008, China was exporting more in a single day than it had done in the entirety of 1978.[3]

The industrialisation of the Chinese economy ushered in a mass urbanisation of the country's population. When Deng launched his programme of reforms, fewer than two in ten Chinese people lived in urban areas. Over the next four decades, roughly 500 million

Chinese migrated into cities, lifting the share of people living in urban areas to nearly 60% by 2017.[4]

The Chinese economic boom started almost immediately after Deng unveiled his reforms in 1978, but it didn't make a significant impact on commodity markets until much later. To understand why, it's necessary to examine the relationship between a nation's wealth and its consumption of natural resources.

The amount of commodities that a country consumes is, for the most part, a function of two factors: the number of people in the country, and their income. The relationship with commodity demand isn't a straight line, however.[5] As long as a country remains relatively poor, with annual per capita income below about $4,000, people spend most of their income on the basics they need to survive: food, clothes and housing. What's more, the governments of poor countries don't have the money to make major investments in commodity-intensive public infrastructure, such as power plants and railways. Even if a very poor country grows rapidly, it doesn't translate into much extra demand for commodities.

The same is true for a very rich country. Once a nation's income rises above roughly $18,000–$20,000 per capita, households spend any extra income on services that require relatively small amounts of commodities: better education and health, recreation and entertainment. Governments of such wealthy countries have usually already built the bulk of the public infrastructure they need.

In between the two extremes, there's a sweet spot for commodities demand. After per capita income rises above $4,000, countries typically industrialise and urbanise, creating a strong, and sometimes disproportionate, relationship between further economic growth and extra commodity demand. China hit the commodity sweet spot around the time that Davis wrote his Xstrata memo: its GDP per capita reached $3,959 in 2001.[6] Davis's analysis wasn't based on detailed economic modelling, but he knew from his travels there that something big was happening in China that could supercharge the commodity markets.

Chinese households were beginning to spend their extra income on consumer goods, such as refrigerators, washing machines and other appliances, and to swap their bicycles for cars. The national diet was changing too: bowls of rice gave way to pork and poultry. At the same time, Beijing and its provincial governments embarked on an infrastructure buildout comparable in scale only to the reconstruction of Europe and Japan after the Second World War. Thousands of kilometres of new highways and railways were laid, dozens of power plants and airports were built, whole cities sprouted up in just a few years, complete with hospitals, schools and shopping centres.

Just as China was passing the commodity demand tipping-point, another momentous event supercharged its economy. On 11 December 2001, China formally became a member of the World Trade Organization.[7] The move heralded an even more intense phase of economic growth. Foreign investment into China surged. The Chinese economy, which had grown 50% between 1980 and 1989, and 175% the following decade, now expanded by more than 400% in the decade after its accession to the WTO.[8]

The impact on commodity demand was seismic. In 1990, China consumed roughly as much copper as Italy did, accounting for less than 5% of the world's demand. By 2000, China's consumption was nearly three times as much as Italy's. By 2017, China accounted for half of global copper demand, making its consumption nearly twenty times that of Italy.[9]

Or take oil. Until 1993, China had been a net exporter, selling more oil on the world market than some members of the OPEC cartel. But China's oilfields were soon unable to meet its domestic demand. From 1993, the country became a net importer. Then, as it entered the commodity sweet spot, demand skyrocketed. In 2001, China's imports were 1.5 million barrels a day. By 2009, they were triple that level, and by 2018, China had become the world's largest oil importer, buying nearly 10 million barrels a day on the international market, equivalent to the entire production of Saudi Arabia.

In just a few years, China had become the world's biggest consumer of commodities by far.

China was the most important country to enter the commodity sweet spot, but not the only one. Across the world, many countries outside the industrialised nations of North America, Europe and Japan were reaching a level of economic development that required far more natural resources than before. The synchronised, resource-intensive growth created what economists call a commodity 'supercycle': an extended period during which the price of raw materials is well above its long-run trend, lasting beyond a normal business cycle, and often extending for decades.[10]

A normal commodity price cycle, the result of a supply shock, such as a crop failure or a mine closure, tends to be short-lived: the rise in prices stimulates additional supply and cools demand, and the market rebalances. Supercycles are demand led, and last longer. They tend to coincide with periods of rapid industrialisation and urbanisation in the global economy. The first modern commodity supercycle, for example, was triggered by the industrial revolution in the nineteenth century in Europe and America; the second, by the global rearmament before the Second World War; the third, by the economic boom of the Pax Americana and the reconstruction of Europe and Japan in the late 1950s and early 1960s.

The fourth began around the turn of the millennium, as China and other emerging economies entered the commodity sweet spot.[11] It fundamentally altered the structure of the global commodity markets. Between 1998 and 2018, the seven largest emerging markets (the BRIC group of Brazil, Russia, India and China, plus Indonesia, Mexico and Turkey) accounted for 92% of the increase in the world's metals consumption, 67% of the increase in energy consumption, and 39% of the increase in food consumption.[12]

The commodity industry was ill prepared to meet the increase in demand. The low prices of the 1990s had forced many miners, oil companies and farmers into savage cost-cutting, so when consumption surged they were unable to boost production.

The combination of runaway demand and stagnant supply had an explosive impact on prices. Crude oil, which in 1998 hit a low of less than $10, rose to more than $50 by the middle of 2004. The price of nickel quadrupled over the same period. Copper, coal, iron ore and soybean prices all surged higher. But that was just a prelude of what was to come. By the end of the decade they would all have smashed records.

The surge in prices filled the coffers of commodity-rich countries, such as Australia, Brazil, Chile, Saudi Arabia and Nigeria, creating a virtuous cycle in which economic growth in China and elsewhere drove commodity demand and prices, stimulating further growth in commodity-rich nations, which in turn demanded more manufactured goods from China. Global economic growth accelerated to more than 5% on average between 2004 and 2007, with emerging markets averaging nearly 8% – in both cases, the highest rate in more than thirty years.

Davis hadn't anticipated all that when he sat down to write his memo in 2001. But within a few years, the commodity boom would turn Xstrata from a financially challenged nuisance into the most valuable part of Glencore. At the helm of the commodity trading house there was a man who would end up doing better from the supercycle than almost anyone else on the planet. And he and Davis would become a tandem that took on both the trading and the mining industries. That man was Ivan Glasenberg.

Born on 7 January 1957, Glasenberg had grown up in a middle-class family in Johannesburg. Most of the city's tight-knit Jewish community hailed originally from Lithuania, and the Glasenbergs were no exception: Ivan's father had been born there, while his mother's, maiden name was Vilensky – meaning 'from Vilnius'.

The young Glasenberg grew up in a comfortable suburb in the north of Johannesburg, where the streets were lined with trees and

the large houses were protected by concrete walls and iron fences. He attended the nearby Hyde Park high school, where he was an unremarkable student but confident and forthright. 'He was not a terribly shy person,' one teacher recalled, 'and did not always accept that the teacher was correct.'[13]

One thing Glasenberg did have was a drive to succeed. While his brother Martin took over running the family business – importing and distributing bags and suitcases – Ivan, once he had completed his military service, took a junior accounting job for a monthly salary of about 200 rand ($230). At the same time, he enrolled in the University of Witwatersrand to study accounting. In 1982, he moved to Los Angeles to study for an MBA at the University of Southern California.

His competitive instinct was not limited to his career. He was an athlete from an early age, and soon started competing in race walking, the hip-wiggling sport in which competitors must cover a distance as fast as possible while maintaining contact with the ground at all times. Glasenberg had hoped to compete in the Olympics in Los Angeles in 1984, but South African athletes were barred from taking part amid a wave of anti-apartheid campaigns.

He would remain a fitness fanatic throughout the rest of his life, running or swimming most mornings, and creating a sports-mad culture within Glencore where whole teams of traders would go for group runs or bike rides in the hills around Zug in lieu of a lunch break. Commodity trading would soon supplant sports as the main focus of Glasenberg's time and energy. Still, he ran the New York marathon in 1994, aged thirty-seven, in the respectable time of 3 hours, 34 minutes, and continued to compete in triathlons in Switzerland into his fifties.[14]

Glasenberg had joined Marc Rich + Co in April 1984, when the company was still under the spotlight of the US justice system. (The case against the company wouldn't be settled until later that year.) Glasenberg started working in the Johannesburg office, where there was a separate room with a padlocked door for organising the oil

imports to South Africa that were, in spite of the UN embargo, one of the company's main lines of business. Once asked how he felt about helping apartheid South Africa to sidestep the embargo, Glasenberg responded with a chuckle and said that the company hadn't broken any laws and had delivered coal to countries that wanted it.[15]

The coal business that Glasenberg joined was a sleepy backwater that made a few million dollars in a good year. Its boss was Udo Horstmann, an old-school German trader whose main passion was collecting indigenous African art. Horstmann sensed Glasenberg was a threat. He once complained to Felix Posen, then one of the senior partners of the company, that the young South African would ruin the coal business.[16]

In reality, the opposite was true. There was no futures market in coal, limiting the potential for sophisticated trading strategies. Instead, the key was wheeling and dealing, haggling with the miners in South Africa, Australia or Colombia who produced the coal, and with the power plants in Japan, South Korea and Germany that consumed it, building and exploiting relationships with both sides.

At this, Glasenberg excelled. He was a 'doer', says Posen, who helped to hire him. He got to know every buyer and seller of coal worth knowing. The market was slow enough that it was possible to keep track of every trade that took place – and Glasenberg's knowledge was encyclopaedic. Soon he moved to Australia to run the coal division there, and then to run Glencore's office in Hong Kong. In 1990 he replaced Horstmann as the company's head of coal in Zug.[17]

Already he was seen as one of the rising stars of the company, and within a few years he would cement his position as its future leader. 'When I came into the company, and Ivan came to Zug, already he was the star,' says Josef Bermann, who joined in 1990 and would go on to become head of aluminium. Rich was already in the twilight of his career, but the hungry young coal trader caught his eye. 'Marc always told me, after I left, he always told me that he could see already that [Glasenberg] is the guy which basically will take Glencore to its next stage,' Bermann recalls.[18]

Glasenberg stayed on the sidelines as infighting consumed Marc Rich + Co in 1992 and 1993. But when the dust cleared and Willy Strothotte emerged victorious in the battle for the future of the company, Glasenberg was at his side as one of the dozen department heads who now owned a sizeable chunk of the company.

Strothotte and Glasenberg, increasingly the two most important people in the company, had complementary styles that were almost comically different. The tall, suave, German Strothotte occupied an ambassadorial post at the helm of Glencore. He would fly the world on his private jet, comfortably tailored in monogrammed shirts, schmoozing suppliers, customers and bankers in the half-dozen languages he spoke flawlessly. He did not live for work: he would, on occasion, call one of Glencore's top executives and tell them to cancel their meetings for the afternoon to come and play golf with him at the elite Schönenberg club near Zurich, where he was a member.[19]

Glasenberg was the exact opposite. Short and slight, with his fine brown hair combed back, he was a dynamo with a belligerent intensity that few inside or outside Glencore could match. With his clipped South African accent and blunt, abrasive style of talking, peppered with profanities, he had none of Strothotte's smoothness. One Australian newspaper described him as 'an excitable terrier'.[20] He had no interest in the luxuries that came with his station: he cut costs without remorse, and for years liked to boast that Glencore didn't own a corporate jet. (In fact, Strothotte owned one that he leased to the company, and Kazzinc, a Glencore subsidiary, owned another.)[21] And, for Glasenberg, work was everything: on weekends, bored, he was known to call up colleagues to meet up and talk business.

Glasenberg was of a different background and generation to Marc Rich, but the two men were similar in many ways. They shared a passion for the business of commodity trading that eclipsed every other aspect of their lives, a Stakhanovite work ethic that put all others to shame, and a personal style that relied on force of will rather than charm.

Glasenberg, an early riser, would greet colleagues arriving at Glencore's headquarters at 8.30 a.m. with a sarcastic 'good afternoon'.[22] It was the very same joke that Rich had made, several decades earlier, to his colleagues at Philipp Brothers in New York.

After Strothotte stepped back and Glasenberg took over in 2002, he built Glencore ever more in his own image. That meant a company where everyone worked at his relentless pace; where traders spent more time on the road than with their families; and where every detail of a deal should be haggled and re-haggled to squeeze out a few extra dollars of profit. Glasenberg also centralised power, ending the autonomy of regional offices and insisting that senior traders be in Baar, the village next to Zug where Glencore now had its headquarters.

Glasenberg also took over Strothotte's role as the steward of Glencore's most important relationships. During his time as chief executive of Glencore, he became friendly with oligarchs like Alexander Mashkevich of Kazakhstan and politicians like South African president Cyril Ramaphosa. He was ready to jump on a plane with a moment's notice in order to smooth over some difficulty in a contract or seal a deal.

But few who have worked with him doubt that, for Glasenberg, relationships were only a means to an end. And that extended to his traders at Glencore. He would call them time and time again, regardless of the time of day, if he wanted something from them. He had little patience for his employees' personal lives. And he quickly turned against people who he felt were no longer giving 100% to the Glencore cause.

'Either you're in the family or you're out,' says one former Glencore employee. 'After I said I was leaving, Ivan didn't speak to me again.'[23]

Years before the commodity supercycle started, Glasenberg had embarked on a series of trades that would transform the company's

fortunes, thanks to the rise of China. In 1994, when few in the natural resources world had any hope of higher prices, he started buying coal mines for Glencore.

It was a new direction for the company, which until recently had focused on trading commodities rather than owning production assets. At this stage, there was no grand strategy – coal prices were low, coal miners were struggling, and so Glasenberg took advantage. His first deal was with Tselentis Mining, a family-owned coal miner in South Africa. Glencore had been buying coal from the company and providing it with some financial support; eventually, it converted its debt into a controlling equity stake. The same year, Glasenberg bought a stake in Australia's Cook Colliery.

These early deals were small, involving investments of \$5 or \$10 million each. Glencore, still struggling from its association with Marc Rich, had little ability to borrow long term and so had to fund the deals entirely from its own retained profits.

'Each time an asset was acquired, you had to demonstrate that Marc Rich was not a shareholder in the company,' recalls Greg James, who worked on the deals as part of Glasenberg's coal team. 'There was no real support from any of the banks. They didn't understand what we were doing.'[24]

It was not just Glasenberg's optimism about the future of coal that drove him. He was also pessimistic about the future of trading. The trading industry was no longer the preserve of a few companies in the know – competition was relentless. And as mobile phones, the internet and email revolutionised communications, the advantage of a traditional trading organisation in the Philipp Brothers style was waning. Maintaining offices in dozens of countries around the world was expensive, and each year it was less certain that the trading profits would be enough to cover those costs.

Buying mines was one way to address the issue: now Glencore's traders would have a guaranteed flow of commodities to sell, without having to outbid their competitors to secure them. 'I've always said,

pure commodity trading without the assets backing up the trading is very difficult,' Glasenberg says today.[25]

It was one thing to buy a few coal mines. But if Glencore could accumulate enough mines, it would bring another advantage: an influence over prices, in particular in the annual negotiations with Japanese power plants where the price of much of the world's coal was set. At the time, the Australian coal industry was made up of dozens of small and mid-sized players, while the Japanese power industry was represented by a few giant companies. The Japanese had little difficulty dominating the discussion. If Glasenberg could buy up a large enough share of the Australian coal industry, he would be able to change that.

In 1998, the coal market entered a broader downturn and Glasenberg's chance came. The price of a tonne of coal dropped to the lowest point since the mid-1980s.[26] Much of the coal mining industry was losing money. Glasenberg became convinced that prices could only rise. But in coal, with no futures market, there was nowhere to place a bet on rising prices. The only way was to buy entire mines. So that's what Glasenberg did. Over the next four years he bought more than a dozen mines in Australia and South Africa, in addition to deals in Colombia.

By the end of the decade, Glencore was the world's largest shipper of thermal coal, trading 48.5 million tonnes in 2000 – one in every six traded on the seaborne market.[27] Glasenberg's investments hadn't been premised on a coming Chinese economic boom, but they would soon be transformed by it. Even before that happened, they were successful enough to catapult him to the top of the ranks of Glencore's hungry young department heads. When Strothotte told the partners he was looking to step back from the day-to-day running of the company, there were only a few likely contenders to replace him: Glasenberg; Paul Wyler, the Swiss head of copper and nickel, who had been at the company since the 1970s; and Ian Perkins, the smooth British head of alumina. Over a few weeks, Strothotte took each of the department

heads to one side and asked them who they thought should succeed him. There was little contest – Glasenberg was anointed CEO-designate.

In 2001, Glasenberg's bet on coal came good: by the middle of the year, prices had risen 35% from their lows. 'Everyone's horny as hell for coal,' Glasenberg bragged in an interview.[28] If he had any concerns about the impact of burning millions of tonnes of coal on the climate, he didn't show it. In another interview the same year, he even described Glencore's coal production in Australia as 'environment-friendly'.[29]

The China boom had yet to transform the market, but Glencore's coal business was already humming. The company had a pressing problem, however: it needed to buy back the 15% stake that Strothotte had sold to Roche in 1994 to finance the management buy-out from Marc Rich. Until now, the pharmaceutical company had been an entirely silent investor, happy with the promise of a guaranteed return on its investment and with no involvement in Glencore's affairs.

But that wouldn't last for ever. Under the original deal, Roche had the right to force Glencore to buy back the stake – known as a 'put option' over its Glencore shares – at any time from November 1999 onwards. It wasn't clear whether Glencore would be able to afford it, however. So the two sides negotiated a compromise: Roche would defer its right to have the shares bought out, giving Glencore until January 2003 to find the money. If it did not, Roche would have the right to sell some or all of its shares 'to the public or ... to another investor', according to one prospectus published by the trading house.[30]

That was an intolerable thought for the Glencore traders. Another investor was likely to be more involved in their business than Roche had been. Strothotte had battled Marc Rich to secure Glencore's independence, and he wasn't about to surrender it. And if Roche sold its shares to the public, Glencore would effectively become a public company. Strothotte had no desire to be forced to publish Glencore's financials and submit to questions about its activities from

investors. 'Culturally, I don't think it makes sense,' he said at the time. 'I don't think we can operate in a way that we have to look over our shoulders, I think you have to have the entrepreneurial freedom.'[31]

The race was on to find a source of cash to buy out Roche. The price that the two sides had negotiated was $494.3 million. That would soon seem a trifling sum, but in the early 2000s, it was still a meaningful amount of money for Glencore to have to raise. It was more than the company's combined net profits in 1998 and 1999. 'It is our intention to acquire the shares from the Investor [Roche] as soon as the financial condition of Glencore will permit,' the company said in another prospectus.[32]

Glasenberg found a solution to the problem. The trading house, he thought, could put all the coal mines he had been buying into a new entity. Rather than selling shares in Glencore to raise money, it could instead sell shares of the coal empire that he had just built. Glencore would raise enough money to buy out Roche, and the trading house would only have to tell investors the secrets of its coal mining business, rather than of the whole company.

For Glencore, it was a tried and tested model. The trading house had done something similar before, using the company that ultimately became Xstrata. The mining group had started life in 1926, when it was established under the name Südelektra in Switzerland as a vehicle to finance electricity projects in South America.[33] By 1990, when Marc Rich bought a majority stake, it was a largely dormant investment vehicle. But under Rich's ownership, it took on a different function. Rich's status as a fugitive from US justice made it near-impossible for his company to raise long-term funding of the kind needed to buy assets – banks thought he was toxic.

Südelektra offered a solution: Marc Rich + Co, and later Glencore, could use it as a vehicle to raise long-term money and so buy assets while using less of its own capital. The company was already listed on the Zurich stock market, so it was easy to raise money by selling shares, and its board of directors was a who's who of the Swiss

establishment. So Südelektra, under the advice of Rich, invested into an oilfield in Argentina, a Chilean forestry company and a South African ferrochrome business.

For years, the Zurich-listed company was the main way for Marc Rich + Co to buy assets. Then, when the traders bought the last of Marc Rich's shares in 1994, Glencore itself was welcomed back into the international financial system. With Marc Rich gone, the renamed company was able to tap a wider range of lenders. Now traders like Glasenberg no longer needed to use Südelektra as a vehicle for their asset purchases. Still, they hadn't forgotten how useful the structure could be.

Glasenberg, faced with the need to pay back Roche, now sought to create a new version of the old Südelektra structure with the coal assets he had accumulated. He started working on an initial public offering of the coal mines on the Australian Stock Exchange, grouping together the assets into a new company called Enex. For Glencore, it would be an ideal manoeuvre: in addition to raising the money it needed, it would retain roughly a third of the equity in its coal mines and so continue to trade the coal they produced.

Glasenberg's timing was almost perfect: few investors had seen it coming, but the price of coal would soon soar as Chinese demand ballooned and the country, at that point still a major exporter of coal to the global market, began to import more and more.

But the timing was not quite perfect. Glasenberg's ingenious plan was scuppered when terrorists hijacked two planes and flew them into the World Trade Center in New York on 11 September, 2001. Another plane hit the Pentagon in Washington; a fourth crashed in rural Pennsylvania. It was the worst terror attack on US soil in history, and it had struck at the heart of Wall Street. Financial markets ground to a halt.

Glasenberg was in New York with his team on 10 September to meet with potential investors for the Enex IPO. He had flown back to Switzerland that evening, and he was back in Glencore's office in Baar, where it was early afternoon on 11 September, when the phone rang.

It was Greg James, the coal department's finance specialist, who had been doing the rounds of investors on the other side of the world in Sydney. 'Take a look at what's happening on CNN,' James told him. 'The listing's off.'

The Glencore team and its bankers spent a couple of weeks trying to revive the Enex IPO, but the events of 9/11 had sent a chill through financial markets.

The failed coal listing was not Glencore's only headache at the time. Xstrata, as Südelektra had been renamed by now, was also struggling. It had borrowed 600 million euros earlier that year to buy Asturiana de Zinc, one of the world's largest zinc producers, located in the north of Spain. It had planned to issue more shares in Switzerland to pay back the loan. But the equity market slump meant that that plan, too, was on hold, and the company was on course to breach its covenants with its lenders – which could have forced Glencore to provide financial support. 'We were solvent but we were certainly nowhere within covenants,' says Mick Davis of the company he took over in mid-2001.[34]

Davis and Glasenberg were old acquaintances: Davis had taught seminars at the University of Witwatersrand when Glasenberg was a student there, and the two men had got to know one another. Two decades later they found themselves on opposite sides of coal deals in Colombia and South Africa. When Glasenberg and Strothotte were looking for a new CEO for Xstrata, his name had come up.

Now Davis was trying to work out a way to extricate Xstrata from its financial mess – at the same time as capitalising on the commodities boom he was anticipating. Glasenberg was still trying to find a way to raise money to buy back the stake in Glencore owned by Roche.

A few weeks after the 9/11 attacks, Davis flew in to Baar to introduce his new chief financial officer, Trevor Reid, to Glasenberg and Strothotte. On the plane back to London, Davis and Reid started discussing the predicament of their new company. Suddenly, the idea occurred to them of solving both Xstrata's and Glencore's problems

in one single transaction. Davis grabbed a piece of paper and started sketching out the details – Xstrata would buy the coal business that Glencore had failed to float, selling shares to new investors in London to finance the purchase. He quickly jotted down a few key numbers: how much they would pay Glencore for the mines, and how much money they would have to raise in order to do so.[35]

When the plane landed, Davis phoned Glasenberg and Strothotte and told them he was coming back to Baar. With the support of a handful of London fund managers, who told him they would back a potential share sale, Davis set about negotiating a deal with Glasenberg to buy the mines.

It was to be the first of a series of combative negotiations between the two men over the next eleven years that would culminate in one of the largest and most bitterly fought mergers in the history of the London market. It was a complicated relationship: Davis ran Xstrata as an independent vehicle, but Glasenberg effectively had the final say in all big decisions, thanks to the large stake that Glencore owned in the mining company.

For now, though, they just needed to agree on how much Xstrata would pay Glencore for the coal mines. Glasenberg kept haggling, telling Davis that he might return to the original plan of an IPO of Enex in Australia, until finally Strothotte intervened to break the deadlock.

On 19 March 2002, Xstrata sold $1.4 billion of shares to new investors in London, using that money plus additional shares to buy the coal assets from Glencore. For a while, it looked like Glasenberg had had the better end of the negotiations. Glencore used the money it got from Xstrata to buy back its shares from Roche, completing the deal in November. The coal price fell, and the $2.57 billion price tag that Xstrata had paid for Glencore's Australian and South African coal operations looked steep.

But soon Davis's optimism about the coming commodities boom would prove justified. As the coal price rose from less than $25 a tonne in mid-2002 to nearly $40 by the end of 2003, Davis was

positioned to take advantage of it. With hindsight, Glasenberg had sold cheap. The China-led supercycle was about to transform the fortunes of both Xstrata and Glencore – and with them, the whole commodity trading industry.

'We need to put XSTRATA into "big bang" territory,' Davis had written in his June 2001 memo, setting out a two-step plan to catapult the company into the mining big league. First, he would try to expand the company's investor base and boost its valuation to around $2–2.5 billion, giving it the scale to pursue a 'big bang' deal. The goal was to turn Xstrata into a $5 billion company within three years.

Fuelled by Davis's optimism about China, the Xstrata team set about hunting for companies to buy. Even as commodity prices started to rise in 2002 and 2003, most executives in the mining industry, still bearing the scars of the downturn, were wary about betting on a boom. The price of futures for metals such as copper for delivery in two, three or five years was lower than spot prices – a condition known as 'backwardation' – and most mining executives worked on the assumption that prices would indeed drop. So did the Xstrata team: they just assumed that prices would drop a little more slowly.

'We took the view that the commodity prices would stay high for longer,' Davis recalls. 'We didn't have an aggressive assumption on what the long-term price would be. But the backwardation, which the industry relied upon, was formed from assumptions about commodity prices falling off a cliff from the prevailing spot price. We delayed falling prices and assumed a slower return to the mean.'[36]

Within a few months of closing the deal to buy Glencore's coal mines, he had launched a takeover bid for Mount Isa Mines, an Australian producer of copper, lead and zinc, and eventually bought the company for a little over $2 billion. Other miners looked at making a counterbid, but none could match Davis's price.

Some Glencore executives, with their life's savings tied up in Glencore shares, were more cautious than Davis on the outlook in the early years of the boom. Willy Strothotte, the patriarch of the company, who was now beginning to eye retirement, had voiced

doubts about the deal for Mount Isa Mines, and needed Glasenberg to talk him round. Telis Mistakidis, a hyperactive Greek, who was the company's top copper trader, even hedged some of Glencore's copper output around this time – effectively, a bet that the high prices might not last.

But it wasn't long before any caution was forgotten. By the end of 2003, Davis had more than achieved his goal for Xstrata: the company, which had been worth as little as $450 million in the middle of 2001, was now worth $7 billion. At its peak in 2008, it would have a market value of $84.2 billion, making it the fifth-most valuable mining company in the world.[37]

Glasenberg's bet on buying assets a decade earlier now helped to deliver profits for Glencore that surpassed even Marc Rich's golden years. In 2003, the company's net income exceeded $1 billion for the first time, and the following year it was more than $2 billion, and in 2007 the trading house made $6.1 billion.[38]

Glencore was not alone. By about 2003, commodity traders across the industry were beginning to wake up to the transformative effect of China on their markets.

In Connecticut, Andy Hall had been beginning to lose his enthusiasm for oil trading. By now, thanks to a series of mergers, Phibro was part of Citigroup. Hall, bored with an oil market that for years had been devoid of the fireworks of the first Gulf war, was spending more and more time competing in rowing competitions and building his art collection.

He was jolted into action by Robert Rubin, who had joined Citigroup after stepping down as US Treasury Secretary. Rubin had asked Hall to put together a presentation on the outlook for the oil market for a group of the bank's top traders. Hall, at a regatta in California at the time, started crunching numbers on the prospects for oil supply and demand over the next few years.

'I really shocked myself,' he recalls. 'I was like, wow, this is unbelievable, the rate at which China imports are growing. And then I started checking all the supply data and I started digging into what the oil companies were doing in terms of adding to reserves, and it just didn't add up.'[39]

Like Mick Davis, Andy Hall believed the market was out of whack when it came to the futures market. By the middle of 2003, spot oil prices had tripled from their low point in 1998 to trade at close to $30 a barrel. But futures for delivery several years later were still trading below $25.

Hall decided to go all in. He asked his bosses at Citigroup to give him more capital to play with – measured according to the statistical concept of 'value-at-risk'. These were the boom years of Wall Street, and they quickly acquiesced. And so Hall placed the biggest bet of his life on long-dated oil futures.

In London, a veteran metals trader called Michael Farmer was also considering giving up on commodity trading. For more than a decade, he'd dominated the global copper market, first as the head of copper at Philipp Brothers, and later as the boss of Metallgesellschaft's physical metals trading unit. Now, after Enron had bought MG and then gone bankrupt, he was out of a job.

A born-again Christian, Farmer had started his career in the rumbustious shouting match that was the London Metal Exchange's trading floor. In the wake of the Enron bankruptcy, he had enrolled in a theology course and considered training to be a priest, but was persuaded to return to commodity trading by a long-time colleague and fellow Christian, David Lilley.

The two men – who acquired the nickname the 'God squad' – soon encountered a problem that turned out to be a blessing. 'We rang around the physical business but there was no copper anywhere, and we slowly learned rapid Chinese growth had left their industry short,' Farmer recalled.[40] If they needed any more indication that the market was about to shoot higher, now they had it. Under the name Red Kite, they started placing bets that copper prices would rise, making a fortune.

In Hong Kong, a British high-school dropout and one-time hippie who had been evangelising about China for years was also seeing his predictions come good. Richard Elman had learnt his trade buying and selling scrap metal in Newcastle, San Francisco and Tokyo, eventually running Philipp Brothers' Hong Kong office before striking out on his own to create Noble Group in 1986.

Elman said he had grown accustomed to friends 'patiently listening to my dreams for Noble while rolling their eyes'.[41] But when China joined the WTO in 2001, he knew his moment had come. 'I think it's singularly one of the most significant things that's happened in world trade in many, many years,' he enthused.[42]

It wasn't long before the whole commodity trading industry was awake to the transformational impact of China's growth. And it was not just commodity traders who got the bug – miners, oil drillers, farmers, financiers, and soon the public at large began to pay attention to the astonishing move in commodity prices. By 2005, the term 'supercycle' had become a buzzword on Wall Street, drawing a wide array of investors to the commodity markets.

The gold rush was on, and anyone who could get their hands on a reliable supply of commodities was all but guaranteed to get rich.

NINE

PETRODOLLARS AND KLEPTOCRATS

No one raised an eyebrow when Murtaza Lakhani strolled into Glencore's offices in Baar on a spring day in 2002.

The Pakistani-born businessman, a schmoozer with a beady gaze and a penchant for two-tone shirts, joined the flow of neatly dressed employees trooping into the boxy building that was the headquarters of the world's largest commodity trader.

In these early days of the commodity boom, it was normal to meet any number of motley characters in Glencore's discreet, glass-fronted lobby, from Central Asian oligarchs and African tycoons to sharp-suited executives from some of the world's largest banks. And in any case, Lakhani was a regular. Proudly describing himself as Glencore's 'man in Baghdad', this was one of at least four visits he would make to Glencore in the first half of 2002 alone.

On this occasion, 15 May, Lakhani passed the small reception area and went into an office. There's no record of who met with him, or how long the conversation took. What is known is what he left with. It was memorialised in an official Glencore receipt: petty cash voucher number 7165, confirmed with the signature of a company cashier. The sum was far from insignificant, however: $415,000 in cash, weighing about four kilogrammes, enough to fill a small briefcase.

Lakhani's next stop was on the other side of Switzerland. Two days after his visit to Glencore, he walked into Iraq's diplomatic office in Geneva, about three hours from Baar by car. He was there to make a deposit. In cash. The amount: $400,000.

The payment, according to Iraqi official records, was to cover a 'surcharge' – something officials at the United Nations considered illegal – paid to Baghdad in exchange for oil contracts that ultimately benefited Glencore.

It was a journey Lakhani made several times that year, always with a similar cargo. On 24 January, he left Glencore's offices with €170,850. On 24 April, he took another €230,000. And on 10 June, he left the building with $190,000. In total, an investigation on behalf of the UN found that Lakhani paid just over $1 million in 'surcharges for oil financed and lifted by Glencore'.

The company has always denied any knowledge of the illicit payments. But it couldn't deny the large amounts of cash that it had handed out to Lakhani. Luis Alvarez, who was in charge of Iraqi oil at Glencore and went on to become head of crude oil trading, later told UN investigators he had orally recommended what he called a 'success fee' of $300,000 or $400,000 for Lakhani. But another senior executive at the company, the head of crude oil operations, told the investigators that, as far as he knew, Glencore never paid bonuses of that size in cash. And Lakhani himself told UN investigators that he periodically received the cash from Glencore for payment of the surcharges.[1]

Lakhani was a natural in the world of oil trading, equally at ease in the presidential palace of an oil-rich megalomaniac or the refined and discreet world of Swiss finance. He was born in Karachi, Pakistan, but had grown up in London and Vancouver.[2] A natural entertainer, he hosted concerts for the diplomatic corps at his bungalow in a wealthy neighbourhood of Baghdad.[3] Later in Erbil, in the semi-autonomous Kurdish region of northern Iraq, he would hold parties with free-flowing champagne and seafood flown in from Dubai where guests would goggle at his collection of paintings by Salvador Dali.

Lakhani's role was a mixture of wheeler-dealer and diplomat. Known variously as 'middlemen', 'agents' or 'fixers' (Lakhani prefers the word 'consultant'), men like Lakhani are hired by commodity traders for their connections and ability to make things happen in difficult parts of the world, where the traders may not have a fully-staffed office. It helps that they are paid as external contractors, rather than in-house staff, giving the trading houses a layer of insulation should anything go wrong. Lakhani once summed up his role, saying: 'I get my hands dirty.'[4]

In the early 2000s, Lakhani's job, for a $5,000 monthly fee, was to represent Glencore 'for the acquisition of Iraqi crude oil'.[5]

It was a moment when acquiring oil had become the key to success for a trading company like Glencore. After a decade of stagnating prices, the Chinese economic boom was just beginning to turn the oil market on its head. As prices rose, money flowed into the coffers of anyone with oil, empowering a new generation of oil barons and kleptocrats. Arab princes, Congolese governors, Russian oligarchs and Kazakh politicians all flooded the hotels and nightclubs of Mayfair and Knightsbridge in London as well as the lakeside hotels of Switzerland. A whole industry of lawyers, accountants and bankers sprung up to service this new class of multimillionaires.

But no one was more critical to their ascent than the commodity traders. It was the traders who ensured that their oil could be sold on the global markets. And it was the traders who ensured that the dollars would flow back to the appropriate bank accounts. As leaders of oil-rich countries like Russia, Oman and Venezuela grew in confidence on the world stage, it was in no small part thanks to the commodity traders.

The dependence was mutual. For the first time in years, oil was in short supply. For the traders, the pressure was on to scour every corner of the world for extra barrels, going wherever necessary and dealing with whomever they had to.

Saddam Hussein, the canny Iraqi leader, spied an opportunity.

After the end of the Gulf War in 1991, the US and its allies convinced the United Nations to keep the embargo on Iraqi oil in place to keep Saddam in check. Without oil money, the Iraqi ruler wouldn't be able to afford more military adventures like his invasion of Kuwait. But the lack of oil money also hit the rest of the country's economy, and it was the Iraqi people who suffered poverty and malnutrition as a result. By 1995, Iraq was in a full-blown humanitarian crisis, and Washington and its allies relented.

The UN created the oil-for-food programme: Iraq could sell its crude on the international market, but all the proceeds would go into an account in New York controlled by the UN, and the money would be used to buy food, medicines and a few other necessities. For the international community, it was a way to keep Saddam under control while alleviating the devastating effect of the sanctions on the Iraqi people.

The commodity traders were the first in line for Iraqi oil: Oscar Wyatt, the founder of Coastal Petroleum, got the first cargo when the embargo was lifted in 1996. He was an old hand in Iraq: it was Wyatt who had travelled to Baghdad in the middle of the Gulf War in 1990 to rescue the Americans that Saddam had been using as human shields. Soon, he was joined by other traders and oil majors seeking cheaper sources of crude in the tough markets of the late 1990s.

For the first four years, the oil-for-food programme worked relatively smoothly. Iraq distributed some oil contracts to its political allies who had spoken out against the sanctions programme – Russia's Communist Party received allocations, and so did several politicians from France, which had argued in favour of lifting the sanctions. The oil was sold slightly below the market price, allowing whoever received allocations to resell them on to traders at a profit. But the petrodollars flowed as intended to the UN-controlled account.

Baghdad got its chance to play with the system after the extraordinary demand from China sent oil prices much higher in 2000. At the OPEC meeting that autumn in Vienna, Iraqi officials spread

the word among oil buyers: if they wanted to keep getting oil cargoes, they would need to pay a 'surcharge' directly to Baghdad, via Iraq's embassies and overseas bank accounts controlled by the Iraqi government. The surcharge amounted to a few cents for every barrel of oil, but UN officials in charge of the oil-for-food pro-gramme warned traders that it was illegal.[6] Most buyers bulked at the request and never got more Iraqi oil. Others found ways to continue buying.

What happened next was the subject of an extensive UN investi-gation chaired by the former head of the US Federal Reserve, Paul Volcker.

In a 623-page report, published in 2005, it offered one of the most comprehensive insights ever into the murky underbelly of the world of oil trading that had blossomed in this era of rising prices and easily grabbed riches.[7] The investigators interviewed traders, politicians and bankers; they got copies of bank transfers, contracts and emails. Crucial to the investigation were the Iraqi government's own meticulous accounts of all the illicit surcharges paid by the commodity traders, which became available to the UN investigators after the toppling of Saddam Hussein following the US invasion in 2003.

The report detailed, barrel by barrel and bank transfer by bank transfer, how Iraq's oil trade moved into the shadows after Baghdad started demanding surcharges.

The oil was handed off from one company to another via a net-work of practically anonymous entities incorporated in tax havens. Trafigura used an off-the-shelf Bahamian company called Round-head; Vitol channelled payments via a mysterious British Virgin Islands outfit called Peakville Limited, whose wire transfers listed as a contact person Vitol's top accountant in Geneva; Oscar Wyatt paid through two companies in Cyprus that had been created just after the surcharges were imposed.

Glencore followed an even more elaborate route: it bought crude the Iraqis had allocated to a Panama-registered company called

Incomed Trading Corporation. In its response to the UN investigators, Glencore said that there was nothing untoward about its purchases of Iraqi oil.

'It was known and accepted by the world community that the Iraqi regime was awarding oil allocations to its political friends and allies,' Glencore said through its lawyer. 'The prevailing understanding in the world community at the time was that recipients of oil allocations were being rewarded by the regime for their loyalty and political support, not because they had paid surcharges to the regime.'[8]

Yet, if anything, Incomed had ties to Glencore, rather than Baghdad. It was owned by relatives of Luis Alvarez, the main Iraqi oil trader at Glencore and the very same man who said he had authorised a $400,000 success fee for Lakhani. Alvarez's father was the main shareholder of Incomed, and his mother was the company's chairwoman.[9]

The UN investigation concluded that Lakhani paid 'approximately $1 million' in surcharges on Incomed Trading's two contracts with Baghdad. Of that, about $710,000 was settled with cash deposited at the Iraqi mission to the UN in Geneva, with cash that Lakhani had received from Glencore. A separate investigation – known as the Duelfer report – described Glencore as one of the 'most active purchasers' of Iraqi oil and quoted Iraqi records showing that Glencore had paid $3,222,780 in 'illegal surcharges' over the course of the oil-for-food programme.[10]

In total, the Iraqi regime earned $228.8 million between 2000 and 2002, the years in which it operated the illicit oil surcharge scheme, from multiple commodity traders and oil companies. Saddam Hussein had ensured that Iraq kept the price of its oil as low as possible in order to leave room for the oil traders to pay Baghdad the surcharges.[11]

Glencore has always denied it made or authorised illegal payments to the Iraqi government. And the company was never charged with any wrongdoing over the oil-for-food affair – neither were Lakhani, Alvarez or any of Glencore's other employees or representatives. Since the company was based in Switzerland, responsibility for

any potential prosecution based on the UN report fell to the Swiss authorities, and none was forthcoming.

Asked years later about his role, Lakhani responded through a spokesman that he 'was asked to attend interviews with the US government to assist it with its investigation, and voluntarily provided his assistance'. 'Since 2006, Mr. Lakhani has had no further involvement with this matter,' the spokesman said.[12]

Glencore didn't appear to see anything wrong with Alvarez securing Iraqi oil through a company owned by his father and chaired by his mother. In fact, it promoted him to run its entire crude-trading operation. When Glencore floated on the London Stock Exchange, Alvarez would emerge as one of the company's largest shareholders with a stake worth $550 million in 2012.[13]

Other commodity traders, after initially issuing blanket denials, eventually admitted to wrongdoing in the oil-for-food scheme. After the Volcker investigation, Vitol pled guilty in the US to grand larceny and paid $17.5 million in fines and restitution.[14] Like Glencore, though, it didn't show any obvious displeasure with the employees involved. Both the trader in charge of handling the Iraqi oil and the accountant named in the UN report continued to work for Vitol or entities associated with it for many more years.

Trafigura pled guilty to a charge of falsely claiming that oil it was selling in the US was compliant with the oil-for-food programme.[15]

The American traders faced the harshest penalties. Oscar Wyatt, the owner of Coastal Petroleum, was sentenced to one year in jail, while his friend David Chalmers, the owner of Bayoil, was sentenced to two years.[16]

The oil-for-food scandal was emblematic of the commodity industry's new era of scarcity. For the next decade, low prices would be a distant memory, and commodity traders would fall over one another to secure the precious raw materials necessary to feed China and

other emerging markets' seemingly bottomless appetites for commodities. And oil was the most prized resource of all.

The commodity boom really picked up steam in the second half of 2003 and into 2004. The oil industry was already operating close to full capacity. Nearly two decades of low prices had curtailed investment in oilfields, pipelines and refineries, so there was not enough new supply to match booming global demand, which in 2004 had the biggest increase since 1978.[17] Prices soared past $40 a barrel for the first time since the first Gulf War, and then surpassed $50 for the first time ever (see graph on page 334).

In many ways, it was a repeat of the 1970s. Politicians in consuming countries showed the same anxiety as OPEC regained its power. The price of gasoline became a staple of news bulletins. There were apocalyptic warnings about the exhaustion of the world's oil reserves.

And for the traders, the race for oil meant a new era of riches. Growing Chinese demand required a drastic increase in China's imports, and that meant that more commodities needed to be shipped around the world. Between 2000 and 2008, global trade in oil increased by 27.2%. That was more than twice the rate of oil demand growth over the same period.[18] That, in turn, meant more business for the traders, whose core business was shipping commodities internationally.

Soaring prices also transformed the way the commodity traders made money. It was a time when pure and simple speculation worked: the market was clearly going up. Unlike the 1970s, it was now possible to bet on the price of oil on the futures markets, and many did. From 2001 until 2008, the average annual price for Brent crude was higher every year – the longest streak of yearly price increases in the history of the petroleum industry, going back to 1861.[19]

But speculation was not the only way that rising prices made the trading business more profitable. In some cases, long-term contracts that the traders had signed years earlier suddenly became enormously profitable. Glencore, for example, was able to buy alumina from

Jamaica at a fixed price under its long-term contract, which had been renegotiated in 2000. When prices soared, the commodity trader was paying less than half the market price for its alumina.[20]

Even commodity deals agreed at market prices became highly profitable in the boom market. That's because most physical commodity contracts include some tolerance on quantity, allowing the trader to buy or supply an agreed tonnage plus or minus a few percent. In normal times, this allowance, known in the industry's jargon as 'optionality', meant that a trader wouldn't be in breach of its contract if a shipment was found to be slightly larger or smaller than planned – an understandable possibility in a large-scale logistics business.

But as prices soared, that optionality became hugely valuable: a trader could buy a little bit more from its supplier at a time when there was lots of demand, or deliver a little less to a buyer at a time when others were willing to pay a premium to get their hands on the commodities they needed. Or, the trader could benefit from its optionality on both sides.

Imagine that a trader has a long-term contract with both an oil producer and an oil consumer for, say, one million barrels per month. The price for each contract is the same: the average price of the month. Each contract allows the trader a 10% volume tolerance. If oil prices were entirely flat, the trader would surely lose money: he would be selling the oil for the same price that he bought it, and so making a profit of zero, before accounting for his shipping and finance costs.

But in a rising oil market, the trader can exploit the optionality in the contract to make a profit. From the producer he will maximise the volume under his contract, securing 1.1 million barrels – 10% more than normal. For the consumer, he will minimise the volume under his contract, supplying just 900,000 barrels, or 10% less than normal. The difference – 200,000 barrels – can then be re-sold. The market is rising, so by the end of the month the price will be higher than the monthly average, and the trader will re-sell his 200,000 barrels at a profit.

Until the 2000s, few commodity suppliers and buyers understood the value of such optionality to the traders – after all, in the era before the supercycle caused prices to soar, it hadn't been nearly as valuable. But, when prices took off, that optionality became a licence to print money. Ton Klomp, who helped build one of the upstart traders of the supercycle era, Mercuria, after a career trading oil at Cargill and Goldman Sachs, remembers that 'in the old days' the traders could take advantage of contracts with wide tolerances: the standard contract for naphtha, a refined product used in the petrochemical industry, allowed the delivery of anything from 17,000 to 25,000 tonnes, at the trader's option. 'Jesus Christ. That's a lot of free money if you know how to optimise those tolerances,' he says.[21]

The boom-time mood, in which buyers were more worried about running out of raw materials than they were about haggling over the last few cents on the price, also helped. The world was crying out for commodities. Oil refineries, facing strong demand for gasoline, diesel, and other products, were willing to pay a premium to secure cargoes of crude oil and so keep meeting demand from their customers.

For the traders, it was a call to action. They set off on a hunt for resources that encompassed every country on the globe. They went to new oil nations, such as Chad and Sudan, which were exporting crude for the first time, and to established producers about to pump more, such as Russia, Azerbaijan, Kazakhstan, Yemen, Brazil, Equatorial Guinea and Angola.

It was a process that drew the traders even closer into the world of oligarchs, despots and dictators, who were getting rich on the commodity boom. They forged alliances, and sometimes joint ventures, with powerful local individuals. Some traders broke the law, as the oil-for-food scandal demonstrated. Others navigated all kinds of dicey situations: wars, coups d'état, corrupt governments and chaotic nations. All in the quest to secure natural resources.

'The trickier the country, the more upside there is,' explains Bob Finch, the former Vitol executive who was one of the company's leading figures during the 2000s.[22]

Anyone who had access to commodities was suddenly in a privileged position thanks to the Chinese demand boom. Companies that had previously been bit players in the global commodity markets suddenly became stars handling tens of billions of dollars' worth of resources a year. They weren't just profitable businesses – in a world where commodities were scarce and China's appetite seemingly insatiable, the traders' ability to keep the flow of commodities moving made them a crucial cog in the global economy.

And the combination of big money and strategic significance gave the traders an important political role in many parts of the world. Their ability to keep the money flowing into the coffers of oil-rich potentates made them powerful allies. It was something Saddam had understood instinctively, prompting him to start demanding kickbacks for Iraq's oil sales. And it was just as true in Russia, where an increasingly muscular Kremlin needed friendly traders to ensure its oil would continue to be sold, even in moments of political tension.

Out of this reactive mix of a world desperate for oil and petrostates hungry for cash sprang two companies that leapt into the big league of global oil trading in just a few years. In many ways, they would be emblematic of the oil market of the 2000s – opportunistic, well-connected, linking rapidly-growing oil producers in emerging markets with China's insatiable demand. They were Mercuria and Gunvor.

The two companies had emerged from the free-for-all of the former Soviet Union in the 1990s at around the same time that David Reuben was turning Trans-World into the world's largest aluminium trader. But for Mercuria and Gunvor, the real big time

was to come not in the 1990s but in the 2000s, when they became critical outlets for Russia's oil, helping to keep the billions of dollars flowing into the Kremlin's coffers that gave a young president Putin the confidence to become more assertive on the world stage.

Mercuria's origins dated back to the days after the break-up of the Soviet Union, when two Soviet-born jobbing musicians named Wiaczeslaw Smolokowski and Gregory Jankilevitsch got a break trading oil. In the 1980s, the pair had made a living playing guitar and piano at gigs in restaurants and clubs in Moscow. They had emigrated to Poland, and were running a small business buying and selling computer equipment and other white goods, when one of their customers in a remote Siberian oil town made them a suggestion: would they like to get into oil trading? He had secured an export licence, a rare and precious thing in the early 1990s. The two traders demurred. They didn't know the first thing about oil. But he was persuasive. 'He said we would learn together,' Jankilevitsch later recalled.[23]

And so, they graduated from refrigerators to tankers of oil. Back in Poland, they struck a deal with a struggling refinery, and soon became the dominant shippers of Russian oil via the Soviet-built Druzhba pipeline into Poland. By the mid-1990s their company, J&S, accounted for 60% of the country's crude supply.

How did the two émigrés manage to establish such a dominant position in the 'wild east' of Russia in the 1990s? 'We meet the requirements of both [producers and consumers]; we take risks,' Jankilevitsch said. 'We have never let our partners in Poland down.'[24]

Others were less enthusiastic about their role. When some of Russia's most powerful oligarchs sued a couple of their own employees, who had been responsible for selling their oil, for taking bribes, the lawsuit uncovered a $1.7 million payment from J&S. The judge described the payment as one of several 'secret commissions or bribes' the employees had received.[25] (Asked about this, Jankilevitsch and Smolokowski note that no claim of impropriety was ever directed

against them, and that they would have 'vigorously defended' any that had been raised.)[26]

Around the same time that Jankilevitsch and Smolokowski were beginning to trade in computers and refrigerators, two other men were also getting their start in trading Russian oil. In St Petersburg, then still called Leningrad, a smooth, confident young electro-mechanical engineer named Gennady Timchenko got a call from a friend asking him if he'd like to go into oil trading. Timchenko jumped at the opportunity.[27]

In the chaotic world of Russian oil trading in the 1990s, Timchenko found himself competing with Torbjörn Törnqvist, a Swede who had set up a new company with the idea of exporting Russian refined products via Estonia. The pair started as rivals, but would end up working together in one of the most successful partnerships in oil trading.

These were dangerous times for anyone doing business in the Russian commodities sector. The aluminium wars became famous, but oil traders were also at risk. One day Törnqvist's business partner vanished, presumed murdered. Törnqvist feared for his own safety. 'Since I was very close to him, I decided to stay out of Russia for at least a year,' he says. 'I was very cautious for a while.'[28]

Törnqvist's fuel oil exports through the Estonian terminal brought him into competition with Timchenko and his partners. Rather than compete in Estonia until one of the two went out of business, the pair decided to go into business together. Timchenko and his partners joined forces with Törnqvist and his partners to create a company – named Gunvor Energy. (Gunvor is a Swedish girl's name meaning 'Vigilant in War' in Old Norse.)[29]

When some of the partners at Gunvor Energy fell out with Törnqvist, Timchenko sided with the Swede over his old colleagues and ejected them. The two men created a new company together in 2000: Gunvor International.

<div align="center">★</div>

Until this point the business of these new oil traders had been profitable, but limited in scope. Their profits measured in the tens rather than the hundreds of millions of dollars each year.

But the really big time was just around the corner. The Chinese economy was booming, providing the opportunity for spectacular profits to anyone with access to oil supplies. It was in this environment that Saddam Hussein had succeeded in persuading international oil traders to pay surcharges under the oil-for-food scheme. Mercuria and Gunvor got lucky: they were in the right place, at the right time, and with the right connections to get access to lots of oil.

Russian oil production was booming too. After a collapse in production in the early 1990s as the Russian economy crashed with the fall of Communism, the country's oil sector recovered just as fast in the early 2000s. By now, the ownership of the industry was well established in the hands of a few powerful oligarchs, and they now turned their focus from protecting their shareholdings to improving their companies. From 1999 to 2005, Russian oil production expanded by more than 50%.[30] Exports surged.

The traders, as the link between the Russian producers and the international financial system, took on a new political significance for the Russian state. The new Russian president, Vladimir Putin, recognised that oil meant money and power. As the Kremlin sought to strengthen its control of the oil sector, Mercuria and Gunvor opened new doors for Russia's oil sales, in different ways helping to maintain the flow of dollars to the Russian state.

For Mercuria, that meant pioneering the trade in oil between two of the most important geopolitical forces of the new century: Moscow and Beijing. As Russian oil production surged in the early 2000s, J&S had started buying more crude than it could sell in Poland. And so the company started exporting, taking oil from Siberia into Poland and to the port of Gdansk on the Baltic Sea coast, and from there, by tanker, to the world.

Jankilevitsch and Smolokowski understood that they wouldn't be able to build an international oil trading business alone, however. So

they got in touch with Marco Dunand and Daniel Jaeggi, a pair of traders with a reputation for matching trading smarts with ruthless ambition. The pair had studied together at the University of Geneva, and gone on to work together at a string of leading trading houses.

In 2004, Jaeggi and Dunand struck a deal with J&S. A new holding company for the J&S Group would be created in Cyprus, called J&S Holding. Jankilevitsch and Smolokowski reduced their stake to 62%, Dunand and Jaeggi got 15% each, while Vadim Linetskiy and Pavel Pojdl, two members of the J&S team, got 7% and 1%, respectively.[31]

Dunand says he and Jaeggi invested 'pretty much all the money' they had to acquire their shares in the company. But they also got a substantial loan from Jankilevitsch and Smolokowski, who agreed that it could be paid back with the future profits of the company. With an initial capitalisation of $250 million, Dunand and Jaeggi's stake in the company was worth $75 million. Under the deal, Dunand and Jaeggi would have full authority to run the company, and Jankilevitsch and Smolokowski would gradually reduce their stake over time. 'They gave us the key and they moved on,' says Dunand.[32]

It turned out to be a smart decision. Dunand had long been a believer that Chinese growth would revolutionise the oil market. Soon, the company was shipping Russian oil, via Gdansk in Poland, to China. The trade flow would grow in importance over the years as other traders got involved, to the point that today Russia is among the largest suppliers of oil to China.

The company grew at an astonishing rate. In 2009, the company's net profit hit a record $454 million.[33] By now the company had changed its name to Mercuria, but Jankilevitsch and Smolokowski remained significant shareholders.[34] They would appear at company parties and – with Jankilevitsch on guitar and Smolokowski on piano – blast out a few rock classics for the assembled Mercuria traders.

Their ability to connect Russian oil supply with Chinese demand at the moment the market was booming had made them all rich.

Between 2007 and 2018, Mercuria had cumulative profits, after tax, of $3.9 billion. And as the original partners reduced their stake, Beijing invested in the company, with the state-owned China National Chemical Corporation buying a minority stake in Mercuria.

If Mercuria had shown the money to be made in bringing Russian oil to China, then its main rival, Gunvor, revealed another way to get ahead: political connections. Timchenko and Törnqvist had long been cultivating relationships with important people in Russian politics and business. But one of those relationships would do more than any other to shape the future of the company, as Vladimir Putin ascended to the Russian presidency on 31 December 1999.

Timchenko and his partners had first dealt with Putin in the early 1990s, when he was in charge of foreign economic relations for the city of St Petersburg. By the end of the decade, Putin was poised to become president, and Timchenko was an established oil trader who had just started working under the name Gunvor. They stayed in touch: in 1998, Timchenko and others sponsored a judo club and made Putin – for whom judo had been a passion since childhood – the honorary chairman.

For many years Timchenko bristled at any suggestion that he and Putin were friends. All the same, by 2014, the Russian president was happy to describe Timchenko as one of 'my close acquaintances – my friends'.[35] Timchenko, in turn, revealed that his pet dog was the daughter of Putin's own Labrador, a gift from the Russian president in 2004.[36]

And it was after Putin became president that Timchenko and Gunvor had their greatest success. After Russia's chaotic 1990s, Putin promised order, stability and strong leadership. Like many ordinary Russians, he was resentful of the oligarch class and the way they had taken advantage of a weak Russian state under the presidency of

Boris Yeltsin, who ruled from 1991 to 1999, to grab the country's resources at knock-down prices.

When he first came to power at the turn of the millennium, Putin had offered the oligarchs an implicit deal: he would not seek to reverse the privatisation deals through which they had acquired their fortunes, but they in turn should stay out of politics. But tension was never far below the surface. Mikhail Khodorkovsky, the owner of oil company Yukos, was the oligarch who more than any other tested the boundaries of Putin's stance.

By 2003, Khodorkovsky, a bookish forty-year-old, had become Russia's number one oligarch and the wealthiest man in the country. Bright and ambitious, he had started a cooperative in the late 1980s as private enterprise was just becoming possible in the Soviet Union. Soon his cooperative, Menatep, had morphed into a bank. And it rapidly became one of the largest and most aggressive private companies in the country, with one of the best networks of government contacts. When the weak Yeltsin government launched an ill-fated loans-for-shares scheme, Khodorkovsky had snapped up a controlling stake in oil company Yukos for just $309 million.[37] A decade later, he had turned it into the darling of the Russian oil industry with a market value of more than $20 billion.

But Yukos was also a poster child for everything that infuriated Putin and his allies about the oligarchs of the 1990s. It was one of the most aggressive users of offshore companies and low-tax special economic zones to reduce its tax bill. It was among the most brazen corporate lobbyists in Russia.

And Khodorkovsky became increasingly bold – even provocative. He challenged Putin over corruption in a televised meeting at the Kremlin. He said that he would retire from Yukos in 2007 – the year before Putin would be required by the constitution to step down – and allowed speculation to build that he might be interested in a move into politics.[38] And he started talks with Chevron and Exxon-Mobil to sell a stake in Yukos. He even came close to a deal to merge

Yukos with Chevron that would have created the world's largest oil company.[39]

On 25 October 2003, Khodorkovsky was flying across Siberia when his plane stopped to refuel, only to find it surrounded by special forces. Russia's richest oligarch was under arrest. He would spend the next decade in a prison camp on charges of fraud, tax evasion and embezzlement. A year later, with the tax claims against Yukos rising, Russia's state oil company Rosneft took control of its main asset – a massive oil production business in the heart of Siberia.

It was one of the defining moments of Putin's presidency: an assertion that no oligarch could hope to be more powerful than the Kremlin, that Russia's businesspeople would enrich themselves only so far as it pleased the president, and that Russia's natural resources ultimately belonged to the state. The event became a lightning rod for critics of Putin at home and internationally, and has been the focus of a protracted, multibillion-dollar legal battle between the Russian government and the former Yukos shareholders.

For Gunvor, it was the ticket to the big time of oil trading.

As Yukos collapsed under the pressure of the Kremlin campaign against it, Gunvor was on hand to help the Russian state keep the oil flowing. The trading house, little known until then, suddenly became an essential cog as Putin sought to re-establish the state's dominance over the Russian oil industry.

For years, Gunvor has guarded its silence about the Yukos affair. Timchenko, asked about it in one of his few interviews, said: 'I don't want to comment on my views about a company with which I had no connection whatsoever.'[40]

But now Törnqvist is willing to talk both about the downfall of Khodorkovsky, and about the role that Gunvor played in helping the Russian state manage the aftermath.

Törnqvist says he knew in advance that Yukos would be taken down. 'I didn't know exactly what's going to happen, I was told something would happen,' he says. He won't say who gave him

the tip. 'I was just told that you should be ready to deal in bigger volumes.'[41]

He says that Khodorkovsky made two mistakes. The first was to ignore Putin's warning not to meddle in Russian politics. The second was his talks to sell Yukos to a US oil company. 'You can imagine the anger. These guys got this for free. They didn't pay for this: they got it. And they're now going to sell it to an American multinational?'

'That was the moment they decided to take him down,' Törnqvist says. 'They're very open about it ... If we allow this to happen, Russia will fall apart. Russia's riches will end up everywhere, and the Russian people will get nothing.'

After Yukos's oilfields were seized, Gunvor was on hand to help sell the oil. The trading house until that point had traded little crude, focusing instead on refined products. Now Törnqvist was suddenly being asked if he could handle huge volumes every month. 'I understood this was the chance of a lifetime,' he said. 'I called my financial officer: I don't know how you do it but you've got to call BNP Paribas and find a credit line *now*.'

Törnqvist says that he was not the only trader who received a call to action. But Gunvor soon became the largest, handling, by Törnqvist's estimate, 60% of Rosneft's seaborne exports at its peak. Other deals followed. From a bit player, Gunvor suddenly became a key part of the global oil market. By 2008, when oil prices skyrocketed above $100 a barrel and control of any oil was a ticket to success, the company was the single largest trader of Russian oil, handling at one point 30% of the country's seaborne exports.[42]

As Vladimir Putin grew bolder at home and abroad, Gunvor was one of the key companies working behind the scenes to keep Russian oil flowing to the world. And Gunvor reaped enormous profits from this work. For years the company's early profits were a matter of speculation and conjecture. But now, Gunvor says that between 2005 and 2009 it averaged annual profits of $347 million.[43] Its equity value rose from $254 million in 2005 to almost $1.4 billion in 2009

– astonishingly rapid growth, even by the standards of the supercycle-era commodity trading industry.

How did a previously unknown trading house make so much money? Were Gunvor's profits made at the expense of the Russian state oil company? 'Rosneft was all of a sudden owning the biggest oil company there ... They had no organisation, they had nothing. Clearly as a trader that's where you want to be. So do you take advantage of the situation? Of course you do,' Törnqvist says. 'That's how traders are. Trying to be there, to take advantage of the situation. So I don't say we took advantage of Rosneft. Yes, we clearly saw the opportunity for us during that situation.'

But questions remained over how Gunvor had risen to such a position of prominence in the Russian oil sector – a key lever of the state's power – so rapidly. Timchenko himself repeatedly denied that he had received any special favours thanks to his relationship with the Russian president.[44] But suspicions about the connection would haunt Gunvor for years to come – and, ultimately, force a dramatic reckoning.

Once again, Russia and the rest of the former Soviet Union had delivered great riches to the commodity traders. Unlike the 1990s, though, this time the profits weren't thanks to the chaos of a collapsing system, but to the region's ability to boost production just as China and other emerging markets were clamouring for oil. Mercuria and Gunvor were the two most obvious winners. By the end of that period, they were comfortably established as the world's fourth- and fifth-largest independent oil traders. In the ten years to 2018, the two companies' combined profits totalled about $6.6 billion – most of it accruing to just six individuals: Jankilevitsch, Smolokowski, Dunand, Jaeggi, Timchenko and Törnqvist.[45]

Their tale, like the oil-for-food programme, was a demonstration of how the soaring oil price had redrawn the contours of the global economy, empowering oil-rich authoritarian leaders and endowing the traders with an influential role funnelling their oil to the market.

But as the commodity boom accelerated, even the natural riches of the former Soviet Union weren't enough to satisfy the market appetite for resources. The commodity traders turned to a new frontier, a continent that was one of the world's richest sources of natural resources, but also one of its most difficult regions to operate in: Africa.

TEN

DESTINATION AFRICA

By seven in the morning, the road out of Kolwezi is already gridlocked.

Everywhere along the way out of town can be found reminders that, on this dusty plateau in the heart of Africa, the mining industry is king. Rows of rudimentary hammers and picks are laid out for sale at the roadside, all to equip the men and boys in muddy clothes who trudge each day to the edge of town and start digging by hand.

The road passes by the stately buildings erected by the Belgian colonialists who first started mining in this region in 1906. And then it passes the fruits of the more modern mining industry: casinos and restaurants, all with signs in English, French and Chinese, to help the fortune-seekers who have been drawn to Kolwezi while away the long evenings and lighten the wads of dollars in their pockets.

No one here drives at night, when the roads are roamed by gangs on motorbikes. And as soon as dawn breaks, everyone has somewhere to be: the trucks loaded with metal and ore, the tankers carrying fuel or acid, the jeeps ferrying foreign executives and consultants.

Out of Kolwezi, the road crosses the Lualaba, the biggest tributary of the mighty Congo River. And then, finally, the destination becomes

clear: a hill rising up in the distance, to which many of the trucks are headed.

This is Mutanda, in the Democratic Republic of Congo, one of the world's richest mineral deposits. Inside the hill there are three enormous pits, each 150 metres deep, where trucks loaded with copper ore snake up and down like ants on an anthill.

The owner of this warren of activity in one of the world's most remote and difficult mining frontiers is none other than Glencore.

Mutanda is a symbol of the scramble for Africa that took hold of the resources industry in the 2000s. As the supercycle gathered pace, miners, oil companies and traders alike could no longer ignore Africa's riches. For decades, the bulk of the continent had been neglected by big Western companies as too remote, too underdeveloped and too corrupt. Now they were falling over one another to invest.

At the vanguard were commodity traders such as Glencore. They bought African commodities, they invested in mines like Mutanda, and they helped to finance African governments. In the process, they propped up many unpopular and authoritarian leaders. And they forged new connections between African commodities and Chinese factories, and between African kleptocrats and bank accounts in London and Switzerland.

For Glencore, emerging from the tussle for resources as the owner of Mutanda, the race for Africa was a blessing but also a curse. It would be the foundation of much of the trading house's wealth, but also the source of the darkest cloud over its future.

Most African countries export commodities, and little else.[1] And that means Africa's economic fortunes have risen and fallen with the commodity markets. The 1950s and 1960s, when many African nations won independence from European colonial powers, were a golden era for the continent. After the Second World War, Europe and Asia

needed commodities for the reconstruction. Traders travelled to Africa for copper and other metals.

But soon Africa's reliance on natural resources became a liability. Low commodity prices, mismanagement, corruption, wars and the legacy of colonialism hampered the continent's development throughout much of the 1980s and 1990s. By 2001, the size of the economy of sub-Saharan Africa was no larger than it had been in 1981.[2]

For the most part, the continent's commodity production also fell. Low prices discouraged investment; ageing infrastructure wasn't replaced; wars ravaged mines, oilfields and farms; and corruption and dictatorship scared off foreign financiers. The country that is now called the Democratic Republic of Congo had been one of the world's largest copper producers, accounting for more than 7% of global supply in 1975. Twenty years later, its output had plunged to just 0.3% of the world total.[3] Zimbabwe went from a breadbasket to a basket case. Nigeria pumped less oil in 1999, when democracy returned after decades of kleptocratic military rule, than it had done in 1979.[4] Africa was, in the eyes of many foreign investors, 'the hopeless continent'.[5]

The commodity traders made money in Africa even during the bad years: this was the period in which Marc Rich and John Deuss defied the UN embargo to supply South Africa with fuel. But, generally, the trading houses focused their attention elsewhere. With commodity production falling through the 1980s and the 1990s, there wasn't much to buy in Africa. And with economic activity falling, there wasn't much to sell to Africa, either.

Then, starting in the early 2000s, the Chinese-led boom upended commodity markets, and the fortunes of the continent changed dramatically. The traditional sources of commodity supply, such as the US, Canada, Australia, the Middle East and Latin America, were no longer sufficient. If the world needed more natural resources, the industry would need to travel further afield. The answer was Africa.

The commodity traders rushed in, not just trading with African countries but investing in mines, oilfields and agricultural processing.

For the African economy, commodities were once again a blessing. In a decade of booming prices from 2001 to 2011, the economy of sub-Saharan Africa quadrupled in size.[6]

The flow of dollars from the sale of commodities enriched a generation of African leaders, entrenching established political elites even when they were blatantly corrupt or widely unpopular. The commodity traders became a key link in a new corner of the international financial system, helping African governments and politicians access the pools of money in the West. Many were soon keeping their own money in the West, too, finalising the details of a commodity deal during the day before spending the evenings in the fleshpots of London or Paris.

In one example that is now public thanks to a US anti-corruption case, from 2011 to 2015 the Nigerian petroleum minister Diezani Alison-Madueke allegedly steered oil contracts to two local businessmen, who rewarded her by funding a lavish lifestyle for her and her family. They bought her gifts including several properties in and around London, and fitted the houses out with millions of dollars' worth of furniture and artwork. The two local businessmen who received the oil contracts were not interested in trading, however. Their companies simply resold the oil to commodity traders – foremost among them Glencore, which bought $800 million of it. While the US hasn't suggested that Glencore did anything wrong, it's clear that, without the involvement of a commodity trader, there wouldn't have been the money to fund the alleged corruption.[7]

The traders also became an important conduit for a new dynamic in the global economy: the rise of trade flows between the emerging market nations that bypassed the West altogether. The boom had started in China, so it was no surprise that much of the commodities that the traders bought in Africa ended up there. Soon, China would be following the trail of the commodity traders to make its own investments directly in Africa, the start of a new phase of Chinese investment that would make Beijing one of the most important actors across much of the African continent.

For the traders themselves, doing business in Africa posed challenges. Dealing on the continent often meant crossing paths with brutal dictators, corrupt politicians, and rapacious local tycoons. In many cases, the commodity traders' solution was to outsource their relationships with local kingpins to a motley crew of agents, fixers and consultants. These were men like Ely Calil, one of the most prominent fixers in the region, whose contact book stretched from Nigeria to Congo, Senegal to Chad.

In some cases, the role of such outside consultants or fixers was extremely simple: putting a layer of deniability between the commodity traders and the bribes and other payments that needed to be made to keep the oil and metals flowing. 'There's no way to do business in the Third World without enriching government leaders,' said Calil. He explained how the practice of greasing the palms of African potentates evolved: 'You used to give a dictator a suitcase of dollars; now you give a tip on your stock shares, or buy a housing estate from his uncle or mother for ten times its worth.'[8]

In other cases, the job of the fixers was more mundane: handling cumbersome logistics in African countries where they had more experience than the commodity traders they were working for, or marshalling a superior network of connections to deal with bureaucratic paperwork and roadblocks.

For Glencore in the Democratic Republic of Congo, this role was fulfilled by an Israeli diamond merchant who had struck up an unlikely friendship with the country's youthful president. His name was Dan Gertler.

About two-thirds the size of Western Europe, the Democratic Republic of Congo contains one of the world's richest tracts of minerals. Known previously as Zaire and the Belgian Congo, it has been one of the most important suppliers of metals to the global market for a century.

Congolese uranium from a mine about eighty kilometres from Mutanda was used in the Manhattan project to produce the first atomic bomb, dropped over Hiroshima in the last days of the Second World War. And Congolese copper was later used to rebuild Japan and Europe. The country is also rich in the minerals that fuel modern life: cobalt, used in high-performance batteries, such as the ones in electric cars, and tantalum, used in mobile phones.

But in 1965, Mobutu Sese Seko came to power. A kleptocratic dictator who would rule the country for more than three decades, Mobutu wasted little time in nationalising the mining industry. Congo's mineral riches paid for Mobutu's extravagant whims, such as turning the village where he was born into a vulgar pleasure palace with a runway hacked out of the forest long enough to land Concorde. As metal prices dropped in the 1980s and 1990s, Congo's mining industry fell into disrepair. With plentiful supplies elsewhere, international miners and commodity traders simply retreated to places where doing business was easier.

Dan Gertler arrived in the Democratic Republic of Congo for the first time in 1997, still in his early twenties, just as Mobutu was deposed in a bloody conflict.[9] Gertler was a young diamond merchant, the scion of a wealthy family of gem dealers, whose grandfather founded the Israel Diamond Exchange. Laurent-Désiré Kabila, the new president of DRC, was fighting a brutal war to consolidate his power, and was desperate for money.[10] Gertler saw an opportunity. In August 2000, his company agreed to pay $20 million to the Congolese government, in exchange receiving a monopoly on diamond sales from the country.[11]

His influence increased when, in 2001, Laurent-Désiré Kabila was assassinated by one of his own bodyguards, and his son, Joseph Kabila, became president. Gertler soon became the confidant of the young president. The two men were the same age. Gertler lived in Israel, but flew every week into Congo.

And he was ready to help in both politics and business. In the mid-2000s, he acted as a go-between for Kabila and US National

Security Adviser Condoleezza Rice when the new Congolese president was still finding his feet on the international stage.[12] Ultimately, Kabila was invited by George W. Bush to the White House in 2007.[13] And Gertler's office in Tel Aviv, which doubles as a Congolese diplomatic post, displays photos of Gertler and Kabila together in their twenties, alongside aerial shots of the copper and cobalt mine he built with Glencore.[14]

It was not just Kabila with whom Gertler cultivated a relationship. He also became close to Augustin Katumba Mwanke, the former governor of the mineral-rich province of Katanga, where the Mutanda mine is located, and Kabila's *éminence grise*. American diplomats, who described Katumba as a 'shady, even nefarious figure', believed that he managed much of Kabila's personal fortune.[15] The tycoon took Katumba and his wife on a yacht trip on the Red Sea and treated them to a performance by the spoon-bending illusionist Uri Geller, according to Katumba's self-published autobiography. In the book, he also recounted how Gertler had saved his life by hiring doctors to treat him. 'From then on, his ideas also became mine,' Katumba wrote. 'Dan, my friend, my twin brother despite everything that appears to make us different, I am proud to be the brother you never had.'[16]

As the Chinese economic boom increased demand for Congolese metals, Gertler was perfectly positioned. He became the gatekeeper to Congo's mineral riches just as the world began to experience a commodity shortage of a kind unseen since the 1970s. He branched out beyond diamonds to start investing in other commodities, such as copper, cobalt and oil. He boasted in an email to one business partner in 2008 that Congo was 'in the making and I am shaping it – like no one else'.

In the same email, he bragged about his own power: 'I facilitated your entry at an attractive time / price knowing that you see there is a bigger picture in all of this. What this bigger picture exactly looks like, is yet to be determined, but it is your partner who is holding the pen – I just need flexibility on the drawing board to create full value for our partnership'.[17]

Gertler got the opportunity to redraw the landscape of the Congolese mining industry in the run-up to the Congolese presidential elections of November 2011. Kabila was short of money, and his right-hand man Katumba worked feverishly to secure a victory.[18] Most of all, he needed to raise money. The Congolese state started selling off stakes in key mineral resources, in a series of deals that only came to light later. The buyers were offshore vehicles that often turned out to be connected to Katumba's 'twin brother', Gertler. Between 2010 and 2012, the Africa Progress Panel, a group led by former UN Secretary General Kofi Annan, estimated that the Congolese state earned $1.36 billion less than it should have done by selling stakes in mines at knock-down prices.[19]

Gertler has rejected the suggestion that the deals were done at below-market prices, arguing instead that he should get a Nobel prize for what he's done in Congo.[20] 'We started to invest in the early days – when nobody else wanted to invest, when the country was at war, when the copper and cobalt prices were at the bottom,' he has said.[21]

The US government disagrees. In 2017, it imposed sanctions on Gertler, saying he used his close friendship with Kabila 'to act as a middleman for mining asset sales in the Democratic Republic of Congo, requiring some multinational companies to go through' him to seal deals. The result, Washington said, was 'hundreds of millions of dollars' worth of opaque and corrupt mining and oil deals'.[22] Gertler has rejected those allegations, and a spokesman for him says that all of his dealings in Congo were lawful and honest, and points out that nothing has been proven against him in a court of law.[23]

The sanctions against Gertler were more than a decade away when Ivan Glasenberg ventured into Congo, hunting for copper. The Glencore boss had been drawn to the country seeking riches, but, in the end, his association with Gertler would become his company's greatest headache.

For years, the Mutanda hill had attracted hundreds of local Congolese people, who came to pick at its streaks of greenish rock with little more than their bare hands. They were not organised into any company; they had no safety equipment; no one regulated them. They would be known, in the jargon of modern-day NGOs, as 'artisanal miners'. Their tools were primitive: hammers, chisels, picks and shovels. Still, they burrowed long holes inside the mountain, as far as seventy metres deep, to reach the richest and most prized veins of ore.[24] It was dangerous work; every year, dozens died in similar operations across the country. But, in one of the world's poorest countries, the rewards were great. In a day, a digger could make more money than a schoolteacher made in a week. For the artisanal miners, the copper and cobalt ore was the only source of income in an otherwise bleak economy.

They were connected to the global market not by the big commodity traders, but by small-scale Indian, Lebanese and later Chinese middlemen. Every evening, the diggers would sell their day's production to the middlemen, who gathered at a hectic village on the outskirts of Kolwezi. In the early 2000s, one of the most successful merchants was a Lebanese man called Alex Hayssam Hamze. His traders bought bags of the green ore – called malachite – that came from Mutanda, piled them high on trucks and drove them along a bumpy road to the nearest smelter, where they could be transformed into pure copper metal.

One such smelter was part-owned by Glencore, about 500 kilometres away and across the border in Zambia. Glencore fed the smelter with ore from its own Zambian mines and any other material it could buy cheaply on the market. Zambia's mines produced excellent ores. But when the Glencore traders saw the ore that was coming over the border from Congo, they couldn't believe their eyes.

The purity of the Congolese ore was off the charts, not just for copper ore, but also for cobalt. The world's average ore grade for a copper mine is about 0.6%. In Chile and Peru, any mine with an average ore grade of more than 1% would be seen as exceptionally

good. In its early days, Mutanda had an average copper ore grade north of 3%.[25]

The Glencore traders asked Hamze to show them the source of this spectacularly rich malachite ore.[26] So, in 2006, Glasenberg travelled first to Kolwezi and eventually to the Mutanda hill. Glasenberg, who had become CEO in large part thanks to his buying spree of coal mines a decade earlier, believed that Glencore's future growth depended on combining its traditional trading smarts with a mining empire. He was convinced that Congo was the opportunity he had been waiting for.

Hamze had evolved from being purely a middleman into a mine investor, winning control of the land around the Mutanda hill. His timing was impeccable: he created Mutanda Mining in May 2001, only a few weeks before Mick Davis wrote his memo arguing that commodity prices could only go up. By the time that Glasenberg reached Mutanda, Hamze needed a partner with the financial strength and expertise to develop the mine. Glasenberg didn't lose any time: in mid-2007, he bought a 40% stake in Mutanda and, with it, operational control, at a valuation of about $150 million.[27]

It was at about this time that Glasenberg first came across Gertler, when the two men became major shareholders in another mine near Kolwezi. It was the beginning of a relationship that would transform Congo's economy.

Until then, Gertler's sway over Congo's mining sector had not been so dominant. He had faced competition from other power-brokers and businessmen. But Gertler and Glencore together were a formidable combination: the commodity trader brought financial firepower and market sway; Gertler opened the doors to Congo's corridors of power.

In 2011, just as Katumba was working to fund the Congolese president's re-election campaign, Gertler joined Glencore as a shareholder in Mutanda. In March, one of his companies bought a 20% stake in the mine from Congo's state-owned mining company,

Gecamines. The price, just $120 million, looked unfathomably low.[28] Copper prices were sky high, and at almost exactly the same time, a mining consultant hired by Glencore valued the whole mine at almost $3.1 billion, suggesting that the true value of the 20% stake that Gertler had bought was $620 million.[29] Only a few months later, Glencore would increase its own stake in Mutanda at a valuation four times higher than Gertler had paid.[30]

Over the course of more than a decade, Gertler and Glencore were involved in more than a dozen transactions, worth over a billion dollars. Glencore bought stakes in mines from Gertler; it provided him with hundreds of millions of dollars in loans; and it paid him copper and cobalt royalties that had originally been meant for the Congolese state. In turn, Gertler became Glencore's business partner, counsellor and fixer in Congo. For years, the trading house didn't have a representative in Kinshasa, the capital, relying instead on Gertler and his team to handle relations with the government.[31]

If Glencore had any doubts about going into business with Gertler, it didn't voice them. 'His involvement has helped to attract much-needed foreign investment to the DRC,' Glasenberg said in 2012.[32] But Gertler's reputation as a businessman involved in opaque deals in Congo was already well-established as Glencore did deal after deal with him.

When, in early 2008, another investor in the Congolese mining industry sought information about Gertler, the report it received from a due diligence company, disclosed in later legal filings, read like a cautionary tale. Gertler kept 'what can only be described as unsavory business associates', according to the report, which was prepared for Och-Ziff Capital Management, a multi-billion-dollar US hedge fund. Gertler, it added, was using 'his significant political influence' in Congo 'to facilitate acquisitions, settle disputes and frustrate competitors'.[33]

Och-Ziff eventually paid more than $400 million in September 2016 to settle a case with the US regulators involving, among other things, its deals with Gertler in Congo.[34] In the deferred prosecution

agreement with the hedge fund, the US government laid bare the influence of the tycoon, alleging that Gertler, together with others, paid more than $100 million in bribes to Congolese officials.[35]

In February 2017, a few months after the details of the Och-Ziff case became public, Gertler cashed in his chips. Glencore bought out his stakes in its two main mines in Congo. The price was a cool $960 million.[36]

The Congolese deals appeared to have been a coup for Glasenberg. He had seized on other big companies' hesitancy to invest in Congo and established a huge position there for Glencore, making the company a leading supplier of copper and cobalt, two metals used in electric cars and batteries whose future prospects looked bright. For Kabila, too, Glencore's bet on the Congo was a boon. The company led a wave of investment into the Congolese mining sector, and soon became one of the country's largest taxpayers.

Then, on 3 July 2018, the music stopped. Glencore announced that it had been subpoenaed by the US Department of Justice in a wide-ranging probe into corruption and money-laundering that included its dealings in Congo dating back to 2007 – the year it first invested in Mutanda, and the year it started dealing with Gertler. The company's share price tumbled.[37]

Glasenberg's African adventure was no longer a triumph of canny investment, but a stain on the Glencore chief's legacy.

Despite the dangers, the resource riches of Africa drew commodity traders of all stripes.

Trafigura, for example, moved beyond its early focus on Latin America and Eastern Europe and threw itself into the booming continent. In Angola, it partnered with a former army officer, General Leopoldino Fragoso do Nascimento, popularly known as 'General Dino'.

A close ally of Angolan President José Eduardo dos Santos, General Dino became a shareholder in two of the most important subsidiaries

of Trafigura – Puma Energy, which owns oil terminals and hundreds of fuel stations across Africa and Latin America, and DT Group, a joint venture focused largely on Angola.[38] Through DT Group, Trafigura and General Dino delivered a large chunk of Angola's fuel imports, generating profits of more than $500 million in the six years to 2018.[39]

For all that they liked to think of themselves as the wiliest investors on the planet, some of the commodity traders were driven to Africa by a motive familiar to anyone: the fear of missing out. 'Everyone was in Africa. So we've got to be in Africa,' Torbjörn Törnqvist, the Gunvor CEO, says of those days.[40] He later came to regret his foray into the continent.

Even Cargill, whose staid Midwestern origins made it relatively cautious by the standards of its industry, dived in. The venerable grain trader would seem an unlikely candidate to set itself up as an alternative to a country's central bank. But, in Zimbabwe, that's exactly what it did.

In the middle of 2003, Zimbabwe was in the throes of a financial and economic crisis. The supermarkets in Harare, the capital, were half empty. Inflation was spiralling out of control. The Zimbabwean central bank couldn't print new banknotes fast enough to keep up with the devaluations of the Zimbabwean dollar, creating a shortage of banknotes. Bank lines stretched several blocks and account holders occasionally resorted to violence.[41]

For Cargill, which had entered the cotton sector in Zimbabwe in 1996, this represented a serious headache. The commodity trader had built a large operation in Zimbabwe, with several ginneries to separate the cotton fibre from its seeds, buying stations across the country, and contracts with 20,000 farmers to buy their produce.[42] With Chinese demand for cotton surging, Cargill needed all the supplies it could get. But the banknote shortage meant it could no longer pay the small-scale farmers, who relied on cash, for their cotton.

Faced with the impossible task of buying cotton without banknotes, Cargill hit on a novel solution: it would simply print its own.

And so it asked a local company to print 7.5 billion Zimbabwean dollars, worth about $2.2 million, in 5,000- and 10,000-Zimabwean dollar bills. To guarantee the notes, it deposited funds at a local bank.[43]

This Monopoly money, which looked a bit like a cheque, carried the logo of Cargill Cotton and the signatures of two of its top local executives. It didn't matter that the bills didn't bear the signature of the governor of the Zimbabwean central bank, or the wildlife scenes that typically decorated Zimbabwean banknotes. They were soon being accepted alongside the country's official currency at shops across Harare.

In all but name, Cargill was acting as the country's bureau of engraving and printing and its central bank. It took out adverts in a local newspaper, instructing Zimbabweans that the banknotes 'should be treated as cash'.[44] It issued more banknotes in 2004, with denominations as high as 100,000 Zimbabwean dollars.

At the trading house's headquarters in the outskirts of Minneapolis, finance employees jokingly called the banknotes 'Staley bucks', after Cargill's chief executive at the time, Warren Staley. 'That was seen as more reliable than the Zimbabwean currency,' says David MacLennan, one of Staley's successors.[45]

The Monopoly money was no joke, however, for Cargill. The company told the Zimbabwean government, which had been largely unaware of Cargill's parallel printing press, that it was helping the country by alleviating the shortage of banknotes. But, for the trading house, issuing its own money was also a lucrative business. Cargill executives told US diplomats they were 'making a killing' printing their own money.

The reason was simple. Zimbabwe was suffering from hyperinflation, with consumer prices increasing at a rate of about 365% per year. With banknotes in short supply, the recipients of Cargill's Monopoly money tended to spend it rather than take it to the bank. When the notes finally trickled into the bank, their value had been eaten away by inflation, sharply reducing Cargill's actual payout in

dollar terms. 'That makes monopoly money even better business than cotton in this oddball economy,' the deputy chief of the American embassy in Harare wrote in a diplomatic cable.[46]

As the commodity supercycle matured, it created other opportunities for inventive commodity traders in Africa. The boom lifted economic growth across the continent, creating a broadening African middle class that could afford to buy cars, televisions and mobile phones. And that rewired Africa's role in the global commodities trade.

The business of buying commodities in Africa and exporting them to the world continued to draw commodity traders to the continent. Africa was still what it had always been – in the jargon of the traders, an 'origination' business. It was the origin of raw materials for the world markets: gold from South Africa, coffee from Ethiopia, crude oil from Nigeria, cocoa from Ivory Coast and copper from Zambia.

But, at the same time, a new business emerged – a 'destination' business. As economic activity across the continent increased, so did demand for commodities from Africa itself. The new demand redrew supply chains: Saudi fuel oil flowed into Kenyan power stations; wheat from Kansas arrived at flour mills in the Tanzanian port of Dar es Salaam; Peruvian copper turned up in Namibia, and Thai rice became a staple in Nigeria.[47]

One reason why so many African countries were an attractive destination business was that quality regulations were often far less strict than in the developed world, allowing the traders to supply products that would be considered substandard in the West. In Europe, oil traders can't legally sell diesel with more than 10 parts per million of sulphur, a cause of acid rain. In some African nations, however, they can sell the same diesel with sulphur content as high as 10,000 ppm without breaking local rules.[48] As such, commodity traders can buy cheap cargoes of low-quality refined products from unsophisticated refineries in Latin America and Russia, and ship them to Africa.

Or take copper. Much of the world's copper ore contains a small amount of arsenic, a toxic substance known for its use as a rat poison. Many governments have attempted to address the risks posed by arsenic in the copper industry with ever stricter regulations. The government of China, for example, has banned traders and smelters from importing copper ore with an arsenic content of more than 0.5%. But Namibia has no restrictions on the arsenic content of its copper ore imports, making it a useful destination for a savvy trader.

By the mid-2000s, Africa, in the traders' eyes, had become a place where the commodities that no one else wanted could be disposed of. It was not just the supplier of last resort, but also a buyer of last resort. And for the least scrupulous, it became a dumping ground.

The sun was setting over Abidjan in Ivory Coast on 19 August 2006, when a truck drove up to the entrance to a rubbish dump on the outskirts of the city. The site was a large, rancid, open-air dump called Akouédo, where residents of the commercial capital of the country had been throwing away their rubbish for decades. Each day, a battalion of the city's poorest residents would descend on the tip to pick over it for scraps that could be sold.

The truck paused by the small concrete hut that marked the entrance to the dump. It drove over a weighbridge to measure the size of its load – 36.2 tonnes – and continued to a corner of the site reserved for 'private' waste. The time was 7.06 p.m. Other trucks soon followed.[49]

The following morning, people living in the ramshackle villages near Akouédo awoke to a repulsive stench of rotten eggs.[50] Thousands soon started experiencing flu-like symptoms. The trucks had contained a toxic residue, so noxious that few companies in Europe would touch it.

The company responsible for shipping the cargo to Ivory Coast was Trafigura.

The resulting international outcry would see the commodity trader lambasted in the media and hauled in front of courts in London and Amsterdam. Ultimately the scandal cost the company more than $200 million and ruined its reputation.

The thousands of pages of inquiries and lawsuits that followed exposed the inner workings of the commodity trading industry to unprecedented scrutiny, reinforcing the public image of the traders as amoral cowboys. The scandal also showed how Africa had become a free-for-all for the least scrupulous commodity traders, a place where there were few rules and those that did exist could easily be circumvented.

Trafigura's foray into Africa had coincided with its ascent to the big leagues of commodity trading. When the boom began in the early 2000s, the company was still struggling. But as demand for commodities raced up, so did its profits. By 2005, Trafigura was earning nearly $300 million, and in 2006, it earned more than $500 million for the first time. The upstart company was establishing its place as a leading oil and metals trader alongside Vitol and Glencore.[51]

Even then, Trafigura still held on to the feeling of being the underdog of the trading industry, always ready to scrap for a few dollars of profit or jump at an unconventional deal. That was how the saga that ended at the waste dump in Abidjan had begun. In late 2005, the Mexican state oil company Pemex had offered to sell an unusual cargo of coker gasoline, a form of fuel that contains high quantities of sulphur and other impurities, at a knock-down price. Trafigura's traders could smell the chance to make a profit. In a series of emails that bounced around the company, from Houston to London and Geneva, the traders enthused about the money-making opportunity. 'This is as cheap as anyone can imagine and should make serious dollars,' wrote one.[52]

Trafigura sprang into action. Pemex was a desperate seller: it was out of storage space for coker gasoline and needed a buyer for a product that had very few markets. The commodity trader thought it could secure the cargo, in the words of one trader, 'bloody cheap'.[53]

If all went as planned, the company would make $7 million per cargo.[54] Not a fortune, but still a decent profit.

But there was a good reason why Pemex was selling the product cheap. Removing sulphur from coker gasoline, a necessary step before the fuel is usable, typically requires processing it in a specialised unit of an oil refinery – and that's expensive.

There is another way to remove the sulphur without paying a refinery to do the job. But it is a primitive process that is banned in much of the Western world. The reason is that this alternative process, called caustic washing, produces a noxious residue with a potent and revolting smell.

Yet this is what Trafigura was planning for the dirt-cheap cargoes it was buying from Pemex. It proved more difficult than anyone at Trafigura had thought. The traders first tried to find a port where they could unload the coker gasoline and perform the caustic washing. But, one by one, all the ports said no. One trader informed his colleagues that American and European terminals 'no longer allow the use of caustic soda washes since local environment agencies do not allow disposal of the toxic caustic after treatment'.[55]

Trafigura was starting to run out of options. If it could not carry out the caustic washing, the company would be forced to re-sell the coker gasoline to a refinery, which would most likely wipe out any potential profit. Claude Dauphin, the tireless Trafigura boss, instructed his team to be creative.[56] It took a few weeks, but the traders came up with an imaginative solution. Rather than shipping the coker gasoline to a terminal for treatment, they would perform the caustic washing on board the tanker that was transporting it. Then, they thought, they could ship the toxic residue to wherever they could find someone willing to take it.

Caustic washing is a nasty process. Not only does it release foul-smelling chemicals, but the caustic soda is highly corrosive. So the best solution, one of the traders thought, would be to find an oil tanker about to be scrapped and park it off the coast of West Africa. Was that possible? Could it be done on the cheap? 'That implies you

do not want insurance ... and you do not care if she sinks,' replied a shipping broker who acted on behalf of Trafigura.[57]

The sacrificial ship that the Trafigura traders found was the *Probo Koala*. The 182-metre-long tanker had seen better times: built in 1989, it was nearing the end of its serviceable life, with rusty patches showing through the paintwork on its hull.

But the *Probo Koala* was able to do the job. On 15 April, the ship's captain radioed a message to confirm that the caustic washing had been completed. He was instructed to pump the toxic residue into the vessel's slop tank, used in normal circumstances to collect the mixture of oil, water and other chemicals left over from cleaning the ship's tanks.

By this point, the ship was floating near Gibraltar. It now contained a cargo of treated coker gasoline that could be sold. But it was also carrying another, nastier cargo: 528 cubic metres of the toxic residue in its slop tank. Trafigura was still looking for a way to dispose of the toxic residue. In the meantime, it would not help for its contents to become widely known. 'Kindly do not, repeat do not disclose the presence of the material,' the captain was instructed.[58]

Trafigura thought it had found a solution, as a terminal in Amsterdam was willing to help to dispose of the residue. But then the terminal demanded a small fortune for the service. So the *Probo Koala* headed to Africa. At Lagos, the commercial capital of Nigeria, Trafigura tried again to unload the toxic residue, but, again, it was unable to do so.[59]

Inside Trafigura, tempers were rising. The traders had been trying to find a home for their cargo for several months. The emails bouncing back and forth between the different Trafigura offices were no longer full of optimism about the deal. Everyone in the oil department, from Dauphin down, was involved in finding a solution. None of their ideas worked, and by mid-August, the *Probo Koala*, still carrying the waste, was near Abidjan. Here, Trafigura finally found a company willing to take the waste off its hands. Its name was Compagnie Tommy.

In the wake of the scandal, Trafigura laid much of the blame at the door of Compagnie Tommy. The Ivorian company, Trafigura says, produced its operating licences on request, and acknowledged 'the necessity for correct and legal treatment' of the waste.[60]

But Compagnie Tommy didn't sound much like a serious company, and it wasn't. It had only secured a permit to deal with waste in the port of Abidjan on 9 August, little more than a week before it signed a contract with Trafigura.[61] An official investigation in Ivory Coast concluded that the speed with which Compagnie Tommy obtained its permits was 'troubling and suggested fraudulent collusion'.[62]

If that wasn't enough to raise alarm bells, the price Compagnie Tommy charged to do the job might have done. Where the Amsterdam waste disposal company had asked for nearly $700,000, Compagnie Tommy was willing to dispose of the very same waste for just $20,000.[63]

Disposing of toxic waste is a specialised job, the kind of thing that prompts company lawyers to draft dense legal contracts. Yet the contract between Trafigura and Compagnie Tommy, dated 18 August, was a single, handwritten page of just 108 words. It stated that, due to the 'high smell of this product', it was planning to 'discharge your chemical slops in a place out of the city properly prepared to receive any type of chemical product called Akouédo'.[64]

Of course, Akouédo was an open-air dump, in no way set up to handle toxic waste. A matter of hours after the contract was signed, the first truck arrived. A few hours after that, the residents of Abidjan began waking up to its rotten stench. And the crisis began.

The scandal soon exploded into an existential issue for Trafigura. The Ivorian government asked for international help to deal with the toxic waste. Dauphin, sensing the magnitude of the threat, flew in to Abidjan to try to smooth things over. But instead, he was thrown into jail, where he would spend the next five months in pre-trial detention. The next year, to secure Dauphin's release, Trafigura paid $198 million to the Ivorian government for clean-up costs and compensation to more than 95,000 victims who said they had fallen

ill. Later, the company would pay another £30 million to settle a case against it in the UK.[65] The stigma, however, would remain.

'It was so obviously stupid,' says Mark Crandall, one of Trafigura's co-founders, who had left the company just before the scandal.

He doesn't believe that anybody in Trafigura knew that Compagnie Tommy was going to dump the toxic waste in a built-up area, but that hardly exonerates the trading house.

'Somebody must have been saying ... "This all looks a little bit dodgy, but if we don't know about it, we're not responsible",' Crandall says. 'If a newly created company in Côte d'Ivoire says, I'll take this stuff off your hands for less money than you think it costs to treat it, my working assumption would have been ... they were planning to load it on a barge and take it out to sea.'[66]

Trafigura says it has learnt its lesson from the crisis. 'Trafigura has expressed, and reiterates, its deep regret of the impact the incident had, both real and perceived,' it said in a statement.[67] Yet José Larocca, who is today one of the company's three top executives and who was closely involved in the *Probo Koala* affair, believes the company's main mistake was not how it handled the toxic waste, but how it handled the negative media attention that followed. 'The media co-ordinated amongst them: it was a mafia,' he says.[68]

ELEVEN

HUNGER AND PROFIT

Wen Jiabao tried to sound calm. It was April 2008, and the Chinese premier had been at the helm of the world's fastest-growing power for half a decade. But as he toured the wheat fields of Hebei province, near Beijing, he needed to summon all of his powers of leadership. 'With grain in our hands there is no need to panic,' he told a small gathering of farmers and local officials.[1]

The Chinese government was in the midst of an increasingly desperate campaign to allay fears of food shortages. For weeks, Chinese newspapers had been printing photographs of state larders stocked high with frozen meat, sacks of grain and vats of cooking oil. Now Wen insisted that China's stocks of grain were sufficient to meet its needs. 'We Chinese are entirely capable of feeding ourselves,' he said.[2]

In private, however, the Chinese leadership was terrified. The price of food staples had been ratcheting higher since 2006, buoyed by demand from China and other emerging markets. For the first time in decades, the world's farmers were unable to keep pace with the rising consumption of a global population that was not only growing rapidly, but also growing rapidly wealthier. Then, beginning in early 2008, the world's key crop-growing regions were hit by a spell of bad weather. From Argentina to Canada, Vietnam to Russia, the

weather was hot when farmers needed it to be temperate, dry when they needed it to be wet.

Now, prices were skyrocketing. A bushel of soybeans had cost just $5.40 in the middle of 2006. By the time Wen was touring farms in Hebei province, it was more than double that. The spike in wheat, rice and corn prices around the world was just as dramatic. Even as a banking crisis was brewing on Wall Street, a food crisis was brewing on the streets of Dhaka, Cairo and Mexico City.

Soaring food prices were the culmination of a decade of the commodity supercycle. And it wasn't just food. Booming demand had reconfigured the flow of oil around the world, opened up Africa's mineral resources to new investment, and filled the pockets of commodity producers and traders the world over. For the first few years of the China-led supercyle, most people had barely noticed the changes sweeping through the commodity markets. But now the world of the commodity traders collided with the world of ordinary citizens as the cost of everyday goods shot higher.

The impact was felt almost immediately by the world's poorest people. Those already struggling to afford enough to eat were forced to go even hungrier. The World Food Programme, a UN agency that supports the world's poorest, nearly ran out of money and was forced to cut the size of the daily rations it distributed to refugees.[3]

The commodity traders were at the centre of the storm. For all his rhetoric, Wen was far from certain that China could ride out the crisis without help. His major concern was soybeans. For a long time, Beijing had insisted on total self-sufficiency in agriculture. But in the mid-1990s, as an increasingly wealthy and urban population demanded more meat, it had rewritten its policy to allow soybean imports to feed growing numbers of pigs and chickens. At first, China's imports of the beans were unremarkable. But then, just as had happened with other commodities, China's appetite shot up. By 2008, its purchases accounted for more than 50% of the global trade in soybeans.

Faced with spiralling prices and a population fearful of shortages, China's premier turned to the only group of people who could be relied on to secure food supplies no matter what the weather: the commodity traders.

Beijing didn't have to phone many traders. If Vitol, Glencore and Trafigura were the leading traders of oil and metals, the trade in food commodities was dominated by four companies, known as the 'ABCD': Archer Daniels Midland, Bunge, Cargill, and Louis Dreyfus. 'I had to go there,' recalls Alberto Weisser, who at the time was head of Bunge. 'It was non-stop, working with the Chinese government.'[4]

China was not alone. As a new wave of food inflation swept the world, rich and poor governments alike began to realise that the rise in prices was a threat not just to development, but also to security. 'Massive hunger poses a threat to the stability of governments, societies and borders,' said Hillary Clinton, who was US Secretary of State from 2009 to 2013. 'Food security is not just about food. But it is all about security – economic security, environmental security, even national security.'[5]

Across the Middle East and North Africa, where bread is the staple food for millions, presidents fretted about the price of wheat. In Saudi Arabia, the world's largest barley importer, the king and his entourage were worrying whether they would have enough barley to feed their camels. In Asia, governments in the Philippines and Vietnam were worried about the spiralling cost of rice.

The commodity traders weren't just ferrying shipments of grain around the world to satisfy the needs of nervous politicians, however. Their position at the heart of global trade gave them unmatched insight into the increasingly fragile state of the world economy. At the same time as they were advising governments and selling commodities around the world, the traders were also placing massively profitable bets on the future direction of the markets.

It was a time when millions of additional people were going hungry, when the banking crisis triggered chaos in financial markets, and when the world experienced the deepest recession in generations.

But for the commodity traders, it would turn out to be the most profitable period they had ever seen.

From their offices on a leafy Geneva backstreet, the traders of Cargill were surveying the mayhem engulfing the global economy with growing interest. Since John H. MacMillan Jr had established Tradax as the company's international arm in Geneva in 1956, the unit had become the nerve centre of Cargill. Information would flow from the company's offices in seventy countries around the world to the traders in Geneva, who in turn would use it to place bets on the global commodity markets.

The traders had understood how valuable the insight from Cargill's physical trading business could be since the days of the Great Grain Robbery, when the company had taken a small loss on its deals with the Soviet Union but the traders in Geneva had made a killing with their bets that prices would rise. From that point on, a hush would fall over the trading floor in Geneva whenever the Soviets called up to trade. One trader would whisper to another, 'the bear is on the phone,' and everyone would know it was time to buy grain futures in anticipation of a jump in prices.[6]

By 2008, Cargill's Geneva operation was a well-oiled machine, synthesising information and adjusting trading positions with practised ease. And so, as Cargill's executives were sent to reassure panicking governments about the state of global food supplies, the traders in Geneva were using that information to form a picture of the health of the global economy. Soon, they realised that it was running on vapours. The massive expansion over the previous decade had driven commodity prices to record highs, but now it was commodity prices that were hampering the global economy. Soaring gasoline prices meant drivers stayed at home, high food prices forced families to cut back on purchases, and manufacturers' profit margins were eroded by high metals prices. Add to that the crisis in credit

markets that, by the spring of 2008, was imperilling the global bank-
ing sector, and the economic boom was rapidly going into reverse.

Cargill's traders followed the Andy Hall school of commodity
trading: quiet and unassuming, but self-assured enough to bet vast
sums of their company's money. So many of them came from the
Netherlands or the UK that office wags referred to them as the 'Dutch
mafia' and the 'British mafia'. Now, increasingly certain that the
global economy was poised for a sharp contraction, they began to
place substantial bets on the futures markets that oil prices and ship-
ping rates were about to fall. At first, the bets – short positions, in
the market's parlance – lost money as prices continued to climb. But
the traders didn't lose their nerve. Soon they were proved right: in
September, Lehman Brothers filed for bankruptcy, triggering a drastic
loss of confidence in financial markets. From a peak in the summer,
commodity prices tumbled as it became clear that the world was
heading for recession. Oil, which had traded at $147.50 a barrel in
early July, tumbled to a low of $36.20 a barrel by the end of the
year. Soybean prices peaked above $16 a bushel, before falling to less
than half that level.

Cargill has never said anything publicly about the speculative
trades, nor has it revealed how much money it made from them.
But, according to two people with direct knowledge of them, the
company made more than $1 billion between late 2008 and early
2009 from its short positions in oil and freight.[7] It was a demonstra-
tion of the ease with which, for the world's largest agricultural
commodity trader, the turmoil shaking global markets could be
turned into profit.

Speculation had always been a central element of commodity trad-
ing, although over the years many commodity traders have denied
that their business involves placing bets on the future direction of
prices. Of all the commodity trading houses, however, it is the agri-
cultural traders whose business model has traditionally relied the most
on speculation. That may be unsurprising: the agricultural traders
had decades of trading in the Chicago futures markets, which had

been founded in the nineteenth century, before there was even such a thing as an oil futures market.

But it was also a function of the different structure of the agricultural commodity markets. In oil or metals, there are a few key suppliers – government agencies of oil-rich countries and large oil and mining companies. That means that, for oil and metals traders, winning large and favourable contracts with those organisations is one of the keys to success. But it also means that being a trader, in and of itself, doesn't confer such a large informational advantage.

Agricultural commodity traders, on the other hand, buy from thousands of individual farmers. That makes the traders' job harder, but it also provides an opportunity: dealing with so many farmers gives the largest traders valuable information. Long before the concept of 'big data' became popular, the agricultural traders were putting it to work, aggregating information from thousands of farmers to get a real-time insight into the state of the markets. Each month, when the US Department of Agriculture published its update on the world's key crops, the agricultural houses' traders were able to bet on what it would say with near-certainty that they were right. Within most trading houses, there was a group of traders whose sole job was to speculate profitably with the company's money – they were known as the proprietary, or 'prop', traders.

'In all the companies that I have worked for, most of the money was made trading prop,' says Ricardo Leiman, an agricultural trader by background who worked for Louis Dreyfus and then went on to become CEO of Noble Group and Engelhart Commodities Trading Partners.[8]

It wasn't just agricultural traders who made money speculating as commodity prices soared and then crashed in 2008–09. Some trading companies were more comfortable with speculation than others. But, to a greater or lesser degree, all traders speculated – whether through a dedicated proprietary desk, or by choosing when and how to hedge their commodities, or simply by doing deals in the physical markets that would pay off if prices moved as they expected. 'We're

speculators,' says Mark Hansen, chief executive of Concord Resources, a metals trader. 'We don't apologise for the fact that we do speculatively trade. The worst things that have happened in this industry have happened when people pretended there wasn't a speculative element to what they were doing.'[9]

Not of all of the traders' speculative bets were successful. As prices plunged in 2008, for example, Glencore lost money speculating in the aluminium market.[10] Even the world's largest metal trader couldn't get the market right every time.

But, in general, the late 2000s were a boom time for speculation. And the commodity traders' run didn't end in 2009. While the global economy had taken a punishing blow from the collapse of some of the largest banks, the main driver of the commodity supercycle – China – soon recovered, thanks to an enormous wave of stimulus spending by the Chinese government. Commodity prices rapidly picked up again, and by 2010 they were scaling new heights.

Once again, the food markets were hit by bad weather. This time it was Glencore that used its position at the heart of a politically sensitive flow of commodities to profitable effect. The company had been in the grain trade ever since Marc Rich + Co had bought a Dutch trader, Granaria, in 1981. In the 1980s, it had been a major supplier of grain to the Communist Bloc. Since the collapse of the Soviet Union, however, the countries of the region had become major exporters of agricultural commodities – particularly wheat, which was shipped from the Kazakh steppe and Russia's Volga basin to the world via ports on the Black Sea.

Glencore had kept up its good relations in the former Soviet Union, and by the late 2000s it was the largest wheat exporter from Russia, buying from farmers up and down the country. So its traders were well placed to respond rapidly when a drought devastated Russia's key growing region in the summer of 2010.

The wheat market was already growing fearful that the Russian government, concerned about domestic prices, could impose restrictions on grain exports, as it had done a few years earlier. Then

Glencore intervened. On 3 August, Yury Ognev, the head of the trading company's Russian grain business, went on TV to publicly encourage such a move. But Ognev wasn't just calling for some export restrictions – he was calling for a complete ban. 'From our point of view, the government has all the reasons to stop all exports,' he said.[11] His deputy emailed journalists with the same message.[12]

If the Russian government was struggling to decide how to respond to the crisis, Glencore provided it with the political cover to make a decision. Two days later, on 5 August, Moscow followed Ognev's advice and imposed an export ban, sending the price of wheat 15% higher in just two days.

Why would Glencore, a company whose business had benefited so spectacularly from the expansion of unrestricted trade around the world, call for such a retrograde measure? The company distanced itself from Ognev's comments, saying he and his deputy were not speaking for Glencore. Some rival traders speculated that Glencore was hoping to use the export ban as an excuse to get out of onerous contracts.

What they didn't know was that, in the weeks before Ognev and his deputy had spoken out in favour of a grain export ban, Glencore had been quietly placing a bet that grain prices would rise. Realising the seriousness of the situation in Russia, the company's traders had bought up corn and wheat futures in Chicago – 'going long', in trader-speak – putting themselves in a position to profit from a jump in prices.

The trade would never have become public but for Glencore's decision to float its shares in London the following year. As it briefed the bankers whose job it was to persuade investors to buy Glencore's shares, the trading house boasted about its superior market insight. Glencore received 'very timely reports from Russia farm assets that growing conditions were deteriorating aggressively in the spring and summer of 2010, as the Russian drought set in', according to one bank report based on meetings with Glencore executives. 'This

put it in a position to make proprietary trades going long wheat and corn.'[13]

Between June 2010 and February 2011, the price of wheat more than doubled. Glencore was perfectly positioned to profit from the crisis it had played a role in stirring up. The company's agricultural trading unit reported earnings of $659 million in 2010, the best year it had ever had and well above the earnings of Glencore's oil and coal traders combined.[14]

Of course, the drought would have devastated the Russian crop regardless of Glencore's statements or Moscow's decision to impose a ban. But the ban triggered a ripple effect that had wide-ranging ramifications for the region that relied on Russian wheat more than any other: the Middle East.

As Russia had become a more important wheat exporter, the bread-eating nations of the Middle East and North Africa had become its most important customers. By 2010, Egypt was buying half of its supplies from Russia. Now the news of a Russian export ban threw the governments of the region into a panic.

The traders did their best to offer reassurance, rerouting large volumes of French and American wheat to the region. Nonetheless, the reaction of the frightened governments was to redouble their wheat buying, adding to demand for the grain just as supplies were particularly tight. The panic buying pushed prices even higher, exacerbating the dissatisfaction that had been brewing across the Middle East and North Africa for years. The region was already afflicted by high unemployment, corruption and a lack of political freedom. Its youthful population was clamouring for reform.

When, in December 2010, a young Tunisian fruit seller doused himself with petrol and set himself on fire in protest at his country's corrupt bureaucracy, he started a chain of events that reshaped the history of the Middle East. Within months, protest movements had swept lifelong dictators from power in Tunisia, Egypt and Yemen. The civil war began in Libya that would topple Muammar Gaddafi;

and a protest movement began in Syria that would become one of the longest and bloodiest conflicts in the region's history.

The series of revolutions soon became known as the Arab Spring. And rising food inflation in 2010 was one of the sparks that helped to trigger it. 'I wouldn't contend it was caused by food, but food was certainly part of the equation,' says Ian McIntosh, the CEO of Louis Dreyfus until 2020. 'The easiest way to create political problems is to have hungry people.'[15] Once again, a spike in the price of food had helped to throw the lives of many of the world's poorest people into chaos; once again, for the commodity traders, it had been a lucrative opportunity for speculation.

For the traders, this climactic period of the supercycle brought profits on an unprecedented scale. Cargill, by this point the unchallenged leader in agricultural commodity trading, epitomised the scale of the windfall. In 2000 its net profits were just under $500 million. As the supercycle picked up steam in 2003, its earnings surpassed $1 billion for the first time, and then $2 billion two years later. And in 2008, as the traders in Geneva were placing their timely bet on a global economic meltdown, the company delivered record profits of nearly $4 billion.

Across the commodity trading industry, it was a time of spectacularly lucrative trades. In the decade to 2011, the world's largest oil, metal and agricultural trading houses – Vitol, Glencore and Cargill, respectively – enjoyed a combined net income of $76.3 billion (see table on page 332). That was an astonishing amount of money. It was ten times the profits the traders were generating in the 1990s.[16] It was more than either Apple or Coca-Cola made over the same period.[17] And it would have been enough money to buy entire titans of corporate America, such as Boeing or Goldman Sachs.[18]

Even adjusting for inflation, it was by far the most profitable period the industry had seen in modern history, surpassing the wild years of

the 1970s, when traders like Philipp Brothers and Marc Rich made hundreds of millions of dollars in the oil market, and Cargill and Continental did the same in grains. And it had accrued to just a small handful of people. Cargill was still owned by the Cargill and MacMillan families, which between them now had fourteen billionaires – more than any other family in the world outside of royalty.[19] Glencore, Vitol and Trafigura were still owned by their staff, meaning the commodity trading bonanza made a few top executives fantastically rich.

Not all of the traders' profits in this period came from speculating on futures markets. Rising prices also meant that their investments in mines, oil refineries, feedlots and other assets generated outsized returns. And the volatile markets of the times threw up all sorts of other ways of spinning money out of commodities.

As commodity demand tumbled in the wake of the financial crisis, oil traders like Vitol made a killing buying up unwanted oil and storing it – doing a version of the deals that Andy Hall had done nearly twenty years earlier. It was a trade they would repeat to great profit every time the market was oversupplied – not least in 2020, when the coronavirus pandemic struck. Aluminium traders were also cashing in enormous profits by funnelling surplus metal into warehouses. 'We milked the cow every day,' recalls one top aluminium trader of his profits in that period.[20]

The commodity traders were enjoying a bounty, but for a world that was suffering from hunger and recession, their success was an affront. It was only a matter of time before the traders' huge profits made them a target for politicians seeking scapegoats.

Campaigners asking who was responsible for the wild swings in the price of basic goods soon turned their ire on speculators – among them, the commodity traders. 'Oil speculators are making money by betting against the American consumers at the pump,' complained Nancy Pelosi, speaker of the US House of Representatives.[21]

It was only a short step from there to call for greater regulation of the trading industry. 'As traders continue to exert a great deal of influence over the global food system, they should be held accountable to be responsible actors,' said Jeremy Hobbs, the executive director of Oxfam.[22]

It wasn't the first time that the traders had caught the eye of politicians. In the 1970s, when grain and oil prices spiked, the first response was to push for more information about markets that were at the time inscrutable to anyone but the commodity traders themselves. But the push for better information did little to address the actual regulation of the activities of the commodity traders. A second push came in the mid-1990s, after Yasuo Hamanaka, a copper trader at Sumitomo, a Japanese trading firm, lost more than $2 billion in a series of deals that his employers said weren't authorised.[23] The scandal engulfed the whole copper market, triggering a chain of lawsuits, and prompting a consortium of regulators from sixteen nations to look once again for ways to better regulate the commodity markets.

'The increasingly global nature of commodity pricing, production, storage and delivery and the diverse regulatory treatment of these markets compounded the potential for market integrity and confidence issues,' the regulators said after meeting in Tokyo in 1997. 'In physical delivery markets with finite supply, information is a critical tool for maintaining fair and orderly markets and ensuring market integrity.'[24]

By 2008, however, as their bets during the food crisis showed, all the best information was still in the hands of the commodity traders. While they had begun to recognise the importance of the physical markets, governments had done very little to regulate the activities of the trading houses. At the peak of the commodity boom, the UK regulator, the Financial Services Authority, was asked by British lawmakers why prices were so high, and how it was overseeing the market. In a memorandum to parliamentarians, the FSA explained in strikingly blunt terms: 'We do not regulate physical (spot) trading in the underlying commodities.'[25]

But was speculation by the commodity traders really responsible for the super-spike in commodity prices? The answer is almost certainly not. There's no doubt that the commodity traders could influence prices, and had done throughout history. As the market's buyers and sellers of last resort, they were often involved in trades for the marginal barrel of oil or bushel of wheat that set the price. And, while big producers and consumers tended to use mainly long-term contracts, commodity traders were more active in the spot markets, where benchmark prices used by everyone else were set.

It's clear they could also manipulate prices – principally by buying physical stocks of a commodity and hoarding them, in that way attempting to push prices up. In the metals markets, the first major corners began in 1887, just a few years after the London Metal Exchange was founded, and by the 1980s they were a fairly regular occurrence.[26] But it was a truth widely acknowledged that it would be a struggle for any trader, no matter how big, to push the price in one direction for long, if the fundamentals of supply and demand dictated it should move in the opposite direction. It was something Marc Rich had learnt to his cost with his misguided zinc trade of 1992.

By the 2000s, the markets for most commodities were much larger and had more participants, meaning that cornering a significant chunk of global stocks was financially unviable even for the biggest traders. Certainly, in some corners of the market, squeezes and other distortions did still occur. But they tended to be limited to particular locations or sub-categories of product, and they didn't last for long. In 2010, for example, one trader bought up nearly all the available stocks of cocoa in one fell swoop, helping to push the cost of the commodity used to make chocolate to a thirty-three-year high and earning himself the nickname 'Chocfinger'.[27] But even Chocfinger couldn't change the weather, and the market soon came back down to earth when Ivory Coast, the main grower, produced a harvest that wasn't as small as feared.

It was tempting to blame commodity speculators for the food crises – throughout history, when commodity prices surged, politicians had found an easy scapegoat in the form of speculators. In AD 301 the Roman Emperor Diocletian imposed a cap on the prices of hundreds of goods in response to 'greed' which 'raves and burns and sets no limit on itself'.[28] In 1897, Germany's Reichstag banned trading in wheat futures after a disastrous harvest sent prices soaring.[29] And in the 1950s, US politicians outlawed the trading of onion futures – a ban that has remained in place to this day.[30]

Again, as commodity prices spiked, crashed and then spiked again in 2007–11, there was a heated discussion about the role of financial speculators in the markets. Scholars, researchers, traders and bankers offered arguments for and against. While most believed that financial speculators may have amplified short-term price swings, even helping to inflate some bubbles,[31] for the most part they argued that supply and demand factors were the main reason for the moves in prices.[32] Academics found some support for this conclusion in an obscure niche of the global economy: the price of some raw materials that weren't traded on financial markets, including the likes of burlap, hides and tallow, rose in tandem with the price of those traded on exchanges, suggesting that financial investment had had little effect on commodity prices.[33] The IMF concluded that 'recent research does not provide strong evidence that commodity market financialization has had obvious destabilizing effects'.[34]

But there is one way in which the commodity traders did bear some responsibility for the surge in food prices in 2008 and again in 2010. For decades, one commodity trading house in particular had been promoting a policy that had exacerbated the squeeze on global food supplies. It was a masterclass in the ability of the commodity traders to exert political influence – even inside the White House. And by

the late 2000s, its fruits were felt all over the world as food prices surged, millions went hungry and unrest swept the Middle East.

The policy was the use of ethanol – a type of alcohol derived from grains or sugars – to fuel cars. It was not a new idea: ethanol had been used as a fuel since the dawn of the automobile. German inventor Nikolaus Otto used ethanol to power an early version of his internal combustion engine, and Henry Ford designed his popular Model T car in 1908 to run on it.[35] But soon ethanol lost ground as a motor fuel to gasoline and diesel.

The idea of mandating ethanol derived from corn to be used to power cars started to gather steam during the oil crises of the 1970s, and over the next four decades it garnered more and more support. Some traders were worried about the impact of this massive diversion of global food supplies into fuel. Warren Staley, chief executive of Cargill until 2007, argued that the promotion of ethanol could end up taking food out of people's mouths. 'The world will have to make choices,' he warned.[36]

But one trading house was not worried; in fact, it had made ethanol the centrepiece of its strategy for four decades. That trading house was the 'A' in the ABCD: Archer Daniels Midland, or ADM. Its story is a testament to the fact that the commodity traders are often every bit as influential in Western capitals as they are in developing countries.

ADM had been a mid-sized grain processer of little note until, in 1970, it appointed Dwayne Andreas as chief executive. Andreas, who had cut his teeth at Cargill, was a diminutive dynamo. With a jockey's build and eyes that twinkled beneath his bushy eyebrows, he was a master manipulator, who saw politicians and governments as the playthings of companies like his.[37]

Installed at the helm of ADM, Andreas set about using his political connections to lobby for the ethanol industry. Under Andreas, ADM ploughed lobbying dollars towards politicians who advocated for tax breaks and loan guarantees for the ethanol industry. The targets of Andreas's lobbying included Bob Dole, who would run as the Republican candidate for president in 1996.

They even included the President of the United States. Andreas personally delivered $100,000 in cash to Richard Nixon's secretary in 1971 – a year before such anonymous campaign contributions would become illegal. It wasn't the only time that Andreas gave cash to Nixon – another payment of $25,000 from the ADM boss found its way, via one of Nixon's fundraisers, into the bank account of one of the five Watergate burglars whose bungled break-in at the headquarters of the Democratic National Committee would ultimately lead to Nixon's downfall.[38]

Andreas's lobbying paid off: the US government introduced tax breaks for blending ethanol into gasoline; it imposed tariffs on foreign ethanol suppliers; and it offered loan guarantees to build ethanol plants. ADM, which accounted for nearly 80% of US corn-made ethanol production by the mid-1990s, was the biggest beneficiary of the government's largesse. By the end of the 1990s when he retired, Andreas had transformed ADM into an agricultural commodity giant involved in processing, ethanol production and trading that called itself the 'supermarket to the world'.[39]

ADM didn't much change its style or its strategy once Andreas had stepped down. It kept investing in the ethanol industry, and kept funnelling cash and favours to politicians who could help its cause. In perhaps the clearest sign of the company's future priority as a producer of fuel rather than food, ADM even hired a new chief executive from the oil industry: Patricia Woertz, the former head of refining at Chevron, who joined in 2006.

Woertz, to date the only woman to become chief executive of a major commodity trading house, was every bit as driven as Andreas had been. Tough, impatient and ferociously ambitious, she'd always known she wanted to be a CEO. She overcame the sexism of the oil industry in the 1980s and 1990s to rise through its ranks, and brought the same spirit of defiance to her role at ADM. 'I'm outside the company, outside the industry, outside the family, outside the gender expectations,' she said.[40]

At Chevron, Woertz had warned about the 'unintended conse-
quences' of mandating the use of corn-based ethanol.[41] But now,
with the faith of a convert, she applauded Washington's support for
ethanol: 'Biofuels are good for the environment, for energy security
and for the American economy.'[42]

With Woertz at the helm, ADM would expand its ethanol capacity
with giant new plants across the US Midwest. At the same time, the
company increased its lobbying spend from about $300,000 in 2006
to nearly $2.1 million in 2008.[43]

ADM's efforts were not in vain. In the early 2000s, as oil prices
began to rise, the policy of promoting ethanol united a set of unlikely
political bedfellows: right-wing security hawks worried about US
dependence on Middle Eastern oil; farmers seeking higher corn prices;
and some left-leaning climate change activists pushing for an alterna-
tive to fossil fuels.

It was a formidable network of supporters, and it made ethanol
politically irresistible. In 2005, George W. Bush approved legislation
that mandated oil refiners to blend billions of gallons of ethanol into
gasoline. Ethanol production ballooned. In 2000, the US distilled
roughly two billion gallons of ethanol from corn; by 2006, the new
law mandated consumption of at least four billion.

As oil prices soared above $100 a barrel, a fresh set of US govern-
ment regulations forced even greater use of ethanol on the energy
industry. By 2011, as the Arab Spring engulfed the Middle East, the
US ethanol industry was consuming one in every six bushels of corn
on the planet.[44]

Of course, ethanol wasn't solely responsible for the rise in agri-
cultural commodity prices, but there's little doubt that it was a
contributing factor. Even ADM now disavows the fuel: the company
has put its ethanol plants up for sale. 'We've been very clear that
ethanol is not a strategic focus area for us going forward,' a spokes-
woman says.[45]

But by the time ADM pivoted away from ethanol, the effects of
its lobbying had already been felt around the world. The food crises

of 2008 and 2010 were a demonstration of the influence of the commodity traders. A policy pushed for by a trading house had helped cause the chaos on world markets. That, in turn, helped make commodity traders more central than ever in feeding the world – which allowed them to make the biggest profits they'd ever seen. The whole affair marked the culmination of the commodity supercycle, a process that had elevated the traders to a position of great strategic significance, and had delivered them spectacular riches.

But this collision between the world of the commodity traders and that of ordinary people would have long-lasting consequences for the trading industry. It would mark the beginning of the traders' emergence from the shadows. And the world was about to get a much greater insight into the business of the commodity traders and the wealth they had accumulated.

TWELVE

THE BILLIONAIRE FACTORY

The traders started arriving before dawn.

One by one, some of the world's most powerful businesspeople pulled in to Glencore's headquarters in the sleepy Swiss village of Baar. Their boss, Ivan Glasenberg, was not a fan of flashy cars, so most of them left their Porsches at home.

But by 6.06 a.m., when the sun rose over the hills around Baar, the car park in the basement of the building was packed. The traders had rushed into the office at an hour that was early even by Glencore's own punishing standards for a simple reason. On this Wednesday morning in early May 2011, one of the biggest secrets in the commodities industry was about to be revealed: who owned Glencore.[1]

For a year, Glasenberg, his team, and an ever-expanding coterie of bankers, had been preparing for an initial public offering. For the finance industry, an IPO is an event with all the choreographed pomp and ceremony of a royal wedding. Before a company can sell shares to the public for the first time, it must go through a series of rituals: choosing bankers, meeting with investors, and preparing reams of information about its history, its management and its finances.

Over the previous months, the Glencore team had written up a prospectus running to more than 1,600 pages. It explained in

painstaking detail the company's activities in the global commodity markets – that Glencore handled more than half of the world's traded zinc and copper, a quarter of world coal exports, and 24% of world barley exports. Lengthy addenda were added detailing the mineralogy of its assets in the Democratic Republic of Congo, Colombia and Kazakhstan; the legal boilerplate alone was dozens of pages long. But in the countless versions of the prospectus that had been drafted and redrafted, passed around and pored over, one page had always been blank. It was the page marked 'Interests of significant Shareholders'.

The size of each employee's shareholding had been the one taboo subject at Glencore ever since the traders had bought the company from Marc Rich two decades earlier. Even the question of which employees were shareholders was considered a secret. Each year, white envelopes would be delivered around the office to those who were shareholders informing them how the value of their shares had changed. The nosier traders would rush around, trying to see who had received an envelope and who had not.

One former Glencore employee, who had casually mentioned his share allocation to a colleague, remembers being called into the office of Eberhard Knoechel, the company's long-time accountant and keeper of secrets. Knoechel rebuked him for his indiscretion, saying: 'At Glencore, there's one thing you don't speak about – your shares.'[2]

Even Glasenberg's closest lieutenants, the dozen powerful heads of individual commodity departments, were in the dark about the size of everyone's shareholding but their own, and those of the traders working directly for them. The only three people in the company who knew everyone's shareholding were the company accountant, Glasenberg and Willy Strothotte, who by now was Glencore's chairman.

That's why the car park was full at six in the morning on the day the prospectus was due to be published. This was the day that the traders would find out which of their colleagues were the largest shareholders of the world's largest commodity trading

company. They would find out at exactly the same time as the rest of the world.

The scale of the riches that the prospectus revealed would shock even some Glencore old hands. Ivan Glasenberg, the CEO, owned 18.1% of the company, giving him a fortune worth $9.3 billion on the day the IPO was launched, and making him one of the richest 100 people on the planet.[3]

But he was far from alone – the IPO would mint no fewer than seven billionaires. Daniel Maté and Telis Mistakidis, the analytical Spaniard and the hyperactive Greek who were the co-heads of copper, lead and zinc, had shareholdings worth $3.5 billion each. Tor Peterson, the foul-mouthed American head of coal, was worth $3.1 billion, while Alex Beard, the cocksure Brit who ran oil, had $2.7 billion. Also in the billionaires' club were Chris Mahoney, the head of agriculture, and Gary Fegel, head of aluminium.[4]

The top thirteen employee-partners, who had owned 56.6% of Glencore immediately before the IPO, were worth a collective $29 billion. Below them, there were dozens whose stakes in the company were worth tens or hundreds of millions.

Glencore's IPO marked the crystallisation of the riches of the commodity boom. In some ways, it was the pinnacle of the commodity traders' rise from relative obscurity: a decade of astonishing Chinese growth had made Glencore and its competitors indispensable cogs in the world's new economic order, at the same time making the Glencore traders some of the richest people on earth.

It brought into the public eye a corner of the global economy that had, until now, operated in the shadows. Until the Glencore IPO, the commodity trading companies were largely anonymous. They supplied the raw materials essential to modern life: the energy, metals and food. There can have been few people among the 7 billion on earth who had not at some point used their services; but only a very few even knew their names. When Glencore published its prospectus, it was as if Glasenberg had flipped a light switch and illuminated an entire industry. Perhaps unintentionally, Glencore, which for decades

had worked hard to remain behind the scenes, had invited public scrutiny not just of itself but also of the whole world of commodity trading.

It was a change that would have momentous consequences for the commodity traders. Everyone from journalists to campaigners and mining executives to regulators would now have a window on the activities of the commodity traders, and a reminder in Glencore's annual results of their scale and profitability. Whether or not Glasenberg and his traders knew it, the Glencore IPO would mark a turning point. The traders would no longer be able to go unnoticed as they wielded their enormous financial power and influence around the world.

The IPO was also a recognition of the changing shape of the industry. The boom had been gloriously profitable for the commodity traders, but it masked a long-term trend that was making their business more challenging. Information was becoming faster, cheaper and more widely available, eroding the edge that had, in previous decades, allowed the traders to steal a march on the rest of the market. An increasingly transparent world made it ever harder for less scrupulous commodity traders to make money through corruption or bribery. And the miners and oil majors who were their principal suppliers had gone through a phase of consolidation, leaving a few large players who had little need of the traders to help them handle logistics.

The old-fashioned business model of the commodity trader, buying in one place and selling in another at a profit, was becoming all but impossible to sustain. The traders could have taken their cash out of their companies and gone home, but that was not their style. Instead, most of the commodity traders followed the path pioneered by Glencore and Cargill of investing in assets, using their profits to build their own supply chains, including mines, oil tankers, warehouses, flour mills and more.

It was an approach Glasenberg had been advocating since the 1990s, when he had started accumulating coal mines. He maintained that

there would be fewer and fewer opportunities for traders who didn't own assets such as mines. 'The perfect example: we don't have assets in aluminium and iron ore,' Glasenberg says, naming two commodities that have become also-rans within Glencore's trading machine. 'You're not going to make bonanzas, you're going to do a lot of volume, with small margins, and you'll make decent money but nothing spectacular.'[5]

As others followed his example on an ever larger scale, the trading houses became not just middlemen, buying and selling oil, metals and grains around the world, but little empires of infrastructure critical to the flow of global trade, much of it in emerging markets. In 2011, Vitol invested in a network of petrol stations in Africa that made it the second-largest retailer in the whole continent, excluding South Africa.[6] The same year, Cargill bought one of the world's largest manufacturers of animal feed, with processing plants from Vietnam to Russia. The family of Theodor Weisser, the man who had traded Soviet oil in the 1950s for Mabanaft, emerged as the owner of one of the world's largest networks of oil-storage tanks.

When, a few years later in 2015, soaring production of oil from shale rock formations turned the US into a meaningful crude oil exporter for the first time in forty years, the commodity traders were first in line not only to buy the oil, but also to build the infrastructure needed to connect American oilfields with the rest of the world.[7] Trafigura, for example, spent $1 billion building a terminal in Texas able to berth large tankers.[8] Mercuria also invested in a US port facility, which the company used to ship crude from as far away as North Dakota to the global market.

Investing in assets may have made good business sense, but – as Glencore had learnt when it started investing in mines – it was expensive, requiring long-term capital. Now Glencore's competitors were also looking for ways of raising longer-term financing. One option was to sell shares, as Glencore did. None of Glencore's competitors followed it down the path of becoming a public company

(a few, like ADM, Bunge and Noble Group, had been public already for years). But many raised money from public markets in the form of bonds. In the period between 2010 and 2013, Trafigura, Louis Dreyfus and Gunvor all issued bonds for the first time. Others found different ways to tap outside investors, such as sovereign wealth funds and private equity. Vitol, for example, set up a new company to invest in assets using its own funds together with investments from George Soros, the sovereign wealth fund of Abu Dhabi, and a rich Saudi family. Noble Group sold shares to China Investment Corporation, a sovereign wealth fund, while Mercuria sold a stake to a state-owned Chinese company.

This new capital gave the commodity traders the firepower to do bigger deals and make big-ticket investments. But it also forced them to reveal much more information about themselves than they ever had before, bringing an unwelcome glare of publicity to an industry that had long operated in the shadows. Glencore, a company few had heard of even in the world of finance, became regular fodder for front-page headlines. Traders who had been used to jetting around the world anonymously now found photographers camped outside their homes. Even those companies that opted to issue bonds rather than going public as Glencore had done still had to publish a lot of information for their bondholders.

It was a shift that some in the industry would later come to regret, as the greater publicity of the public markets also meant greater awareness of the scale and significance of the commodity traders. The flotation of Glencore, in May 2011, marked the point when, for investors, journalists and governments, the traders became too big to ignore.

The path to Glencore's IPO had begun four years earlier.

In 2007, Glasenberg gathered together his most senior traders and presented them with a dilemma. As a private company, Glencore

couldn't afford to keep doing deals at the rate it had been. The only way the company could keep growing was to become public.

The relentless rise in commodity prices meant that Glasenberg's time-honoured strategy of investing in assets – particularly mines – was becoming impossible to sustain. Glencore simply couldn't afford to keep buying. It had become too expensive to buy more assets, and Glencore, as a private company, couldn't pay for its acquisitions using its shares as public companies could.

What's more, the commodity trader had become a victim of its own success. It had made so much money in the previous two years that it would be potentially devastating if several of its top trader-shareholders quit at once. That was because, whenever traders left Glencore, the company would buy back their shares and then, over a five-year period, pay them the accumulated value of their equity.[9] Effectively, the departure of a shareholder meant a reduction in Glencore's shareholder capital at the same time as an increase in debt – a double-whammy for the company's balance sheet.

That had been manageable when the size of the company's historical profits was relatively small, and it was making enough money that it could afford to pay out departing shareholders. But then came the China boom and, with it, skyrocketing profitability. In 2006–7, Glencore made more money than it had done in the previous eight years combined.[10] Now, if several big shareholders left, the company's debt would increase by potentially billions of dollars.

The options Glasenberg presented to the partners were straightforward: they could stay private, but they'd have to stop making acquisitions and build a pot of cash to be able to pay out the larger shareholders as they left. Or they could go public.

There was another dynamic motivating Glasenberg. The relationship between Glencore and Xstrata had started to chafe. Xstrata had grown at a spectacular rate, becoming one of the largest mining companies in the world. And Glencore had also been doing larger and larger mining deals in its own right, such as its foray into the Democratic Republic of Congo. The two sister companies had started

to clash: when BHP Billiton was looking to sell a copper mine in Peru, for example, both companies expressed an interest.

So Glasenberg started talking to Davis about a plan to merge Glencore and Xstrata. For Glencore, the merger with Xstrata, which was already listed in London and Zurich, would have achieved the same result as an IPO but without the rigmarole of the IPO process. If the Glencore traders agreed on the need to become a public company, it was clear that a merger with Xstrata was their preferred means to achieve it. Inside Glencore, many joked that Xstrata's name, a consultancy's invention combining 'extraction' and 'strata', actually stood for Glencore's 'exit strategy'.

'In 2007, we agreed on a way to do it,' Glasenberg says.[11] The idea was for Xstrata to absorb Glencore, which still owned about 34% of the mining company. The Glencore managers would get Xstrata shares in exchange for their Glencore shares.

That would solve both of Glasenberg's problems. As part of a public company, the Glencore traders would be able to buy much bigger assets: they could now use their own shares as a currency, handing them to the shareholders of any company they decided to buy instead of cash. And when the traders retired, it would no longer imperil the entire company – they would simply have publicly traded shares that they could sell whenever they wanted. 'It was a logical thing to put these companies together,' Davis says.[12] But the negotiations stumbled. Glasenberg and Davis couldn't agree on a valuation, even if both men agreed that putting the two companies together made sense.

Their talks were soon to become a sideshow to a much bigger deal. In November 2007, Davis was approached by Roger Agnelli, the ambitious chief executive of Brazil's state mining giant and number-one iron ore producer globally, Vale. Agnelli wanted Vale to buy Xstrata, creating the world's largest mining company. For Davis, it was the natural culmination of his time at Xstrata – after a whirlwind six years riding the wave of the commodity supercycle, now he and his shareholders could cash out.

But there was a hitch: Glasenberg. With Glencore owning over a third of Xstrata's shares, the South African trader effectively had a veto over any deal. Glasenberg, Davis and Agnelli, on occasion mediated by a clutch of the world's best-paid investment bankers, spent several months haggling over the details. But Glasenberg dragged his feet.

The Glencore boss spent weeks going over apparently minor details, such as the duration of a deal for Glencore to trade the combined company's nickel production. But, in Davis's view, that was merely an excuse. 'The transaction failed because Ivan wanted it to fail,' he says. 'Ivan valued control above value.'[13] Davis, frustrated and upset, was ready to quit Xstrata. He and Glasenberg resumed their discussions about a merger between Glencore and Xstrata.

Then the global financial crisis hit, and suddenly both men had to focus on their companies' survival. In theory, Xstrata's situation should have been more precarious than Glencore's: it was a mining company, and the plunge in commodity prices directly fed through into lower profits at its mines. Glencore, as a trader, could simply bet against commodity prices and keep making money. And falling prices would mean it had less need to borrow, since the cost of each cargo of oil, metals or grain was lower.

That was the theory, but in practice the two companies' fates were intertwined. In its quest to keep buying things, Glencore had mortgaged its Xstrata shares to raise loans. As Xstrata's share price tumbled in late 2008 and early 2009, the risk was growing that Glencore would be forced to hand over its Xstrata stake to its banks. It became a self-reinforcing cycle: hedge funds bet against Xstrata, knowing that doing so would put further pressure on Glencore and make a fire sale of its Xstrata shares more likely.

At the same time, they were betting against Glencore on the credit markets. The cost of insuring against a Glencore bankruptcy skyrocketed. In the wake of the collapse of Lehman Brothers, when every company in the world was worrying about who might be next, that caused deep concern among Glencore's banks and trading counterparties.

Credit is the lifeblood of commodity trading. It's what allows traders to handle vast quantities of raw materials without having to pay upfront every time. Without it, the business grinds to a halt. Now, suddenly, Goldman Sachs was calling up Glencore and suggesting politely that it might be better for everyone if the next time it wanted to do a trade, the trading house should approach a different bank. Some industrial companies started making Glencore pay upfront for shipments of metal.

Even the Glencore traders started to doubt their company's future. 'It wasn't a pleasant time,' says one senior executive from that period, whose shareholding would make him a billionaire at the time of the IPO. 'If you had asked me what my Glencore shares were worth in September 2008, I would have said nothing.'[14]

The clammy fear of the financial crisis soon subsided as China led a global economic recovery with a massive wave of spending on infrastructure that boosted demand for commodities. But the experience changed Glencore profoundly. At the height of the crisis at the end of 2008, Glasenberg had been quizzed by one of the ratings agencies that assess companies' creditworthiness on how Glencore would cope if twenty of the top shareholders all left at once.[15] Glasenberg called round his partners: within 24 hours they had all agreed not to leave the company for at least three years.

For Glasenberg, it was a rare moment of vulnerability. The company was under pressure and he needed to ask his lieutenants for their support. If one of them had used the moment as an opportunity to negotiate, Glasenberg would have been powerless to resist. The power dynamic had shifted, and the atmosphere inside the company became harsher. Where the Glencore traders had been a band of brothers, sharing pranks and punishing travel schedules, they became more suspicious, more ruthless, more aggressive. The experience of having to fight for Glencore's survival during the financial crisis made Glasenberg even more certain that he needed to remove the risk of a mass departure of partners and address the constraints on the company's growth.

And that put Glencore firmly on the path to an IPO. Soon, Glasenberg and his traders were pitching themselves to some of the world's biggest sovereign wealth funds and other money managers. In December 2009, the company raised $2.2 billion from a group of those investors in the form of debt that, under certain circumstances, could be converted into Glencore shares. For the first time since Roche's investment in 1994, an investor outside the trading company had put a valuation on Glencore – in this case, $35 billion.[16]

Glasenberg kept pressing Davis for a merger between Glencore and Xstrata. But the two men still couldn't agree how to put a valuation on Glencore. So, in around May 2010, a small team of Glencore's in-house financiers, lawyers and accountants began preparing in earnest for the IPO. The trading house was heading inexorably for life as a public company.

For Glasenberg, one of the main tasks was to find new directors to sit on Glencore's board. Until now, the company's board had consisted of Glasenberg himself and a few insiders. Its role was largely ceremonial: rubber stamping the company's results each year and waving through a few key decisions. Board meetings typically lasted about 10 minutes.

Glasenberg might have been quite happy to continue with that sort of arrangement, but to persuade London's money managers to invest in Glencore he knew he'd need a board that looked more robust. He started calling round his contacts in the world of commodities and finance and signed up a few new directors. But Glasenberg still needed a chairman. Strothotte was too intertwined with the history of the company to stay on. Glencore started drawing up a shortlist of potential candidates.

By early April 2011, when the IPO was ready to go, the leading candidate was John Browne, a former chief executive of BP. A day before Glencore planned to make a formal announcement of its IPO – a stage of the ritual akin to sending out wedding invitations – Glasenberg and several of his top lieutenants went to Browne's house in Chelsea to get to know their new chairman a little better.

Browne, a small man with a lightning-sharp mind and an imperious manner, had built BP through a series of deals into one of the world's dominant oil companies. By the time he was approached by Glasenberg, Browne had little left to prove. He had turned a painful personal scandal – when he was outed by a former boyfriend, and then had to leave BP after lying about the affair in court – into a platform to champion workplace diversity. He was a member of the House of Lords and chair of the trustees of the Tate art galleries.

Browne gathered the Glencore traders in the library of his tastefully luxurious home, where they sat on chairs upholstered in Venetian silk velvet, surrounded by Browne's collection of rare books and antiques. In his BP days, Browne had been nicknamed the 'Sun King of the oil industry'.[17] Now he held court, surrounded by a group of men who would soon be billionaires, against a backdrop of a ceiling papered with gold leaf.[18]

Browne started asking questions about the company he was due to chair. It soon became clear that he was making the Glencore traders uncomfortable. Different people who were at that meeting have different accounts of what went wrong. The Glencore traders, who since the buyout from Marc Rich had been masters of their own destiny and answerable to no one, were affronted by Browne's domineering style. They left muttering about the former BP boss's arrogance and worried that he wanted to run their company himself.

For his part, Browne felt that the Glencore traders hadn't been entirely open with him about how they actually made their money. And he was disinclined to lend his reputation to a company that wanted him to be a figurehead and nothing more.[19]

By the time Glasenberg and his partners left Browne's house and stepped out on to his Chelsea street with its view over the Thames, the deal for Browne to become Glencore's chairman was off. There was just one problem: the choreography of the IPO was already in train. The plan for Browne to chair the Glencore board had been months in the making, and the company was due to announce the

appointment the very morning after Glasenberg and his team had visited Browne at home. The press releases had been drafted: Browne's appointment was due to be revealed as Glencore officially announced its long-awaited IPO.

But now there was no chairman, and Glasenberg had to find a plan B. He settled on Simon Murray, a former legionnaire with a taste for adventure, who had built his career in Hong Kong, where Glencore was also planning to raise money. But by the time Glasenberg had decided on his pick, there were only a few hours to go until the announcement. Murray couldn't be reached by phone. And so the press release went out with a blank space where the chairman's name should have been.

'Glencore has made its decision regarding the new Chairman and is in the final stages of making the appointment, which will be communicated shortly,' the announcement read.[20]

In the end, the somewhat slapdash nature of Glencore's preparation mattered little. With investor enthusiasm for commodities reaching fever pitch, the company raised $10 billion. It was the largest listing ever in London, catapulting the company into the ranks of the FTSE 100 and into the pension funds of Britain's retirees.[21]

Throughout this period, Glasenberg had barely stopped negotiating with Davis to merge Glencore with Xstrata.[22]

At last, Glasenberg had a market valuation, and one that wasn't far below that of Davis's company. (Glencore's value at its IPO was just under $60 billion, while Xstrata's was $67 billion.) But the relationship between the two men had soured. Davis blamed Glasenberg for blocking the Vale deal. Glasenberg resented Davis for having asked Xstrata shareholders for more cash at the low point for the equity markets in January 2009.

For Glasenberg, the IPO had always been a stepping stone on the path to a merger with Xstrata. Now, with Glencore's IPO done, the

negotiations began in earnest. Glasenberg and Davis disagreed on almost everything: how the deal should be structured; what the relative valuation of the two companies should be; and who would be in charge of the new company.

In a nod to the challenge of reaching a deal, the two sides gave their discussions the codename 'Everest'. By the end of 2011, Glasenberg and Davis had battered each other into a compromise. Davis took the deal to the Xstrata board. Was it his best ever deal? No. But, he told the board, it was the best deal he could extract from Glasenberg.

At the same time, Glasenberg was holding a pow-wow of his top traders. Not all of them were happy with the plan to merge with Xstrata. In particular, Mistakidis, the copper trader, argued that Glencore was overpaying for Xstrata's assets and was appalled at the thought of having to work alongside Xstrata's bosses, whom he regarded as ineffective and lazy. Steve Kalmin, the finance chief, was also reluctant.

Still, Glasenberg prevailed. The two companies announced a deal on 7 February 2012. Formally, Glencore would buy Xstrata, issuing new Glencore shares to Xstrata shareholders; the price would be 2.8 Glencore shares for every Xstrata share, valuing the company slightly above where the market had been trading; Davis would stay on as chief executive, and Glasenberg would be his deputy with responsibility for trading.[23]

Almost immediately, the tensions at the heart of the plan became apparent. Glasenberg's traders had barely disguised contempt for Davis and his team of mining executives. But the two sides would have to work together side by side, in a structure where, at least on paper, the Xstrata group was equal or even senior to the Glencore traders. At the same time, the Glencore traders would remain owners of a substantial chunk of the combined company's shares.

Few observers inside and outside the companies believed the arrangement could last. It was only a matter of time, they assumed, before Glasenberg's band of traders would assert the power that their

shareholdings gave them. 'None of us thought it would last very long, and we were all pretty clear who's going to come out on top,' says a person who was involved in the negotiations on Glencore's side.[24]

Davis had come to the same conclusion. It was what drove the miscalculation that would lead to his downfall.

As Xstrata and Glencore had grown side by side through the commodity boom, Davis had become increasingly resentful of the phenomenal wealth that had accrued to the Glencore traders. The Xstrata CEO had also become very wealthy by any normal standard: by the time of the merger, the *Sunday Times* Rich List estimated his wealth at £80 million ($130 million), about half of it coming from his shareholding in Xstrata.[25] But Glasenberg's wealth was on another scale – and it was built to a significant extent on the success of Xstrata, the company Davis had been running. Glasenberg had become the largest shareholder of Glencore while it remained private, whereas Davis was a relatively small shareholder of publicly listed Xstrata, behind various pension funds and other institutional investors.

With the merger looming, Davis realised that it was surely only a matter of time before he and his lieutenants would be ejected from the combined company. So he negotiated a generous package of 'retention bonuses' for himself and his team – worth more than $200 million – that they would receive for staying at the company, or if they were forced out by Glasenberg's traders.

The timing couldn't have been worse. A wave of shareholder activism was sweeping the UK, with investors threatening to vote down executives and board directors whom they considered to be greedy or inept. The movement would become known as the 'shareholder spring', and outsized executive pay packets were a key focus. Some of Xstrata's top shareholders publicly voiced their disgust at Davis's pay deal.

The fight over the retention bonuses galvanised opposition to the deal among Xstrata's shareholders. Already, some of them felt that Glasenberg should be offering a higher price for Xstrata. In parallel,

Qatar's sovereign wealth fund had started buying shares in Xstrata. Within just a few months, the fund had amassed a stake of more than 10%. It demanded that Glencore increase its offer.[26] The deal was on the rocks.

Again, Glasenberg held a discussion with his top traders. Some had been reluctant to go ahead with the initial deal; they were even more reluctant to pay more. Mistakidis, together with some of the other large shareholders, argued that they should only increase their offer if they could take control of the management of the company. Glasenberg played tough, and for weeks adamantly refused to raise his offer. But he was bluffing, and the Qataris knew it. They repeated their demand: raise the offer, or the deal is dead.

Glasenberg, a man who had built a personal myth as the shrewdest dealmaker of the natural resources industry, was forced to admit defeat. It was late in the evening on 6 September when Glasenberg walked into Claridge's, the London hotel known for hosting visiting royalty. Glasenberg was there to meet the prime minister of Qatar, in a last-ditch attempt to save his merger with Xstrata.

Also in attendance was Tony Blair, the former British prime minister, who had a close relationship with the Qataris. The horde of investment bankers who had tens of millions of dollars of fees riding on the success of the deal had suggested calling in Blair to try to smooth things over.

It worked. Glasenberg, the consummate trader, had come ready to negotiate. Sometime after midnight, he emerged with a deal: he had needed to increase his offer to 3.05 Glencore shares for every Xstrata share, but he had won Qatar's approval. The Glencore boss headed straight to a nearby bar where Glencore's coal traders were drinking.

At around 2 a.m., he telephoned Davis. He had a deal with the Qataris, he told his rival, but there was just one catch: Glasenberg, not Davis, would be chief executive of the combined company.

The next morning, Xstrata's board of directors gathered in Zug for a meeting where the company's shareholders were due to vote

on the deal. A few minutes before the meeting was set to begin, a piece of paper was delivered to the board detailing the new terms of Glencore's proposal. Xstrata's chairman dutifully read them out to the assembled shareholders. 'Bloody hell,' muttered one.[27]

Eight months later, the deal was finally completed, and the curtain was drawn on one of the greatest corporate melodramas that had ever played out on the London stage. Davis, who went on to become chief executive and treasurer of the UK's Conservative Party, remained upset about how the deal between Xstrata and Glencore had played out. He believed that Glencore undermined the deal from the beginning, helping to stir up shareholder dissent over the retention bonuses, while the Qataris reneged on a promise to back his team.

But Glasenberg and his team were on top of the world. Between them, Glasenberg and his traders owned around a third of the combined company, which would soon be the world's third most valuable mining company, behind only BHP Billiton and Rio Tinto.[28] Glencore was no longer just the world's largest trader of commodities, but also one of the largest producers of natural resources on the planet. It was the world's largest exporter of thermal coal, used to fire power stations in China, Japan and Germany; the largest miner of ferrochrome and zinc, key metals for the steel industry; and the top producer of cobalt, crucial for the batteries used in mobile phones and electric cars. It also had the firepower to make investments at every point of the supply chain – in oilfields in Chad and Equatorial Guinea; in grain silos and ports in Canada, Australia and Russia; and in petrol stations in Mexico. It was, in Glasenberg's words, 'a new powerhouse'.[29]

Glencore's IPO had not just made Glasenberg and his traders rich; it had allowed them to expand even more aggressively. At the same time as he was negotiating with Mick Davis to buy Xstrata, Glasenberg was also putting together a $6 billion deal to buy Viterra, a Canadian

grain trader. Little over a year later he was on the phone to the chairman of Rio Tinto, proposing that the two companies should consider a deal to create the world's largest mining company.

The IPO was a step in what appeared to be an inexorable march towards greater openness that – however much it was resisted by some commodity traders – was increasingly essential. Just as it had been necessary to jettison Marc Rich, their fugitive founder, for the traders at Glencore to start doing business with Wall Street banks, so greater publicity was a price the trading industry paid as it became larger and more integrated into the global financial system.

But being public also brought new challenges for which Glasenberg and his team were ill prepared. They had to submit themselves – and their results – to public examination every six months. Their every move was chronicled in elaborate detail in the press. More than anything, the IPO had revealed astonishing profits that made everyone, from Glencore's competitors to its customers, from investors to journalists, NGOs to governments, sit up and pay attention. The trading house was under scrutiny like never before.

That kind of scrutiny was something the company had long sought to avoid, preferring to operate quietly and in the shadows. Partly that was to avoid awkward questions about who it was dealing with and how. But it was also simply a question of not wanting to disclose, in an era when the company's global network put it at a significant advantage to many other market participants, any of its insights to outsiders. That was the reason why, on previous occasions, the company had turned down the opportunity to go public.

In the Marc Rich era, the company had never even had a discussion about going public, according to Felix Posen, one of the company's earliest partners. 'Certain things you preferred not to make public,' he said. 'And it's I think also what you're used to. We were all used to being in private companies.'[30]

Then, in the late 1990s, when the company was looking for a way to buy back the stake that it had sold to Roche, several investment bankers suggested it should go public.[31] But Willy Strothotte's

generation of Glencore traders was unmoved by the bankers' over-tures: going public, he said, would restrict Glencore's 'entrepreneurial freedom'.[32]

Paul Wyler, one of company's three executive directors throughout the 1990s, put it more bluntly: 'We had advantages if we wanted to pay commissions. So if we wanted to pay certain things, we didn't have to declare it in our annual report.'[33]

Still, those advantages were already fading in the late 1990s. Legis-lation such as the Convention on Combating Bribery of Foreign Public Officials in International Business Transactions, adopted in 1997 by the members of the OECD, and the UN's Convention against Corruption in 2003, made it harder for companies to pay commis-sions or bribes. And the value of Glencore's insights into the global economy declined as news and information became cheaper and more widely available. 'There are some advantages, but we knew this is going to come to an end,' says Wyler. 'The company just grew too big for it to remain private, in my opinion.'

All the same, the publicity generated by the IPO had a ripple effect that the Glencore traders had barely anticipated. The miners, oil companies, farmers, refiners and manufacturers that were Glencore's suppliers and buyers had always known that the company was making money, but until the IPO they hadn't been forced to reckon with quite how much money the company was making. It added urgency to the question of whether the money was being made at their expense. And Glencore didn't just lift its own veil of secrecy: its IPO made the profitability of the trading industry as a whole impossible to ignore.

'You always had this tension with your customers: well, if you're being a fair trader how come you guys are making so much money out of everything?' says David Issroff, who was head of Glencore's ferroalloys department until 2006. Until the IPO, he says, 'people knew we were making money; ... nobody knew the extent.'

It was a familiar argument against going public – indeed it was the main reason some commodity traders had decided against an IPO. In

the 1940s, Philipp Brothers had considered information about its balance sheet and annual profits to be in the 'same secret category as the development of the atom bomb', according to one executive at the time.[34] The company later changed tack, however, becoming one of the first examples of a publicly traded commodity trader when, in 1960, it merged with the listed Minerals & Chemicals Corporation.

More than anything, being public meant that, when something went wrong, it played out in lurid detail on a public stage. Glasenberg didn't have to wait long to experience that: even as the company was preparing its IPO, the cotton price had soared to an all-time high. Glencore, a relatively new entrant to the cotton market, was on the wrong side of the move. When Glasenberg came to announce the company's full-year results for the first time as a public company, he had to reveal a cotton-trading loss in excess of $330 million.[35] The Glencore traders' aura of invincibility, so carefully cultivated during the IPO, was shattered.

Worse was to come only a couple of years after Glasenberg had sealed his deal to take over Xstrata. In 2015, the price of commodities from oil to copper plunged on the back of slowing Chinese growth, just as many boom-era investments were bearing fruit in the form of increased production. Glencore's debt load was high thanks to Glasenberg's passion for expansion, and hedge funds started betting against the company's shares.

Glasenberg was rattled. For weeks, the company was silent as its share price plunged. Then, reluctantly, Glasenberg approved a plan to issue new shares, sell assets and pay down debt. For a few weeks it seemed that it might not be enough. On one occasion the company's share price plummeted 29% in one day, an extraordinary fall for a blue-chip member of the FTSE 100 index. Eventually, the market turned and Glencore's share price recovered, but it was a harrowing experience that the company probably wouldn't have gone through if it had been a private company.

It was a salutary lesson on the downsides of a public listing, and it was not the only one among the commodities traders. Noble Group,

the Hong Kong trading house founded by one-time scrap dealer Richard Elman, suffered a spectacular fall from grace after an ex-employee started alleging it had used accounting trickery to inflate its profits. The company's troubles played out in gruesomely public fashion. Every new problem triggered a flurry of newspaper stories and a swoon in Noble's share price; in the end, the company was taken over by its creditors.[36]

Stories like these led many traders to conclude that the commodity trading industry works best as a partnership. 'It's a business that shouldn't be public,' says David Tendler, the former chief executive of Philipp Brothers.[37] Indeed, no other large trader followed Glencore into the public markets. Those that were private by the mid-2000s had made a conscious decision to remain so. Vitol had flirted with the idea of an IPO in the early 1980s, going as far as hiring an investment bank, Kleinwort Benson, which proposed a valuation of $650–$750 million.[38] Again, around 2006, the company considered hiring a bank to explore going public, but ultimately decided against it.[39] Louis Dreyfus also briefly considered an IPO.[40]

Others remained vehemently opposed to the idea. 'The biggest advantage that we have is that we have close to 700 shareholders in the company. Their business interests are aligned with the company,' says Jeremy Weir, Trafigura's CEO.[41]

Among all the large traders, Cargill was the one which worked most feverishly to avoid going public. For more than a century, the company had been owned by the Cargill and MacMillan families, the descendants of the pioneers of the grain trade.

Then, in 2006, Margaret Cargill, the granddaughter of the company's founder, passed away. Margaret was one of America's richest women, but the bulk of her fortune was tied up in a stake of about 17.5% in Cargill. After her death, the charities she had founded looked to cash in their investment. They started lobbying the trading house to arrange an IPO, at least for Margaret's stake in the business.

The rest of the Cargill and MacMillan families were dead set against the idea. For five years, a behind-the-scenes conflict raged between

the different groups of Cargill shareholders. Eventually, the company found a solution: it bought back Margaret's stake in Cargill from the charities she had set up. In exchange, the charities would get almost $9.4 billion worth of shares in Mosaic, a publicly traded fertiliser company in which Cargill held a majority stake.[42] Other Cargill and MacMillan family shareholders received a further $5.7 billion in Mosaic shares. The deal solved two problems for the company: it satisfied the requests of the charities founded by Margaret, and it raised billions of dollars for the rest of the family shareholders, thereby undercutting potential support for a future IPO.[43] It also put a public valuation on Cargill itself for the first time – about $53.5 billion.[44] 'This is probably the best evidence one can imagine of the family's commitment to remaining private,' said Gregory Page, Cargill's chief executive at the time.[45]

And yet, despite the best efforts of companies like Cargill, Vitol and Trafigura to remain private and to stay out of the public eye, the IPO of Glencore inevitably raised the profile of the entire sector. Suddenly Glencore shares were a sizeable component of every British retiree's pension fund, and the company and its rivals made for more interesting headlines than FTSE 100 peers like Vodafone, the telecoms company, or GlaxoSmithKline, the pharmaceuticals group.

In 2008, for all the furore over high oil and food prices, there were only 385 articles in major global newspapers that mentioned one of the top trading houses. By 2011, the number of articles was 1,886.[46] Newswires started hiring correspondents whose main brief was to write about the commodity trading houses. In turn, the traders were forced to beef up PR teams – in some cases that meant hiring a PR specialist for the first time. Trafigura even hired the former editor of the *Financial Times*.

Inexorably, the veil of secrecy that had shrouded the commodity traders for decades was being lifted. At times, the transition to a life in the public eye was painful. Some still think it was a mistake. Zbynek Zak, the former chief financial officer who was a member of Glencore's board of directors until the IPO, says: 'The company

should not have gone public.' He attributes the decision to IPO to 'greed and arrogance'.[47]

Whatever the potential downsides of going public, the industry's shift towards the public markets brought with it considerable benefits. Whether they pursued an IPO, a bond sale, or partnerships with private equity investors, the commodity traders' ability to tap a wider pool of investors gave them the ability to raise much more money.

As never before, they had the financial firepower to shape global events.

THIRTEEN

MERCHANTS OF POWER

—————————

It's not likely that any of Pennsylvania's public school teachers paid attention to it, but a brief announcement in early 2018 held some unwelcome news for their retirement savings.

The pension pots of Pennsylvania's teachers are overseen from a red-brick office in Harrisburg, the state capital, from which the Public School Employees' Retirement System manages more than $50 billion of savings on behalf of 500,000 teachers and former teachers. Public pension funds have a reputation for being extremely conservative investors. Traditionally, they put safety above outsized returns. They hardly fit the stereotype of swashbuckling investors in hairy parts of the world.

Yet, on 19 March 2018, a terse notice from one of their holdings alerted the Pennsylvania teachers to the fact that their latest investment was anything but conservative.

'We hereby inform you that as a result of the independence referendum held by Kurdistan Regional Government on 25th September 2017, KRG's exports have decreased by almost 50% due to the takeover of Kirkuk oilfields which has had an adverse effect on the ability to supply the minimum contractual volumes,' the notice read.[1]

Pennsylvania's teachers may not have been aware of it, but a few months earlier, a small sliver of their retirement savings had been

directed to Kurdistan. They were far from alone. In South Carolina, the savings of over 600,000 police officers, judges and other public sector workers had been funnelled into the same investment. So had the savings of the teachers, firefighters and police officers of West Virginia.

The investment that connected them to one of the most febrile regions of the Middle East could have been a parable for the modern-day financial system, where money is passed between anonymous vehicles in low-tax, low-scrutiny jurisdictions. Their money's journey from Pennsylvania, South Carolina and West Virginia to northern Iraq had involved stops in George Town, the capital of the notoriously opaque tax haven of the Cayman Islands; Dublin, the finance-friendly Irish capital; Mayfair, the moneyed district at the heart of London; and Dubai, the glitzy emirate that is a hub for Middle Eastern money.

If the American pensioners had looked at the annual reports of their funds, they probably wouldn't have been any the wiser. Buried in the list of investments held by their pension funds, they would have seen the name 'Oilflow SPV 1 DAC'. Dig a little deeper, and they would have found that Oilflow SPV 1 DAC was an Irish company whose address was a bland, four-storey building in central Dublin where some 200 other companies were also formally incorporated.[2]

Its official purpose, according to a filing with the Irish authorities in 2016, was to 'acquire, manage, hold, sell, dispose of, finance and trade in all forms of financial assets'.[3] Then, in early 2017, Oilflow SPV 1 DAC registered on the Cayman Islands Stock Exchange. It had raised $500 million in 'secured amortising notes', an investment akin to a bond, due to be repaid by 2022.[4]

The most unusual element of Oilflow SPV 1 DAC was how good an investment it looked to be. In a world of ultra-low interest rates, the anonymous-sounding Irish company offered a surprisingly high yield. The notes promised to pay 12% annually over five years, more than six times the interest rate on US government debt at the time.

Of course, the high yield reflected the fact that the investment product carried a significant risk. Franklin Templeton, the fund manager that steered the American pension funds' money into the notes, described them simply as 'US-dollar bonds backed by oil from northern Iraq'.[5]

In reality, the bonds were part of a complex financial structure that had channelled the savings of American pensioners to help finance an independence movement in Iraqi Kurdistan. It was an investment that plunged the pension funds into a great game involving centuries of Middle Eastern history, the struggle for oil riches, and the daredevil world of the commodity traders. For Oilflow SPV 1 DAC was not just some anonymous investment vehicle. It was controlled by none other than Glencore.[6]

Commodity traders had been willing to put themselves and their money in places few others dared to tread since at least the days of Theodor Weisser's trip to the Soviet Union. And since at least the 1980s, they'd been arranging financing for more challenging countries by using the flow of commodities as a guarantee. In the early 1980s, for example, Marc Rich + Co agreed to advance about $80 million to Angola's government in the midst of a civil war. It was one of the first times that a country's oil had been used as security for a loan – a type of deal that would, in later years, become enormously popular.[7]

Now, the industry's shift towards raising outside capital – epitomised by Glencore's IPO in 2011 – had handed the commodity traders unprecedented clout. American pension funds would not have dreamt of lending to Marc Rich + Co. But they were happy to put their money in a vehicle created and controlled by its modern incarnation. After all, their reasoning might have gone, Glencore was a public company and a constituent of the prestigious FTSE 100.

Their new financial might made the commodity traders an even more important part of the global economic system, and it gave them the means to influence global politics as never before. The traders were guided by money, but in their pursuit of profit they inevitably

played a political role. Suddenly, they had the financial means to bankroll entire countries, to provide access to the global financial system for individuals and countries that had previously been frozen out of it, and even to play a decisive role in politically charged conflicts, such as Libya's civil war or Kurdistan's independence struggle. From their comfortable offices in London, Zug and Houston, the traders were shaping history.

Numbering about 30 million people spread across Iraq, Syria, Turkey and Iran, the Kurds are often described as the world's largest ethnic group without their own country.[8] Since the end of the first Gulf War in 1991, the Kurds had enjoyed a semi-autonomous state in northern Iraq, despite the protests of Saddam Hussein's government in Baghdad. When American forces toppled Saddam in 2003, the region emerged from the war enjoying even greater autonomy from Baghdad.

Still, their autonomy fell short of the fully independent state that most Kurds yearned for. But for Kurdistan to be a workable country, it would have to be able to stand alone economically. And the best hope of establishing an economically viable country was oil.

In early 2014, the Kurds' chance came. Civil war had been raging in neighbouring Syria for three years. Out of the wreckage, a new and dangerous force was growing stronger: Islamic State, the jihadist group known as ISIS. In 2014, with its stronghold in Syria established, the group turned its attention to Iraq.

ISIS first captured cities in the west of the country, including restive spots like Ramadi and Fallujah. Then, in June, it launched an offensive that overwhelmed the Iraqi army in the north, and captured Mosul. In the panicked retreat that followed, the Iraqi army all but abandoned Kirkuk, an important city to the south of Mosul. Kirkuk didn't fall to ISIS, however. Instead, a Kurdish guerrilla force, the Peshmerga, filled the void.

For the Kurds, it was an unusual victory. Since the creation of the modern nation state of Iraq in the 1920s, the oil of Kirkuk had been controlled by the central government in Baghdad. But the Kurds had always coveted the city, a melting pot of civilisations with thousands of years of history. And now they had gained control without even having to fight for it.

The Kurdish troops secured the fabled site of Baba Gurgur, whose name means 'father of fire' in Kurdish. For thousands of years, fire has burnt from the ground there, fed by natural gas escaping from a giant oilfield beneath the surface. Some believe the flames of Baba Gurgur are the fiery furnace of the Old Testament, into which Nebuchadnezzar, king of Babylon, threw three Jews who refused to bow down in front of a golden image.

By 2014, the Iraqi Kurds had spent more than a decade since the fall of Saddam lobbying the international community to recognise their push for independence. After South Sudan broke away from Sudan in 2011 with international recognition, the Kurds had hoped that they would be viewed similarly. But Washington and other Western capitals resisted.

The unexpected capture of Kirkuk's oil riches gave the Kurds a chance to build an economically autonomous country. A motley array of fixers and consultants soon appeared to help guide them. For oil, they hired a man who knew how to get it into the market: Murtaza Lakhani, the very same fixer who had been Glencore's man in Iraq a decade earlier and had played a role in the oil-for-food scandal. Now working as an independent consultant, Lakhani helped the Kurds connect with the commodity traders.[9] Among the other fixers who cropped up in Kurdistan was Paul Manafort, the former campaign chairman for Donald Trump, who would later be jailed for financial fraud. In Iraqi Kurdistan, Manafort's role was to help organise an independence referendum.[10]

But to convert their new oil into money, the Kurds needed to find a way to sell it. And that was not an easy task: Baghdad had threatened legal action against buyers of the crude, considering it stolen

property of the Iraqi state. The warning deterred many refiners, for whom the central government in Baghdad was a much more important oil supplier than the fragile Kurdish region could ever hope to be.[11]

Oil refiners may have been running scared from Baghdad's threats, but the commodity traders weren't so easily intimidated. Some of them had been buying the relatively small amounts of oil sold by the Kurds before the capture of Kirkuk, and they were happy to help handle a bigger volume. Kurdistan's oil attracted all the large traders, with Trafigura, Glencore and Vitol all descending on Erbil, the region's capital, in search of barrels.

Even for the commodity traders, dealing with the Kurdistan Regional Government, the entity that ruled over the semi-autonomous region of northern Iraq, was extremely politically sensitive. Just like the rebels in Vitol's adventure in war-torn Libya, the government in Erbil wasn't internationally recognised. And, of course, the very ownership of the oil was disputed: the Kurds claimed it as their own, while Baghdad argued that only the federal government could legally sell it. The threat of legal action hung over every deal the commodity traders did.

'The early business was: Can you take some crude oil and help us find homes for it? Because, obviously, it was more of a disputed commodity at the time,' says Ben Luckock, head of oil at Trafigura, who helped to organise some of the shipments.[12] 'It was really very difficult,' he added. 'We had no homes [for the oil] for a period of time.'

The traders went back to the smoke-and-mirrors techniques they had used in the 1970s and 1980s to evade embargoes. From northern Iraq, the Kurdish oil flowed 1,000 kilometres by pipeline through Turkey to Ceyhan, a port on the Mediterranean (see map on page 333). There, it was loaded into tankers, and then, as if by magic, it vanished.

For Trafigura, one of the pioneers of the Kurdish oil trade, the magic trick involved the Eilat–Ashkelon pipeline, the very same route that Marc Rich had employed in the 1970s to bring Iranian oil via Israel into Europe. The pipeline was, by now, able to pump oil in

both directions. And so Trafigura sent its tankers to Ashkelon to discharge the Kurdish crude, which then travelled across Israel to the Red Sea port of Eilat, where the trail became impossible to follow. Some of the oil ended up in Israel itself; some made its way to the independent oil refineries in China that are known, because of their often rudimentary design, as teapots.[13]

Just as in the 1970s, the use of the Eilat–Ashkelon pipeline was diplomatically charged. Iraq had formally been in a state of war with Israel since 1948, and Baghdad didn't recognise the Jewish state. But Claude Dauphin, the Trafigura chief executive, worked his own magic, and soon Israel was allowing Kurdish oil from northern Iraq to flow through its territory. 'The Israelis made a choice, that's clear,' says Luckock. 'The political situation was that the Israelis didn't mind.'[14]

Not every Kurdish oil deal worked out as planned, however. On one occasion in mid-2017, Vitol loaded a tanker called *Neverland* with about one million barrels of Kurdish crude and sent it towards a refinery in Canada. The government in Baghdad leapt into action – a delivery of crude to North America would be an intolerable political victory for the Kurds' campaign to sell their oil independently. The central Iraqi government publicly claimed the oil was stolen, and filed a lawsuit to impound the vessel and its cargo, as well as seeking $30 million in damages from Vitol. The Federal Court of Canada ordered the seizure of the vessel if it entered its territorial waters.

The entire global oil industry – not to mention countless diplomats, lawyers and court-appointed bailiffs – was fixated on the location of a single tanker. But the *Neverland* simply vanished. It had turned off its radio beacon, the signal that allows commodity wonks to follow cargoes of oil around the world, effectively becoming a ghost vessel. What happened next is a mystery. But nearly four weeks later, the tanker turned its beacon on again. It was back near Malta, where it had last been seen. But now it was empty. Vitol had, somewhere, offloaded the Kurdish oil. How? Where? To whom?

Several years later, the Vitol partners are still coy about it. 'Every-one knows a cargo disappeared and everyone knows that it didn't discharge in Europe or North America,' says Chris Bake, a senior partner at Vitol. 'So it went east.'[15]

The battle over Kurdish oil was one that Baghdad was destined to lose. The flow of money and oil was too beguiling, and the commod-ity traders found it too easy to sidestep any obstacles the Iraqi government might throw in their way. 'In the end, they realised that this wasn't a fight they were going to win a cargo at a time,' Bake says.

With the help of the commodity traders, the regional government of Kurdistan was shipping nearly 600,000 barrels a day at its peak – equivalent to about half of Norway's oil exports. And half of the Kurdish oil was coming from the oilfields that the Peshmerga had seized around Kirkuk.[16] Yet Erbil was still short of money. If the region was to push for independence, it would need a sizeable injec-tion of cash. The Kurdish leadership once again turned to the commodity traders. Would they lend the government some money in exchange for future oil shipments? The traders agreed. With oil as a guarantee, Vitol, Trafigura and Glencore, together with the Russian oil company Rosneft and another smaller trader called Petraco, advanced the Kurdistan Regional Government as much as $3.5 billon.[17] For Kurdistan that was a staggeringly large sum, equiva-lent to some 17.5% of the region's economy.[18] The loans would be repaid over several years with crude exports. Some trading houses lent the money using their own funds; others enlisted the help of their banks.

But Glencore took the most unusual route: the trading house decided Kurdistan was too risky for its own money; so it turned to international investors for cash, selling them an oil-backed bond that paid a high rate of interest. The note, in turn, would fund its advances to the Kurds. Oilflow SPV 1 DAC was born.

The risks for all the traders involved were significant: Baghdad continued to view the oil from Kirkuk as stolen; the borders between the semi-autonomous region and the rest of the country were, at

best, fluid; the risk of a civil war was ever present; and, to make things worse, ISIS was threatening the whole region.

Of course, the risks were also significant for the American pensioners whose savings were backing Oilflow SPV 1 DAC. A third of the investor presentation for the notes was spent enumerating the various risks involved. They included 'terrorism, religious conflicts, civil wars, border disputes, guerrilla activities, social unrest, economic difficulties, volatility in currency exchange rates and high inflation'. The presentation also alluded to the possibility that investors' money could be used for corruption, noting that Kurdistan was 'a high risk region with regards to governance practices'.[19]

What's more, Glencore had organised the deal so it would not buy the oil directly from the Kurdistan Regional Government, but through an intermediary company. Like the other oil traders, Glencore was risking the wrath of Baghdad by facilitating Kurdistan's oil sales, and its solution was to use a middleman. In exchange for $500 million of the investors' money, the Kurdish government would sign a contract not with Glencore, but with the intermediary company. It, in turn, would then have a contract with Glencore.

The intermediary wasn't a well-known company, and in its presentation to investors, Glencore didn't even name it. But it was rather well known to Glencore. The middleman for Glencore's Kurdish oil deal was a company established a little over a year earlier in Dubai, called Exmor Group. Operating from a forty-seven-floor skyscraper overlooking Palm Jumeirah, an artificial island off the coast of Dubai, Exmor was set up by a trader by the name of Josef Drujan, who had previously spent fifteen years working for Glencore across Asia and the former Soviet Union.[20] Glencore was using one of its longstanding former employees as a middleman between itself and the Kurdish government.

The money flowing from the oil deals with the trading houses became the main means of survival for the Kurdish region.[21] But the cash did a lot more than pay the salaries of teachers and policemen. The petrodollars also emboldened Kurdistan's independence

movement. Before its deals with the commodity traders, the Kurdish government had had little source of income other than handouts from Baghdad. Now, for the first time, local politicians felt that true independence from Baghdad was within reach – and for the first time, they might have the money to pay for it.

In September 2017, only a few months after Glencore had raised money for the region through Oilflow SPV 1 DAC, the politicians of Kurdistan took a fateful decision, and attempted to turn their new-found economic independence into political liberation. With its financial security guaranteed by the oil deals with Glencore and the other trading houses, the Kurdish government defied the central government in Baghdad and held an independence referendum. The result was overwhelming: 93% of the population voted to part ways with the rest of the country.[22]

But if the Kurds had hoped that the international community would welcome a new nation as it had done with South Sudan only a few years earlier, they had miscalculated: with ISIS in retreat, the West was no longer so reliant on the Kurds as military allies. Washington and other Western governments had warned Erbil against holding an independence referendum. The last thing they wanted was another fragile nation in an already fragile region. Now, their warnings ignored, the US and Europe did little to deter Baghdad's response.

Within days of the referendum, the central government reasserted its authority. Baghdad sent the federal army north to recapture the city of Kirkuk and its oilfields. The Kurdish region's hope of independence was in tatters. The economic autonomy that might have been possible, thanks to the oil riches of Baba Gurgur, now seemed like a fantasy. For the commodity traders, who had helped the independence movement with billions of dollars, it was a worrying development.

That's when Oilflow SPV 1 DAC started posting notices about the military manoeuvres in Iraq to the Cayman Islands Stock Exchange. Glencore had set up the vehicle with plenty of leeway to

manage either a drop in exports or in oil prices, and its ability to repay its lenders wasn't immediately affected by the drastic reduction in the amount of oil production under the Kurdish government's control. But when, in 2020, oil prices also tumbled, even the head-room Glencore had built into Oilflow SPV 1 DAC wasn't sufficient. The vehicle was no longer able to meet its commitments, and its investors had to agree to a delayed repayment schedule.

For pension funds like that of the Pennsylvanian teachers, the investment in Oilflow SPV 1 DAC had been a way to generate more income for their growing ranks of retirees than most conventional investments could offer. It's not clear they even considered what effect their money would have on Middle Eastern politics. The invest-ment in Oilflow SPV 1 DAC by Pennsylvania's Public School Employees' Retirement System, for example, was part of a wide portfolio of emerging market debt holdings, which was managed for it by Franklin Templeton, according to a spokesman.

'PSERS' investment professionals and consultants are well aware of the risks involved with this type of emerging market investment as well as the pros and cons involved in all its investment strategies and portfolios,' the spokesman said.[23]

Commodity traders like to say they are apolitical – they don't take sides; they are guided simply by their financial interest. It has been a mantra of the industry throughout its modern history. Challenged over his dealings with Iran in the midst of the hostage crisis, Marc Rich said: 'In our business we're not political. We never have been. That's the philosophy of our company.'[24]

Certainly, some commodity traders have used their personal wealth to push a political agenda. The Koch brothers, owners of Koch Industries, have spent hundreds of millions of dollars backing con-servative candidates and policies in the US. On a smaller scale, Vitol's Ian Taylor donated several million pounds to Britain's Conservative

Party and used his personal wealth to support the 'Better Together' campaign for Scotland to remain within the UK during the 2014 Scottish independence referendum.

Nonetheless, in their commodity deals, the traders' motivation is almost always coldly financial. If a trade is legal and profitable, most commodity traders don't pause to consider whether the political ramifications are desirable. 'We deal with the physical flow of oil up until the point where we feel it's right or allowable,' says Chris Bake of Vitol. 'I don't think we sit back and pull out a cigar and say, let's make some history here. I wish we had time to do that.'[25]

But even if political influence isn't their goal, that doesn't mean that the commodity traders are not influential. In a world where commodities are a direct route to money and power, the traders have the ability to change the course of history. For Kurdistan, the commodity traders helped to free the region from economic dependence on Baghdad and gave it the confidence to push for independence.

The traders may have disavowed any political pretensions, but Ashti Hawrami, Kurdistan's minister for natural resources, was under no illusions about the significance of their role. His philosophy was that economic independence was a precondition for political independence. 'The economy can take a lead ahead of politics and force politicians to take decisions,' he said.[26] And the commodity traders' cash? 'This helps our economic independence,' he said.[27]

A few weeks after the independence referendum, Taylor, the CEO of Vitol, was asked at a conference whether the traders had been instrumental in pushing Kurdistan over the line. After a pause, he acknowledged: 'We were, yeah.'[28]

Kurdistan wasn't the only place where the commodity traders deployed their new-found financial might. The combination of boom-time profits and expanded access to public markets gave them the ability to spread their largesse far and wide. From Libya to Kazakhstan, from Congo to South Sudan, the commodity traders became the major financiers of the kind of politically brittle but resource-rich countries that made other investors queasy.

Increasingly, the commodity traders were not risking their own money, but acting as links to international financial markets, channelling dollars from banks, pension funds and other investors into commodity deals in far-flung countries. It was a role that was familiar – after all, the traders had always acted as middlemen in the commodity markets. Now they were simply expanding to act as middlemen for money too.

It was no coincidence that this was happening in the wake of the global financial crisis of 2008. The American, British and European investment banks that had epitomised the freewheeling expansion of the finance industry were now in retreat. If they had not gone bankrupt or been nationalised, they were under the thumb of increasingly stringent regulations. They hardly needed to be told to pull back from the difficult, resource-rich countries that were known in bankerspeak as 'frontier markets'.

The commodity traders, not subject to anything like the degree of regulatory scrutiny that the banks faced, were only too willing to fill the void. Glencore's Oilflow SPV 1 DAC deal was a perfect example. But it was one of many similar deals, in similarly challenging parts of the world. In its 2016 presentation to prospective investors, the commodity trading house boasted that, in the previous six years, it had arranged over $17 billion in oil prepayments, that it had never lost money on a deal, and that it had a close relationship with 'more than 150 financial institutions around the world including all major banks and leading institutional investors'.[29]

The growing role of the commodity traders as large-scale financiers was also a reflection of changes in the business of commodity trading, particularly in oil. As their traditional model was eroded by the world's growing access to information, the traders prioritised size and scale to help maintain their profitability. Their investments in networks of pipelines, ports, storage tanks and refineries helped – and into this 'system' of assets they sought to feed ever larger volumes of oil. Rather than making a large amount of money on buying and selling a few cargoes of oil, they would aim to make

tiny individual profits on huge volumes. In the mid-1980s, Marc Rich + Co, then the largest oil trader, had been handling about 1.3 million barrels a day of crude and refined products.[30] By 2019, Vitol, which had taken the crown as the largest oil trader, was handling 8 million barrels a day. And Vitol wasn't an outlier: Trafigura was trading 6.1 million barrels a day, and Glencore 4.8 million barrels a day.

'At the end of the day our business does need scale,' said Ian Taylor. 'I hate to say it: size matters.'[31]

With sufficient scale, the traders could exploit their oil contracts and assets in response to minute moves in market prices. Perhaps a cargo that was due to head to the US could be redirected to Asia? Or a refinery could switch the blend of different types of crude it was processing to take advantage of price differences? Maybe one contract allowed the trader to deliver a few days later, or to deliver a few barrels fewer or more? Or perhaps a few million barrels could be parked in storage tanks, awaiting the next jump in prices?

This kind of system became the model for commodity trading – particularly oil trading, but also in metals and grains. And for it to work, the traders needed to have large volumes of oil flowing through their system, ready to respond to any opportunity the market might present. The best way to secure large volumes of oil was to finance the producers, locking them in to a multiyear relationship.

And so the commodity traders plunged in. They put their money (and that of others) to work wherever there was oil to buy and oil sellers in need of cash. It took them from the battlefields of the Libyan civil war to the gilded halls of the Kremlin.

The rise of these large-scale finance deals would mark a new era in the development of the commodity traders: with bigger deals, they oversaw larger amounts of money. Now, they had the ability to finance entire nations – and to help others into being. They were no longer just traders of commodities, but merchants of power.

★

There are few places in the world where a commodity trader has played such a dominant role in one country's economy as in Chad. Glencore's dealings in the African nation showed how some traders were prepared to put their financial resources to work alongside some of the most unsavoury figures in international politics.

Landlocked, desperately poor and relentlessly corrupt, Chad is an uninviting prospect for international investors.[32] Since a coup d'état in 1990, it has been ruled by Idriss Déby, a battle-hardened army general whose commitment to Chivas Regal whisky has often run deeper than his commitment to democracy.[33] Fending off attempts to oust him from inside and outside the country (the French government once offered him a pension and a comfortable apartment in exchange for stepping down),[34] Déby has maintained his grip on power, becoming one of the world's longest-serving leaders.

The people of Chad haven't shared his good fortune, despite the development of the country's modest oil resources. Life expectancy is the third-lowest on the planet;[35] nearly half the population lives below the World Bank poverty line;[36] and the country has been blighted by conflict and unrest.

By 2013, Chad was facing its latest threat in the shape of Islamist militants. Al-Qaeda was strong in central Africa, and Déby deployed his army to fight jihadists in neighbouring Mali and on Chad's border with Nigeria.

But the Chadian president had a problem. He didn't have enough cash to pay for his military adventures. Widely seen among international investors as an economic disaster zone, Chad couldn't simply call up banks and ask for a loan. And governmental donors like France, the former colonial power, and the World Bank and the IMF had grown wary of giving Déby generous handouts and by now were insisting on the strict ring-fencing of any loan to ensure that it would only be spent on poverty reduction.

Shunned by every other lender, Chad's president turned for help to a company that was comfortable with the risk involved in lending

to his country and nonchalant about the ripple effects its money could have throughout the region: Glencore.

In May 2013, Déby received a $300 million influx of cash from Glencore, in the form of a loan backed by future oil supplies, a type of arrangement known as a prepayment. By the end of the year, the trader had doubled the size of the loan to $600 million.[37] The cash came with a proviso: the money could only be used 'for civil purposes to support the state budget'.[38] But this seemingly restrictive clause was a gimmick: Chad could use the Glencore money for non-military expenses, freeing up the rest of its budgetary resources to fund the military. In effect, Glencore was helping to finance Déby's wars against jihadist Islam in his neighbouring countries.

With oil prices above $100 a barrel, Déby found in Glencore a bank that was willing to lend him vast sums of money despite an appalling human rights track record and international concerns about economic mismanagement. Soon, he was back for more: in 2014, he borrowed a further $1.45 billion from Glencore, this time in order to buy out Chevron's stake in Chad's oilfields.[39]

Just as in Kurdistan, Glencore didn't lend Chad all the money itself. Instead, it persuaded a group of banks and other investors to back the deal.[40] And just as in Kurdistan, the investors included some of the largest US pension funds – according to one corporate filing, the Public Employees Retirement System of Ohio and the West Virginia Investment Management Board contributed funds to Glencore's Chad deals.[41]

Glencore's dealings with Déby had been friendly enough while oil prices were above $100 a barrel, but when, in late 2014, they began to fall, the relationship soured. With output rising from the US shale oil industry, the oil price tumbled from a peak of $115 a barrel in 2014 to just $27 in early 2016. Chad simply couldn't repay its debts in the new oil price environment. The African nation asked to renegotiate the deal, and after protracted talks, Glencore agreed to restructure the loans. But the restructuring demonstrated quite how

important a force Glencore had become in Chad: with oil prices still low, the poverty-stricken country owed Glencore and its partners almost \$1.5 billion, equivalent to 15% of its gross domestic product.[42]

Even after it had been restructured, the Glencore loan imposed punishing austerity on the Chadian government. The country was forced to slash education, health and investment spending, and struggled for months to pay salaries – all so it could meet its repayment obligations to the world's largest commodity trader. Even the IMF, well known for imposing fiscal discipline on struggling countries, described Chad's spending cuts as 'dramatic'.[43]

Déby came to regret his deal with Glencore, calling the loan a fool's bargain. 'I must admit that the loan obtained from Glencore was irresponsible,' he said.[44] With his country on the brink of collapse, Déby asked for another revision of the terms of the debt, which Glencore eventually agreed to in 2018, giving Chad more time to repay and halving the interest rate.[45]

Today, the Glencore loan is so important for Chad that, when the IMF publishes reviews of the country's economy, the commodity trading house merits its own mention in the analysis of the African nation's government finances. Even before coronavirus struck, the country didn't expect to finish paying back Glencore until 2026.[46] Despite his near absolute control in Chad, Déby has become suspicious about his deal with the commodity trading house, leading him to comment: 'When I welcomed the head of Glencore here, I asked him: "Are there any people to whom you have paid commissions?"'[47]

If Glencore was the lender of last resort in Chad, in Kazakhstan that role was performed by Vitol. While Glencore's deals in Chad had been relatively straightforward, advancing money in exchange for future oil supplies, Vitol's many years of dealings in Kazakhstan were

a demonstration of the complex network of relationships commodity traders were willing to build to maintain their business in resource-rich countries – and the rewards for doing so.

In the era of the commodity boom, Kazakhstan had been a hot new frontier for oil companies to invest in. Sparsely populated Kazakh plains were suddenly awash with geologists and engineers from Texas, Scotland and Canada on the hunt for oil riches. The dollars flowed in, and a futuristic new capital sprouted out of the Kazakh steppe, while the country's politicians and oligarchs filled the clubs and hotels of Mayfair and Dubai.

By the early 2010s, the Central Asian nation had lost its shine for many international investors. They were frustrated with the country's sclerotic post-Soviet bureaucracy, its frequent rule changes, and the avarice of its elites. The flagship Kazakh oil project, Kashagan, had been beset by so many delays and cost blow-outs that the engineers nicknamed it 'cash all gone'.

When the oil price plunged in 2014, it threw the Kazakh authorities into panic. Since before the collapse of the Soviet Union, the country had been ruled by just one man, Nursultan Nazarbayev. The Kazakh president's authoritarian rule had been tolerated, for the most part, by a population that had been growing wealthier every year. But now that was no longer true, Nazarbayev's reign was looking increasingly brittle.

One area of particular concern was the state oil company, Kaz-MunaiGas (KMG). It was a vast enterprise, responsible for the employment of whole towns. An oil workers' strike in 2011 in western Kazakhstan had ended in deadly clashes with police, in one of the darkest moments in the country's post-Soviet history.

After the oil price fall at the end of 2014, KMG needed money so desperately that it was forced to beg for a cash injection from the Kazakh central bank. But that was only a stopgap solution. For a more permanent fix, Kazakhstan's state oil company turned to Vitol.

Starting in early 2016, the oil trader channelled a total of more than $6 billion in loans to KMG in exchange for future oil supplies.[48]

In effect, the deals made Vitol the largest financier of the Kazakh state oil company, and probably the single largest financier of the Kazakh state.[49] It was the same type of prepayment deal – loans for future oil supplies – that traders had done in Chad and Kurdistan. Just as in those deals, the money ultimately came from a group of banks. But it couldn't have happened without Vitol.[50]

Nazarbayev's presidency survived the downturn in the oil price, allowing him to effect a long-planned succession and oversee the country in his dotage from his post as 'Leader of the Nation'. And Vitol, in exchange for the billions of dollars it steered into Kazakhstan's state coffers, received hundreds of millions of barrels of Kazakh oil.

But these were far from being Vitol's first deals in Kazakhstan. The trading house had assiduously cultivated ties in the country for more than a decade. As long ago as 2005, an entity by the name of Vitol Central Asia was the dominant buyer of oil from KMG's trading unit.[51]

For all the world, Vitol Central Asia looks like just another subsidiary of the giant oil trading house. It shares an address in Geneva with Vitol. Its directors are two of Vitol's most senior partners.[52]

But Vitol Central Asia was not just another Vitol subsidiary. In fact, it was only 49% owned by Vitol itself.[53] The majority stake in the company was owned by a man called Arvind Tiku. (Later, his stake would be reduced to just under 50%.)

It might seem odd for the world's largest oil trader to allow an outsider to hold a majority stake in a company that bears its name, but Tiku was not just anyone. He had been an important player in the Kazakh energy industry for a number of years, starting out in the country in the 1990s trading oil and grains, including a stint working for Marc Rich after his exit from Glencore. And he became a business associate of Timur Kulibayev, the Kazakh president's son-in-law, widely viewed as the most powerful individual in the Kazakh oil sector and at times seen as a possible successor to Nazarbayev.[54]

In response to questions, Vitol said it 'does not believe Mr Tiku's relationship with Mr Kulibayev has benefited Vitol meaningfully'. A spokesman for Tiku pointed out that he had not had any business relationship with Kulibayev until 2006, several years after he first went into business with Vitol. 'Mr Tiku did not use any relationship with Mr Kulibayev to obtain any favours or favourable terms for VCA [Vitol Central Asia], Vitol or any other business', the spokesman said.[55]

The alliance between Vitol and Tiku has been an extremely profitable enterprise. Between 2011 and 2018, for example, the holding company for Vitol Central Asia – which included several other joint ventures between Vitol and Tiku, with names like Wimar, Titan Oil Trading, and Euro-Asian Oil – paid more than $1 billion in dividends to its shareholders.[56]

And, after more than a decade, Vitol remains the dominant international oil trader in Kazakhstan – a testament to the rewards on offer for a trader willing to commit to a long-term relationship.

In Kazakhstan, Chad and Kurdistan, the traders had used their financial heft to great effect. But nowhere did they funnel more dollars to a state than in Russia. In the process, they probably did more to help Vladimir Putin remain in power than anyone else in the international business community – even as he was engaged in a hostile geopolitical standoff with Europe and the US.

For much of the boom era of the 2000s, Russia hadn't really needed the commodity traders' money. It was a darling of Western investors, one of the BRIC economies whose rapid growth and burgeoning middle class made it an irresistible bet on the future of commodity-rich emerging markets. Even after the shock of the takeover of Yukos's assets by the State, and the imprisonment of Mikhail Khodorkovsky, Russian companies and the Russian state alike could borrow easily from Western investors and banks.

Then, in 2012, Igor Sechin, a powerful confidant of president Vladimir Putin, who had long pushed for the consolidation of Russia's oil assets under the state champion Rosneft, agreed to buy the privately owned TNK–BP. At a valuation of $55 billion, the acquisition was one of the largest in the history of the energy industry. Western banks lined up to lend Rosneft money, but Sechin needed more cash than the global banking system was able to muster, even for one of the world's largest oil companies.

And so the commodity traders stepped in. Since Sechin had taken over as chief executive of Rosneft, Gunvor had fallen out of favour with the state oil company (Sechin and Timchenko, while both friends of Putin, had a tense relationship and sometimes weren't even on speaking terms with one another).[57]

Now, needing money in a hurry, Sechin phoned two of Gunvor's competitors: Ivan Glasenberg of Glencore and Ian Taylor of Vitol. Within a few weeks, the traders had rustled up a staggering $10 billion that they would give Rosneft in exchange for future supplies of oil.[58] It was the largest oil-for-loans deal ever: since the first such deal thirty years earlier between Marc Rich + Co and Angola, the traders had gone from lending $80 million to more than one hundred times that amount.

For Glencore and Vitol, it was a lucrative foothold in one of the world's largest oil exporters. Soon, however, the traders would become even more important to Rosneft, Sechin and Russia itself.

On 18 March 2014, Putin signed a decree to incorporate Crimea into Russia following a hastily arranged referendum. The West, describing the move as an illegal annexation of part of Ukraine, responded by ramping up the economic pressure on Russia through sanctions. Washington began by placing sanctions on influential individuals who were close to the Kremlin, including Sechin, citing his 'utter loyalty to Vladimir Putin'.[59]

Over the summer, fighting escalated in eastern Ukraine, and the West imposed ever more restrictive sanctions against the Russian economy – including on Rosneft itself. The sanctions on Rosneft

did not block all dealings with the Russian oil company, but they specifically prohibited long-term lending to it.

That created an enormous headache for Sechin. The problem almost became fatal for the entire Russian financial system. On top of the $10 billion it had got from Vitol and Glencore, Rosneft had borrowed about $35 billion from Western banks and investors to consummate the TNK–BP deal. In late 2014 and early 2015, some of the loans were due to be repaid. It seemed that the only solution for Rosneft, frozen out of international debt markets by the sanctions, would be to borrow in roubles and convert the currency into dollars. As Rosneft's loan deadlines neared, the rouble went into freefall, losing a quarter of its value in just a few hours.

The commodity traders were unfazed by Rosneft's troubles – in fact, they were queueing up to see what they could do to help. Trafigura drastically expanded its dealings with Rosneft, with chief executive Jeremy Weir describing the environment in early 2015 as a business opportunity. 'We have seen a niche,' he said.[60]

But it was Glencore that pulled off perhaps the biggest coup in Russia. In 2016, with the oil price still in the doldrums, the Russian government was short of money. Sechin, ever the bold and aggressive empire-builder of the Russian energy sector, persuaded Putin to allow Rosneft to take over a smaller, private Russian oil producer. In exchange, he promised that he would be able to sell part of the Russian government's stake in Rosneft – and so deliver a windfall to the Russian budget by the end of the year.

But with the deadline nearing, buyers were thin on the ground. Sechin shuttled between talks with Middle Eastern and Asian investors, but none was willing to stump up billions of dollars for a stake in Rosneft.[61] Once again, Glencore came to Sechin's rescue. The trading house wasn't willing to put up all the money itself, so it called on the government of Qatar. The very same Qatari sovereign wealth fund that Glasenberg had battled with over the Xstrata deal was now Glencore's largest shareholder. Now, Glencore and Qatar were

joining forces as co-investors in an $11 billion deal to buy part of the Russian government's stake in Rosneft.

Sechin was triumphant – the deal had defied predictions that no investor would dare buy a stake in Rosneft, given the sanctions. And with the traders' help, Putin had weathered a sharp economic down-turn. It would be an exaggeration to say that the commodity traders saved the Russian president's political career, but there's no doubt their actions helped.

At a reception in the Kremlin, a smiling Putin reminded Glasenberg of his humbler beginnings trading coal.[62] 'I want to express my con-fidence that your business in Russia will develop and will develop successfully,' the president said, awarding Glasenberg and the other participants in the deal Russia's Order of Friendship.[63] Six decades after a fearful Theodor Weisser had travelled to Moscow in search of oil to buy, the commodity traders were now being welcomed with open arms in the citadel of Russian political power.

All over the world, the commodity traders' cash was changing the course of history. Yet there was no guarantee that the traders – many of whom travelled the world on British and American passports and operated from bases in Europe and America – would be acting in line with Western political interests.

In some cases, such as the war in Libya, when Vitol shipped more than $1 billion of fuel to the rebels, they were clearly pulling in the same direction as the foreign ministries of their home governments. In some cases, such as in Kazakhstan, Western governments were more or less indifferent to their activities.

But in other cases their deals went squarely in the face of Western policy. The traders' money helped spur a Kurdish independence referendum in the face of strong opposition from the US, which argued it could jeopardise the fight against ISIS.[64] In Chad, Glencore's money helped bankroll Idriss Déby's government even as Western-led

institutions, such as the World Bank and IMF, were trying to impose strict conditions on him. In Russia, the traders' cash very directly flew in the face of Western policy, by helping Rosneft and Putin weather the impact of US and EU sanctions against them.

And as they realised that the commodity traders had become enormously important actors in global finance and politics, Western politicians and regulators also began to realise that they had terrifyingly little oversight of what the commodity traders were doing. Even as the traders had accumulated unprecedented financial power, their activity remained almost entirely unregulated.

There had been a push for greater regulation of futures markets in the wake of the wild price gyrations of 2007–2011, but it had left the physical commodity markets largely untouched. The issue was not lost on the regulators themselves. For the most part, however, they lacked the legal authority, the political support, or simply the resources to do much about it. But there was one aspect of their business where the commodity traders were potentially vulnerable to aggressive regulation. They were reliant on a relatively narrow group of banks to provide them with huge sums in credit. And, more than anything, they relied on being able to access those sums in US dollars.

CONCLUSION

A LOT OF SKELETONS

The phone call that almost killed Trafigura came on a summer's day in 2014.

By now, the trading house was no longer the scrappy upstart it had once been. Symbolising its arrival at the top table of global commodity trading, Trafigura had just taken over an entire office building, its top floor fitted out with meeting rooms with tinted glass walls and leather seats from which its tireless boss Claude Dauphin could look out over the rooftops of Geneva.

Trafigura's success had been built overwhelmingly thanks to money from one bank: BNP Paribas. Since the beginnings of the spot oil market in the 1970s, the French lender had been the king of commodity trade finance, the lifeblood of the whole industry. It provided the billions of dollars in short-term loans that allowed the traders to buy and sell oil, metals and grains around the world without using much of their own money. For Dauphin, the relationship with BNP Paribas was indispensable: since Trafigura's earliest days, the French bank had been its largest lender, at times accounting for half of all its financing. It had stuck by Trafigura's side through thick and thin, even at Dauphin's personal low point, when he was thrown into a jail cell in Ivory Coast in the midst of the toxic waste scandal.

So when Dauphin answered the phone to his banker at BNP Paribas, he might have expected a friendly catch-up. He might have assumed the BNP Paribas executive was calling to ask after his health – a few months earlier, Dauphin had been diagnosed with lung cancer. He may have also been ready to commiserate: BNP Paribas had been going through one of the darkest spells in its history, under pressure from the US government for violating sanctions.

But Dauphin hadn't expected what he heard next. This was not a social call. BNP Paribas was telephoning to inform the Trafigura boss that the bank no longer wanted to do business with him. The French lender was pulling about $2 billion in credit lines from Trafigura. Their relationship, forged over decades of trading commodities on every corner of the planet, was over.[1]

It was a cataclysmic moment for Dauphin, who had poured his life into Trafigura. Chain-smoking, relentless, charming and witty, he was the last of a generation of traders who had been seen as the heirs to Marc Rich in the 1980s, trading missionaries who brought Rich's style of trading to all corners of the globe. He had built Trafigura in that image, driving the upstart trading house into the big league alongside companies like Vitol and Glencore almost through force of will alone.

It was also a moment that would mark the beginning of a new era for the commodity traders. Just as they had reached the zenith of their wealth and influence around the world, their industry was about to change for ever. After decades in which they had expanded their reach around the world in the almost total absence of regulation or oversight, there was now an aggressive and unpredictable policeman in town: the US government.

BNP Paribas had just pled guilty to violating US sanctions against Cuba, Sudan and Iran, and agreed to pay nearly $9 billion.[2] It was a landmark case that shocked both the French elite and the global banking industry – the first time US officials had pursued such a large case against a major bank in a foreign country that was also a US ally.

In a devastating statement of its case, the US government set out how BNP Paribas had 'knowingly, intentionally and willfully' moved billions of dollars through the US financial system in breach of sanctions. Among the trades that had violated the sanctions were US dollar loans that BNP Paribas had provided 'to a Dutch company'.[3] The loans had been designed to 'finance the purchase of crude oil products destined to be refined in and sold to Cuba'.

The US didn't name the Dutch company, nor did it suggest it had done anything wrong. But its presence in the list of charges against BNP Paribas was the reason a senior executive from the bank was phoning Claude Dauphin. Unknown to everyone but a small circle of insiders, the mysterious Dutch company shipping oil to Cuba was Trafigura.[4]

Trafigura and BNP Paribas had been working together in Cuba since the 1990s, when Dauphin had elbowed his way into the country in a challenge to the dominance of Vitol. Dauphin agreed to help finance inventories of crude oil and refined products in storage tanks at a refinery on the outskirts of Havana. And Trafigura had continued doing so ever since. 'We would finance these stocks with a bank, which was BNP Paribas, and they [the Cuban state-owned oil company] would buy the oil when needed for cash,' recalls Eric de Turckheim, who was Trafigura's head of finance at the time.[5]

The deal had helped the government of Fidel Castro conserve its cash at a time of hardship, winning Dauphin his desired foothold in the Cuban market. For Trafigura, it was a relatively small deal, as the inventories involved at any one time were only worth about $40 million.[6] But repeated many times over the years of Trafigura's dealings in Cuba, it added up to hundreds of millions of dollars in sales.

For years, the Americans were unaware. The US had outlawed American companies from dealing with Cuba, but European governments opposed the ban and many European companies were happy to invest there. The problem for BNP Paribas was that its loans to support Trafigura's Cuban business were in US dollars, meaning that they had to be routed through the American financial system.

Aware of the US sanctions, the French lender concealed the connection to Cuba. Rather than make direct payments, the bank set up layers of accounts to disguise the origin of the deals and instructed other banks involved that 'they should not mention CUBA in their transfer order'.[7]

When Washington uncovered the plot, it moved aggressively against BNP Paribas. The $9 billion settlement in 2014 was one of the largest ever fines imposed on a single financial institution. Just as damaging, the US blocked parts of BNP Paribas from accessing the US dollar system for one year – a punishment of unprecedented severity for a bank operating in the global financial markets where the US dollar is king.

Back at Trafigura's Geneva headquarters, Dauphin quickly understood the magnitude of the problem. The phone call from BNP Paribas was an existential threat to his company. The French bank wasn't just Trafigura's largest financier, it was a trendsetter for the mostly European banks that financed the commodity traders. If other banks saw BNP Paribas dropping Trafigura, they might also run for the exit. Dauphin started phoning around his other banking contacts, begging them not to pull the plug.

The case against BNP Paribas highlighted the US government's changing philosophy to the world beyond its borders: from now on, it would aggressively prosecute behaviour that ran counter to its foreign policy – even if that meant attacking major companies in countries that were US allies.

And its main weapon was the US dollar, whose singular importance to the global banking system gave Washington enormous power to enforce its will. No bank could afford to be locked out of the US dollar system, as BNP Paribas had been. And so every bank around the world would effectively become an extension of US law enforcement, proactively hunting for any behaviour that ran counter to US policy.

Announcing the BNP Paribas fines, Eric Holder, the US attorney general, sent a warning to companies around the world: the US would no longer look the other way just because they were not American.

'This outcome should send a strong message to any institution – any-where in the world – that does business in the United States: illegal conduct will not be tolerated,' Holder said. 'And wherever it is uncovered, it will be punished to the fullest extent of the law.'[8]

The episode marked the beginning of the end of the era in which the traders had jetted around the world, doing deals in corrupt countries or with pariah governments with impunity. The huge fines against BNP Paribas only tangentially touched the commodity traders – Dauphin's campaign to keep his other bankers onside was successful, and Trafigura survived – but it was a sign of things to come. Soon the commodity traders, too, would be in the crosshairs of the US government, and the future of trading as an industry would be under a cloud.

For years, many commodity traders had looked on sanctions and embargoes as an opportunity rather than a threat. Countries under embargo had fewer choices about whom to trade with, and so the profits for those who found ways to do business with them were proportionately higher. That's what had allowed Marc Rich and John Deuss to make astronomical profits from subverting the oil embargo against apartheid South Africa in the 1980s.

It was possible because the embargoes were poorly enforced. If they were put in place by only a few countries, then it was easy enough for the traders to open up a subsidiary in a country that hadn't imposed sanctions, and deal through that subsidiary. Much of the traders' activity took place in international waters, and so went ungoverned by any one nation's laws. And the traders' businesses similarly operated in the most opaque corners of the international financial system, where they might use a Cayman Islands shell company one day and a Maltese shell company the next; and where ships could sail under the flag of any number of nations, from Panama to Liberia or the Marshall Islands.

It was rare for sanctions to be imposed on a truly global basis. Until the collapse of the Soviet Union, the United Nations Security Council had only imposed economic sanctions twice, against Southern Rhodesia in 1966 and South Africa in 1977. Once Moscow dropped its perennial opposition to the use of economic penalties after 1991, the UN imposed sanctions more than twenty times, in countries from Somalia to Yugoslavia.[9] But still, they were easy enough to circumvent: Switzerland, where many of the commodity traders were based, would not become a member of the UN until 2002. Even if the commodity traders did do something wrong in Switzerland, Swiss prosecutors were rarely aggressive in prosecuting companies that were some of their country's major taxpayers.

For many years, the traders had lived by Marc Rich's maxim of walking on the edge of the knife – going as close as possible to the line of what was legal, using every loophole they could find. If they didn't break the letter of the law, they made a mockery of its spirit. Vitol, for example, used its subsidiary in Bahrain to skirt European sanctions on Iran in 2012.[10]

It was a similar story regarding corruption. Cultivating cosy relationships with powerful officials had long been at the heart of the business of commodity trading, and in many countries in Africa, the former Soviet Union and the Middle East, that meant finding ways to pay them off.

The commodity traders certainly hadn't been alone in seeing bribery as an unavoidable cost of doing business in the 1970s. After the Watergate scandal, American officials started to investigate companies' payments to politicians in the US and beyond. What they uncovered shocked the foundations of corporate America. More than 400 companies admitted to having made questionable or outright illegal payments overseas.[11] Ashland Oil, the American refiner that had traded with Marc Rich in his last days at Philipp Brothers, admitted to having paid thousands of dollars in bribes to foreign officials, including on one occasion when its chief executive officer 'personally delivered $7,500 to an official' of a foreign nation.[12] Cook Industries, one of

the traders that sold grains to the Russians in 1972, said that some of its employees 'may have been involved in violations relating to grain transactions and other such matters as bribery and intimidation of federally licensed grain officials'.[13]

Until then, the US had not considered the bribing of foreign officials for business purposes to be illegal. But in 1977, the Foreign Corrupt Practices Act was passed, making it illegal for US individuals or companies to pay bribes overseas. Step by step, many other countries tightened their laws on bribery too.

But some, notably Switzerland, were extremely slow to act. Paying bribes to foreign officials was not only widely accepted within the business community, but the bribes were even tax deductible. It was only in 2016 that Swiss companies stopped being able to claim a tax credit against the bribes they had paid to businesspeople abroad, with the approval of new legislation. 'Bribery payments to private individuals should no longer be allowed as expenses that are justified for business purposes', the Swiss government wrote.[14]

Switzerland also dragged its feet in prosecuting bribery of foreign government officials. Its first foreign corruption case against a company in Switzerland came only in 2011.[15] And the penalties, beyond public shame, remained very low. For companies whose employees bribe a foreign official, the maximum penalty is five million Swiss francs, plus forfeiture of profit. The IMF has described the fines as 'not effective, proportionate or dissuasive'.[16]

Thanks to antiquated regulations and the willingness of countries like Switzerland to turn a blind eye, many commodity traders had little trouble finding ways to keep their most important relationships sweet. Marc Rich publicly admitted to having paid bribes during his golden years. Vitol admitted to paying kickbacks to Iraq in the oil-for-food scandal. Trafigura, in 2006, paid $475,000 to the ruling party in Jamaica, where the trader had a big oil contract. The Jamaican government, which had benefited from the money, called it a campaign donation; Trafigura said it was a commercial matter.[17] A subsidiary of ADM paid $22 million via intermediaries to Ukrainian

government officials between 2002 and 2008 to win a $100 million tax rebate.[18]

At Glencore, there were traders who would fly the world carrying briefcases full of cash. 'I used to go with 500,000 pounds to London,' says Paul Wyler, who was one of Glencore's most senior executives until 2002. Once, he was stopped in Heathrow airport by customs officials shocked at the amount of cash in his luggage. They asked him what he planned to do with such a lot of money. Knowing that he wouldn't be able to get a receipt for what he was planning to spend it on, Wyler calmly replied: 'I go gambling.'

Still, he says there was less corruption in Glencore's history than is commonly believed. 'It's not like that we got the business only because we paid everybody off,' he says. 'In many countries it was just a no-go. You couldn't pay commissions in Japan, or you couldn't pay commissions in Chile, or in most of Western Europe it wasn't really that widespread. In South America, yes . . . And, yes, in China it was very corrupt.'[19]

But in 2014, when the US levied its enormous fine on BNP Paribas, the world was changing. For decades, the US had imposed its will around the world using its pre-eminent military might. But now, after years of fighting in Iraq and Afghanistan, the US public was tired of wars. Under President Barack Obama, Washington found a new method to enforce its will: using the power of the dollar in the global financial system as a weapon.

Sanctions programmes proliferated as a tool of US foreign policy – against countries that were America's foes, and individuals who, in the opinion of the US government, were responsible for corruption and human rights abuses around the world. All of this was possible because of the overwhelming importance of the US dollar. As the US became the world's dominant economy in the second half of the twentieth century, a large proportion of global trade was priced in

US dollars – including almost all commodities. Because any US dollar transaction must be cleared through an American bank, US sanctions took on 'enormous weight and influence beyond our borders', according to Jack Lew, the Treasury secretary from 2013 to 2017.[20]

But the US went further still, introducing a new concept called 'secondary sanctions' that would use the global significance of the dollar to police trade that wasn't even conducted in US dollars. Secondary sanctions involved the threat to block access to the US financial system to companies that had done business with sanctioned entities, even if they hadn't done so in dollars. The effect was to make the US the world's policeman. Lew himself acknowledged that such secondary sanctions 'are viewed, even by some of our closest allies as extra-territorial attempts to apply US foreign policy to the rest of the world'.[21]

The first target was the banks. BNP Paribas was not alone. The US forced HSBC to pay $1.9 billion for allowing itself to be used to launder Mexican drug money;[22] Credit Suisse paid $2.6 billion for helping US citizens to avoid taxes.[23]

For the commodity traders, too, the world was changing. Trafigura had survived the loss of BNP Paribas as its main banker. But the incident was a warning shot to the industry: it was only a matter of time before the traders would find themselves in Washington's sights. For decades, trumpeting that they were apolitical, the traders had rushed to do business with all kinds of individuals and regimes that were unloved by the US government. But as the US started to use its economic dominance rather than its military might to enforce its foreign policy, it was increasingly unwilling to tolerate the traders' propensity to undermine it.

US sanctions started to target many of the countries where the traders had done most business – including Iran, Russia and Venezuela. And the US placed many of the traders' closest friends and allies on the sanctions list it had previously reserved for terrorists and drug dealers.

Washington imposed sanctions on Oleg Deripaska, the aluminium magnate with whom Ivan Glasenberg had watched football, citing 'allegations that Deripaska bribed a government official, ordered the

murder of a businessman, and had links to a Russian organized crime group'.[24] (Deripaska denies those allegations and has filed a lawsuit against the US government.) Dan Gertler, Glencore's longstanding business partner, was placed under sanctions for his allegedly 'opaque and corrupt mining and oil deals in the Democratic Republic of the Congo'.[25] (Gertler has also denied the allegations.) And so was Didier Casimiro, the Belgian-born boss of Rosneft's trading unit who was, for many years, a key contact for many of the commodity traders.[26]

It wasn't just the traders' business partners that were in the firing line. Increasingly, the traders themselves seemed to be the targets of the US. At Gunvor, Gennady Timchenko, the company's co-founder, was placed under sanctions in the wake of Russia's annexation of Crimea in 2014. Describing him as a member of the Russian president's 'inner circle', the US Treasury stated: 'Timchenko's activities in the energy sector have been directly linked to Putin. Putin has investments in Gunvor and may have access to Gunvor funds.'[27]

It was a bombshell for the company – an apparent confirmation of all the rumours that had long swirled around its success in Russia. Could Gunvor, so dependent on credit from banks, survive the association? In the hours after the sanctions hit, the company's situation looked bleak. But Gunvor had a rabbit to pull out of the hat. Within hours of the US Treasury's statement, it announced that Timchenko had sold his stake – a day earlier, just before the sanctions had been imposed. Timchenko's lobbyists in Washington had heard that sanctions on Putin's circle were coming, and so he'd rushed to put together a deal whereby his partner Törnqvist would buy him out, according to the Gunvor CEO.[28]

In the years after the BNP Paribas settlement in 2014, a profusion of investigations sprang up into the murkier side of the traders' business practices. In Brazil, local prosecutors, with the help of the FBI, the US Department of Justice, and the Swiss attorney general, started investigating payments made by a number of international trading houses to employees of the Brazilian state oil company Petrobras in exchange for supply contracts. The prosecutors alleged that Vitol, Trafigura and Glencore had paid a total of $31 million in bribes to

Petrobras employees and intermediaries between 2011 and 2014.[29] One former Petrobras trader, who went by the nickname 'Phil Collins', testified that Vitol had paid him bribes. 'In trading, when you want to get a bribe, you don't make $10 a barrel in one cargo,' he said. 'It's the perpetuity of a few cents in each sale, in each product, that provides the illicit gain.'[30] In December 2020, Vitol agreed to pay $164 million after admitting to bribing officials in Brazil, as well as Ecuador and Mexico. Trafigura denied the allegations, while Glencore said it was cooperating with investigators.

In Switzerland, Gunvor was forced to pay $95 million after one of its employees bribed officials in the Republic of the Congo and Ivory Coast to secure oil deals – the largest penalty the Swiss prosecutor had ever issued against a commodity trader.[31] And prosecutors began investigating Glencore, a symbolic strike against the world's largest commodity trader and the heir to the empire of Philipp Brothers and Marc Rich + Co. In July 2018, Glencore announced that it had been subpoenaed by the US Department of Justice as part of a corruption and money-laundering probe. The investigation covered eleven years of the company's activity at its copper and cobalt mines in the Democratic Republic of Congo, as well as its oil deals in Nigeria and Venezuela.[32] A year later, the UK's Serious Fraud Office announced that it, too, was investigating 'suspected bribery' at Glencore.[33] In 2020, the Swiss attorney general followed suit.[34]

Glasenberg's adventure in the Congo, which had once seemed like a stroke of dealmaking brilliance, now cast a long shadow over his company's future. The Glencore share price collapsed, wiping billions of dollars off the company's value and the fortunes of its top traders.[35] Glasenberg, facing a barrage of questions from investors about his and the company's future, announced he would soon step aside as chief executive.[36]

US government officials didn't explain why their focus appeared to have landed on the commodity traders, but there was no doubt

in the minds of the traders themselves that they were in Washington's sights. Much as the BNP Paribas case in 2014 changed the behaviour of the global banking industry, the US appeared to be determined to set a new benchmark for what would count as acceptable behaviour for international commodity traders.

Jeremy Weir, the successor to Claude Dauphin as CEO of Trafigura, summed up the feeling of being the target of Washington's new offensive: 'The industry – like the banking industry was – is under a bit of a microscope.'[37]

This book has told the story of how the commodity traders rose, almost unnoticed, to the pinnacle of global power. With little fanfare, the commodity traders helped to free the global oil market from the grip of the Seven Sisters, re-carved the economic landscape of Russia and the rest of the former Soviet Union, and empowered resource-rich governments from Congo to Iraq.

But seemingly from every side, the industry is under fire. It's not just the corruption probes that are darkening the outlook. Following a boom in the first decade of this century, the profitability of the traders has levelled off. The industry is still able to turn a healthy profit – many traders made a killing as oil prices plunged in 2020 – but it's becoming clearer and clearer that another meaningful step up in profitability is out of reach.

In part that's because the great engine of the commodity boom, China, is slowing down. The Chinese economy, which was growing at a rate of more than 14% in 2007, had slowed down to just 6% even before the coronavirus pandemic knocked it further off course. Commodity prices have fallen sharply from the records many hit in 2007–2011. The profits of the trading industry as a whole have flatlined.

But the economic slowdown in China is only part of the reason why commodity traders' earnings are no longer growing. The traders have several far deeper and more structural problems.

The first is the democratisation of information. For decades, the commodity trading houses enjoyed a tremendous information advantage over the rest of the market. Their vast networks of offices around the world provided them with up-to-the-minute intelligence about economic activity, commodity supply and demand, and a multitude of other data. If workers at a key copper mine in Chile went on strike or if a new oilfield started producing in Nigeria, the traders would be the first to know. In many cases, they built their own telecommunications networks at a time when long-distance phone calls had to be booked well in advance. They often knew more than most governments. 'The CIA used to come to us,' recalls David Tendler, who ran Philipp Brothers from 1975 until 1984. 'They used to visit us: "talk to us about the economy, talk to us about what you're seeing …" They felt we were a source of information on countries.'[38]

Information was the most valuable resource. And the traders controlled it. Even the most basic piece of information, the exact price of each commodity, wasn't readily available to everyone. In the 1980s or the 1990s, a metals trader could turn up in Zambia, Peru or Mongolia and buy a cargo of copper at the price of a week earlier, booking an immediate profit. The easy money wasn't just limited to developing countries. Before the launch of oil futures in London, the UK subsidiary of Exxon used to sell its North Sea crude based on the price quotation of the previous day.[39] If prices were going up, traders could buy from Exxon with near certainty of a profit.

The situation began to change in the 1980s, with the arrival of new technologies that allowed the publication and distribution of news and data in almost real time. Ironically, the development was prompted by one of the commodity trading industry's biggest deals: the merger of Philipp Brothers and Salomon Brothers. When they joined forces, the two firms fired some staff. Among them was Michael Bloomberg, an executive at Salomon. He walked away with $10 million and used the money to build a data company that would become ubiquitous on trading floors around the world, helping to erode the commodity traders' informational advantage.[40]

As the speed and availability of information increased exponentially with the spread of the internet, the traders' advantage was slowly whittled away. In the early 2000s, trading houses still had far superior information than what was available to non-physical traders about shipments of oil around the world – something that could be crucial in determining where a shortage or a glut was emerging. But even that advantage was eroded as satellite images became widely available, spurring a profusion of companies tracking tankers and selling the information.

The democratisation of information means that it has become more difficult to make money from simply moving commodities around the world. The traditional business model of the traders, spotting market dislocations and being able to take advantage of them before anyone else, is becoming harder and harder to sustain in an age when all market participants have access to the same information. Of course, occasional supply or demand shocks can still cause wild swings in prices, which traders can benefit from if they have a large enough presence in the market. But it is an unpredictable business model that relies on a war, crop failure, mine strike or pandemic to save the day.

A second challenge to the traders' profitability comes from the reversal of one of the trends that has benefited them most over the past three-quarters of a century: the liberalisation of global trade. From the world's first modern free trade treaty, the General Agreement on Tariffs and Trade in 1947, to China's accession to the WTO in 2001, the trend after the Second World War was for open borders, frictionless trade and globalisation. For the commodity houses, that meant growing global trade and markets that were more easily connected: in a truly globalised market, a trader can just as easily sell Chilean copper to China or to Germany, and so can direct it to wherever the price is best. The final boost for the traders came in 2015, when the US ended a de facto export ban on American crude oil, opening a new trade flow for the global oil market.

Since then, however, the zeitgeist has shifted against globalisation and free trade. Donald Trump was elected president in 2016 on an

explicitly anti-free trade platform. And he delivered on it, tearing up free-trade agreements and launching a trade war with China, which led to new tariffs on everything from steel to soybeans. The tariffs caused trade flows to be redirected: US exports of soybeans to China, for example, previously worth $12 billion a year, were for a couple of years displaced by Brazil. Some traders were wrongfooted by those moves; others made money from them. More worrying, however, is what the trade wars could mean for the overall volume of global trade: just as the traders profited from decades of expanding international trade, so they are likely to suffer as that trend goes into reverse.

The fragmentation that is taking place in global trade goes beyond US trade policy. Consumers increasingly care about traceability and ethical sourcing of their products – whether that means a Fair Trade chocolate bar or conflict-free minerals in their mobile phones. And that means they can't buy just any cocoa beans or cobalt. They must know exactly where the raw materials have come from. The result is a more fragmented market, in which the commodity traders are less able to buy from anywhere and sell to anyone.

A third challenge for the traders strikes at the core of their business: climate change. Much of the industry's profits come from trading fossil fuels, such as oil, gas and coal. If Big Oil and Big Coal are responsible for polluting the planet, the traders are their enablers, shipping their production to global markets.

As the world increasingly turns against oil and coal consumption, the traders' business will suffer. At Glencore, coal is one of the biggest money makers. The company is not only the top coal trader, but also one of the world's largest coal miners. Vitol, Mercuria, Gunvor and Trafigura rely on oil trading for the bulk of their profits.

Already, many economists – and some traders – believe oil demand may peak in around 2030 if not earlier. 'Our business will probably die over the next ten years because the demand for oil probably will start peaking – we think in 2028–2029,' said Ian Taylor. 'The use of renewables will go up and eventually electric cars will take over significant chunks of the market.'[41]

Climate change needn't be a wholly negative story for the commodity traders. The shift towards electric vehicles, for example, is triggering a massive expansion in the markets for cobalt, lithium and nickel, used to make batteries. It's also likely to make the electricity market more interesting for the traders. Nonetheless, it's tough to see how those markets will replicate the billions of dollars the commodity traders currently make each year from trading oil.

Finally, the traders have become victims of their own success. The industry's tentative move out of the shadows, epitomised by the Glencore IPO, has laid out the traders' enormous profits for all to see. It has not just been US policymakers and law enforcement officials that have been dismayed by some of the details of the traders' activity. It's also the traders' clients – the producers and consumers of natural resources – who have begun to wake up to the profits the traders have been making, in some cases at their expense.

In response, many of them are getting smarter about how they buy and sell commodities. State companies owned by oil-rich governments have started setting up their own in-house trading operations – if not to compete barrel for barrel with the likes of Vitol, then at least to ensure that they can sell their own oil in the most profitable way possible.

Among the oil producers to start their own trading operations are Saudi Aramco and the Abu Dhabi National Oil Company, two state companies with massive oil resources in the Middle East; and Rosneft of Russia and Socar of Azerbaijan, which in 2015 bought the remnants of the oil trading business of Philipp Brothers.[42] It's not only state-owned producers that are getting into trading: so is ExxonMobil, the largest oil major, and so are mining companies such as Anglo American. For the traders, that's a challenge. As more oil producers do their own trading, an ever-larger chunk of the market is effectively walled off from the commodity traders. It's a reversal of the trend that has been in place since the Seven Sisters lost control of the oil market in the 1970s.

The biggest threat of all comes from the traders' biggest client: China. For the past two decades, the trading industry's profits have

been driven by China's appetite for raw materials. But, just like the rest of the resources industry, the Chinese government has also woken up to the enormous profits of the trading industry. And so, while China remains a large and important market for the trading houses, Beijing is increasingly pushing to build its own commodity trading capability. The clearest example is in agriculture: the Chinese state agriculture trading agency, Cofco, has spent $4 billion since 2014 to establish an international food trading arm. In metals, Chinese companies have bought several mid-sized trading firms in recent years, including the metals business of Louis Dreyfus. And in oil, trading companies, such as Unipec, ChinaOil and Zhuhai Zhenrong, are handling a significant share of China's import needs.

For trading houses like Glencore and Vitol, the Chinese traders pose a double threat. Not only does their presence reduce the potential for the traders to sell to China, but also if anyone is able to operate in defiance of US regulators and Western societal pressure, it is the Chinese, with less need to access the global banking system and the US financial markets than other trading companies. And so, as American sanctions have proliferated and Western commodity traders have been forced to step back from certain markets, the Chinese traders have benefited.

In Iran, for example, Western traders have been forced to stop all business as the US has tightened sanctions. But Zhuhai Zhenrong, a Chinese trading house set up in the mid-1990s with links to the military, has managed to continue buying from Iran. Its maverick leader, Yang Qinglong, who died in 2014, was a Chinese version of Marc Rich or John Deuss: a hard-drinking trader famous for his hospitality who went by the nickname 'Crazy Yang'. He turned Zhuhai Zhenrong into the world's largest trader of Iranian crude, at one time supplying a sixth of all the oil that China bought overseas.[43] With no assets in the US and little need to use the American financial system, Zhuhai Zhenrong was able to ignore the threat of US sanctions. And, indeed, Washington has imposed sanctions on Zhuhai Zhenrong twice: first under the Obama administration in

2012 for selling gasoline to Tehran, and in 2019 under the Trump administration for buying Iranian crude oil.[44] For the Chinese company, it was only a minor inconvenience.

'Bluntly, the Chinese probably are willing to take much more risk than we are,' said Ian Taylor.[45]

But if anyone had thought the commodity traders were going to sail off quietly into the sunset, or that the world could somehow find a way of functioning without them, they would have been sorely mistaken. There may be pressure on the business model the commodity traders have hewn to over the past half century, but their position at the heart of the world's commerce in natural resources means that they remain as essential to the global economy as ever.

The events of 2020 provided the ultimate proof. As a novel coronavirus spread lethally around the world, plunging the global economy into the deepest crisis since the Great Depression in the 1930s, the commodity traders sprang into action. Just as they had done many times before, they stepped in as the market's buyers of last resort. But this market needed buyers of last resort on a scale never seen before. It was a call to arms for the commodity traders: none of their challengers or critics could match their capacity to deploy billions of dollars of firepower at lightning speed.

Many in the West were still blasé about the threat posed by the coronavirus even as it began to spread beyond China's borders to South Korea, Iran and Italy in February 2020. But inside Glencore's unassuming headquarters in Baar, the traders were anything but relaxed about the impact on world economy. The trader's staff in China had been relaying messages about the deadly seriousness of the new virus for weeks. It seemed inevitable that as other countries around the world confronted the same threat, they would need to take similar measures to the ones China had taken, shutting down large swathes of their economies and instructing citizens not to

travel. That could only mean one thing: that demand for oil, the commodity that had fuelled the human race's vastly increased mobility over the previous century, was going to fall dramatically. If a price crash was to be averted, producers would have to cut output just as aggressively.

Yet Glencore also knew that a coordinated production cut was unlikely. The company had counted on a network of high-level contacts in Moscow since the days of Marc Rich, and now, once again, they came into their own. As a key partner of OPEC, Russia would have to participate in any joint production cut. But Glencore's contacts told it that Moscow was dead set against the idea of reducing output.[46]

The trading house started to prepare itself for a world awash with oil. Its traders in Singapore began calling up brokers to hire ships, ready to store a wave of unwanted crude. It was an exact replica of the trade that Andy Hall had executed three decades earlier. Only now the scale was even more gigantic. In March, Glencore hired the *Europe*, the world's largest oil tanker, capable of storing 3.2 million barrels of oil beneath a deck that is longer than the Eiffel Tower is tall.

Even Glencore hadn't foreseen the magnitude of the coming collapse, however. By mid-March, Russia's intransigence had plunged it into a price war with Saudi Arabia. Instead of reducing output, Riyadh increased the amount of oil it was pumping. And at the same time countries around the world began to impose draconian lockdowns in an attempt to control the coronavirus. The effect of billions of people around the world suddenly staying at home was hard to overstate. Demand for oil simply dried up. In normal times, a severe recession might see global oil demand drop by 4% – now, as planes were grounded, factories closed, and city centres deserted, it plunged by as much as 30%.

For the oil market, it was a cataclysmic moment. It was not just that oil prices were falling. Storage tanks were filling close to the brim, leading producers to fear they'd have to shut down simply because there was nowhere to put the oil. Oil companies

were desperate. 'We will disappear as an industry, like the coal industry,' warned Scott Sheffield, the chief executive of a US shale producer.[47]

From around $60 a barrel before the virus struck, oil prices tumbled to less than $30, then less than $20. And then, for a few hours in April, the commodity that Theodor Weisser had coaxed out of the Soviet Union, that Marc Rich had bought and sold in the midst of wars and embargoes, that had been coveted to such a degree that it was known as 'black gold', became literally worthless. Parts of the world, like Texas, the heart of the US shale revolution, were so awash with oil that you couldn't give it away. For a brief period of time, oil prices fell below zero.

And so the commodity traders stepped in. Just as Andy Hall had done in 1990, they bought oil and stored it, using the futures market to lock in profits. With a flotilla of some of the world's largest tankers to fill, Glencore traders did the rounds of despairing US oil producers, buying oil everywhere from the Bakken oilfields of North Dakota to the Permian basin in Texas and New Mexico. From the shale wells, Glencore shipped some of the crude by pipeline down to tankers waiting off the Gulf of Mexico coast; from there to a larger vessel, the *New Comfort*, which sailed halfway across the world to the Strait of Malacca, off the coast of Singapore. There, it unloaded its cargo of American oil into the enormous hull of the *Europe*.

And then the *Europe* did nothing. When Glencore was buying from the shale producers of the Bakken and the Permian, the cost of the oil it was snapping up was as low as $10 a barrel. But the market situation was so extreme that futures for delivery only three months later were trading at three times that price. All Glencore had to do was buy oil, store it and sell futures, and it would triple its money. Even after taking into account the cost of renting the tankers and financing its oil purchases, the trading house was making returns of 50%–100% on the deals.[48] And so the *Europe* waited at anchor, its vast bulk becoming a temporary island in the Strait of Malacca – and a cash machine for Glencore.

Then, as demand began to recover, Glencore started to unwind the trade. Countries in Asia had weathered the first wave of the pandemic more successfully than their counterparts in the West, and their economies were driving a rebound in the oil market. The *Europe* was located in just the right spot. In early July, one million barrels of its cargo was unloaded on to another tanker and sent to the port of Onsan, in South Korea, home to one of the world's largest oil refineries.

To the producing companies, the oil had been worthless. But for Glencore and the other traders, it was a lucrative prize. A world in which oil demand was collapsing had a great need of the traders, who were always prepared to buy, no matter how dire the circumstances. And they bought and bought, all the while guaranteeing eye-popping profits by selling futures at much higher prices. In just a few months, about a billion barrels of unwanted oil and refined products had been stored around the world, much of it by the traders.[49] It was such an audacious trade that even Donald Trump remarked upon it. 'There's oil all over the oceans right now. The boats are all filled … That's where they are storing oil – they're sent out to sea and they sit there for long periods of time,' the US president said. 'We've never seen anything like it.'[50]

When the dust settled, it would turn out to have been one of the most profitable periods in the history of oil trading. Glencore made $1.3 billion from trading energy in the first six months of 2020 – a record performance by its oil traders.[51] Trafigura and Mercuria also enjoyed record oil trading profits.[52]

But the episode was more than just an opportunity for profit. It was a reminder that, for all the challenges they face in the coming years and decades, the commodity traders still play an essential role in the modern economy. As much as some politicians in the West may disdain the traders' political dalliances in tricky parts of the world, those same politicians are still reliant on their ability to buy, sell and store natural resources around the globe.

Oil remains one of the world's key currencies of power. And the traders are still masters of the oil market. Without their ability to

step in and buy the oil that the world suddenly had no need of, there would have been no buyers at all for one billion barrels of oil. At the time of writing, the trajectory of the global oil industry's recovery from the pandemic-induced price slump is still unclear. But there's little doubt that without the traders' ability to buy and store vast quantities of oil at their moment of greatest need, more Texas oil companies would have faced bankruptcy, more roughnecks would have lost their jobs, and government budgets in Nigeria, Angola and Iraq would have suffered even more swingeing cuts.

Their industry may be under fire as never before, but the events of 2020 showed that the commodity traders are still powerful actors in the global economy.

But if the traders are likely to remain an important force for years to come, it won't be the same individuals who have dominated the pages of this book. Many of the characters at the heart of our story are no longer active. Marc Rich died in 2013; Claude Dauphin in 2015; and Ian Taylor in 2020. John Deuss has retired into obscurity at his base in Bermuda; Andy Hall is enjoying his art collection; even Ivan Glasenberg, the most relentless and driven trader of them all, has announced plans to retire in 2021. There are few in the commodity trading industry who do not feel the winds changing.

It's not just a few individuals who are giving way to a new generation, but a whole philosophy of trading that is at risk of extinction. Increasingly, it may no longer be viable for the commodity traders to operate right up to the edge of what is legal or acceptable, to deal unapologetically in polluting commodities, or to have boardrooms filled exclusively with white men.

The most aggressive enforcers of the new order are the European banks, terrified of a repeat of the BNP Paribas fine. The fact that some of the largest banks, stung by losses, are stepping back from financing the commodity trade altogether has only given more weight

to the voices of those that remain. The traders, who are extremely reliant on them for financing, have had little choice but to fall into line. Many trading houses have announced they will stop using agents, the third-party fixers who in some cases had become a means of outsourcing bribe-paying. But it is not just banks enforcing a change of culture. The world as a whole has moved on.

'It's not just the banks or the regulators,' says Muriel Schwab, the chief financial officer of Gunvor. 'Society is putting more pressure towards sustainability, climate change and ethical ways of doing business.'[53]

Even on the issue of gender diversity, where the trading industry is one of the most backward in the Western world, Schwab believes that things are changing. As one of the most senior women in the commodity trading industry, she has plenty of experience of 'men who have this perception that only men can do the job'. But, she says, the commodity traders are already evolving, under pressure from their newest recruits.

'Today, if you want to hire young talent … they don't want to work for a dirty company that drops dirty oil in some places,' she says. 'I really think that the younger generation will shape the industry, and the industry will have to change. And it is changing, actually.'[54]

Of all the companies whose stories we've traced, Cargill is the one most secure of its place in the world – and that's largely because it has moved the focus of its business away from trading. Cargill is still the world's leading agricultural commodity trader, but over the years it has recycled its profits into investments in corn mills, soybean crushers and meat-packing plants, which are far outperforming its trading business. The company now plans for trading to make up just a third of its profits. In a bad year for Cargill's traders, it could be just 10%.[55]

It's a model others are beginning to follow. Ivan Glasenberg now talks about Glencore as if it were any other mining company. 'Trading is not a big part of the company any more,' he says. 'We treat the trading as a good way to understand markets and make sure we are also selling our products well into the markets.'[56]

It's an extraordinary statement from the man who has inherited the mantle of Ludwig Jesselson and Marc Rich. It would be tempting to conclude from Glasenberg's words that the commodity trading industry is dying. And it may well be the case that a certain style of trading is on the way out, notwithstanding the example of Chinese traders like Zhuhai Zhenrong. The conclusions of many of the most significant corruption probes are still to come, but the business model of many of the commodity traders has already been forced to change. The style of trading epitomised by the dynasty that started with Philipp Brothers and continued in Marc Rich + Co and now Glencore – go anywhere, deal with anyone, walk on the edge of the knife – may soon be consigned to the history books. As Torbjörn Törnqvist, chief executive of Gunvor, puts it: 'I think the old-style traders, the Marc Rich diehard breed, some of them don't quite get it. Until they're sitting and talking with the FBI. Then they get it.'[57]

Or as Ian Taylor told us in 2019: 'We've changed. We accept it's very, very important to have a good reputation. And we accept totally that that means you can't do certain things and you shouldn't do certain things. So we don't, basically.'[58]

But predictions of the death of the commodity trading industry are almost certainly premature. As long as natural resources continue to be exported around the world, there will continue to be a role for the commodity traders. For all the attempts by producers and consumers to expand into trading, there is little hope that they will match the commodity traders' combination of financial firepower and agility any time soon. And for all that climate change poses a threat to the commodities at the heart of the traders' business, even the most ardent environmentalists recognise that oil is likely to be a critical part of the world's energy supply for many years to come.

Despite the pressure on their business, the traders remain profitable. The industry probably does face a reckoning at some point in the coming years, the oil market bonanza of 2020 notwithstanding. But as long as markets are less than perfectly efficient, there will still be money to be made – even without walking the knife-edge between

legal and illegal – by exploiting inefficiencies and moving commodities around the world in response to price signals from the markets.

And the traders' role as a clearing-house for the world's essential goods still endows them with an almost unique sort of economic and political power. It was as recently as 2017 that the traders' money helped pay for Kurdistan's independence push. It was the same year that Ivan Glasenberg was awarded a medal by Vladimir Putin for his services to the Russian state. And the oil companies and petrostates that emerge intact from the trials of 2020 will in no small part have the traders to thank for their survival.

The world is changing, but its natural resources still need to be bought and sold. And commodities are still a sure-fire path to money and power. The traders may well remain powerful actors in world affairs for years to come. But after decades in the shadows, their influence can surely no longer be ignored.

ACKNOWLEDGEMENTS

The commodity trading industry has never been renowned for its transparency. We have been more than usually reliant on the willingness of our sources to open up to us – from those who first helped us to understand their business many years ago, to the dozens who more recently agreed to sit down for taped, on-the-record interviews for this book. Speaking to journalists was not a familiar or a comfortable experience for many of them, and we are deeply grateful that they did so all the same. Thanks also to Bassam Fattouh and Andrew Hudson, who generously opened the Oxford Institute for Energy Studies' library to us.

Over the years, our reporting has taken us to dozens of countries. We are particularly indebted to the drivers, translators and fixers who often risked their own safety to make sure that we came back in one piece.

Our bosses at Bloomberg News were unflinchingly supportive, even when writing this book took us away from our day jobs. Thanks to Will Kennedy, Emma Ross-Thomas, John Fraher and Heather Harris, who not only encouraged us to write the book but also read early drafts and made many helpful comments and suggestions. Stuart Wallace, Reto Gregori and John Micklethwait supported us from the beginning. Yuliya Fedorinova and Irina Reznik helped us track down contacts.

Many other colleagues across the newsroom made sure our beats were well covered while we were away researching and writing.

We first got interested in writing about the commodity traders while working at the *Financial Times*. Our editors there, Lionel Barber and Gillian Tett, needed no persuading to allow us to devote our time to this as yet unproven beat (we also have Gillian, together with Alec Russell, to thank for assigning us to work together for the first time). Diana Whittington was a rock through many late nights and last-minute panics putting together the *FT* Global Commodities Summit.

Our agent Andrew Wylie was an early enthusiast for the project, and together with James Pullen helped turn it from idea into reality.

Rowan Borchers at Penguin Random House has been everything two first-time authors could ask for in an editor. He grasped what we were trying to achieve from the first time we met, and set about improving everything we sent him with sensitivity and verve. Thanks also to Lucy Middleton, who provided sage and level-headed counsel; Nigel Wilcockson, who was a valuable sounding board; Anna Herve, who polished our copy; and Ceara Elliot, who designed the cover. At OUP, thanks to David Pervin, who first took an interest in the book; and James Cook, who saw it home. Isabelle Ralphs and Cayla DiFabio got the word out.

The idea of writing this book was a long time in the germination, and our friends patiently listened to our musings about the commodity traders over a period of many years. Peter and Amy Bernstein were generous in helping us to organise our thoughts and to understand the world of publishing. Sam Pritchard, Ed Cumming and Clem Naylor read early drafts and made thoughtful comments. Thanks to Carola Hoyos for her mentorship and her friendship.

We are extremely fortunate to have loving families that have supported us in more ways than we can put into words. Sandra Farchy turned her house into a writing retreat (and got Javier into cycling). Jan Collings would have loved every moment of this, including seeing her name in print. José Blas and Mari Carmen Otín never wavered in their encouragement for this project, even when it kept us apart. Thank you for your love and support.

APPENDICES

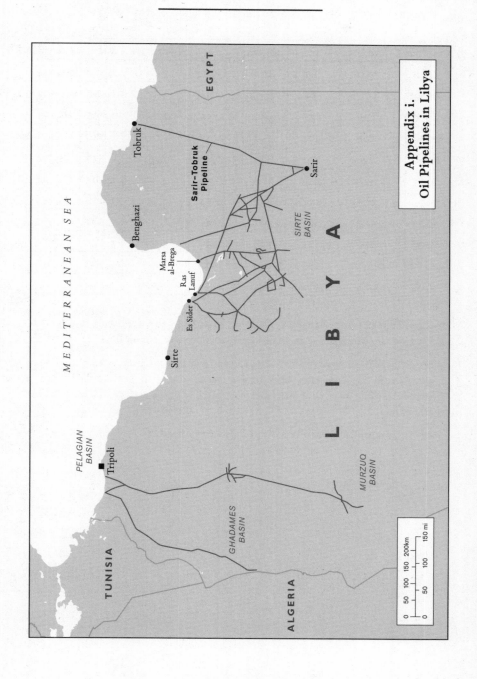

Appendix i.
Oil Pipelines in Libya

Appendix ii. Commodity trading giants' net profits, million US dollars, 1998–2019

	Glencore	Vitol	Cargill		Glencore	Vitol	Cargill
1998	192	24	468	2009	1,633	2,286	3,334
1999	277	68	597	2010	3,751	1,524	2,603
2000	420	290	480	2011	4,048	1,701	15,735*
2001	708	271	358	2012	1,004	1,080	1,175
2002	939	214	827	2013	-7,402	837	2,312
2003	1,120	422	1,290	2014	2,308	1,395	1,822
2004	2,208	634	1,331	2015	-4,964	1,632	1,583
2005	2,560	1,097	2,103	2016	1,379	2,081	2,377
2006	5,296	2,222	1,537	2017	5,777	1,525	2,835
2007	6,114	1,120	2,343	2018	3,408	1,660	3,103
2008	1,044	1,372	3,951	2019	-404	2,320	2,564

* Cargill's 2011 result includes the sale of its stake in the fertiliser group Mosaic. Excluding the Mosaic sale, its earnings in 2011 were $2,693 million.

Notes: Cargill's entries refer to its fiscal year, which runs from 1 June to 31 May. Glencore and Vitol's entries refer to the calendar year. Before 2011, figures for Glencore include profits attributable to equity holders and profit participation shareholders.

Source: Companies' annual reports and bond prospectuses.

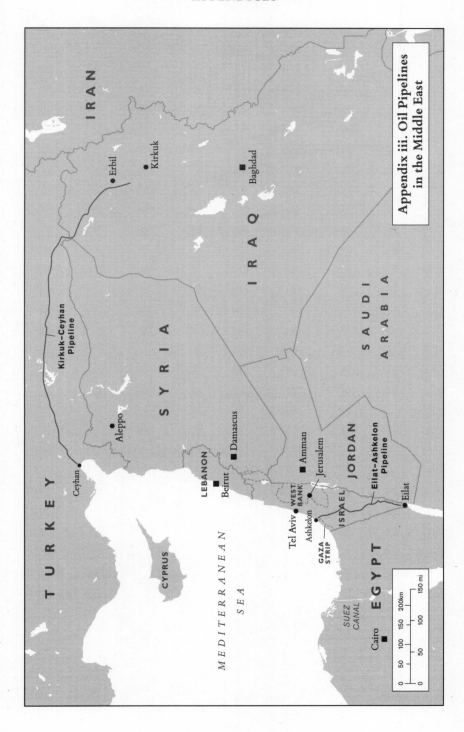

Appendix iii. Oil Pipelines in the Middle East

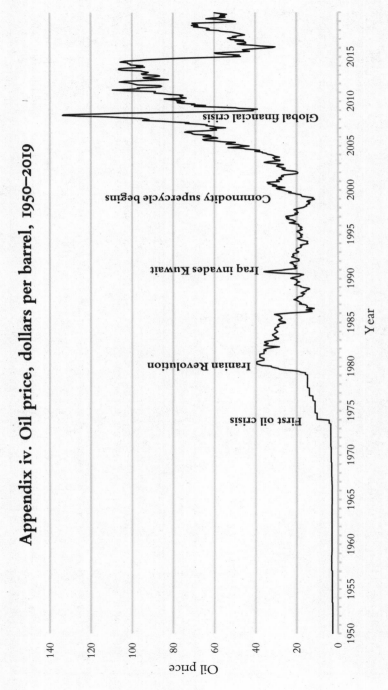

Appendix iv. Oil price, dollars per barrel, 1950–2019

Source: Rapidan Energy Group, based on American Petroleum Institute, Federal Reserve, Energy Information Administration, and Bloomberg. Crude oil price is monthly "posted price" for US mid-continent 36 degrees crude up to 1982, and WTI since then.

NOTES

Introduction: The Last Swashbucklers

1 This account of Vitol's adventure in Libya is based on the authors' reporting for a piece published in *Bloomberg Markets* magazine in June 2016, called 'Inside Vitol: How the World's Largest Oil Trader Makes Billions', as well as the authors' previous and subsequent interviews with Vitol executives.

2 In 2019, Vitol traded 8 million barrels a day of crude oil and refined products – '2019 volumes and review', Vitol, 27 March 2020, accessed: https://www.vitol.com/vitol-2019-volumes-and-review. According to the International Energy Agency, Germany, France, Spain, the UK and Italy consumed 8.15 million barrels a day in 2019.

3 'Risky Oil Supply Deal Pays off For Vitol', *Financial Times*, 5 September 2011, accessed: https://www.ft.com/content/93aecc44-d6f3-11e0-bc73-00144feabdco.

4 'Vitol's Ian Taylor on oil deals with dictators and drinks with Fidel', *Financial Times*, Lunch with the FT, 3 August 2018, accessed: https://www.ft.com/content/2dc35efc-89ea-11e8-bf9e-8771d5404543.

335

5 'Libya on the brink as protests hit Tripoli', *Guardian*, 21 February 2011, accessed: https://www.theguardian.com/world/2011/feb/20/libya-defiant-protesters-feared-dead.

6 Op. cit., *Financial Times*, 5 September 2011.

7 Vitol says it supplied fuel 'for humanitarian use' rather than to the military (Vitol, email to the authors, February 2020). Regardless, the fuel was used by the rebel army, according to Abdeljalil Mayuf, an official at rebel-controlled Arabian Gulf Oil in Benghazi.

8 Chris Bake, interview with the authors, London, April 2016.

9 'US Says $300 Million in Libyan Assets Unfrozen to Pay Vitol', Bloomberg News, September 2011, accessed: https://www.bloomberg.com/news/articles/2011-09-01/u-s-says-300-million-of-libya-assets-freed-to-pay-vitol-for-rebels-fuel.

10 David Fransen, interview with the authors, London, February 2019.

11 Ian Taylor, interview with the authors, London, March 2016.

12 Op. cit., *Financial Times*, 5 September 2011.

13 'Final report of the Panel of Experts established pursuant to resolution 1973 (2011) concerning Libya', United Nations Security Council, New York, 9 March 2013, accessed: https://www.securitycouncilreport.org/atf/cf/%7B65BFCF9B-6D27-4E9C-8CD3-CF6E4FF96FF9%7D/s_2013_99.pdf.

14 'Ian Taylor: the oilman, his cancer and the millions he's giving the NHS', *The Sunday Times Magazine*, 8 June 2019, accessed: https://www.thetimes.co.uk/article/ian-taylor-the-oilman-his-cancer-and-the-millions-hes-giving-the-nhs-wnwbtpq2h.

15 'Phibro's New Commodity: Money', *New York Times*, 9 August 1981, accessed: https://www.nytimes.com/1981/08/09/business/phibro-s-new-commodity-money.html.

16 Data for 2019 for Vitol, Trafigura, Glencore, Mercuria and Gunvor, based on the companies' reporting.

17 Kingsman, Jonathan, *Out of the Shadows: The New Merchants of Grain* (2019), introduction.

18 Darton Commodities, 'Cobalt Market Review, 2019—2020'.

19 Ian Taylor, interview with the authors, London, February 2019.

20 'Glencore appoints first woman director', *Financial Times*, June 2014, accessed: https://www.ft.com/content/9c46d148-fcf8-11e3-bc93-00144 feab7de.

21 'There are 316 Men Leading Top Commodity Houses and Only 14 Women', Bloomberg News, 19 March 2018, accessed: https://www. bloomberg.com/news/articles/2018-03-19/there-are-316-men-leading-top-commodity-houses-and-only-14-women.

22 Glencore annual report, 2019.

23 Pirrong, Craig, 'The Economics of Commodity Trading Firms', University of Houston, 2014, p. 8, accessed: https://trafigura.com/media/1192/2014_trafigura_economics_of_commodity_trading_firms_en.pdf.

24 Jim Daley, interview with the authors, London, August 2019.

25 World Trade Statistical Review 2018, World Trade Organization, Geneva, pp. 41–44, accessed: https://www.wto.org/english/res_e/statis_e/wts2018_e/wts2018_e.pdf.

26 David MacLennan, interview with the authors, Minneapolis, August 2019.

27 World Bureau of Metal Statistics.

28 Authors' calculation based on company reports of Vitol, Glencore, Trafigura and Cargill for each company's 2019 financial year; Japanese trade data from http://www.customs.go.jp.

29 '2016 America's Richest Families', *Forbes*, 29 June 2016, accessed: https://www.forbes.com/profile/cargill-macmillan-1/#3961c31223b6.

30 'Commodity Traders – Impact of the New Financial Market Regulation', Pestalozzi Attorneys at Law, 25 December 2016, accessed: https://pestalozzilaw.com/en/news/legal-insights/commodity-traders/legal_pdf/.

31 Torbjörn Törnqvist, interview with the authors, Geneva, August 2019.

32 Paul Wyler, interview with the authors, Zurich, June 2019.

33 Mark Hansen, interview with the authors, London, February 2019.

34 Based on Vitol's accounts from 2000 to 2019.

35 'The World is Hungry for Coal, Glencore Says', *Coal Week International*, August 2001.

36 'Glencore CEO Slams Fight Against Developing New Coal Mines', Bloomberg News, 24 October 2019.

One: The Pioneers

1 This account is based principally on the authors' interview with Hellmuth Weisser, Theodor's son, Hamburg, May 2019.

2 'Utka neftyanykh monopolii zapada', TASS, 20 March 1963, interview with Gurov.

3 'A Journey Through Time: Milestones of Success', Marquard & Bahls, accessed: https://www.marquard-bahls.com/en/about-us/history/details/event/show/founding-of-the-gefo-society-for-oil-shipments.html.

4 US Census Bureau: 20th Century Statistics, accessed: https://www.census.gov/prod/99pubs/99statab/sec31.pdf.

5 'Post-war reconstruction and development in the Golden Age of Capitalism', UN World Economic Survey 2017, accessed: https://www.un.org/development/desa/dpad/wp-content/uploads/sites/45/WESS_2017_ch2.pdf.

6 Bernstein, William, *A Splendid Exchange: How Trade Shaped the World* (London: Atlantic Books, 2008), p. 8.

7 Information on the history of Philipp Brothers is based largely on Waszkis, Helmut, *Philipp Brothers: The Rise and Fall of a Trading Giant* (Metal Bulletin, 1992). Waszkis, a former Philipp Brothers executive, kept meticulous notes on his research, which are stored at the Leo Baeck Institute in New York. Items from Waszkis's notes are referred to as 'Philipp Brothers Collection', followed by their box, folder and page number. The collection is accessible online at: https://digifinding aids.cjh.org/?pID=431072.

8 Philipp Brothers Collection: box 1, folder 3, p. 40.

9 As described by Charles Bendheim, Philipp Brothers Collection: box 1, folder 16, p. 157.

10 David Tendler, interview with the authors, New York, August 2019.

11 Memoir of Norbert Smith, a former Philipp Brothers executive, that was serialised in *The Jewish Link of New Jersey*, part 19, accessed: https://www.jewishlinknj.com/features/23920-my-stories-19.

12 'Philipp Brothers in Tito deal', *New York Times*, 13 October 1950, accessed: https://www.nytimes.com/1950/10/13/archives/philipp-brothers-in-tito-deal.html.

13 Philipp Brothers' 1973 annual report, Philipp Brothers Collection: box 2, folder 7, p. 95.

14 MacMillan, William Duncan, *MacMillan: The American Grain Family* (Afton Historical Society Press, 1998), p. 304.

15 Broehl, Jr, Wayne G., *Cargill: Trading the World's Grain* (University Press of New England, 1992), p. 787.

16 Testimony from Cargill executives at the 'Multinational Corporations and United States Foreign Policy' hearings before the Subcommittee of Multinational Corporations of the Committee on Foreign Relations, part 16, p. 101, Washington 1973–76.

17 Morgan, Dan, *Merchants of Grain* (An Authors Guild Backinprint.com Edition, 2000; originally published by Viking, 1979), p. 122.

18 Broehl, Jr Wayne G., *Cargill: Going Global* (University Press of New England, 1998), pp. 36–46.

19 David MacLennan, interview with the authors, Davos, January 2020.

20 Wiener, Robert J., 'Origins of Futures Trading: The Oil Exchanges in the 19th Century', L'Université Laval, Quebec, Canada. 1992.

21 Hellmuth Weisser, interview with the authors, Hamburg, May 2019.

22 Ermolaev, Sergei, 'The Formation and Evolution of the Soviet Union's Oil and Gas Dependence', 2017, accessed: https://carnegieendowment.org/2017/03/29/formation-and-evolution-of-soviet-union-s-oil-and-gas-dependence-pub-68443.

23 Yergin, Daniel, *The Prize* (New York: Simon & Schuster, 1993), p. 497.

24 'Impact of Oil Exports from the Soviet Bloc', National Petroleum Council, Washington, 1962, p. 25, accessed: https://www.npc.org/reports/1962-Impact-Oil_Exports_From_The_Soviet_Bloc-Vol_I.pdf.

25 Philipp Brothers Collection: box 1, folder 2, p. 48.

26 Helmut Waszkis interview with Ernst Frank, June 1978; Metallgesellschaft Collection; AR 25149, p. 271; Leo Baeck Institute.

27 Jean-Pierre Adamian and Antoine Carassus, interview with the authors, Geneva, February 2019.

28 'The Colossus of Phibro', *Institutional Investor*, 1981. Philipp Brothers Collection: box 1, folder 17, p. 158.

29 Broehl, Jr, Wayne G., *Cargill: Trading the World's Grain* (University Press of New England, 1992), p. 793.

30 Felix Posen, interview with the authors, London, May 2019.

31 'The Colossus of Phibro', *Institutional Investor*, 1981.

32 1940 profit number from Broehl, Jr, Wayne G., *Cargill: Trading the World's Grain* (University Press of New England, 1992), p. 879; 1970 profit number from Broehl, Jr, Wayne G., *Cargill: Going Global* (University Press of New England, 1998), p. 379.

33 Philipp Brothers Collection, 1947 accounts: box 1, folder 11, p. 55.

34 Philipp Brothers Collection: box 1, folder 11, p. 143.

35 The best chronicle of the Soviet grain purchases is Trager, James, *The Great Grain Robbery* (New York: Ballantine Books, 1975). In addition, the US Congress held hearings into the purchases, including 'Russian Grain Transactions' (Senate Permanent Subcommittee on Investigations, July 1973) and 'Sale of Wheat to Russia' (House Agriculture Committee, September 1972). Both hearings included first-hand and detailed testimony from trading executives and government officials.

36 'Some Deal: The Full Story of How America Got Burned and the Russians Got Bread', *New York Times*, 25 November 1973, accessed: https://www.nytimes.com/1973/11/25/archives/some-deal-the-full-story-of-how-amepnka-got-burned-and-the-russians.html.

37 Luttrell, Clifton, 'The Russian Wheat Deal – Hindsight vs. Foresight', US Federal Reserve of St. Louis, October 1973, accessed: https://www.staff.ncl.ac.uk/david.harvey/MKT3008/RussianOct1973.pdf.

38 Broehl, Jr, Wayne G., *Cargill: Going Global* (University Press of New England, 1998), p. 224.

39 Morgan, Dan, *Merchants of Grain*, p. 168.

40 Broehl, Jr, Wayne, G., *Cargill: Going Global*, p. 224.

41 Ibid., p. 225.

42 Fortune 500 list, 1972, *Fortune Magazine*, accessed: https://archive.fortune.com/magazines/fortune/fortune500_archive/full/1972/.

43 US General Accounting Office, "Exporters' Profits On Sales of US Wheat to Russia", p. 2, accessed: http://archive.gao.gov/f0302/096760.pdf.

44 'Soviet Grain Deal is Called a Coup', *New York Times*, 29 September 1972, accessed: https://www.nytimes.com/1972/09/29/archives/soviet-grain-deal-is-called-a-coup-capitalistic-skill-surprised.html.

Two: The Godfather of Oil

1 The President's Daily Brief, CIA, 25 April 1968, accessed: https://www.cia.gov/library/readingroom/docs/DOC_0005974399.pdf, declassified in 2015.

2 Yergin, Daniel, *The Prize*, pp. 523–524.

3 For a detailed overview of the negotiations for the construction of the pipeline, see Bialer, Uri, 'Fuel Bridge across the Middle East— Israel, Iran, and the Eilat-Ashkelon Oil Pipeline', Israel Studies, vol. 12, no. 3, accessed: http://ismi.emory.edu/home/documents/Readings/Bialer_Fuel_Bridge_Israeli_oil_pipline.pdf. In addition, a recent Swiss ruling contains information about the ownership structure: Suisse, Tribunal Fédéral, 27 June 2016, accessed: https://res.cloudinary.com/lbresearch/image/upload/v1469537636/suisse_tribunal_f_d_ral_arr_t_du_27_juin_2016_4a_322_2015_266116_1354.pdf.

4 'The Time Has Come for Israel to Expose Its Most Secret Firm', *Haaretz*, 18 September 2016, accessed: https://www.haaretz.com/opinion/the-time-has-come-for-israel-to-expose-its-secret-firm-1.5437187.

5 Biographical details from Ammann, Daniel, *The King of Oil: The Secret Lives of Marc Rich* (New York: St Martin's Press, 2009) and *Petition for Pardon for Marc Rich and Pincus Green*, 2001, included in US House of Representatives, *Justice Undone: Clemency Decisions in the Clinton White House*, 107th Congress, 2nd session, Report 107-454, 14 May 2002, accessed: https://www.congress.gov/107/crpt/hrpt454/CRPT-107hrpt454-vol3.pdf.

6 Ammann, Daniel, op. cit., p. 36.

7 Felix Posen, interview with the authors, London, May 2019.

8 Waszkis, Helmut, *Philipp Brothers: The Rise and Fall of a Trading Giant*, p. 207.

9 Isabel Arias, interview with the authors, Lima, April 2019.

10 Danny Posen, interview with the authors, London, February 2019.

11 Roque Benavides, interview with the authors, Lima, April 2019.

12 Copetas, A. Craig, *Metal Men: Marc Rich and the 10-Billion-Dollar Scam* (London: Harrap Limited, 1986), p. 51.

13 Ammann, Daniel, *The King of Oil: The Secret Lives of Marc Rich* (New York: St Martin's Press, 2009), pp. 58–59.

14 'Mystery of the Disappearing Tankers', *The Sunday Times*, 13 December 1970, p.11.

15 'Minerals Yearbook 1970, Chromium', United States Geological Survey, p. 302, accessed: http://images.library.wisc.edu/EcoNatRes/EFacs2/MineralsYearBk/MinYB1970v1/reference/econatres.minyb1970v1.jmorning00.pdf.

16 Fraenkel, Ernst, verbatim notes of interview with Helmut Waszkis, in Philipp Brothers Collection; AR 25131; box 1, folder 9, p. 6.

17 Ammann, Daniel, op. cit., p. 67.

18 Garavini, Giuliano, *The Rise & Fall of OPEC in the Twentieth Century* (Oxford: Oxford University Press, 2019), p. 203.

19 Akins, James, 'The Oil Crisis: This Time the Wolf Is Here', *Foreign Affairs*, vol. 51, no. 3 (April, 1973), pp. 462–490, accessed: https://pdfs.semanticscholar.org/7e25/19e3a8f85571946eb76785c43cd1a493cafo.pdf.

20 Waszkis, Helmut, *Philipp Brothers: The Rise and Fall of a Trading Giant*, p. 212.

21 Ibid., p. 211.

22 Ibid., footnote on p. 292.

23 Yergin, Daniel, *The Prize*, p. 581.

24 The description of the meeting at Yamani's suite in Vienna comes from 'How the Oil Companies Help the Arabs to Keep Prices High', *New York Magazine*, 22 September 1975.

25 Yergin, Daniel, op. cit., p. 585.

26 Ibid., p. 588.

27 The President's Daily Brief, CIA, 18 October 1973, declassified in part on 20 June 2016, accessed: https://www.cia.gov/library/readingroom/docs/DOC_0005993960.pdf.

28 'Markets Pointers', Europ-Oil Prices (London), 3 December 1973, p. 1.

29 'Milestones in the History of U.S. Foreign Relations: Oil embargo 1973–74', US State Department, accessed: https://history.state.gov/milestones/1969-1976/oil-embargo.

30 Broehl, Jr, Wayne G., *Cargill: Going Global*, p. 237.

31 Milton Rosenthal, president and CEO of Engelhard, quoted in 'Engelhard's Gold', *Dun's Review*, April 1975, in Philipp Brothers Collection: box 2, folder 2, p. 17.

32 Waszkis, Helmut, *Philipp Brothers: The Rise and Fall of a Trading Giant*, p. 215.

33 Rich told Daniel Ammann (op. cit., p. 73) that Jesselson offered $150,000 each to him and Green; Jesselson told Helmut Waszkis (*Philipp Brothers: The Rise and Fall of a Trading Giant*, p. 215) that he was willing to let their pay rise to $250,000 each.

34 Ammann, Daniel, op. cit., p. 73.

35 'Inside Philipp Brothers, a $9 billion supertrader most people don't know', *BusinessWeek*, 3 September 1979. Philipp Brothers Collection: box 2, folder 10, p. 207.

36 Ammann, Daniel, op. cit., p. 75.

37 'Secrets of Marc Rich', *Fortune*, 23 January 1984.

38 Gerard F. Cerchio, the president of Sun International Inc., the trading arm of the Sun Company, quoted in 'The Man Behind Marc Rich', *New York Times*, 18 August 1983, accessed: https://www.nytimes.com/1983/08/18/business/the-man-behind-marc-rich.html.

39 Isaac Querub, interview with the authors, Madrid, June 2019.

40 Isaac Querub, email to the authors, June 2019.

41 Manny Weiss, interview with the authors, London, March 2019.

42 'Le Pape Du Negoce', *Le Temps*, 30 October 2008, accessed at: https://www.letemps.ch/opinions/pape-negoce.

43 Ammann, Daniel, op. cit., p. 82.

44 Philipp Brothers Collection: box 1, folder 11, p. 143.

45 Philipp Brothers, 1977 annual report, in Philipp Brothers Collection: box 2, folder 9.

46 Razavi, Hossein, 'The New Era of Petroleum Trading: Spot Oil, Spot-Related Contracts, and Futures Markets', World Bank Technical Paper, Number 96, Washington, 1989.

47 Tetreault, Mary Ann, *Revolution in the World Petroleum Market* (Quorum Books, 1985), p. 55.

48 'Die Knochen sind noch nicht numeriert', *Der Spiegel*, 17 February 1986, accessed: https://www.spiegel.de/spiegel/print/d-13517991.html.

49 'Oil: The Great Noses of Rotterdam', *New York Times*, 8 July 1979, accessed: https://www.nytimes.com/1979/07/08/archives/oil-the-great-noses-of-rotterdam-a-market-that-runs-on-the-telex.html.

50 'Etude Sur Le Trading Petrolier', Ministere de la Mer, 14 June 1983, accessed: http://temis.documentation.developpement-durable.gouv.fr/docs/Temis/0002/Temis-0002860/7522.pdf.

51 Bill Emmitt, interview with the authors, May 2019.

52 'Deuss: From Second-Hand Car Dealer to Controversial World Figure', *Bermuda Sun*, 18 February 1994, accessed: http://bermudasun.bm/Content/Default/NewsOlder20120206/Article/Deuss-From-second-hand-car-dealer-to-controversial-world-figure/-3/1294/31102.

53 Boon, Marten, 'Deuss' demise: an oil trader's struggle to keep up with the market, 1970s-1990s', MPRA Paper, 2019, accessed: https://mpra.ub.uni-muenchen.de/95460/1/MPRA_paper_95460.pdf.

54 Sanoff, Jonathan, 'Soyuznefteexport v JOC Oil Ltd: a Recent Development in the Theory of the Separability of the Arbitration Clause', in *The American Review of International Arbitration*, 1990 (Sanoff was an associate general counsel for Transworld Oil, and as such an adviser to JOC Oil).

55 Levine, Steve, *The Oil and the Glory* (New York: Random House, 2007), p. 133.

56 Deposition of Francis V. Elias, in US v Advance Chemical Company, case no. CIV-86-1401-P, US District Court for the Western District of Oklahoma. Elias was at the time the secretary of Transworld Oil Ltd.

57 'Energy: JOC Oil Bona Fides', US State Department, cable from US embassy in Valletta, Malta; Washington, May 1974, via WikiLeaks, accessed: https://wikileaks.org/plusd/cables/1974VALLET00848_b. html.

58 'Request for Information on Petroleum Company', US State Department, cable from US embassy in Gaborone, Botswana; Washington, January 1975, via WikiLeaks, accessed: https://wikileaks.org/plusd/ cables/1975GABORO00154_b.html.

59 'Request for Background Information on World Oil Bank', US State Department, cable from US embassy in Ankara, Turkey; Washington, May 1978, via WikiLeaks, accessed: https://wikileaks.org/plusd/cables/ 1978ANKARA03599_d.html.

60 'Iran-Contra Investigation', US Senate, appendix B, vol. 25, Deposition of Theodore G. Shackley, pp. 20–23 and 377–383. The name of Transworld Oil is misspelled as Trans-World, and John Deuss is misspelled several times as 'John Dois', accessed: https://ia902906.us.archive. org/25/items/reportofcongress25unit/reportofcongress25unit.pdf.

61 'Deuss: From Second-Hand Car Dealer to Controversial World Figure', *Bermuda Sun*, op. cit.

62 'Ayatollah Khomeini returns to Iran', *The Associated Press*, 1 February 1979, accessed: https://www.apnews.com/3042785d564d4acaa2e4a18bf c206d25.

63 Yergin, Daniel, op. cit., pp. 656–680.

64 'Middleman Made a Fortune in the Good Old Days Of Oil Crisis', *Washington Post*, 15 February 1983.

65 Yergin, Daniel, *The Prize*, p. 679.

66 Copetas, A. Craig, op. cit., p. 72.

67 Ammann, Daniel, *The King of Oil*, p. 177.

68 Hellmuth Weisser, interview with the authors, Hamburg, May 2019.

69 Philipp Brothers Collection: box 1, folder 11, p. 143.

70 Broehl, Jr, Wayne G., *Cargill: From Commodities to Customers* (University Press of New England, 2008), p. 38.

71 Group of Seven, 'Declaration 1979', Tokyo, 29 June 1979, in Oxford Institute of Energy Studies archive, grey literature, box 79.

Three: The Last Bank in Town

1 This account of Jamaica's dealings with Marc Rich + Co is based primarily on the authors' interviews with Hugh Hart, Manny Weiss, Vincent Lawrence and Carlton Davis. The story of the country's Friday night crisis was told to the authors by Hart.

2 In the first half of the 1980s, Jamaica was the third-largest bauxite producer after Australia and Guinea, and the fourth-largest alumina producer after Australia, the US and the USSR, according to the US Geological Survey.

3 'History of Aluminum', The Aluminum Association, 2019, accessed: https://www.aluminum.org/aluminum-advantage/history-aluminum.

4 US Geological Survey data.

5 Stuckey, John A., *Vertical Integration and Joint Ventures in the Aluminum Industry* (Harvard University Press, 1983), p. 84.

6 European Commission decision on aluminium imports from Eastern Europe, 19 December 1984, accessed: https://eur-lex.europa.eu/legal-content/EN/TXT/HTML/?uri=CELEX:31985D0206&from=GA.

7 US Geological Survey data.

8 'World Bauxite Industry: Recent Trends and Implications of Guyana's Nationalization Moves', CIA, April 1971, accessed: https://www.cia.gov/library/readingroom/docs/CIA-RDP85T00875R001700010006-3.pdf.

9 Waszkis, Helmut, *Philipp Brothers: The Rise and Fall of a Trading Giant*, p. 120.

10 'Guyana's Bauxite Industry Since Partial Nationalization', CIA, December 1972, accessed: https://www.cia.gov/library/readingroom/docs/CIA-RDP85T00875R001700040056-5.pdf.

11 'Bodies on the Doorstep: Jamaica in the 1970s', Association for Diplomatic Studies and Training, accessed: https://adst.org/2016/12/bodies-doorstep-jamaica-late-1970s/.

12 'Rules Bent for Jamaica, Helping US Industry', *New York Times*, 1981, accessed: https://www.nytimes.com/1982/04/28/business/rules-bent-for-jamaica-helping-us-industry.html.

13 Davis, Carlton, *Jamaica in the World Aluminium Industry*, 2011, vol. 3, p. 67; and USGS yearbooks.

14 Hugh Hart, interview with the authors, Kingston, March 2019, and Manny Weiss, interview with the authors, London, March 2019.

15 'What's Behind the Govt., Marc Rich Relationship?', *The Daily Gleaner*, 5 August 1985, p. 1, accessed: https://newspaperarchive.com/kingston-gleaner-aug-05-1985-p-1/. Also confirmed in authors' interviews with Manny Weiss and Hugh Hart.

16 Ken Hill, a US marshal who spent years trying to arrest Rich, quoted in 'The Face of Scandal', *Vanity Fair*, June 2001, accessed: https://www.vanityfair.com/news/2001/06/rich200106.

17 Hugh Hart, interview with the authors, Kingston, March 2019.

18 Jamaica Bauxite Institute.

19 Hugh Hart, interview with the authors, Kingston, March 2019.

20 Davis, Carlton, *Jamaica in the World Aluminium Industry*, vol. 3, p. 90.

21 'Implementation Completion Report – Clarendon Alumina Production Project', World Bank, 1995, accessed: http://documents.worldbank.org/curated/en/326311468043471038/pdf/multi-page.pdf.

22 Manny Weiss, interview with the authors, London, March 2019.

23 'Marc Rich "Tolling" Deals Reopen US Aluminium Plants', *Financial Times*, 17 October 1986.

24 'Electric Shocks for Aluminium Producers', *Financial Times*, 11 September 1987.

25 US Bureau of Labor Statistics, producer price index, aluminium foil, accessed via the FRED database: https://fred.stlouisfed.org/series/WPU10250111.

26 Manny Weiss, interview with the authors, London, March 2019.

27 Ibid.

28 According to Rich, quoted in 'Alchemist At Large', *Financial Times*, 1 September 1988.

29 Manny Weiss, interview with the authors, London, March 2019.

30 Hugh Small, interview with the authors, Kingston, March 2019.

31 According to Hugh Small and Vincent Lawrence in interviews with the authors, Kingston, March 2019.

32 'PM Confirms Rich Deal', *The Daily Gleaner*, 30 June 1989, accessed: https://newspaperarchive.com/kingston-gleaner-jun-30-1989-p-1/.

33 Based on data in Clarendon Alumina Production 2006 bond prospectus.

34 $313m from 1982–1987, $365m from 1988–1999, $125m in 2000 and $65m in 2003. See, Davis, Carlton, '2009: Fiscal Budgets (Part 1) Prepayment of bauxite and alumina earnings' at http://old.jamaica-gleaner.com/gleaner/20090308/focus/focus5.html and Clarendon Alumina Production 2006 bond prospectus.

35 Carlton Davis, interview with the authors, Kingston, March 2019.

36 Copper Handbook, World Bank, 1981 (The Democratic Republic of Congo was known as Zaire between 1971 and 1997), accessed: http://documents.worldbank.org/curated/en/543761492970653971/pdf/multi-page.pdf.

37 'What's in a name?', *The Economist*, 5 October 2017. The economist was Antoine van Agtmael, who worked at the International Finance Corporation, a branch of the World Bank.

38 Ricardo Leiman, interview with the authors, London, August 2019.

39 Quoted in 'Why Marc Rich is Richer than Ever', *Fortune*, 1 August 1988, accessed: https://archive.fortune.com/magazines/fortune/fortune_archive/1988/08/01/70845/index.htm.

40 'While Marc Rich Was Fugitive, Firm Dealt With Pariah Nations', *Wall Street Journal*, 23 April 2001, accessed: https://www.wsj.com/articles/SB982885815892990443.

41 Eric de Turckheim, interview with the authors, Geneva, March 2019.

42 Ammann, Daniel, *The King of Oil*, op. cit., p. 194.

43 Macmillan, Harold, 'The Wind of Change', Cape Town, 3 February 1960, accessed: http://www.africanrhetoric.org/pdf/J%20%20%20Macmillan%20-%20%20the%20wind%20of%20change.pdf.

44 Ivan Glasenberg, who would become CEO of Glencore, couldn't participate in the Los Angeles Olympics in 1984 as a consequence of the boycott.

45 Shipping Research Bureau, 'Embargo: Apartheid Oil's Secrets Revealed' (Amsterdam University Press, 1995), in the collection of the International Institute of Social History, Amsterdam, p.192, accessed: https://

archief.socialhistory.org/sites/default/files/docs/collections/embargo_
apartheids_oil_secrets_revealed_0.pdf#overlay-context=nl/
node/4708.

46 Ford, Jonathan, *Depression, Oil Trading & a Mind at War With Itself*
(Chipmunkapublishing, 2016), a memoir written by a former Vitol
trader.

47 Mark Crandall, interview with the authors, London, May 2019.

48 David Issroff, interview with the authors, New York, August 2019.

49 Shipping Research Bureau, op. cit., p. 326.

50 'South Africa's Secret Lifeline', *Observer*, 3 June 1984.

51 Van Vuuren, Hennie, *Apartheid, Guns and Money* (London: Hurst &
Company, 2018).

52 Shipping Research Bureau, op. cit., p. 258.

53 Van Vuuren, Hennie, op. cit., p. 103.

54 Quoted in Shipping Research Bureau, op. cit., p. 149. The BBC didn't
broadcast the interview with John Deuss, but the tape resurfaced years
later when it was used by the Dutch television investigative programme
Gouden Bergen, on 10 September 1989.

55 Ammann, Daniel, op. cit., p. 195.

56 Authors' interview with former senior Marc Rich + Co executive, who
declined to be named.

57 Authors' interview with 'Monsieur Ndolo' (pseudonym used by the
Marc Rich trader who set up Cobuco in the early 1980s).

58 GDP per capita database, World Bank, accessed: https://data.world-
bank.org/indicator/ny.gdp.pcap.cd?most_recent_value_desc=true.

59 The US Federal Reserve effective rate peaked above 22% in 1981.

60 Based on EIA data showing Burundian oil consumption at 700–800 barrels
a day in 1980–1983, and a standard VLCC carrying 2 million barrels.

61 Authors' interview with a trader, who requested anonymity.

62 Ammann, Daniel, op. cit., p. 93.

63 'Executive Order 12205', US Government, Washington, 7 April 1980,
45 FR 24099, 3 CFR, 1980 Comp., p. 248, accessed: https://www.archives.
gov/federal-register/codification/executive-order/12205.html.

64 NBC interview with Rich, 1992.

65 'Indictment: United States of America vs Marc Rich et al.', United States District Court, Southern District of New York, September 1983.

66 Ibid.

67 'The Lifestyle of Rich, the infamous', *Fortune*, 30 June 1986, accessed: https://fortune.com/2013/06/30/the-lifestyle-of-rich-the-infamous-fortune-1986/.

68 'Judge Orders Exxon to Repay $895m', *Financial Times*, 26 March 1983.

69 'Arco to Pay $315 Million to Settle Claims of Price Control Violations, Overcharges', *Wall Street Journal*, 2 May 1986.

70 Thomas, Evan, *The Man to See* (New York: Simon & Schuster, 1991), p. 417. Rich, however, denied the account, saying there was 'not a shred of truth in it'. Rich said his lawyer never asked him to return to the US.

71 'The controversial pardon of international fugitive Marc Rich', US Congress, Washington, 8 February and 1 March 2001, pp. 73 and 303, accessed: https://upload.wikimedia.org/wikipedia/commons/1/12/2001_The_Controversial_Pardon_of_International_Fugitive_Marc_Rich.pdf.

Four: Paper Barrels

1 Andy Hall, interview with the authors, Derneburg, March 2019.

2 BP Statistical Review of World Energy. Kuwait pumped 1.4m b/d and Iraq pumped 2.8m b/d – total global oil production was estimated at 63.8m b/d.

3 UN Security Council Resolution 661 of 6 August 1990, accessed: http://unscr.com/en/resolutions/doc/661.

4 Andy Hall, interview with the authors, Derneburg, March 2019.

5 'Will Phibro's Daddy Squash Its Ambitions?', *Business Week*, 25 March 1991.

6 Colin Bryce, interview with the authors, London, February 2019.

7 'Dojima Rice Exchange', Japan Exchange Group, accessed: https://www.jpx.co.jp/dojima/en/index.html.

8 Wiener, Robert J., 'Origins of Futures Trading: The Oil Exchanges in the 19th Century', L'Université Laval, Quebec, Canada. 1992.

9 Andy Hall, interview with the authors, Derneburg, March 2019.

10 'Salomon Inc.'s Powerful Oil Man, Andrew Hall, Leads a Resurgence of Traders on Wall Street', *Wall Street Journal*, 11 January 1991.

11 Oil Monthly Market Report, International Energy Agency, Paris, January 1990, p. 11.

12 'Saddam's Message of Friendship to President Bush', US State Department, cable from US Embassy in Baghdad, 25 July 1990, accessed: https://wikileaks.org/plusd/cables/90BAGHDAD4237_a.html.

13 Andy Hall, interview with the authors, Derneburg, March 2019.

14 Ibid.

15 'Iraq Threatens Emirates and Kuwait on Oil Glut', *New York Times*, 18 July 1990, accessed: https://www.nytimes.com/1990/07/18/business/iraq-threatens-emirates-and-kuwait-on-oil-glut.html.

16 'Invading Iraqis Seize Kuwait and Its Oil', *New York Times*, 3 August 1990, accessed: https://www.nytimes.com/1990/08/03/world/iraqi-invasion-invading-iraqis-seize-kuwait-its-oil-us-condemns-attack-urges.html.

17 'Meaner than a Junkyard Dog', *Texas Monthly*, April 1991, accessed: https://www.texasmonthly.com/articles/meaner-than-a-junkyard-dog/.

18 Andy Hall, interview with the authors, Derneburg, March 2019.

19 Waszkis, Helmut, *Philipp Brothers: The Rise and Fall of a Trading Giant*, pp. 232–233.

20 Philipp Brothers Collection: box 1, folder 11, p. 143.

21 David Tendler, interview with the authors, New York, August 2019.

22 'Behind the Salomon Brothers Buyout', *Fortune*, 7 September 1981, accessed: https://fortune.com/1981/09/07/salomon-brothers-buyout/.

23 Waszkis, Helmut, *Philipp Brothers: The Rise and Fall of a Trading Giant*, p. 251.

24 Ibid.

25 David Tendler, interview with the authors, New York, August 2019.

26 'Voest-Alpine Plight Affects All Austria', *New York Times*, 20 January 1986, accessed: https://www.nytimes.com/1986/01/20/business/voest-alpine-plight-affects-all-austria.html.

27 Klöeckner corporate website, accessed: https://www.kloeckner.com/en/group/history.html.

28 'Ferruzzi Group – Trading Activities May Post $100m Loss for 1989', *Wall Street Journal*, 25 September 1989.

29 Serge Varsano, interview with the authors, Paris, November 2019.

30 'OPEC Keeps Oil Traders Guessing', *Financial Times*, 12 April 1988.

31 Authors' interview with former executive of Transworld Oil, who declined to be named.

32 Ibid.

33 The size of estimated losses varies according to sources, but most put it between $200 and $660 million. Bower, Tom, *The Squeeze* (London: HarperPress, 2010), pp 63–65.

34 'Oil Trader Big Winner in Atlantic Sale to Sun', *New York Times*, 7 July 1988, accessed: https://www.nytimes.com/1988/07/07/business/business-people-oil-trader-a-big-winner-in-atlantic-sale-to-sun.html.

Five: The Fall of Marc Rich

1 The description in this chapter of the fall of Marc Rich is based primarily on the authors' interviews with people involved, including Zbynek Zak, Josef Bermann, Paul Wyler, Manny Weiss, Ivan Glasenberg, Mark Crandall, Graham Sharp, Danny Posen and Isaac Querub, as well as on Ammann, Daniel, *The King of Oil* (op. cit.).

2 Jim Daley, who joined Marc Rich + Co in 1977 to run oil financing; interview with the authors, London, August 2019.

3 Interview with Rich in 'Fugitive Marc Rich Prospers Abroad, Hopes to Settle US Criminal Charges', *Wall Street Journal*, 1 February 1994.

4 'Smoking Out Marc Rich', *Institutional Investor*, 1 August 1992.

5 Danny Posen, interview with the authors, London, February 2019.

6 Mark Crandall, interview with the authors, London, May 2019.

7 'A definition of Richness', *Financial Times*, 10 August 1992.

8 Mark Crandall, interview with the authors, London, May 2019.

9 'Aide to Marc Rich Quits Post', *New York Times*, 4 June 1992, accessed: https://www.nytimes.com/1992/06/04/business/aid-to-marc-rich-quits-post.html.

10 Manny Weiss, interview with the authors, London, March 2019.

11 Ibid.

12 Isaac Querub, interview with the authors, Madrid, June 2019.

13 Ibid.

14 Bloomberg data.

15 Zbynek Zak, interview with the authors, Zug, June 2019.

16 Ammann, Daniel, *The King of Oil*, p. 226.

17 Manny Weiss, interview with the authors, London, March 2019.

18 Mark Crandall, interview with the authors, London, May 2019.

19 'What Makes $1 Billion a Year and Oils the Global Economy While Rebuilding Its Reputation?', Bloomberg News, 2018, accessed: https://www.bloomberg.com/news/features/2018-05-31/oil-trader-trafigura-rebuilds-reputation-while-making-billions.

20 'Marc Rich Cedes Majority Stake in Commodities Firm He Founded', *Wall Street Journal*, 9 March 1993; 'Marc Rich Hopes For Resolution of Tax Case', *Financial Times*, 12 March 1993.

21 As told by Zbynek Zak, who was present; interview with the authors, Zug, June 2019.

22 Authors' correspondence with Zbynek Zak, February 2020.

23 'Marc Rich Passes Control of Company to Employees', *Wall Street Journal*, 10 December 1993, and Amman, Daniel, op. cit., p. 233.

24 Isaac Querub, interview with the authors, Madrid, June 2019.

25 According to several people involved in the deliberations, but Ebner doesn't remember any discussion with Strothotte, and says he's never invested in commodities (Martin Ebner, interview with the authors by telephone, February 2020).

26 'Roche's 93 net rose by 29%', *Wall Street Journal*, 20 April 1994.

27 The company's structure before 1994 was complicated, and different partners remember different things about the details of the buyout deal. Rich, asked by his biographer to confirm that he had received about

$600 million from the sale of the company, said that that was 'not far from the truth' (Ammann, Daniel, *The King of Oil*, op. cit., p. 235).

28 Ammann, Daniel, op. cit., p. 233.

29 Mark Crandall, interview with the authors, London, May 2019.

30 Trafigura, internal publication.

31 Danny Posen, interview with the authors, London, February 2019. The group bought Skydiver as well as Trafigura, but left Blackheart on the shelf.

32 Edmundo Vidal, interview with the authors, Lima, April 2019.

33 Authors' interview with a former Trafigura executive, who declined to be named.

34 Zbynek Zak, interview with the authors, Zug, June 2019.

35 Authors' calculation based on Glencore's trading profit in this period.

36 Lucio Genovese, interview with the authors by video call, October 2020.

37 Based on accounts published in bond prospectuses from 1998, and interviews with former partners.

38 Blank v. Commissioner of Taxation in Australia's High Court, 2016, accessed: http://www.hcourt.gov.au/assets/publications/judgment-summaries/2016/hca-42-2016-11-09.pdf.

39 Mark Crandall, interview with the authors, London, May 2019.

Six: The Biggest Closing-Down Sale in History

1 This account of Trans-World in Russia is based on the authors' interviews with several former Trans-World employees and executives; Lev Chernoy and Michael Cherney's emailed responses to questions from the authors; archived copies of the Reubens' website, containing biographical details; and various other published interviews given by Reuben and other protagonists, including: 'Russia's Aluminium Tsar', *The Economist*, 21 January 1995; 'Grabbing a Corner on Russian Aluminum', *Businessweek*, 16 September 1996; 'Helter-Smelter: Amid Russia's Turmoil, UK Firm Wins Slice of Nation's Aluminum', *Wall Street Journal*, 28 January 1997; 'Transworld Group: Pitfalls for Pioneers', *Financial Times*, 17 June 1998; and 'Aluminium "Risk Taker" Changes Tack in Russia', *Financial Times*, 11 April 2000.

2 Felix Posen, interview with the authors, London, May 2019.

3 Tarasov, Artem, *Millionaire* (2004). Authors' translation from the Russian text, accessed at http://lib.ru/NEWPROZA/TARASOW_A/millioner. txt.

4 Ibid.

5 'Soviets buy American', *New York Times*, 10 May 1989, accessed: https:// www.nytimes.com/1989/05/10/opinion/foreign-affairs-soviets-buy-american.html.

6 According to a senior Marc Rich + Co executive at the time, who requested anonymity.

7 According to David Lilley, who worked for Philipp Brothers and then Metallgesellschaft. When the Phibro metals trading team moved to Metallgesellschaft, the German company took over a significant part of the nickel deal.

8 According to his son, in 'The Reuben Show: The Hottest Property Tycoons in London', *Evening Standard*, 25 June 2010, accessed: https:// www.standard.co.uk/lifestyle/the-reuben-show-the-hottest-property-tycoons-in-london-6484966.html.

9 'Baby Reuben', *Estates Gazette*, 24 June 2006.

10 'Brothers Go Public Over Their Success', *Jewish Chronicle*, 28 March 2003, accessed: https://www.reubenbrothers.com/brothers-go-public-over-their-success/.

11 David Issroff, interview with the authors, New York, August 2019.

12 Ibid.

13 Danny Posen (who was head of Marc Rich + Co's office in Moscow at the time), interview with the authors, London, February 2019.

14 Lev Chernoy, emailed response to questions from the authors, February 2020.

15 'We Saved the Industry', *Rosbalt*, 25 November 2006 (interview with Lev Chernoy), accessed: http://chernoi.ru/top/publikatsii/publitsistika/105-my-spasli-promyshlennost-rossii-intervyu-informatsionnomu-agentstvu-rosbalt-25-11-2006.

16 'Grabbing a Corner on Russian Aluminum', *Businessweek*, 16 September 1996.

17 'Aluminium "Risk Taker" Changes Tack in Russia', *Financial Times*, 11 April 2000, accessed: https://www.reubenbrothers.com/aluminium-%e2%80%b2risk-taker%e2%80%b2-changes-tack-in-russia/.

18 Ibid.

19 Lev Chernoy, emailed response to questions from the authors, February 2020.

20 'Trans-World – Establishment of a New Aluminium Company', Macquarie Equities Limited, December 1995.

21 'King of the Castle', *The Economist*, 21 January 1995, accessed: https://www.reubenbrothers.com/king-of-the-castle-russianaluminium/.

22 Ibid.

23 'It's Lawyers at Dawn in the Wild East', *Guardian*, 1 March 2000, accessed: https://www.reubenbrothers.com/it%e2%80%b2s-lawyers-at-dawn-in-the-wild-east/.

24 Gary Busch, interview with the authors, London, May 2019.

25 'Helter-Smelter: Amid Russia's Turmoil, UK Firm Wins Slice of Nation's Aluminum', *Wall Street Journal*, 28 January 1997.

26 Bloomberg data.

27 Op. cit., *Financial Times*, 2000, via Reuben Brothers website.

28 Berezovsky v Abramovich – Gloster judgment, 2012, paragraph 1044. [2012] EWHC 2463 (Comm).

29 'Smert' predprinimatelya', *Kommersant*, 12 September 1995, accessed: https://www.kommersant.ru/doc/117306.

30 Igor Vishnevskiy (former head of Glencore's Moscow office), interview with the authors, London, June 2019.

31 David Issroff, interview with the authors, New York, August 2019.

32 Op. cit., *Financial Times*, 2000, via Reuben Brothers website.

33 Ibid.

34 Ibid.

35 Ibid.

36 US State Department, 2005 Kazakhstan investment climate statement, accessed: https://2001-2009.state.gov/e/eeb/ifd/2005/42065.htm.

37 Archive of Reuben Brothers website, accessed: http://web.archive.org/web/20060419184709/http://www.reubenbrothers.com/transworld.html.

38 Ibid., *Financial Times*, 2000, via Reuben Brothers website.

39 'Reuben Brothers give Tories nearly £200,000', *Financial Times*, 29 July 2008, accessed: https://www.ft.com/content/4cc2e73c-5dc2-11dd-8129-000077b07658.

40 'Reuben Foundation donates £80 million for first new Oxford college in 30 years', Oxford University, 11 June 2020, accessed: https://www. ox.ac.uk/news/2020-06-11-reuben-foundation-donates-80-million-first-new-oxford-college-30-years.

41 Igor Vishnevskiy, interview with the authors, London, June 2019.

42 According to a person who attended a game with them, who requested anonymity.

43 'Lev Chernoy: Almost half the business elite of the country are my protégés,' *Komsomlskaya Pravda*, 15 November 2004, accessed: https://www.kp.ru/daily/23403/33998/.

44 Lucio Genovese, interview with the authors by video call, October 2020.

45 Klebnikov, Paul, *Godfather of the Kremlin: Life and Times of Boris Berezovsky* (Mariner Books, 2001), p. 71.

46 Klebnikov, Paul, Ibid., p. 182, and authors' interview with Raymond Cretegny, Geneva, May 2019.

47 Igor Vishnevskiy, interview with the authors, London, June 2019.

Seven: Communism with Capitalist Influences

1 'El Hotel Parque Central de La Habana Cumple ya 20 años', *Cibercuba*, 6 May 2018, accessed: https://www.cibercuba.com/noticias/z2018-05-06-u1-e196568-s27316-hotel-parque-central-habana-cumple-20-anos.

2 'Search for New Capital Sources', *Cuba Business*, October 1994, vol. 8, no. 8.

3 Ian Taylor, interview with the authors, London, February 2019.

4 Colin Bryce, interview with the authors, London, February 2019.

5 David Jamison, interview with the authors, Graffham, February 2019.

6 Ford, Jonathan, *Depression, Oil Trading & A Mind At War With Itself* (Chipmunkapublishing, 2016), p. 130.

7 'Ian Taylor: the oilman, his cancer, and the millions he's giving the NHS', *The Times*, 8 June 2019, accessed: https://www.thetimes.co.uk/article/ian-taylor-the-oilman-his-cancer-and-the-millions-hes-giving-the-nhs-wnwbtpq2h.

8 Blasier, Cole, 'El fin de la Asociacion Sovietico-Cubana', Revista del Instituto de Estudios Internacionales de la Universidad de Chile, accessed: https://revistaei.uchile.cl/index.php/REI/article/download/15377/28489/ and TASS, 'Trade, Credit Pact Signed with USRR', Moscow, 12 January 1964.

9 Authors' interview with former senior Marc Rich + Co trader, who requested anonymity.

10 Fidel Castro speech, 28 January 1990, Castro Speech Data Base, Latin American Network Information Center, University of Texas at Austin, accessed: http://lanic.utexas.edu/project/castro/db/1990/19900129.html.

11 Ian Taylor and David Fransen, interview with the authors, London, February 2019.

12 Vitol brochure, 2010.

13 Vitol annual report, 1994.

14 *Cuba Business*, op. cit., October 1994.

15 *Team spirit* (Paris: Sucres et Denrées, 2012), a book printed to commemorate the 60[th] anniversary of the company.

16 David Fransen, interview with the authors, London, February 2019.

17 Perez-Lopez, Jorge, 'The Restructuring of the Cuban Sugar Agro-industry: A Progress Report, Association for the Study of the Cuban Economy', 2016, accessed: https://www.ascecuba.org/asce_proceedings/the-restructuring-of-the-cuban-sugar-agroindustry-a-progress-report/.

18 United States Department of Agriculture, Foreign Agriculture Service database.

19 David Fransen, interview with the authors, London, February 2019.

20 The ownership structure of Sunrise (Bermuda) Ltd is shown in Vitol's 1994 annual report.

21 Ford, Jonathan, op. cit.

22 'Vitol's Ian Taylor on oil deals with dictators and drinks with Fidel', *Financial Times*, 8 April 2018, accessed: https://www.ft.com/content/2dc35efc-89ea-11e8-bf9e-8771d5404543.

23 'Lured by Sun and Socialism, Tourists Flocking to Cuba', *Washington Post*, 1999, accessed: https://www.washingtonpost.com/archive/politics/1999/01/09/lured-by-sun-and-socialism-tourists-flocking-to-cuba/f5ec77c7-95ed-4b6b-b318-d12b47a74ea9/.

24 Igor Vishnevskiy, interview with the authors, London, June 2019.

25 Danny Posen, interview with the authors, London, February 2019.

26 Interview with former senior Cargill executive, who declined to be named.

27 Raymond Cretegny, a former managing director of André; interview with the authors, Geneva, May 2019.

28 Data provided to the authors by Vitol, February 2020.

29 Offering circular, Vitol Master Trust, 1999.

30 'Inside Vitol: How the World's Largest Oil Trader Makes Billions', Bloomberg News, 2016, accessed: https://www.bloomberg.com/news/features/2016-06-01/giant-oil-trader-vitol-makes-billions-in-volatile-times.

31 Vitol 1967 annual report.

32 David Jamison, interview with the authors, Graffham, February 2019.

33 Philipp Brothers Collection: box 1, folder 11, p. 143.

34 Brochure, Vitol Holding NV, 1974, p. 11.

35 David Jamison, interview with the authors, Graffham, February 2019.

36 'Fasting on the Oil Glut', *Texas Monthly*, October 1984.

37 David Jamison, interview with the authors, Graffham, February 2019.

38 Vitol's 1970 annual report.

39 Ford, Jonathan, op. cit., p. 120.

40 Euromin's 1995 annual report, available via Companies House in the UK, accessed: https://beta.companieshouse.gov.uk/company/FC016897/filing-history.

41 Ibid.

42 Ian Taylor, interview with the authors, London, February 2019.

43 In 1999, Vitol traded about 3 million barrels a day of oil and products, according to data provided to the authors by the company. A Glencore bond prospectus puts its oil and products trading volume at 2.5 million barrels a day the same year.

44 Raznjatovic (Arkan) indictment, International Criminal Tribunal for the Former Yugoslavia, 1997, accessed: https://www.icty.org/x/cases/zeljko_raznjatovic/ind/en/ark-ii970930e.pdf.

45 'Oil chief paid $1 million to warlord', *Guardian*, 1 July 2001, accessed: https://www.theguardian.com/world/2001/jul/01/balkans.warcrimes2

46 Vitol, email to the authors, February 2020.

47 OMV Petrom SA *v.* Glencore International AG, England and Wales High Court (Commercial Court), 13 March 2015, [2015] EWHC 666 (Comm), accessed: http://www.bailii.org/ew/cases/EWHC/Comm/2015/666.html; compensation figure from Glencore's 2015 annual report.

48 Graham Sharp, interview with the authors, London, February 2019.

49 Vitol Holding BV, the holding company for the group, reported a $6.6 million profit for the year, but Vitol Holding II SA, the Luxembourg entity through which Vitol's managers held shares in the group, reported a $6 million loss.

50 US Department of Justice, US *v.* Cargill, Inc., and Continental Grain Co., US District Court for the District of Columbia, Civil No. 1:99CV01875, Washington, 8 July 1999, accessed: https://www.justice.gov/atr/case-document/file/490676/download.

51 Brian Gilvary, interview with the authors, London, November 2019.

52 A gripping and comprehensive account of the rise and fall of Enron is McLean, Bethany, and Elkind, Peter, *The Smartest Guys in the Room* (New York: Portfolio, 2003).

53 'Enron Will Pay $445 Million to Buy Metals Merchant MG', *Wall Street Journal*, 23 May 2000, accessed: https://www.wsj.com/articles/SB959026617606197228.

54 'Inside Vitol: How the World's Largest Oil Trader Makes Billions', Bloomberg News, 1 June 2016, accessed: https://www.bloomberg.com/news/features/2016-06-01/giant-oil-trader-vitol-makes-billions-in-volatile-times.

55 McLean, Bethany, and Elkind, Peter, op. cit., p. 225.

56 Ibid., p. 224.

57 'Timeline: A Chronology of Enron Corp.', *New York Times*, 18 January 2006, accessed: https://www.nytimes.com/2006/01/18/business/world business/timeline-a-chronology-of-enron-corp.html.

58 US Department of Justice, US *v*. Cargill, Inc., and Continental Grain Co., US District Court for the District of Columbia, Civil No. 1: 99CV01875, Washington, 8 July 1999, accessed: https://www.justice. gov/atr/case-document/file/490676/download.

Eight: Big Bang

1 'XSTRATA – A Leap Upwards', memo sent by Mick Davis to Brian Azzopardi, Gavin Foley and Benny Levene, 27 June 2001, copy in the authors' possession.

2 Deng Xiaoping, 'Emancipate the Mind, Seek Truth From Facts and United as One in Looking to the Future', Beijing, 13 December 1978, accessed: http://cpcchina.chinadaily.com.cn/2010-10/15/content_13918199.htm.

3 Leung, Guy C. K., Li, Raymond, and Low, Melissa, 'Transitions in China's Oil Economy, 1990–2010.

4 Yiping Xiao, Yan Song, and Xiaodong Wu, 'How Far Has China's Urbanisation Gone?', *Sustainability*, August 2018, accessed: https://res. mdpi.com/sustainability/sustainability-10-02953/article_deploy/ sustainability-10-02953.pdf.

5 Eslake, Saul, 'Commodity Prices', Paper Presented to the International Conference of Commercial Bank Economists, 23 June 2011, accessed: https://grattan.edu.au/wp-content/uploads/2014/04/092_ICCBE_ commodities.pdf.

6 IMF data, gross domestic product per capita, constant prices, measured using purchasing power parity, 2011 international dollar, accessed: https://www.imf.org/external/pubs/ft/weo/2019/01/weodata/ weorept.aspx?pr.x=61&pr.y=11&sy=1980&ey=2024&scsm=1&ssd= 1&sort=country&ds=.&br=1&c=924&s=NGDPRPPPPC%2 CNGDPDPC%2CPPPPC&grp=0&a=.

7 'Protocol on the Accession of the People's Republic of China', World Trade Organization, November 2001, accessed: https://www.wto.org/english/thewto_e/acc_e/a1_chine_e.htm.

8 International Monetary Fund data.

9 World Bureau of Metal Statistics.

10 'Commodity Supercycles: What Are They and What Lies Ahead', Bank of Canada, Bank of Canada Review, Autumn 2016, accessed: https://www.bankofcanada.ca/wp-content/uploads/2016/11/boc-review-autumn16-buyuksahin.pdf.

11 Ibid.

12 'The Role of Major Emerging Markets in Global Commodity Demand', World Bank, June 2018, accessed: http://documents.worldbank.org/curated/en/865201530037257969/pdf/WPS8495.pdf.

13 'Glasenberg was a cheeky kid – ex teacher', *Sunday Times* (South Africa), 22 May 2011, accessed: https://www.timeslive.co.za/news/south-africa/2011-05-22-glasenberg-was-a-cheeky-kid-ex-teacher/.

14 NYC Marathon results, Glasenberg's page at https://results.nyrr.org/runner/5960/result/941106.

15 'Der Reichster Haendler der Welt', *Bilanz*, 1 May 2011, accessed: https://www.handelszeitung.ch/unternehmen/der-reichste-handler-der-welt.

16 Felix Posen, interview with the authors, London, May 2019.

17 According to official Glencore biography, accessed: https://www.glencore.com/en/who-we-are/our-leadership.

18 Josef Bermann, interview with the authors, Zurich, May 2019.

19 Zbynek Zak, interview with the authors, Zug, June 2019.

20 'Enex Float Lifts Veil on Glencore's $10bn Empire', *Sydney Morning Herald*, 1 September 2001.

21 According to two senior Glencore partners, speaking on condition of anonymity.

22 Paul Wyler, interview with the authors, Zurich, June 2019.

23 Authors' interview with former Glencore employee, who declined to be named.

24 Greg James, interview with the authors by telephone, June 2019.

25 Ivan Glasenberg, interview with the authors, Baar, August 2019.

26 By the end of 1998, Australian export prices for thermal coal had dropped to $26.1 a tonne, the lowest since 1987, according to IMF data.

27 Glencore May 2002 prospectus.

28 'The World is Hungry for Coal, Glencore Says', *Coal Week International*, August 2001.

29 'Glencore's Glasenberg on Enex IPO, Coal Potential: Comment', Bloomberg News, 4 September 2001.

30 Glencore's August 2000 prospectus.

31 'Enex Float Lifts Veil on Glencore's $10bn Empire', *Sydney Morning Herald*, 1 September 2001.

32 Glencore's May 2002 prospectus.

33 Xstrata, IPO prospectus, 2002.

34 Mick Davis, interview with the authors, London, June 2019.

35 This account is based on the authors' interviews with Mick Davis, Ivan Glasenberg, other executives of the time, and their advisers, as well as contemporaneous company reports.

36 Mick Davis, interview with the authors, London, September 2019.

37 According to Bloomberg data.

38 Glencore's historical financial data compiled by the authors based on bond prospectuses and related disclosures.

39 Andy Hall, interview with the authors, Derneburg, March 2019.

40 'Profile: Michael Farmer', *Metal Bulletin*, March 2014.

41 Noble Group's 2016 annual report.

42 'Born to be a Noble Man', *South China Morning Post*, 27 May 2002.

Nine: Petrodollars and Kleptocrats

1 This account of Glencore's role in the oil-for-food scandal is based on the lengthy and detailed report of the inquiry led by Paul Volcker:

'Report on Programme Manipulation', Independent Inquiry Committee into the United Nations Oil-for-Food Programme, 27 October 2005. The roles of Glencore, Lakhani and Incomed Trading are detailed on pp. 143–156.

2 'Pakistani broker fuels Iraqi Kurdistan oil exports', *Financial Times*, 29 October 2015, accessed: https://www.ft.com/content/02a7065a-78cd-11e5-933d-efcdc3c11c89.

3 'Music and message of Baghdad's Concert for Peace expected to fall on deaf ears in Washington', *Irish Times*, 1 Feb 2003, accessed: https://www.irishtimes.com/news/music-and-message-of-baghdad-s-concert-for-peace-expected-to-fall-on-deaf-ears-in-washington-1.347379.

4 'Pakistani broker fuels Iraqi Kurdistan oil exports', *Financial Times*, 29 October 2015. A spokesman for Lakhani later told Bloomberg News that he had meant he was 'prepared to work hard in a 'hands on' manner, often in a small team'.

5 'Report on Programme Manipulation', Independent Inquiry Committee into the United Nations Oil-for-Food Programme, 27 October 2005, p. 154.

6 The surcharge was initially set at 50 cents per barrel, but was soon lowered to between 30 and 25 cents per barrel, depending on the destination. By late 2002, it was lowered again to 15 cents per barrel.

7 The full report can be found at the archived version of the Independent Inquiry Committee's website: http://web.archive.org/web/20071113193128/http://www.iic-offp.org/documents/IIC%20Final%20Report%2027Oct2005.pdf. Some of the individuals whom the report accused of involvement in the manipulation of the oil-for-food programme have publicly criticised the inquiry's methods and conclusions, arguing that it was politically motivated. However, the inquiry, which was endorsed by the UN Security Council, was praised by UN Secretary General Kofi Annan as an 'extremely thorough investigation', and information from it was cited in numerous anti-corruption cases.

8 Independent Inquiry, op. cit., p. 198.

9 Ibid., p. 152.

10 'Comprehensive Report of the Special Advisor to the DCI on Iraq's WMD', Iraq Survey Group (the report is otherwise known as the Duelfer report, after its lead author, Charles Duelfer, special advisor to the US Director of Central Intelligence), 30 September 2004, p. 39.

11 Ibid., p. 38.

12 'The Billion-Dollar Broker Who Managed a Nation's Oil Wealth', Bloomberg News, 16 July 2020, accessed: https://www.bloomberg.com/news/articles/2020-07-16/billion-dollar-broker-how-one-man-managed-a-nation-s-oil-wealth.

13 'Glencore reveals more IPO rewards', *Financial Times*, 17 February 2012.

14 New York County District Attorney's Office Press Release, 20 November 2007, accessed: https://star.worldbank.org/corruption-cases/printpdf/19592.

15 'Firm Pleads Guilty in Oil-For-Food Case', *Houston Chronicle*, 26 May 2006, accessed: https://www.chron.com/business/energy/article/Firm-pleads-guilty-in-Oil-for-Food-case-1862731.php.

16 'Houston Oil-For-Food Trader Gets 2 Years', *Houston Chronicle*, 8 March 2008, accessed: https://www.chron.com/business/energy/article/Houston-Oil-for-Food-trader-gets-2-years-1779305.php.

17 BP Statistical Review of World Energy database.

18 Ibid.

19 Ibid.

20 Clarendon Alumina Production 2006 bond prospectus.

21 Ton Klomp, interview with the authors, London, July 2019.

22 Bob Finch, interview with the authors, London, April 2019.

23 Polish Investigative Committee hearing on allegations about PK Orlen, 30 March 2005, accessed: http://orka.sejm.gov.pl/Biuletyn.nsf/0/9BF787564C6DC12DC1256FDA00469547?OpenDocument.

24 Ibid.

25 Crown Resources AG *v*. Vinogradsky et al., 2001. A copy of the judgment is at: https://www.ucc.ie/academic/law/restitution/archive/englcases/crown_resources.htm.

26 Jankilevitsch and Smolokowski, email to the authors, February 2020. Their full statement reads: 'It is true that Crown Resources brought

a claim and obtained Judgement in 2001 against two of its former employees (and their respective Companies) regarding their receipt of certain payments many years earlier from several companies who were not a party to the Action. No assertion of any impropriety was ever directed against J&S and had one been raised and had proceedings been pursued against J&S in relation thereto they would have been vigorously defended. As it happens, and not surprisingly, they were not.'

27 Biographical details on Timchenko are taken from authors' interview with Törnqvist, Geneva, May 2019, as well as Timchenko's 2008 interview with the *Wall Street Journal* (https://www.wsj.com/articles/SB121314210826662571), a 2008 profile in the *Financial Times* (https://www.ft.com/content/c3c5c012-21e9-11dd-a50a-000077b07658), and a 2013 profile in *Vedomosti* (https://www.vedomosti.ru/library/articles/2013/01/21/chelovek_s_resursom).

28 Torbjörn Törnqvist, interview with the authors, Geneva, May 2019.

29 'Gunvor pins future on Swedish CEO after Russian co-founder exits', Reuters, 24 March 2014: https://uk.reuters.com/article/uk-ukraine-crisis-gunvor/gunvor-pins-future-on-swedish-ceo-after-russian-co-founder-exits-idUKBREA2N05K20140324.

30 BP Statistical Review of World Energy database.

31 Cyprus corporate registry data.

32 Marco Dunand, interview with the authors by telephone, August 2019.

33 Mercuria company accounts filed in the Netherlands and Cyprus.

34 The holding company changed its name to Mercuria Energy Group Ltd in January 2007.

35 On his annual 'Direct Line' call-in show, broadcast on 17 April 2014, accessed: https://www.vesti.ru/doc.html?id=1488888.

36 'Timchenko: Everything has to be paid for, and acquaintance with top officials as well', Timchenko interview with TASS, 4 August 2014, accessed: https://tass.com/top-officials/743432.

37 Freeland, Chrystia, *Sale of the Century: The Inside Story of the Second Russian Revolution* (Abacus, 2005), p. 178.

38 'Khodorkovskiy otmeril sebe srok', *Vedomosti*, 3 April 2003 (Khodorkovsky measured out his term) and 'Ritt auf der Rasierklinge', *Spiegel*, 3 May 2003 (Ride on the razorblade).

39 Gustafson, Thane, *Wheel of Fortune* (Harvard University Press, 2013), pp. 297–300.

40 Interview with Timchenko, *Forbes Russia*, 2012, accessed: https://www.forbes.ru/sobytiya/lyudi/181713-tot-samyi-timchenko-pervoe-intervyu-bogateishego-iz-druzei-putina.

41 Torbjörn Törnqvist, interview with the authors, Geneva, May 2019.

42 Gunvor, email to the authors, February 2020. The company says it bought oil from many Russian companies, with the bulk of its supplies coming from TNK-BP.

43 Ibid. The company says that, between 2005 and 2014, it paid average dividends of 18.5%.

44 In a letter published in the *Financial Times* on 14 May 2008, he said: 'My career of more than 20 years in the oil industry has not been built on favours or political connections', accessed: https://www.ft.com/content/c3c5c012-21e9-11dd-a50a-000077b07658.

45 Authors' calculation based on company earnings data.

Ten: Destination Africa

1 Deaton, Angus, 'Commodity Prices and Growth in Africa', *Journal of Economic Perspectives*, vol. 3, no. 3, summer 1999, pp. 23–40, accessed: https://www.princeton.edu/~deaton/downloads/Commodity_Prices_and_Growth_in_Africa.pdf.

2 World Bank data. Sub-Saharan Africa GDP was $381.8 billion in 2001 – compared to $381.2 billion in 1981. GDP per capita was much lower in 2001 than in 1981, as during those two decades the sub-continent's population increased by roughly 75%, going from 394.2 million people to 682.9 million. https://data.worldbank.org/region/sub-saharan-africa.

3 US Geological Survey, Copper, Minerals Yearbook, accessed: https://s3-us-west-2.amazonaws.com/prd-wret/assets/palladium/production/mineral-pubs/copper/240497.pdf.

4 'BP Statistical Review of World Energy', June 2019. Nigeria produced 1.895 million barrels a day in 1999, compared to 2.302 million barrels a day in 1979. By 2010, Nigerian output had risen to 2.5 million barrels a day.

5 Cover story, 'The hopeless continent', *The Economist*, 13 May 2000, accessed: https://www.economist.com/node/21519234.

6 World Bank data. Sub-Saharan Africa GDP was $1.55 trillion by 2011.

7 United States of America *v.* The M/Y Galactica Star et al.', United States District Court, Southern District of Texas, Houston Division, 14 July 2017, and 'Department of Justice Seeks to Recover Over $100 Million Obtained from Corruption in the Nigerian Oil Industry', US Department of Justice, Press Release, 14 July 2017, accessed: https://star.worldbank.org/corruption-cases/sites/corruption-cases/files/DOJ-Galactica-Complaint.pdf and https://www.justice.gov/opa/pr/department-justice-seeks-recover-over-100-million-obtained-corruption-nigerian-oil-industry.

8 Silverstein, Ken, *The Secret World of Oil* (London: Verso, 2015), p. 53.

9 'Congo Bribery Probe Puts Israeli Billionaire's Future on Hold', Bloomberg News, 23 February 2018, accessed: https://www.bloomberg.com/news/articles/2018-02-23/he-got-rich-on-congo-mines-until-bribe-probe-put-future-on-hold.

10 'Congo war-driven crisis kills 45,000 a month: survey', Reuters, 22 January 2008, accessed: https://www.reuters.com/article/us-congo-democratic-death/congo-war-driven-crisis-kills-45000-a-month-study-idUSL2280201220080122.

11 'Report of the Panel of Experts on the Illegal Exploitation of Natural Resources and Other Forms of Wealth of DR Congo', United Nations, 12 April 2001, accessed: https://reliefweb.int/report/democratic-republic-congo/report-panel-experts-illegal-exploitation-natural-resources-and.

12 'Gertler Earns Billions as Mine Deals Leave Congo Poorest', Bloomberg News, 5 December 2012, accessed: https://www.bloomberg.com/

news/articles/2012-12-05/gertler-earns-billions-as-mine-deals-leave-congo-poorest.

13 'President Bush Meets with Democratic Republic of Congo President Kabila', White House, 26 October 2007, accessed: https://georgewbush-whitehouse.archives.gov/news/releases/2007/10/images/20071026-1_d-0061-3-515h.html.

14 'Congo Bribery Probe Puts Israeli Billionaire's Future on Hold', Bloomberg News, 23 February 2018.

15 'Augustin Katumba, President's Alleged Treasurer and Enforcer, Steps Out as Head of National Assembly's Ruling Coalition; His Influence Could Remain', US Department of State, Diplomatic Cable from US Embassy in Kinshasa, Washington, 14 December 2009, accessed: https://wikileaks.org/plusd/cables/09KINSHASA1080_a.html.

16 'Trouble in the Congo: The Misadventures of Glencore', *Bloomberg Businessweek*, 16 November 2018, accessed: https://www.bloomberg.com/news/features/2018-11-16/glencore-s-misadventure-in-the-congo-threatens-its-cobalt-dreams.

17 Email dated 16 March 2008, from Dan Gertler, described as 'DRC Partner', to an Och-Ziff executive, in US District Court Eastern District of New York, 'US vs Och-Ziff Capital Management Group LLC', Cr. No. 16-516 (NGG), Deferred Prosecution Agreement, Page A-12. A later judgment dated 28 August 2019 identified Gertler as 'DRC Partner' (16-CR-515 (NGG), order and memorandum signed by Judge Nicholas Garaufis).

18 'The Kingmaker is dead', *The Economist*, 20 February 2012, accessed: https://www.economist.com/baobab/2012/02/20/the-kingmaker-is-dead.

19 'Equity in Extractives: Stewarding Africa's Natural Resources for All', Africa Progress Panel, 2013.

20 'Gertler Earns Billions as Mine Deals Leave Congo Poorest', Bloomberg News, 5 December 2012.

21 'Congo Bribery Probe Puts Israeli Billionaire's Future on Hold', Bloomberg News, 23 February 2018.

22 US Department of the Treasury press release, 21 December 2017, accessed at: https://home.treasury.gov/news/press-releases/sm0243.

23 Gertler spokesman, emailed response to questions, March 2020.

24 Glencore, 3 May 2011, IPO Prospectus, p. 859, accessed: https://www.glencore.com/dam/jcr:268b58d2-61b8-44d1-997a-17e76bb66f93/Final-Prospectus-3-May-2011-lowres.pdf.

25 Glencore, IPO Prospectus, p. 77.

26 'Glencore Faces New Legal Challenge Against Congo Cobalt Mine', Bloomberg News, 8 June 2018, accessed: https://www.bloomberg.com/news/articles/2018-06-08/glencore-faces-new-legal-challenge-against-cobalt-mine-in-congo.

27 Glencore, annual report 2007, p. 31. Glencore disclosed in its annual report that it paid $296 million in total for two deals: the 40% stake in Mutanda Mining and the purchase of several oil tankers.

28 'Equity in Extractives', Africa Progress Panel, 2013.

29 Golder Associates, a consultant, valued the whole of Mutanda at $3,089 million in May 2011, as part of Glencore's IPO process, p. 130 of the report, in Glencore, IPO Prospectus, 3 May 2011.

30 'Glencore takes control of Mutanda with $480 million deal', Reuters, 22 May 2012, accessed: https://www.reuters.com/article/glencore-mutanda/update-2-glencore-takes-control-of-mutanda-with-480-mln-deal-idUSL5E8GM5RO20120522.

31 The details of Glencore's relationship with Gertler have been reported extensively, including in 'Trouble in the Congo: The Misadventures of Glencore', *Bloomberg Businessweek*, 16 November 2018; 'Congo Bribery Probe Puts Israeli Billionaire's Future on Hold', Bloomberg News, 23 February 2018; and 'Gertler Earns Billions as Mine Deals Leave Congo Poorest', Bloomberg News, 5 December 2012.

32 Bloomberg News, 5 December 2012, op. cit.

33 Email dated 21 February 2008 from an unnamed due diligence firm to Och-Ziff employees. Gertler is referred to as 'DRC Partner', in 'US vs Och-Ziff Capital Management Group LLC', US District Court Eastern District of New York, Cr. No. 16-516 (NGG), Deferred Prosecution Agreement, p. A-9.

34 'US vs Och-Ziff Capital Management Group LLC', US District Court Eastern District of New York, Cr. No. 16-516 (NGG), Deferred Prosecution Agreement, accessed: https://www.justice.gov/opa/file/899306/download.

35 'US vs OZ Africa Management GP, LLC', US District Court, Eastern District of New York, Cr. No. 16-515 (NGG), Plea Agreement, accessed: https://www.justice.gov/opa/file/899316/download.

36 'Glencore purchases stakes in Mutanda and Katanga', Glencore press release, 13 February 2017, accessed: https://otp.investis.com/clients/uk/glencore2/rns/regulatory-story.aspx?cid=275&newsid=843557.

37 'Subpoena from United States Department of Justice', Glencore press release, 3 July 2018, accessed: https://www.glencore.com/media-and-insights/news/Subpoena-from-United-States-Department-of-Justice.

38 'Puma International Financing SA, $750,000,000 5% Senior Notes due 2026 Prospectus', Puma Energy, 31 January 2018, and 'Share Purchase Agreement', Puma Energy LLC, 21 August 2013.

39 Trafigura's annual reports 2014–2018.

40 Torbjörn Törnqvist, interview with the authors, Geneva, August 2019.

41 'Banknote Shortage Still Acute', US State Department, cable from US embassy in Harare, Zimbabwe, Washington, 28 July 2003, via WikiLeaks, accessed: https://wikileaks.org/plusd/cables/03HARARE1521_a.html.

42 'Cargill closes local cotton business', *The Herald*, 15 October 2014, accessed: https://www.herald.co.zw/cargill-closes-local-cotton-business/.

43 'Cargill Makes Bootleg Currency', US State Department, cable from US embassy in Harare, Zimbabwe, Washington, 6 August 2003, via WikiLeaks, accessed: https://wikileaks.org/plusd/cables/03HARARE1577_a.html.

44 'Zimbabwe plunging toward total collapse', *Chicago Tribune*, 8 June 2003.

45 David MacLennan, interview with the authors, Minneapolis, August 2019.

46 'Cargill Makes Bootleg Currency', US State Department, 6 August 2003.

47 'Commodities: Destination Africa', *Financial Times*, 11 November 2013, accessed: https://www.ft.com/content/817df4c2-35c0-11e3-952b-00144feab7de.

48 'Dirty Diesel: How Swiss Traders Flood Africa with Toxic Fuels', *Public Eye*, September 2016, accessed: https://www.publiceye.ch/fileadmin/doc/Rohstoffe/2016_PublicEye_DirtyDiesel_EN_Report.pdf.

49 'Rapport de la Commission Nationale d'Enquête sur les Déchets Toxiques dans le District d'Abidjan', Republic of Côte d'Ivoire, pp. 27–28, accessed: https://www.trafigura.com/media/1440/2006_trafigura_rapport_commission_nationale_enqu%C3%AAte_district_abidjan_french.pdf.

50 'Trafigura & the Probo Koala', Trafigura, pp.8–9, accessed: https://www.trafigura.com/media/1372/2016_trafigura_and_the_probo_koala_english.pdf.

51 'Trafigura Beheer BV Investor Presentation', Trafigura, March 2010.

52 Trafigura email dated 27 December 2005, 4.54 PM, from James McNicol to other oil traders, accessed: https://www.trafigura.com/media/1374/2009_trafigura_emails_published_by_the_guardian_english.pdf.

53 Trafigura email dated 27 December 2005, 1.12 PM, from James McNicol to other oil traders.

54 Trafigura email dated 28 December 2005, 9.30 AM, from James McNicol to other executives.

55 Trafigura email dated 27 December 2005, 7.29 PM, from Naeem Ahmed to other executives.

56 Trafigura email dated 28 December 2005, 9.30 AM, from James McNicol.

57 Trafigura email dated 13 March 2006, 9.15 AM, from Toula Gerakis to other executives.

58 Email from *Probo Koala* captain acknowledging receipt of instructions, 15 April 2006, 4.26 PM.

59 Second Interim Report, *Probo Koala* Inquiry, conducted by Lord Fraser Carmyllie, accessed: https://www.trafigura.com/media/1382/2010_trafigura_second_interim_report_of_lord_fraser_of_carmyllie_qc_probo_koala_report_english.pdf.

60 Trafigura report on the *Probo Koala*, 2016, p. 8.

61 'Rapport de la Commission Nationale d'Enquête sur les Déchets Toxiques dans le District d'Abidjan', Republic of Côte d'Ivoire, p. 46.

62 Ibid., p. 45.

63 'Neglect and Fraud Blamed for Toxic Dumping in Ivory Coast', *New York Times*, 24 November 2006, accessed: https://www.nytimes.com/2006/11/24/world/africa/24ivory.html.

64 The contract between Trafigura and Compagnie Tommy is quoted in full (in French) in 'Rapport de la Commission Nationale d'Enquête sur les Déchets Toxiques dans le District d'Abidjan', Republic of Côte d'Ivoire, p. 19. An image of the original letter (in English) showing the letterhead of Compagnie Tommy is reproduced in 'The Toxic Truth', Greenpeace and Amnesty International, 2012, p. 46.

65 Details of the cases are taken from Trafigura's own summary of the scandal, 'Trafigura and the *Probo Koala*', accessed: https://www.trafigura.com/media/1787/2016_trafigura_and_the_probo_koala.pdf.

66 Mark Crandall, interview with the authors, London, June 2019.

67 Trafigura, email to the authors, February 2020.

68 José Larocca, interview with the authors, Geneva, May 2019.

Eleven: Hunger and Profit

1 'The ravening hoards', *The Economist*, 17 April 2008, accessed: https://www.economist.com/asia/2008/04/17/the-ravening-hoards.

2 'Wen Jiabao Inspects Agriculture and Spring Farming in Hebei', BBC Monitoring translation of Xinhua, 6 April 2008.

3 'Funds crunch threatens world food aid', *Financial Times*, 12 June 2009, accessed: https://www.ft.com/content/524d50da-56ae-11de-9a1c-00144feabdc0.

4 Alberto Weisser, interview with the authors, London, March 2019.

5 'Remarks at the Clinton Global Initiative Closing Plenary', US State Department, 25 September 2009, accessed: https://2009-2017.state.gov/secretary/20092013clinton/rm/2009a/09/129644.htm.

6 Ton Klomp, who worked at Cargill in the 1980s, interview with the authors, London, July 2019.

7 Authors' interviews with two Cargill executives, who requested anonymity.

8 Ricardo Leiman, interview with the authors, London, August 2019.

9 Mark Hansen, interview with the authors, London, February 2019.

10 Interviews with two senior Glencore executives, who declined to be named.

11 'Moscow Urged to Ban Grain Exports', *Financial Times*, 3 August 2010, accessed: https://www.ft.com/content/dfa6ba3a-9f27-11df-8732-00144feabdc0.

12 'Russian Officials Mull Grain Export Curbs, Union Says', Bloomberg News, 4 August 2010: accessed: https://www.bloomberg.com/news/articles/2010-08-03/russia-should-ban-grain-exports-as-drought-withers-crops-glencore-says.

13 'Glencore reveals bet on grain price rise', *Financial Times*, 24 April 2011, accessed: https://www.ft.com/content/aea76c56-6ea5-11e0-a13b-00144feabdc0.

14 See Glencore's IPO prospectus, May 2011, p. 50, for agricultural and oil/coal trading profitability. For historical data of the agricultural division's profitability, see 'Olympian Expands Glencore's Empire With Emerging Food Colossus', Bloomberg News, 3 May 2017, accessed: https://www.bloomberg.com/news/articles/2017-05-03/olympian-expands-glencore-empire-with-emerging-food-colossus.

15 Ian McIntosh, interview with the authors, London, June 2019.

16 Based on annual average profits for Vitol, Glencore and Cargill of $813 million in 1998–1999.

17 Apple's cumulative net income over the period was $61.5 billion; Coca-Cola's was $61.2 billion.

18 At the end of 2011, Boeing had a market cap of $55 billion and Goldman Sachs $45 billion, source: http://media.ft.com/cms/73f82726-385d-11e1-9f07-00144feabdc0.pdf.

19 'Cargill-MacMillan family', *Forbes*, 29 June 2016, accessed: https://www.forbes.com/profile/cargill-macmillan-1/#5095a3cd23b6.

20 Authors' interview with a trader, who requested anonymity.

21 'Dems' new gas-pump villain: Speculators', Politico, 8 July 2008, accessed: https://www.politico.com/story/2008/07/dems-new-gas-pump-villain-speculators-011583.

22 'Cereal Secrets', Oxfam, Oxfam Research Reports, August 2012, accessed: https://www-cdn.oxfam.org/s3fs-public/file_attachments/rr-cereal-secrets-grain-traders-agriculture-30082012-en_4.pdf.

23 'Sumitomo Ex-Trader Wants Company to Share Scandal Blame', *New York Times*, 18 February 1997, accessed: https://www.nytimes.com/1997/02/18/business/sumitomo-ex-trader-wants-company-to-share-scandal-blame.html.

24 'Tokyo Commodity Futures Markets Regulators' Conference', October 1997, pp. 4–9, accessed: https://www.cftc.gov/sites/default/files/idc/groups/public/@internationalaffairs/documents/file/oia_tokyorpt.pdf.

25 'Treasury Select Committee, Memorandum from the FSA on Oil Market Regulation', UK Financial Services Authority, 10 July 2008, accessed: https://publications.parliament.uk/pa/cm200708/cmselect/cmtreasy/memo/oilreg/ucm0202.htm.

26 See Tarring, Trevor, *Corner! A century of metal market manipulation* (1998), for an account of the history of metals market corners, including the Secretan copper corner which began in 1887.

27 'Armajaro sells position as it offloads cocoa', *Financial Times*, 16 December 2010, accessed: https://www.ft.com/content/cfb68d4e-094e-11e0-ada6-00144feabdc0.

28 'Edict on Maximum Prices', Diocletian, accessed: http://web.archive.org/web/20060916063955/http://orion.it.luc.edu/~jlong1/priceed.htm.

29 Jacks, David S., 'Populists v. Theorists: Futures Markets and the Volatility of Prices', Simon Fraser University, accessed: http://econ.queensu.ca/CNEH/2005/papers/futures_CNEH_0305.pdf.

30 'Hearings Before a Special Subcommittee of the Committee on Agriculture', US Congress, House of Representatives, 16, 17, 18 and 22 May 1956, Washington, pp. 292–325.

31 'Price Volatility in Food and Agricultural Markets: Policy Responses', joint report by FAO, IFAD, IMF, OECD, UNCTAD, WFP, the World

Bank, the WTO, IFPRI, June 2011, accessed: http://www.fao.org/
fileadmin/templates/est/Volatility/Interagency_Report_to_the_G20_
on_Food_Price_Volatility.pdf.

32 For example, Fattouh, Bassam, Kilian, Lutz, and Mahadeva, Lavan,
'The Role of Speculation in Oil Markets: What Have We Learned So
Far?', *The Energy Journal*, vol. 34, no. 3, accessed: https://www.iaee.
org/en/publications/ejarticle.aspx?id=2536&id=2536 and Irwin, Scott
H., Sanders, Dwight R., and Merrin, Robert P., 'Devil or Angel? The
Role of Speculation in the Recent Commodity Price Boom (and Bust)',
paper presented at the Southern Agricultural Economics Association
Meetings, Atlanta, Georgia, 31 January–3 February 2009, accessed:
https://www.cftc.gov/sites/default/files/idc/groups/public/@swaps/
documents/file/plstudy_24_ism.pdf.

33 'Financial Investment in Commodity Markets: Potential Impact on
Commodity Prices and Volatility', Institute of International Finance,
September 2011, accessed: https://www.eia.gov/finance/markets/
reports_presentations/2012PaperFinancialInvestment.pdf.

34 World Economic Outlook, IMF, September 2011, p. 60.

35 'History of Ethanol Production and Policy', North Dakota State Uni-
versity, accessed: https://www.ag.ndsu.edu/energy/biofuels/energy-
briefs/history-of-ethanol-production-and-policy.

36 'Boom in Ethanol Reshapes Economy of Heartland', *New York Times*,
25 June 2006, accessed: https://www.nytimes.com/2006/06/25/business/
25ethanol.html.

37 'Dwayne's World', *Mother Jones*, July/August 1995.

38 'Kenneth H. Dahlberg, Link in the Watergate Chain, Dies at 94', *New
York Times*, 8 October 2011, accessed: https://www.nytimes.com/
2011/10/09/us/kenneth-h-dahlberg-watergate-figure-and-wwii-ace-
dies-at-94.html.

39 The most detailed chronicles of the rise and fall of Dwayne Andreas
at ADM are the detailed biography by Khan, E. J., *Supermarketer to the
World: The Story of Dwayne Andreas CEO of Archer Daniels Midland* (New
York: Warner Books, Inc., 1984) and Eichenwald, Kurt, *The Informant*
(Broadway, 2000).

40 'It's Good To Be The Boss', *Fortune*, October 2006, accessed: https://money.cnn.com/magazines/fortune/fortune_archive/2006/10/16/8390308/index.htm.

41 'A Bet on Ethanol, With a Convert at the Helm', *New York Times*, 8 October 2006, accessed: https://www.nytimes.com/2006/10/08/business/yourmoney/08adm.html.

42 ADM, company statement, 5 June 2009, accessed: https://www.adm.com/news/news-releases/archer-daniels-midland-company-statement-regarding-obama-administration-biofuels-support.

43 Center for Responsive Politics, Archer Daniels Midland, accessed: https://www.opensecrets.org/lobby/clientsum.php?id=D000000132&year=2008.

44 Annual US Fuel Ethanol Production, Renewable Fuel Association, accessed: https://ethanolrfa.org/statistics/annual-ethanol-production/ and WASDE reports, US Agriculture Department, accessed: https://usda.library.cornell.edu/concern/publications/3t945q76s.

45 ADM, email to the authors, February 2020.

Twelve: The Billionaire Factory

1 This account of Glencore's IPO is based on interviews with numerous former and current Glencore traders and executives, as well as public interviews and documents from the time.

2 Authors' interview with former Glencore employee, who declined to be named.

3 *Forbes* magazine's 'The World's Billionaires 2011' didn't include Glasenberg, as it was published in February 2011, ahead of the IPO. If it had included him, he would have ranked 96th.

4 The shareholdings of Mahoney and Fegel were not revealed until a few months later.

5 Ivan Glasenberg, interview with the authors, Baar, August 2019.

6 Vivo IPO prospectus, 2018, p. 64.

7 'First U.S. Oil Export Leaves Port; Marks End to 40-Year Ban', Bloomberg News, 31 December 2015, accessed: https://www.bloomberg.com/news/

articles/2015-12-31/first-u-s-oil-export-leaves-port-marking-end
-of-40-year-ban.

8 'Advancing US Exports', Trafigura, p. 8, accessed: https://www.trafig-ura.com/media/1472/2020-trafigura-us-crude-oil-exports-brochure.
pdf.

9 The structure was somewhat complex. Each share, which carried voting rights, came attached to a profit participation certificate, which entitled its owner to a share of the company's profit for that year. Each year, the company bought back shares from departing shareholders and issued them to rising stars. Then, over the five years after a departing share-holder left the company, Glencore would pay them (quarterly, with interest) for the value of the historic allocation of profit on their profit participation account.

10 Glencore's net profits in 2006–2007 were $11.4 billion, while between 1998 and 2005 they were $8.4 billion, according to accounts published in bond prospectuses.

11 Ivan Glasenberg, interview with the authors, Baar, August 2019.

12 Mick Davis, interview with the authors, London, September 2019.

13 Ibid.

14 Authors' interview with a former senior Glencore executive, who requested anonymity.

15 Kelly, Kate, *The Secret Club That Runs the World* (London: Portfolio, 2014), p. 63.

16 'Glencore issues up to US$2,200 million 5% convertible bonds due 2014', Glencore press release, 23 December 2009.

17 'Sun King of the Oil Industry', *Financial Times*, July 2002, accessed: https://www.ft.com/content/2a42aa08-a261-11db-a187-0000779e2340.

18 'Inside Lord Browne of Madingley's Chelsea Home', *Telegraph*, 25 July 2013, accessed: https://www.telegraph.co.uk/lifestyle/interiors/10199624/Interiors-inside-Lord-Browne-of-Madingleys-Chelsea-home.html.

19 According to several people who were present at or briefed on the meeting, speaking on condition of anonymity.

20 'Announcement of intention to float on the London Stock Exchange and the Hong Kong Stock Exchange', Glencore press release, 14 April 2011, accessed: https://www.glencore.com/dam/jcr:d91c0e46-8b24-48ec-b5f2-4b4637e1b90c/201104140800-Glencore-ITF.pdf.

21 As of late 2020, that's a record it still holds.

22 This account of the Glencore–Xstrata merger is based on the authors' interviews, both at the time and later, with Glasenberg, Davis and numerous others involved in the negotiations.

23 'Recommended all-share merger of equals of Glencore International PLC and Xstrata PLC to create unique $90 billion natural resources group', Glencore press release, 7 February 2012, accessed: https://www.glencore.com/dam/jcr:4fe5ba2e-6abb-41ad-910a-247a39e4e3a6/Everest-Finalversion-Feb.pdf.

24 Authors' interview with a person who requested anonymity.

25 *The Sunday Times* Rich List 2011.

26 'Glencore's $65bn Deal Close to Collapse', *Financial Times*, 27 June 2012, accessed: https://www.ft.com/content/fec63352e-bfb1-11e1-bb88-00144feabdc0.

27 'Glencore chief makes offer with a twist', *Financial Times*, 7 September 2012, accessed: https://www.ft.com/content/ec2167f0-f903-11e1-8d92-00144feabdc0.

28 According to a Glencore presentation on 3 May 2013, Glencore's 'executive management' owned 24.9% of the enlarged company, while its 'employees and management' owned 35.7%.

29 'Recommended All-Share Merger of Equals of Glencore International Plc and Xstrata Plc to Create Unique $90 Billion Natural Resources Group', Glencore press release, 7 February 2012.

30 Felix Posen, interview with the authors, London, May 2019.

31 Zbynek Zak, interview with the authors, Zug, June 2019.

32 'Enex Float Lifts Veil on Glencore's $10bn Empire', *Sydney Morning Herald*, 1 September 2001.

33 Paul Wyler, interview with the authors, Zurich, June 2019.

34 Philipp Brothers Collection: box 1, folder 11, p. 39.

35 'Cotton Trading Costs Glencore $330 Million', *Financial Times*, 7 February 2012, accessed: https://www.ft.com/content/16af8bfe-51b2-11e1-a30c-00144feabdc0.

36 'How a Last-Minute Raid Derailed Noble Group's Story of Rebirth', Bloomberg News, 20 December 2018, accessed: https://www.bloomberg.com/news/articles/2018-12-20/how-a-last-minute-raid-derailed-noble-group-s-story-of-rebirth.

37 David Tendler, interview with the authors, New York, August 2019.

38 David Jamison, interview with the authors, Graffham, February 2019.

39 'Inside Vitol: How the World's Largest Oil Trader Makes Billions', *Bloomberg Markets*, 1 June 2016.

40 'Louis Dreyfus Looks to IPO or Partial Sale', *Financial Times*, 16 October 2011, accessed: https://www.ft.com/content/f8499efe-f813-11e0-a419-00144feab49a.

41 Jeremy Weir, interview with the authors, Geneva, May 2019.

42 'Cargill to Give Up Mosaic Stake in $24.3 Billion Deal', *Wall Street Journal*, 19 January 2011.

43 Tan, Ruth S. K., and Wiwattanakantang, Yupana, 'Cargill: Keeping the Family Business Private', National University of Singapore and Richard Ivey School of Business Foundation, Case Study, 2015.

44 'Commodity Daily: Putting a price on Glencore', *Financial Times*, 20 January 2011.

45 'Cargill agrees $24 billion spin-off of Mosaic', *Financial Times*, 19 January 2011.

46 Annual number of articles mentioning at least one of Cargill, Glencore, Vitol or Trafigura, published in *The New York Times*, the *Wall Street Journal*, the *Financial Times* or *The Economist*, via Factiva's database.

47 Zbynek Zak, interview with the authors, Zug, June 2019.

Thirteen: Merchants of Power

1 'Oilflow SPV 1 DAC: Company Announcement', Cayman Islands Stock Exchange, 19 March 2018, accessed: https://www.csx.ky/companies/announcement.asp?Id=6518.

2 As of mid-2020, there were 198 companies registered at 32 Molesworth Street, according to a list published by the Spanish central bank, accessed: https://www.bde.es/webbde/en/estadis/fvc/fvc_ie.html.

3 Constitution of Oilflow SPV 1 Designated Activity Company, Memorandum of Association, Companies Registration Office, Ireland, 25 October 2016.

4 CSX admits Oilflow SPV 1 DAC to the official list, 13 January 2017, accessed: https://www.csx.ky/companies/announcement.asp?Id=5850.

5 Audited Annual Report, Franklin Templeton Series II Funds, p. 7, accessed: http://www.ftidocuments.com/content-common/annual-report/en_GB/FTSIIF-annual-report.pdf.

6 The 2017 financial statements of Oilflow SPV 1 DAC state that the company is ultimately controlled by Glencore.

7 Jim Daley, interview with the authors, London, August 2019. Daley was the chief financial officer for oil at Marc Rich + Co from 1977 to 1980, and from 1983 to 1990 was the global head of oil trading.

8 Arango, Tim, 'For Iraq's Long-Suffering Kurds, Independence Beckons', *New York Times*, 9 September 2017, accessed: https://www.nytimes.com/2017/09/09/world/middleeast/iraq-kurdistan-kurds-kurdish-referendum-independence.html.

9 'Pakistani broker fuels Iraqi Kurdistan oil exports', *Financial Times*, 29 October 2015, accessed: https://www.ft.com/content/02a7065a-78cd-11e5-933d-efcdc3c11c89.

10 'Manafort Working on Kurdish Referendum Opposed by US', *New York Times*, 20 September 2017, accessed: https://www.nytimes.com/2017/09/20/us/politics/manafort-kurdish-referendum.html.

11 'Under the mountains: Kurdish Oil and Regional Politics', Oxford Institute for Energy Studies, January 2016, p. 12, accessed: https://www.oxfordenergy.org/wpcms/wp-content/uploads/2016/02/Kurdish-Oil-and-Regional-Politics-WPM-63.pdf.

12 Ben Luckock, interview with the authors, Geneva, May 2019.

13 Ibid.

14 Ibid.

15 Chris Bake, interview with the authors, London, April 2019.

16 Iraqi output rises despite threats to KRG oil, International Energy Agency, Monthly Oil Market Report, October 2017.

17 'Iraq Turmoil Threatens Billions in Oil Traders' Kurd Deals', Bloomberg News, 18 October 2017, accessed: https://www.bloomberg.com/news/articles/2017-10-18/iraq-turmoil-threatens-billions-in-oil-trader-deals-with-kurds.

18 The Kurdistan Region Statistics Office estimates the regional GDP at $20 billion in 2011, accessed: http://krso.net/files/articles/240816061824.pdf.

19 Oilflow SPV 1 DAC investor presentation dated 1 December 2016.

20 According to people who had done business with Exmor. Details on Drujan's career are based on his LinkedIn profile, accessed 25 October 2019.

21 Raval, Anjli, 'Kurds defy Iraq to establish own oil sales', *Financial Times*, 23 August 2015.

22 Preliminary results published by the Kurdistan Independent High Elections and Referendum Commission, 27 September 2017, accessed: http://www.khec.krd/pdf/173082892017_english%202.pdf.

23 Email to the authors from PSERS spokesman, April 2019.

24 NBC interview with Rich, 1992.

25 Chris Bake, interview with the authors, London, April 2019.

26 'Iraq's Kurdistan oil minister "pleads" for international support', *Financial Times*, 19 October 2017, accessed: https://www.ft.com/content/586dbee9-8899-39e1-9e9e-82bc8e2d4bff.

27 'Iraq's Kurdistan negotiates new terms, raises oil pre-payments to $3 billion', Reuters, 28 February 2017, accessed: https://www.reuters.com/article/us-iraq-kurdistan-oil-idUSKBN1671F5.

28 'In conversation with Ian Taylor, Chairman and Group CEO, Vitol', Chatham House, 5 October 2017, accessed: https://www.chathamhouse.org/file/conversation-ian-taylor-chairman-and-group-ceo-vitol.

29 Oilflow SPV 1 DAC, investor presentation.

30 Interview with Marc Rich in 'The Lifestyle of Rich, the Infamous', *Fortune*, 1986, accessed: https://fortune.com/2013/06/30/the-lifestyle-of-rich-the-infamous-fortune-1986/.

31 Ian Taylor, interview with the authors, London, February 2019.

32 Transparency International Index. Chad is ranked 165 out of 180 nations. Accessed: https://www.transparency.org/cpi2018.

33 The French government's Chad expert described Déby's 'chronic over-indulgence in Chivaz Regal [sic]' in a conversation described in a US diplomatic cable published by WikiLeaks, 16 November 2005, accessed: https://wikileaks.org/plusd/cables/05PARIS7792_a.html.

34 US diplomatic cable published by WikiLeaks, 13 December 2005, accessed: https://wikileaks.org/plusd/cables/05NDJAMENA1761_a.html.

35 World Bank data for 2018. Only the Central African Republic and Lesotho had a lower life expectancy. Accessed: https://data.worldbank.org/indicator/sp.dyn.le00.in?most_recent_value_desc=false.

36 World Bank data, accessed: https://data.worldbank.org/indicator/SI.POV.NAHC?locations=TD.

37 'Tchad Rapport EITI 2016', Extractive Industries Transparency Initiative, August 2018, p. 52, accessed: https://eiti.org/sites/default/files/documents/rapport_itie_tchad_2016.pdf.

38 Ibid.

39 Ibid.

40 'Glencore arranges $1 billion oil loan for Chad', *Financial Times*, 16 June 2014, accessed: https://www.ft.com/content/1061fc0a-f539-11e3-91a8-00144feabdc0. The interest rate of the loan was revealed on EITI, op. cit., August 2018, p. 175.

41 'Bank Accounts Pledge Agreement between Glencore Energy UK and Natixis and The Original Beneficiaries', Glencore Energy UK Ltd, 9 August 2018, Schedule 1, 'Original Beneficiaries', pp. 12–13, via UK Companies House, received for electronic filing on 16 August 2018.

42 The Glencore debt was consolidated and rescheduled in December 2015 for a total value of $1.488 billion, see 'First Review Under the Extended Credit Facility', International Monetary Fund, April 2018, box 1, p. 11, accessed: https://www.imf.org/~/media/Files/Publications/CR/2018/cr18108.ashx; the GDP of Chad stood at $10.1 billion in 2016, according to the International Monetary Fund.

43 'First Review Under the Extended Credit Facility', International Monetary Fund, April 2018, p. 4.

44 'Idriss Déby: "Je ne suis pas un aventurier, un guerrier, je suis un homme seul"', *Le Monde*, 25 June 2017.

45 'Tchad Rapport EITI 2016', Extractive Industries Transparency Initiative, August 2018, p. 54.

46 'Second Review Under the Program Under the Extended Credit Facility', International Monetary Fund, Chad, August 2018, p. 6, accessed: https://www.imf.org/~/media/Files/Publications/CR/2018/cr18260.ashx.

47 Op. cit., *Le Monde*, 25 June 2017.

48 Vitol's prepayments involved a total of $4 billion in exchange for future supplies from the Tengiz field, and $2.2 billion in exchange for future supplies from Kashagan. KMG investor presentation, October 2019 (http://ir.kmg.kz/storage/files/ad9d29e757f04f5e/NDR_ppt_01112019.pdf).

49 KMG's accounts show its single largest lender, other than its prepayment deal with Vitol, as Eximbank of China with a $1.13 billion loan. Kazakhstan's total external government and SOE debt was 25.5% of GDP, or about $40 billion, at the end of 2017 according to the IMF, making Vitol's prepayments equivalent to well over a tenth of the total.

50 Vitol says the deals were awarded after open and competitive tenders in which other large traders participated. Vitol, email to the authors, February 2020.

51 TH KazMunaiGaz Holding SA, consolidated financial statements 2005, p. 5. The IPO prospectus of KMG EP provides further evidence for Vitol's role: it shows that roughly half of its oil exports were sold to a trading subsidiary called KMG TradeHouse at the port of Odessa in Ukraine, and then 'resold by KMG TradeHouse AG to Vittol [sic]'.

52 Vitol Central Asia SA entry on the Swiss corporate registry, accessed: https://www.monetas.ch/en/647/Company-data.htm?subj=1769122.

53 Vitol's consolidated financial statements, 2005. At the time of writing, Vitol's stake was 42.5%, and Tiku's stake had been reduced to just under 50%.

54 Kulibayev and Tiku had a number of 'shared business interests', according to Nostrum Oil & Gas prospectus, 20 May 2014, accessed: https://www.sec.gov/Archives/edgar/data/1608672/000119312514207809/d728917dex991.htm.

55 Hywel Phillip, AT Capital, email to the authors, February 2020.

56 Ingma Holding BV's annual financial statements. Total payments to shareholders during the period were $1.12 billion.

57 Tornbjörn Törnqvist, interview with the authors, Geneva, May 2019.

58 'Commodities: Tougher Times for Trading Titans', *Financial Times*, 2013, accessed: https://www.ft.com/content/250af818-a1c1-11e2-8971-00144feabdc0.

59 'Announcement Of Additional Treasury Sanctions on Russian Government Officials And Entities', US Treasury press release, 28 April 2014, accessed: https://www.treasury.gov/press-center/press-releases/Pages/jl2369.aspx.

60 'Trafigura Becomes Major Exporter Of Russian Oil', *Financial Times*, 27 May 2015.

61 'Russian State Bank Secretly Financed Rosneft Sale After Foreign Buyers Balked', Reuters, 9 November 2018, accessed: https://www.reuters.com/article/us-rosneft-privatisation-exclusive/exclusive-russian-state-bank-secretly-financed-rosneft-sale-after-foreign-buyers-balked-idUSKCN1NE132.

62 A video of the meeting is available at http://en.kremlin.ru/catalog/persons/61/events/53774/videos.

63 Russian presidential order, dated 10 April 2017, accessed: http://publication.pravo.gov.ru/Document/View/0001201704100002?index=1&rangeSize=1.

64 'US warns Kurdistan over independence referendum', *Financial Times*, 21 September 2017, accessed: https://www.ft.com/content/69b5b776-9e58-11e7-8cd4-932067fbf946.

Conclusion: A Lot of Skeletons

1 'BNP Said to Reduce Commodity-Trading Finance to Trafigura', Bloomberg News, 8 September 2014, accessed: https://www.bloomberg. com/news/articles/2014-09-07/bnp-paribas-said-to-curb-commodity-trade-finance-to-trafigura.

2 'BNP Paribas Agrees to Plead Guilty and to Pay $8.9 Billion for Illegally Processing Financial Transactions for Countries Subject to US Economic Sanctions', US Department of Justice press release, 30 June 2014, accessed: https://www.justice.gov/opa/pr/bnp-paribas-agrees-plead-guilty-and-pay-89-billion-illegally-processing-financial.

3 Statement of Facts, US District Court Southern District of New York, United States of America *v*. BNP Paribas, 30 June 2014, accessed: https://www.justice.gov/sites/default/files/opa/legacy/2014/06/30/statement-of-facts.pdf.

4 Two former Trafigura senior executives with direct knowledge of the situation confirmed, under condition of anonymity, that the Dutch company was Trafigura. Although Trafigura largely operates from its headquarters in Geneva, the company was at the time formally incorporated in the Netherlands. It later moved its incorporation to Singapore.

5 Eric de Turckheim, interview with the authors, Geneva, March 2019.

6 According to a former Trafigura executive, who declined to be named.

7 Email from BNP Paribas employee quoted in Statement of Facts, US District Court Southern District of New York, United States of America *v*. BNP Paribas, 30 June 2014, p. 25, accessed: https://www.justice.gov/sites/default/files/opa/legacy/2014/06/30/statement-of-facts.pdf.

8 'Attorney General Holder Delivers Remarks at Press Conference Announcing Significant Law Enforcement Action', US Department of Justice statement, Washington, 30 June 2014, accessed: https://www.justice.gov/opa/speech/attorney-general-holder-delivers-remarks-press-conference-announcing-significant-law.

9 'What Are Economic Sanctions?', Council on Foreign Relations, 12 August 2019, accessed: https://www.cfr.org/backgrounder/what-are-economic-sanctions.

10 'Vitol trades Iranian fuel oil, skirting sanctions', Reuters, 26 September 2012, accessed: https://www.reuters.com/article/us-iran-oil-sanctions-vitol-idUSBRE88P06C20120926.

11 'Unlawful Corporate Payments Act of 1977', US House of Representatives, 28 September 1977, accessed: https://www.justice.gov/sites/default/files/criminal-fraud/legacy/2010/04/11/houseprt-95-640.pdf.

12 'Report of the Securities Exchange Commission on Questionable and Illegal Corporate Payments and Practices', US Securities and Exchange Commission, May 1976, p. B-4, accessed: https://www.sec.gov/spotlight/fcpa/sec-report-questionable-illegal-corporate-payments-practices-1976.pdf.

13 Ibid., p. 44.

14 'Fines and bribes paid to private individuals should not be tax deductible', Confédération Suisse, Federal Council press release, 18 December 2015, accessed: https://www.admin.ch/gov/en/start/dokumentation/medienmitteilungen.msg-id-60078.html.

15 Phase 4 report on Switzerland, OECD Working Group on Bribery in International Business Transactions, 2018, accessed: http://www.oecd.org/corruption/anti-bribery/Switzerland-Phase-4-Report-ENG.pdf.

16 'Switzerland – 2019 Article IV Consultation', International Monetary Fund, p. 22, accessed: https://www.imf.org/~/media/Files/Publications/CR/2019/1CHEEA2019001.ashx.

17 'Jamaica: a Trafigura Scandal Primer', US State Department, 12 October 2006, in Public Library of US Diplomacy, 06KINGSTON2021_a, WikiLeaks, accessed: https://search.wikileaks.org/plusd/cables/06KINGSTON2021_a.html.

18 'ADM Subsidiary Pleads Guilty to Conspiracy to Violate the Foreign Corrupt Practices Act', US Department of Justice, 20 December 2013, accessed: https://www.justice.gov/opa/pr/adm-subsidiary-pleads-guilty-conspiracy-violate-foreign-corrupt-practices-act.

19 Paul Wyler, interview with the authors, Zurich, June 2019.

20 'Remarks of Secretary Lew on the Evolution of Sanctions and Lessons for the Future at the Carnegie Endowment for International Peace', US Department of the Treasury, 30 March 2016, accessed: https://www.treasury.gov/press-center/press-releases/pages/jl0398.aspx.

21 Ibid.

22 'HSBC Holdings Plc and HSBC Bank USA NA Admit to Anti-Money Laundering and Sanctions Violations', US Department of Justice, 11 Dec 2012, accessed: https://www.justice.gov/opa/pr/hsbc-holdings-plc-and-hsbc-bank-usa-na-admit-anti-money-laundering-and-sanctions-violations.

23 'Credit Suisse Pleads Guilty to Conspiracy to Aid and Assist US Taxpayers in Filing False Returns', US Department of Justice, 19 May 2014, accessed: https://www.justice.gov/opa/pr/credit-suisse-pleads-guilty-conspiracy-aid-and-assist-us-taxpayers-filing-false-returns.

24 'Treasury Designates Russian Oligarchs, Officials and Entities in Response to Worldwide Malign Activity', US Treasury, 6 April 2018, accessed: https://home.treasury.gov/news/press-releases/sm0338.

25 'United States Sanctions Human Rights Abusers and Corrupt Actors Across the Globe', US Treasury, 21 December 2017, accessed: https://home.treasury.gov/news/press-releases/sm0243.

26 'Treasury Targets Russian Oil Brokerage Firm for Supporting Illegitimate Maduro Regime', US Treasury, 18 February 2020, accessed: https://home.treasury.gov/news/press-releases/sm909.

27 US Treasury press release, 20 March 2014, accessed: https://www.treasury.gov/press-center/press-releases/pages/jl23331.aspx.

28 Torbjörn Törnqvist, interview with the authors, Geneva, May 2019.

29 'Trafigura, Glencore and Vitol Probed in Brazil Graft Scandal', Bloomberg News, 5 December 2018, accessed: https://www.bloomberg.com/news/articles/2018-12-05/trafigura-glencore-and-vitol-ensnared-in-brazil-bribery-scandal.

30 'Ex-Petrobras Trader "Phil Collins" Says Vitol Bribed Him', Bloomberg News, 23 November 2019, accessed: https://www.bloomberg.com/

news/articles/2019-11-23/ex-petrobras-trader-phil-collins-tells-judge-vitol-bribed-him.

31 'Trader Gunvor Pays $95 Million to Swiss in Corruption Probe', Bloomberg News, 17 October 2019, accessed: https://www.bloomberg.com/news/articles/2019-10-17/gunvor-strikes-95-million-deal-with-swiss-to-end-congo-probe.

32 Glencore's annual report 2018, p. 126.

33 'SFO Confirms Investigation Into Suspected Bribery at Glencore Group of Companies', Serious Fraud Office, 5 December 2019, accessed: https://www.sfo.gov.uk/2019/12/05/sfo-confirms-investigation-into-suspected-bribery-at-glencore-group-of-companies/.

34 'Investigation by the Office of the Attorney General in Switzerland', Glencore press release, 19 June 2020, accessed: https://www.glencore.com/media-and-insights/news/investigation-by-the-office-of-the-attorney-general-of-switzerland.

35 'Glencore Drops as US Orders Documents in Corruption Probe', Bloomberg News, 3 July 2018.

36 'Glasenberg's Legacy Threatened By Long List of Corruption Probes', Bloomberg News, 5 December 2019, accessed: https://www.bloomberg.com/news/articles/2019-12-05/glasenberg-s-legacy-threatened-by-long-list-of-corruption-probes.

37 'Back to the Marc Rich Days as US Probes Commodity Traders', Bloomberg News, 25 March 2019, accessed: https://www.bloomberg.com/news/articles/2019-03-25/back-to-the-marc-rich-days-as-u-s-probes-commodity-traders.

38 David Tendler, interview with the authors, New York, August 2019.

39 Ian Taylor and David Fransen, interview with the authors, London, February 2019.

40 Bloomberg, Michael, *Bloomberg by Bloomberg* (John Wiley & Sons, 2001), accessed: http://movies2.nytimes.com/books/first/b/bloomberg-bloomberg.html.

41 'Ian Taylor: the oilman, his cancer, and the millions he's giving the NHS', *The Times*, 8 June 2019, accessed: https://www.thetimes.co.uk/

article/ian-taylor-the-oilman-his-cancer-and-the-millions-hes-giving-the-nhs-wnwbtpq2h.

42 'State Commodity Traders Grow to Take On Glencore, Cargill', Bloomberg News, 1 June 2015, accessed: https://www.bloomberg.com/news/articles/2015-05-31/state-commodity-traders-grow-to-take-on-glencore-cargill.

43 'Trader who tapped Tehran to power China', *Financial Times*, 27 June 2014, accessed: https://www.ft.com/content/4ed3edd6-fc69-11e3-86dc-00144feab7de, and 'Iranian Oil, arms, sanctions … and China's 'Crazy Yang', Reuters, 16 January 2012, accessed: http://news.trust.org//item/20120116002600-enu8o/.

44 For the 2012 sanctions, see: 'Three Companies Sanctioned Under the Amended Iran Sanctions Act', US State Department, 12 January 2012, accessed: https://2009-2017.state.gov/r/pa/prs/ps/2012/01/180552.htm. The US State Department called Zhuhai Zhenrong 'the largest supplier of refined petroleum product to Iran' at the time. For the 2019 sanctions, see: 'The United States to Impose Sanctions On Chinese Firm Zhuhai Zhenrong Company Limited for Purchasing Oil From Iran', US State Department, 22 July 2019, accessed: https://www.state.gov/the-united-states-to-impose-sanctions-on-chinese-firm-zhuhai-zhenrong-company-limited-for-purchasing-oil-from-iran/.

45 Ian Taylor, interview with the authors, London, February 2019.

46 This account of Glencore's trading in 2020 is based on an interview with a senior executive, who declined to be named, as well as the company's statements, and publicly-available information on ship movements.

47 'Texas Regulators Weigh Historic Oil Cuts as Coronavirus Pandemic Saps Demand', *Wall Street Journal*, 14 April 2020, accessed: https://www.wsj.com/articles/texas-regulators-weigh-historic-oil-cuts-after-coronavirus-11586886293.

48 Steve Kalmin, Glencore's chief financial officer, told journalists in August 2020 that the return on equity on the company's contango deals was as much as 100% 'in some cases'.

49 According to the estimates of several leading oil traders. For example, Mercuria's Marco Dunand estimated the stock build at 1.25 billion barrels. 'Trader Mercuria Says Oil Has Bottomed With More Shut-ins Coming', Bloomberg News, 29 April 2020.

50 White House Coronavirus Task Force press briefing, 31 March 2020, accessed: https://www.youtube.com/watch?v=c2TRmlsmMNU.

51 Glencore, 2020 Half-Year Report, 6 August 2020, accessed: https://www.glencore.com/dam/jcr:50ad1802-2213-43d8-8008-5fe84e3c65ed/GLEN-2020-Half-Year-Report.pdf.

52 Trafigura, 2020 interim report (https://www.trafigura.com/media/2648/trafigura_interim_report_2020.pdf), and 'Mercuria scores record profit amid oil market chaos', *Financial Times*, 13 July 2020 (https://www.ft.com/content/72300405-20bc-4dde-b145-9ff28f9da69d).

53 Muriel Schwab, interview with the authors, Geneva, August 2019.

54 Muriel Schwab, interviews with the authors, Geneva, August 2019, and by telephone, February 2020.

55 David MacLennan, interview with the authors, Minneapolis, August 2019.

56 Ivan Glasenberg, interview with the authors, Baar, August 2019.

57 Torbjörn Törnqvist, interview with the authors, Geneva, August 2019.

58 Ian Taylor, interview with the authors, London, February 2019.

INDEX